Northampton County Virginia

Register of Deaths

1871–1896

Allen B. Hamilton

HERITAGE BOOKS
2018

HERITAGE BOOKS
AN IMPRINT OF HERITAGE BOOKS, INC.

Books, CDs, and more—Worldwide

For our listing of thousands of titles see our website
at
www.HeritageBooks.com

Published 2018 by
HERITAGE BOOKS, INC.
Publishing Division
5810 Ruatan Street
Berwyn Heights, Md. 20740

Copyright © 2018 Allen B. Hamilton

Heritage Books by the author:
Northampton County, Virginia, Land Tax Records, 1782–1799
Northampton County, Virginia, Land Tax Records, 1800–1825
Northampton County, Virginia, 1890 Personal Property Tax List
Northampton County, Virginia, Personal Property Tax Lists, 1782–1799
Northampton County, Virginia, Register of Deaths, 1871–1896

Cover photo: Old Chapel Cemetery near Townsend, Virginia.
Photo by Sharon Meekins.

International Standard Book Number
Paperbound: 978-0-7884-5820-0

INTRODUCTION

This is Northampton County, Virginia's Register of Deaths for 1871 to 1896, a continuation of Sandra Perkins work 1853 to 1870. Many of the entries between 1873 and 1877 were difficult if not impossible to read because pages are either faint or dark. To compensate, I borrowed the Library of Virginia's copy to make the best and most complete list. In some early years the Occupation and Martial Status was not that of the deceased but of the individual's parents or Head of Family. An example: a 1 day infant cannot be a Laborer and Married. This has been noted in [brackets] following the information of the deceased. The top of each original form states "It is hereby requested that the Commissioner of the Revenue in making up their reports shall certify the aggregate number and also give separately the number of White and Colored". I have included this info for each year. I also have a breakdown of the causes of death by year. This is shown in the 1871-83 & 1884-96 charts. There are 6 years missing. These include 1879 – 1881. I have included the Mortality Schedules from June 1, 1879 to May 31, 1880 to fill in some of this missing gap. This includes 57 from the Capeville District, 34 from Eastville District, 23 from Johnsontown District and 25 from Franktown District for a total of 139. This list of over 2,200 names is in alphabetical order with an index in the back with reference page for the parent's names and sources that provided the information. The following is a breakdown of the order of information contained from the Death Register.

- Name in Full
- Race – White / Colored or Black
- Sex – Male / Female
- Date of Death
- Place of Death
- Name of Disease or Cause of Death
- Age in Years / Months / Days (3 columns)
- Names of Parents
- Where Born
- Occupation
- Marital Status   Consort (Married) or Unmarried
- Source of Information (Name of person giving information of death)
  > (Designation of informant such as physician, surgeon, coroner, head of the family, friend, etc.)

The Mortality Schedule is different because it lacks the deceased parents' names. However the number of the family household where the individual lived is noted before each name in the Mortality Schedule. With this information I referenced the 1880 Census so the parent or parent's names could be included. I have keep the same order as much as possible. I have included the birth state of the Individual's Father and Mother as noted in the 1880 Census. (PR) is noted at the end of some listings. These are Physicians Report. Mortality Schedules only list the month and year of death. 1882 has 3 listings with different death dates, causes and ages. Discrepancies are noted in the back. I have also included 105 deaths 1871-1901 from Will Books 39 & 40 in the back. I referenced the 1870 Census for the 1st parents in the book. Molly's last name could have been Gatewood, Jarvis, Satchel, Spady, Stoakley or Taylor and there was no Travis in the 1870 Census.

Assessors / Commissioners of Revenue

1871	Capeville	L. S. Nottingham
	Eastville	R. H. Read
	Franktown	Geo. H. Thomas
1872	Capeville	Lucius S. Nottingham
	Eastville	R. H. Read
	Franktown	Geo. H. Thomas
1873	Capeville	John C. Dalby
	Eastville	Leonard J. Goffigon
	Franktown	Geo. H. Thomas
1874	Capeville	John C. Dalby
	Eastville	G. R. Jacob
	Franktown	Geo. H. Thomas
1875	County	P. B. Smith
1876	County	Michael E. Underhill
1877	County	Michael E. Underhill
1878	County	M. E. Underhill
1879	Missing	Mortality Schedules June 1, 1879 to May 31, 1880 substituted
1880	Missing	Mortality Schedules June 1, 1879 to May 31, 1880 substituted
1881	Missing	
1882	County	John F. W. Custis
1883	County	Geo. R. Jacob
1884	County	Geo. R. Jacob
1885	County	Geo. R. Jacob
1886	Missing	
1887	County	George Toy
1888	County	George Toy
1889	Missing	
1890	Missing	
1891	County	Zoro Willis
1892	County	Zoro Willis
1893	County	Zoro Willis
1894	County	Zoro Willis
1895	County	Zoro Willis
1896	County	Zoro Willis

Starting in 1875 districts were not noted and the only name was that of the Commissioner of Revenue.

Number of Deaths per Year
by
Race & Sex

	District	White	Colored	Unkn.	Male	Female	Unkn.	Total	
1871	"Capeville"	9	17	.	9	17	.	26	
	"Eastville"	15	9	.	14	10	.	24	
	"Franktown"	18	14	.	11	19	2	32	82
1872	"Capeville"	19	11	.	18	12	.	30	
	"Eastville"	21	16	.	23	14	.	37	
	"Franktown"	25	19	.	26	18	.	44	111
1873	"Capeville"	9	10	.	9	10	.	19	
	"Eastville"	24	36	.	33	26	1	60	
	"Franktown"	19	19	.	25	11	2	38	117
1874	"Capeville"	16	11	.	17	10	.	27	
	"Eastville"	12	8	.	15	5	.	20	
	"Franktown"	10	9	.	10	9	.	19	66
1875	County	46	49	.	50	45	.	95	
1876	County	65	91	.	78	77	1	156	
1877	County	37	46	1	48	35	1	84	
1878	County	36	73	.	60	49	.	109	
1879	MISSING	.	.	.	.	.	.	.	
1880	MISSING	.	.	.	.	.	.	.	
1879-80	"Capeville"	24	33	.	37	20	.	57	
	"Eastville"	8	26	.	16	18	.	34	
	"Johnsontown"	10	15	.	14	11	.	25	
	"Franktown"	17	6	.	11	12	.	23	139
1881	MISSING	.	.	.	.	.	.	.	
1882	County	10	30	1	24	16	1	41	
1883	County	27	21	.	25	23	.	48	
1884	County	29	16	.	21	24	.	45	
1885	County	32	20	.	26	26	.	52	
1886	MISSING	.	.	.	.	.	.	.	
1887	County	37	48	.	51	34	.	85	
1888	County	18	36	.	31	23	.	54	
1889	MISSING	.	.	.	.	.	.	.	
1890	MISSING	.	.	.	.	.	.	.	
1891	County	60	64	.	60	64	.	124	
1892	County	79	71	.	83	67	.	150	
1893	County	96	128	.	130	94	.	224	
1894	County	71	79	.	82	68	.	150	
1895	County	60	85	.	81	64	.	145	
1896	County	62	90	.	83	69	.	152	

*1871 Franktown – 2 Born Dead, Sex not noted

2,091

1871 Deaths
"Capeville District"

Dalby, Tabitha	Hamilton, John	Nottingham, Lilie	Smith, Sallie
Dixon, Infant	Hallett, Eliza	" , William	Stafford, Melvina
" , Samuel	Jarvis, Joshua	Outten, Infant	Stratton, Infant
Fitchett, Violett	" , William S.	Scott, Maggie	Trower, Infant
Fox, James	Mapp, Harriett	Seaton, Tabitha	" , Luke
Griffith, Infant	Morris, Infant	Shackleford, Milley	
" , James	Nottingham, Elizabeth	Smith, Infant	

(26)

"Eastville District"

Allen, Jno.	Fitchett, Georgie S.	Nottingham, Susan A.	Thomas, Dennis
Bell, Not Named	Jackson, Rachael	Purnell, Levin	Weeks, Not Named
Colony, Cincinatus U.	Jacob, Marg't. S.	Stephens, Not Named	Wilkins, Nancy
Dalby, Alberta	James, Napoleon	Stephen, Robert	Wilkins, Not Named
" , Emma D.	Jarvis, William	Taylor, Henry	Willis, Leonard
Dunton, Geo. U.	Kelley, Mary Susan	" , Wm. E.	Wyatt, Betsy

(24)

"Franktown District"

Badger, Mary F.	Harman, Arthur	Mingo, Not Named	Scarborough, Hennie
Bonwell, Alice	Heath, Augustus	Nottingham, Fanny	Smith, Grace
Carpenter, Not Named	Johnson, Jno. Y.	" , Henry	Thomas, Not Named
Charnock, Fanny	" , Wm.	Reid, Anna	Wallace, Andrew
" , Not Named	Kelly, Lizzie	Reid, Edward	" , Rose
Churn, Sally	" , Not Named	" , Jno. W.	Wescoat, Not Named
Doughty, Susan	Mapp, Marg't	" , Lena	" , Not Named
Frances, Sabra	" , Peter	Rufus, Lucinda	Young, Peggy

(32)

82

1872 Deaths
"Capeville District"

-------, Infant	Elliott, Thomas	Kendall, Infant	Nottingham, William
-------, Infant	Fitchett, Infant	Moore, Grace	Simpkins, Laura
Collins, Infant	Fitchett, Maria	Morris, Infant	Spady, Infant
" , James	Goffigon, Obediah	Nottingham, Annie	Trower, Infant
" , William	Griffith, James	" , Chas.	Wilkins, M. S.
Costin, Infant	" , Moses	" , Infant	" , Sallie
" , Joseph	Hallett, Infant	" , Infant	
Dixon, Wesley	Joynes, Infant	" , James	13 infants

(30)

"Eastville District"

Beavins, Shadrack	Giddens, Abram	Nottingham, Not Named	Thomas, Wm. H.
Bradford, Jim	Haley, Not Named	" , Jas. S.	Turner, Not Named
" , Mary	Isdell, John	Rayfield, Fannie S.	Tyler, Sallie
Booker, Henry	" , Sally	Read, Mary	Weeks, Wm.
Carpenter, Geo.	" , Wm. E.	Roberts, Edmd. T.	Wilkins, Not Named
Church, John	Jarvis, Thos. B.	" , Edwd P.	Wyatt, Not Named
Dix, Not Named	" , Virginia	Savage, Anna	Yerby, Tabby
Fitchett, Wilson	Moore, Leonard	Smith, Edward	
Fletcher, James	" , Zack P.	Sturgis, Effie Lee	
Floyd, John	Nottingham, Ellen	Thomas, Virginia	

(37)

"Franktown District"

Ashby, Not Named	Churn, Jno.	Gladson, Sally	Pitts, Major
" , James F.	Doughty, Mary E.	Gunter, Isabella	Reid, Not Named
Bagwell, Comfort	Downing, Herbert	" , Jno.	Satchell, Not Named
Bayly, Not Named	" , Maria	" , Missouri	Savage, George
Bell, Jane	" , Not Named	Harmon, Henry	" , Not Named
Bunting, Alice	" , Sissie	Jarvis, Thomas	Scott, Wm. H.
Carpenter, Henry	Dunton, Devericks	Johnson, Not Named	Ward, Thomas
" , Isiah	" , Thos. R.	Kellam, Edward	" , Missouri
" , Jas.	Fisher, Not Named	Mapp, Kate	Wescoat, Lizzie
Charnock, Alex	" , Not Named	" , Thomas	Not Named
Church, James	" , Not Named	Mingo, James	Not Named

(44)

111

1873 Deaths
"Capeville District"

Andrews, Wm. W.	Fitchett, Margariet S.	Hallett, Sabra	Stoakley, Sarah
Bayly, No Name	Goffigon, Arthur	Mingo, Rachel	Watson, Sally
Brickhouse, Elizabeth M.	" , Severn	Nottingham, James B.	Willis, No Name
Coles, No Name	Hallett, Ed. M.	Powell, Handy	" , No Name
Coffer, No Name	" , No Name	Richardson, Major	

(19)

"Eastville District"

Addison, John Sr.	Darby/Peterson William	Nelson, Amanda	Satchell, Nelson
Bayly, Betty	Dix, Peggy	" , Rosa	" , Not Named
" , Edward P.	Fisher, Miers W.	Nottingham, Florence	Shields, Infant
Becket, Kessiah	Giddins, Infant	" , Joseph D.	Spady, Infant
Bell, Edward	Gunter, William	" , Not Named	" , Infant
Bradford, William	Hack, Alfred	" , Not Named	Thomas, John C.
Bull, Anna	Heath, John	" , Samuel Y.	" , Not Named
Carpenter, Anna	Holt, Ginny	Palmer, Missouri	Upshur, Bennett
" , Becca	House, Not Named	Rayfield, Fanny S.	Van Ness, William
Carter, Infant	Jacob, Susan	Read, Peggy	Vaughn, Mary C.
" , Jesse	Lewis, Littleton W.	Richardson, Georgiana	Wesley, William
Coles, Infant	Mapp, Elizabeth	" , Major	Widgen, Gabe
Collins, Caleb P.	Moore, John W.	" , Thomas	" , Kate
" , Wilcher	" , Pop	Robinson, Mary E.	" , William
" , Victor	" , William P. Jr.	Satchell, George	Wright, Mary E.

(60)

"Franktown District"

Anderson, Not Named	Harman, Not Named	McKandess, Not Named	Thomas, Not Named
" , Not Named	" , Rosey	Roberts, Not Named	Ward, Michael
Bayly, Not Named	Heath, Jno. Arthur	Robertson, William	Wescoat, Jno. B.
Church, James	Jacob, Not Named	Savage, Geo. F.	" , Sally T.
" , Not Named	Johnson, Eliza	" , Lilia	White, Edward T.
Churn, William	Kelly, Not Named	" , Not Named	Wyatt, Amelia
Downing, Not Named	Kennerly, William A.	" , Sam	Wyatt, Not Known
Fisher, Ellyson D.	Maddox, Francis	Scott, Jno. E.	" , Not Known
" , Mary	Mapp, Robins	Thomas, Levin	
Harman, Amy	McRandolp, Not Named	" , Not Named	

(38)

117

1874 Deaths
"Capeville District"

Barcraft, Fanny	Griffith, None	Nottingham, None	Tyler, Robt. E.
Charnick, Leah	Hallett, Elizabeth	Scott, Wm. I.	Whitehead, None
Crow, William	" , None	Simpkins, Jno. A.	Widgen, Patsey E.
Downs, Allice	Hunt, Washington	Smith, Major	Williams, Edward
" , Ed. P.	Kellam, Mary T.	" , None	Wilson, Nancey
Fitchett, Bennet	Lipscome, Charles	" , None	Young, Peggy
Griffith, Alexandrew	McKown, Ann	Travis, None	

(27)

"Eastville District"

Bell, unnamed	Dalby, Mary A.	Matthews, Levi	Scott, unnamed
Bingham, James W.	" , Thomas	Nottingham, Miss Ann	Turner, unnamed
Burris, Caleb	" , unnamed	Pyle, Wm. T.	Wilson, unnamed
Collins, Jim	Garrett, Lucian	Robins, unnamed	Wilkins, James E.
Cook, Wm. Snr.	Jarvis, Geo. T.	Richardson, Thomas	Underhill, Richie P.

(20)

"Franktown District"

Ashby, Jas. H.	Pitts, William	Savage, Not Named	Stewart, Not Named
Church, Charles	Pool, Not Named	Scott, Not Named	" , Not Named
Churn, Eliza	Satchell, Leah	Smith, Caty "Catherine"	Upshur, Sally
Hastings, Rinatha R.	Savage, Edward	" , Not Named	Wise, Seymour
Only, Isaac	" , Elizebeth	Stephens, Not Named	

(19)

66

1875 Deaths

Addison, No Name	Collins, No Name	Leatherbury, Chas.	Spady, Thos. R.
Ames, No Name	Cornell, Ben	Lothand, Garnett	Stephens, Jno.
Andrews, No Name	Costin, Margt.	Mathews, Mary	" , No Name
Antney, No Name	" , No Name	Nottingham, Jno. W.	Tankard, No Name
Baker, No Name	" , No Name	" , Maria	Thomas, No Name
Barcraft, Patsy	" , Susan	" , No Name	Trower, No Name
Bayly, Fanny	Dalby, No Name	" , No Name	" , Rachel
Becket, Sarah	Doughty, Arthur	Only, Isaac	Upshur, Bill
Bell, Allen Mrs.	Downing, No Name	Parsons, Susan	Upshur, Geo.
" , Ezekiel	Dunton, Henry R.	Pearson, Stoakley	Vanness, Jerusha
Benson, Edwd. Jr.	Fatherly, Ellen	Pyle, No Name	Walker, Jno.
Bowdoin, No Name	Fisher, No Name	Read, No Name	Ward, Kate
" , Peter S.	Fitchett, Charles	Revel, Custis	Wescoat, Dennis
Brickhouse, Cora	" , No Name	Richardson, No Name	" , Rich'd
Brown, Caroline	" , No Name	Satchell, Prissy	" , Rose
Brown, No Name	Griffith, No Name	Savage, James W.	West, Caroline
Burtin, James	Hallett, No Name	" , Lettie	Wilkins, Mary A.
Carpenter, Alfred	" , Tamar	" , No Name	Willis, Emily Susan
Chandler, No Name	Heath, No Name	Seaton, No Name	" , No Name
Church, Mary Esther	Hickman, No Name	Simpkins, Geo.	" , No Name
" , Sissy	Johnson, Obedience	Sisco, Margt.	" , No Name
Collins, Annie	" , Wm. G.	" , No Name	" , Susan
" , Arby	Joynes, Margt.	Spady, No Name	Wilson, James B.
" , Lizzy	" ,No Name	" , No Name	

(95)

1876 Deaths

Addison, Henry	Fitchett, Henrietta	Johnson, Edward L.	Saunders, Not Named
Allen, Polly	" , James	Kellam, Kitty	Savage, Indiana
Anderson, Sarah	" , Jas. Sr.	" , Thomas	" , William L.
Andrews, George	" , John S.	Kendall, Mary	Scisco, Not Named
" , Marg. S.	" , Joseph	LaForge, John T.	Scott, Ella G.
" , William W.	" , Not Named	Leatherbury, George	Seeds, Samuel
Baker, Not Named	" , Not Named	Lewis, Margaret E.	Simkins, Margaret S.
Bayly, Elizabeth	" , Not Named	Lingo, Not Named	Smith, Fanny
" , Maria	" , Not Named	Mapp, Not Known	" , Isaac
Bell, Harriet	" , Not Named	" , Not Known	" , Not Named
" , John H.	Giddins, Isaac	Moore, Arameah	" , Not Named
" , Levin	Gladden, Moses W.	" , Catherine	" , Not Named
Belote, John	Godwin, Mary	" , Fanny L.	" ,Not Named
Bevans, Not Named	" , Nicey	" , Ginny	Somers, Not Named
Bradford, Anna	" , William	" , Not Named	Spady, Robert C.
" , Joana	Goffigon, Ben	" , Not Named	Stephens, Adah
" , John	Griffith, Elizabeth	Morris, Jack	Stewart, James H.
Brickhouse, Polly	Gunter, Philip B.	Moses, George	" , Joseph
Brittingham, Joseph B.	Guy, Not Named	Nottingham, John C.	Stoakley, Thos. S.
Bull, Mary F.	James, Not Named	" , L.	Sturgis, Samuel Jr.
Burton, John W.	Jefferson, Ellen	" , Leah	Tankard, Adah
Byrd, Not Named	Johnson, Esther	" , Maria	Taylor, Not Named
Carter, James H.	Joynes, Major	" , Wm. P.	Travis, George
" , Not Named	" , Not Named	Only, Esther	Upshur, Gaddy
Church, Georgiana	Hack, Thomas H.	Peed, Fanny	" , Leah
Churn, Peggy	Hallett, Ibby	" , Isaac	Ward, Minny
Coles, Ellen L.	" , Laura	" , Not Named	Whitehead, Talmadge
Collins, Major	" , Not Named	Philips, Evans	Widgen, Sauky
" , Mary	Hanby, Not Named	Pitts, Sarah	Wilkins, Lottie
" , Noah	Hargis, Not Named	Rayfield, Not Named	" , Maria
Costin, James	" , Not Named	Read, Edward	Williams, Not Named
" , James H.	" , Not Named	" , Maria	" , Puss
" , Mary E.	Harmanson, William	Richardson, Emily S.	Willis, Emily
" , Not Named	Harrison, William	Robins, Not Named	" , Harriett
Coston, Joseph	Heath, Jasper	Rolly, Not Named	" , Not Named
Dixon, John C.	Holt, Joseph	" , Not Named	Window, Alonzo
Dunton, Ellison	" , Lucy	Russel, Emily	Wise, Charles
Easton, Not Named	Hunt, Mary E.	Saddler, Nathan	" , Charlotte S.
Evans, Isaac	Hyslop, Not Named	Satchell, Emily S.	" , Eleanor

(156)

1877 Deaths

Addison, John W.	Dixon, Mary	Morris, Not Named	Spady, John
" , Not Named	Douglass, Not Named	" , Sallie	" , Joseph
Andrews, Not Named	Ephraim, James	Nottingham, Edgar	" , Not Named
Ashby, Darky	" , John	" , Hezekiah	" , Sallie
" , Sarah E.	Fitchett, Francis	" , Leonard B.	Stephens, Not Named
Bayly, Mary D.	Gayle, Lucy	" , Not Named	" , Sallie
" , Thomas W.	Gibbins, Isaac	" , Not Named	Sturgis, Alma
Becket, Not Named	Gladstone, Not Named	" , Sallie	" , Mary
Beloat, Not Named	Goffigon, Not Named	Paremore, Raymond	" , Wm. H.
Brickhouse, Carrie	Griffith, Nathan	Pitts, Parker	Taylor, Not Named
" , Eadmond	Heath, Horace M.	" , Sydney	Thomas, George
" , Emily	Ivins, Robert	Powell, Jackson B.	Trower, Fannie
" , Geo.	Jacob, James	Read, Lucy	Upshur, Wilson
" , James M.	" , Robert C.	" , Maria J.	Ward, Not Named
Brittingham, Elijah	James, Not Named	Rodgers, Lucy	Watson, John B.
Burton, Not Named	Jarvis, Not Named	Rolly, Nettie	Webb, Harriet
Carter, Geo.	Jones, Hebrew	Savage, Fannie	Weeks, Solomon
Coleman, Richard	Justice, Jane	Scott, Not Named	Widgen, John
Collins, John	Mapp, Not Named	Simkins, Not Named	Williams, Edward
Dalby, Not Named	McMath, Samuel	Smith, Annie	Wilson, Margaret
Dixon, James	Moore, Lloyd	Solomon, Adah	" , Samuel

(84)

1878 Deaths

Ashby, Saly E.	Douglass, Madora	Mason, John	Smaw, Emily
" , Mary	Dunton, Adeline	Moore, Arthur	Smith, Abe
Bragg, Severn	" , Not Named	Moses, Not Named	" , Appy
Brickhouse, Ben Sr.	East, Not Named	Neal, Ruth	" , Jacob
" , Polly	Evans, Lambert	Nelson, Sallie	" , Joseph
" , Smith	Exall, George	Nottingham, Ella	" , Moses
" , William	Floyd, Edmund	" , Hezakiah	Spady, Edgar J.
Brooks, John	" , Rachiel	" , Ida	" , Not Named
Bunting, Not Named	Fortune, Not Named	" , Mary	" , Sally
Burroughs, Mary	Francis, Jenny	" , Not Named	Stakes, Not Named
Burtin, Adah	" , William	Paramore, Raymond	Stephens, Susan
" , Walter	Giddings, Colbert	Parker, Wm.	Stott, Lizzie
Carpenter, Ada	Goffigon, Not Named	Perkins, Emily	Stratton, David
" , Nim	" , Susan	" , Mary	Sunkets, Not Named
Carter, Henretta	Griffin, Not Named	Pitts, Nellie	Turner, Henie
Church, Arthur	Hallett, Not Named	" , Parker H.	Upshur, Willie
Churn, Not Named	Harmon, Not Named	Platt, Jobe	Ward, J. D.
Colaway, Ida	Hunt, Belfert F.	" , Wm.	Watson, John B.
Collins, Ann	" , Virginnia	Powell, Levin	Weeks, Ellen
" , Rosie E.	Jacob, Ella	Press, Not Named	" , Major
Conway, Matilda	" , Wm. T.	Richardson, Not Named	Wilkins, Sarah
Costin, Cordellia	Jarvis, Maggie	Riley, Not Named	Wilson, John
Crosby, Thomas	Jones, Geo. T.	Robbins, A.	Wyatt, Isma G.
Cullen, Not Named	" , Jacob	Rooks, James	" , Not Named
Dexter, Sadie	" , Wm.	Savage, Julious	Young, Mary E.
Dilliard, Richard	Major, Not Named	" , Margaret S.	
Doughty, Not Named	" , Olevia	Scisco, Henry	
" , Peggie	Mapp, Annie	Scott, John T. P.	

(109)

1879, 1880, 1881

Missing

Mortality Schedule
June 1, 1879 to May 31, 1880

"Capeville District"
James B. Scott Enumerator

Ames, Juletta	Downing, Maria	Nottingham, R. W.	Stevenson, Susan
Andrews, Custis	Fisher, Thomas H.	Phillips, George	Taylor, William
Bailey, Infant	Floyd, John W.	Platt, Capt.	Tazewell, Infant
Ball, Isaac	" , Maria	Richardson, Infant	Trower, Infant
Bell, William T.	Griffith, Infant	" , James A.	" , Infant
Braxton, Leonard	" , Infant	" , Tabitha S.	Turner, Mary
Brooks, Lucy E.	Hanby, William T.	Rooks, James	Walston, Sam'l J.
Burbridge, Infant	Hickman, John	Satchell, Ester	Ward, John
Carter, Tamer	Hunt, Isaac	Scisco, MIchael	Watson, Walter
Christian, Amanda	James, Isaac	Scott, Infant	Weeks, Nelly
Church, Tony	Little, Robert	Smith, Infant	Widgen, Elizabeth
Costin, Infant	McKown, Infant	Spady, Edy	Wilkins, Origen J.
" , Nathaniel	Morris, Nathaniel	" , Louisa	
Dennis, John	Nottingham, Henry	" , Major	
" , Stephen	" , Infant	Stevens, Infant	

(57)

"Eastville District"
Benj. F. Toy Enumerator

Bailey, Sarah	Fry, Joseph	Randal, Alfred	Stevens, Lillian
Bivins, Samuel	Jarvis, Samuel	Riley, Dianna	Stott, Maietta
Cisco, Emma	Johnson, Grace	Satchell, Schailotte	Stratton, Peter
Cobb, Mary	Little, George	Scarborough, Henry	Tazewell, Emma
Custis, Edward	Mears, Annie	Smith, Goldust?	Thomas, Caleb Jr
" , James	" , Wm. J.	" , Hariet	Upshur, Annie G.
Davis, Sarah	Moore, William	" , Henry	Watson, Thornton
Downing, Lina	Morris, Alfred	" , Patience	
Fry, Joseph	Nelson, Lucy	Stevens, Dara	

(34)

Mortality Schedule
June 1, 1879 to May 31, 1880

"Johnsontown District"
John H. Carter Enumerator

Badger, Edmond	Gladson, Annie T.	Nottingham, John	Stringer, Sallie
Brickhouse, -------	Henry, James	Palmer, Ellen	Weeks, Edmond
Carter, -------	~~Hopkins, Tinnie~~	" , Nim	Wilson, Emily
Coleman, Sallie	Jarvis, Margaret S.	~~Palmer, Rachel A.~~	Winder, Lizzie
Collins, Jacob	Mapp, William	Reed, Ida	
Eshom, Katie B.	Moore, Richard	Savage, Nelson	
Francis, Jeremiah	Nottingham, E. H.	Scott, John T. P.	

(25)

"Franktown District"
John Addison Enumerator

Adams, Viola	Dunton, Adaline	Kelly, Charles	Smith, Julius A.
Addison, Infant	Fisher, Charles	Major, -------	Ward, Eliza
Barrott, William	Garrison, Laura	" , Matilda	Wilkins, Laura
Bull, Major	Giddings, Joshua	McPhearson, -------	Wilson, Severn
Doughty, Archibald	Heath, Augustus C.	Menica, Laura	Wyatt, Isma G.
" , Mary	Kellam, Samuel E. A.	Scott, Ella T.	

(23)

139

1882 Deaths

Ashby, Charles	Collins, Jacob Henry	Kellam, Sam'l E. D.	Smith, Golden
Becket, Mary	" , James	Morris, Nat.	Smith/Riley, Dinah
Bell, Maggie	" , Sallie	Nottingham, Unnamed	" / " , Peter
" , Major	Costin, Nat.	" , Unknown	Stratton, Peter
Braxton, Richard	Custis, James	Richardson, James	Unknown/ Unknown
Brickhouse, Carrie	Downs, Nellie	" , Richard	Weeks, Unnamed
Brooks, Adline	Easter, Mary	" , Tobertha	Wescoat, Easter
Bull, Leah	Floyd, Jno. M.	Riley/Smith, Dinah	Wilson, Emily
Cisco, Henry	Gladson, Annie F.	" / " , Peter	
Collins, Ann	Gunter, Charles	Roberts, Unnamed	
Collins, Henry	Jarvis, Sam'l	Scott, Ella	

(41)

1883 Deaths

Ashby, Mary E.	Dunton, Joe L.	Mapp, Harry H.	Spratley, Marion
" , Navellia E.	Fatherly, Wm. J.	" , Sally	Stevens, Alice
Badger, Unnamed	Fereby, Newman	Martin, Rose	Stewart, Mary
Bayly, Ann	Fitchett, Kessie	Morris, Luke	Stratton, Chas.
Carter, Peggie	Floyd, Unnamed	Nottingham, Ellen K.	Tankard, Alfred
Chandler, Jas.	Goffigon, Solomon	Parker, Ann G.	Turner, Unnamed
Christian, Maria	Harmon, Lloyd	" , Anna	Upshur, Sarah
Colonna, Ella	Harrison, Margt.	Pitts, Unnamed	Warren, Dollie
Conner, Lloyd	Hopkins,	Pyle, Unnamed	Wescott, Jno.
" , Parker	James, Margt.	Robins, Essie	White, Jas. H.
Dennis, Sallie A.	Johnson, Geo. E.	Savage, Jas. H.	Widgen, Ernest
Doughty, Harriett	Jones, Hessie M.	Smith, Unnamed	Wyatt, Wilmer

(48)

1884 Deaths

Ames, Peggy	Griffith, Sallie	Morris, Unnamed	Trower, Clement
Ashby, Mary A.	Hamby, Elizabeth	Nottingham, Mary	" , Daisy
Baker, Sallie	Harcus/Hargis, Unnamed	" , Thos. H.	" , Jesse
Burton, Eva	Hargis, Unnamed	" , Unnamed	Upshur, Sarah P.
Chandler, Unnamed	Hickman, Unnamed	" , Unnamed	Warren, Lukie
Dixon, Mary Susan	Joynes, Garnet	Parker, Unnamed	Wescoat, Sarah
Downing, Luen	Kellam, Southey	Roberts, Unnamed	Wilkins, Unnamed
Dunton, Mary Mrs.	Kelly, Annie	Rose, Unnamed	Willett, Unnamed
Fitchett, Unnamed	Laupheimer, Jacob	Scott, H. Henry	Wise, Unnamed
Giddings, Robert	Mapp, Geo.	" , Unnamed	
Gladson, Vernon	Mears, Esther S.	Skidmore, Unnamed	
Goffigon, Nath'l S.	Metcalf, Wm. T.	Stoakley, Thos. A.	

(45)

1885 Deaths

Ames, Unnamed	Holland, N. L.	Only, Marg't.	Thompson, Unnamed
Bagwell, Susanna	Jacob, C. W.	Parker, Tantha	Turner, Major
Banks, Unnamed	James, Hez. P.	Sample, Octava	Warren, Rebecca
Bell, Lottie E.	James, Jno.	Satchell, Unnamed	Watson, Joseph
Barrott, Tabitha	Jarvis, Wm. S.	Savage, Isaac	Wescott, Comfort
Bloxom, Unnamed	Johnson, Jno. M. H.	Scisco, Etha L.	West, Many A.
Church, Laura Ellen	" , Sydney	Scott, Willie H.	White, Annie
Cobb, Nathan E.	La Peters, Lloyd	Sheppard, Lloyd	Williams, Jno. H.
Collins, Unnamed	Morris, Unnamed	Smith, Unnamed	Wilson, Henna
Dunton, Dana A.	Nottingham, Jno. E.	Spady, Thos.	" , Michael
Fitchett, W. T.	" , Sallie	Sturgis, Lillian L.	" , Recca
Floyd, Ruth	" , Unnamed	" , Vianna	" , Recca
Hemings, Viola	" , Unnamed	Sunket, Unnamed	Wyatt, Virginia E.

(52)

1886
Missing

1887 Deaths

Abbott, Chas. B.	Eastes, Fritz	Morris, Not Named	Sturgis, Wm.
Ames, Jas. P.	Fisher, Elizabeth	Nelson, Laura	Tankard, Maria
" , Not Named	" , Wilmer W.	Nock, Not Named	Taylor, Not Named
Badger, Not Named	Fitchett, Jam	Nottingham, Alonzo	Thomas, Not Named
Baily, Not Named	Giddings, Not Named	" , Sarah	Trehern, Not Named
Baker, Sarah E.	" , Not Named	" , Southy	Upshur, Caroline
Becket, Not Named	Goffigon, Arthur	Parsons, Emily L.	" , Elizabeth
Beloate, Not Named	" , Edward	Sample, Not Named	Walston, Thos. C.
Bott, Jas. S.	" , Jennie	Savage, Not Named	Warren, Mary
Brickhouse, Ether	Goodie, Margaret	" , Wm.	Warrington, Wissie May
Brisco, Susan	Hays, Emma	Scarborough, Not Named	Webb, Rosa
Brown, Isaac	Holt, Not Named	Scott, Not Named	Wescoat, Rose
Carter, Jno.	Hunt, Jane	" , Not Named	Widgen, Alfred
" , Priscilla	James, Arthur	Simpkins, Not Named	Wilkins, Jafus
Collins, Geo.	Johnson, Jacob	Sisco, Annie	Williams, George
" , Susan	Jones, Whittington	Spady, Not Named	Wilson, Annie
Dixon, Not Named	Joynes, Arthur	" , Not Named	Winder, Wesley
Doughty, Annie	Lawson, Edwin	" , George	" , William
Douglass, Frederick	Melson, Wm. Henry	" , Susan	Wise, Horace
Drummond, Robt. A.	Miles, Eliza	Stevens, Robt.	
Dunton, Jas.	Moore, Not Named	Stokley, Thos. S.	
" , L. W.	" , Roland B.	Sturgis, Not Named	

(85)

1888 Deaths

Badger, Sarah	Finney, Edna F.	Massey, Ellen	Stevens, Nancy
Brickhouse, Not Named	Fitchett, Mary	Mears, Samuel	Stiles, Nellie
Burrown, Caleb W. J.	" , Not Known	Moore, Mary	Sutton, Not Known
Cobourn, Jno. C.	" , Susan	Nottingham, Not Known	" , Peter
Coley, Samuel	Floyd, Mary F.	Parmer, Catharn	Thompson, Peter C.
Collins, Not Named	Gladden, Ellen	Pearson, Maria	Trehurn, Not Known
" , Susan	Godwin, Rosie A. P.	Peed, Mary	Turner, Nancy
Custis, Not Named	Griffin, Tabby	Rayfield, Minnie	Underhill, Not Known
Doughty, Albert L.	Hickman, Not Known	Robinson, Delia	Upshur, Demory
" , Geo. T.	Joynes, E. G.	Satchell, Davy	White, L. S.
" , Lloyd	" , Tobitha	Savage, Rufus K.	Winder, Born Dead
Eichelburger, Mary	Mapp, E. D.	Smith, Deann	Wyatt, Jas. T.
Fatherly, Major	Mason, Not Known	" , Zero	
Fenderson, Rosee'	" , Wm. A.	Spady, Not Known	

(54)

1889 & 1890

Missing

1891 Deaths

Abrams, John W.	Giddings, -----	Lingo, F. T.	Stewart, Thos.
Ames, Ambro	", Smith	Mapp, M. S.	Stevens, -----
", Lora	Godwin, Maria	", Tabbie	", -----
Andrews, Jacob	Gordy, -----	", Trower	Stratton, Jennie
Bayly, Missouri	Hack, W. T.	", Victor	Taylor, Mary
Beckett, -----	Hargis, Alice R.	Mariner, Ruth	Thomas, Geo.
Bell, Ellen	", Lovey	Milby, James	", Luke
Bivans, Eliza	Harman, Susan	Nottingham, Sallie P.	", Sophia
Brickhouse, Mary	Harmon, Jane	Pead, Georgianna	Thompson, -----
", Robt.	Henderson, Jacob	", Mary	Travis, -----
Bullman, Virginia	Hunt, Ruth T.	Pitts, -----	", Madaline
Burton, Annie	Hurtt, G. K.	", Annie J.	Trehurne, -----
Carpenter, James	Isdell, Sam'l R.	Read, John W.	Trower, Alfred
", John P.	Jacobs, Susie	", Mary	", Joseph
Collins, Delia	James, Benjamin	Rhea, Rebecca H.	Turner, -----
Copes, Elizabeth	", Toby	Richardson, -----	", Julia
Costen, Mary F.	Jarvis, Virginia	", Sarah	Upshur, -----
Council, Virginia S.	Johnson, Berry	Rippon, Peggie	", Patience
Custis, Jas. S.	", J. C. Jr.	Roberts, -----	", Paul
Dalby, Kate	", Maria	Rolley, C. P.	Walston, Maggie
Davis, E. E.	Kellam, Cora	Sample, -----	Washington, Geo.
Doughty, -----	", Jas. C.	Satchell, Geo. Jr.	Webb, Jno. J.
", -----	Kelly, Obed	Saunders, Jas. T.	White, Annie E.
", Edith	Killmon, Polly	Savage, -----	Willis, Harriet
", Sheppard	Lambertson, Jessie	", Peter	Wilson, Ellen
Dunton, Susan A.	Lane, Mary	Scott, James B.	", Fannie
East, Mollie	Lawson, Isaac	", V. A. Mrs.	", Mary E.
Fitchett, Fred	LeCato, -----	Sheppard, Agnes	Winder, John B.
", Henry I.	", E. F.	Smith, Virginia	Wise, -----
Foreman, -----	", Sallie L.	Spady, -----	", -----
Gibb, Ann W.	Lee, Ella W.	Starchey, -----	Wyatt, Estelle P.

(124)

1892 Deaths

Abott, -----	Doughty, -----	Major, May	Smaw, Edward
Addison, -----	" , James S.	Mallett, Elizabeth	Smith, Edward
Allen, Moses	Downing, Martha S.	Mapp, Harry W.	Smith, J. W.
Ames, Willie F.	Dunton, -----	Mariner, -----	Spady, Patience
Andrews, W. W.	Ephraim, -----	Massey, J. W.	Sterling, L. R.
Ashby, Edward	Fisher, Geo.	Mears, -----	Stevens, -----
" , Harold	Fitchett, -----	" , Lizzie	" , -----
" , Maggie	" , Edith	Melson, Mary	" , Geo.
Badger, Elizabeth	" , Priscilla	Nelson, Rosa	Stewart, -----
Bagwell, Emily	" , W. P.	Nottingham, Ruth V.	" , Mary
Baker, J. R.	Francis, Demorey L.	" , Sallie A.	Stoakley, Henry
Ball, Sam'l	Giddings, -----	" , Virginia F.	" , Milley
Bayly, Geo.	" , Willie	" , W. R.	Sturgis, Leonard
" , John	Goffigon, Arintha S.	" , Wm. R.	Sutton, Hennie
Beckett, Linie	Gordy, James S.	Onley, Frank	Tankard, Ezekiel
" , Patience	Hall, Jacob	Palmer, Ellen	Taylor, Adelaide
Bell, Richard	Hallett, Lee	Powell, -----	" , Jas. W.
Belote, Amanda C.	Hamilton, Lena	" , Bennett	" , Mary
" , Fannie	Harmon, Jane	" , Holland	" , Peter
Boggs, E. T.	" , John	Rayfield, Wm. H.	Thompson, Ella
Bool, Sallie	Heath, Caroline	Read, Geo. H.	Upshur, Arthur
" , Willie	" , Julius C.	" , L. S.	" , Mary E.
Brady, Frank	James, Hezekiah	" , Wm. P., Dr.	" , William
Brickhouse, -----	Jarvis, Jesse N.	Rhea, Rebecca	Webb, D. R.
" , Maggie	Johnson, Berry	Richardson, Mary E.	Whitehead, Edgar
Brown, Major	" , Edward B.	Riley, Peter	" . Wm.
" , Norris L.	" , Isabella	Robins, -----	Wicks, Mattie
Burrows, Eva	" , John C.	Rogers, -----	Wilkins, Anna B.
Carpenter, Rinie D.	" , Maria E.	" , -----	Williams, Nannie B.
" , Stephen	" , W. L.	Sample, Lloyd	Willis, Lola
Collins, -----	Kellam, Zed	Satchel, -----	Wilson, Geo.
Colona, Willie	Kerr, Geo. W., Dr.	" , Julia	" , Martha
Custis, Cordelia	Lewis, Adah	" , Leah	Winder, Alice
Davis, Elijah	Liliston, E. C.	Scott, Ellen	" , E. L.
Dennis, James	Lingo, Ben F.	" , Geo. W.	Wright, Isaac
Dix, Carrie	" , Mary	" , Lucile	" , James
" , John H.	Luker, -----	" , Wesley U.	
" , Martha S.	Major, Clara	Sisco, Henry	

(150)

1893 Deaths

Allen, Moses	Dixon, -----	Heath, Rachel	Nelson, David
Ames, F. Willis	", Bell	", Wm. H.	Nottingham, -----
", Florida	", Lillie	Henderson, -----	", Hattie
Anderson, -----	Doughty, Betsy	Henry, Alex	", Roberta
Ashby, Easter	", John W.	Hodges, -----	", Robt.
", Lizzie	", Martin	", Edith	", Thos. H.
", Wilhemina	", Mary	Horsey, Luther N.	", Wm. J.
Badger, Stepney	", Mary A.	Jackson, Ibbie	Parker, Joseph
Baker, Nancy C.	Douglass, Lummie	Jacob, Sallie	Parramore, Mary
Bailey, Maria	Downing, John H.	Jefferson, -----	Pearson, Emma M.
Bayly, John	", S. B.	Johnson, Annie	Perkins, Patience
", Lillie E.	Drier, Geo.	", Nancy	Phillips, Maude C.
", Mary	Dunton, Juliet	", Ruth	", Zoro.
", Thos. M.	", Peter	", Sudie M.	Powell, -----
Bell, -----	", Peter	", William	", Bennett
", -----	Fenderson, Thos.	Jones, William	", John
", Alfred T. Jr.	Ferby, Milton	Kellam, -----	Pruden, Mamie
", Smith	Finney, Chas.	", Sam'l	Randolph, Geo.
Belote, Fanny	Fisher, Julius	", Sarah	Read, Isaac
Bingham, Charlotte	Fitchett, -----	Kendall, Lucius	Redden, Dolly M.
Bivans, -----	", Isaac	Kishpaugh, W. D.	Riddick, -----
Bloxom, W. F.	Floyd, James B.	Lankford, B. S.	Roberts, E. T.
Booker, Lee	Gaskins, Mary	Lewis, -----	", Grace M.
Bool, Wm. T.	Godwin, Harriet B.	Lindsay, Imogene	Rogers, John
Brickhouse, -----	Goffigon, Mary A.	Mapp, Bessie	Satchell, Juliet
Brown, -----	", Mildred E.	", Bettie H.	", Thos. J.
", -----	", Spencer	", Frank B.	Saunders, Effie
", I. J.	Green, John	", J. A.	Savage, Ann
", Mattie	Griffin, Jacob H.	", John C.	", Geo. W.
", Thos.	", Patsy	", Sarah J.	", Kate
", W. C.	Griffith, Severn	", Severn	", Mary
Burruss, Mary E.	", Severn Sr.	Marriner, -----	", Thos.
Burton, James	Guy, James	Mason, Edward	", Walker
Charnock, Mary	", Lillie M.	Mears, ------	Scott, -----
", Mary E.	Hallett, Comfort	Messick, Sallie A.	", Ibbie
Collins, -----	", Hebrew	Miles, Mary	", S. H.
Colona, Ethel	Hamilton, -----	Milligan, Robt.	", Victoria J.
Copes, Lizzie	", Geo. W.	Moody, -----	Shackleford, -----
Costin, Henry	Harman, -----	Moore, Geo.	Sharpley, James E.
", Robt. S.	", Dolph	", Geo. W.	Sheppard, James
Dennis, Littleton	", Frank	", Levin	Sisco, Leonard
Dix, Mary	Hatany, Arintha	Morris, Wm.	Smith, -----
", Wm. T. Sr.	Hayes, Emma	", Wm. Sr.	", -----

1893 Deaths "cont'd"

Spady, -----	Tankard, Calno	Upshur, Julia A.	Williams, Levin
" , Betsy	Taylor, Levin	" , Wm. B.	" , Lloyd W.
" , Ella	Thomas, Solomon	Ward, Sam'l N.	" , Maria P. H., Mrs.
" , Grace	Thompson, Geo.	White, John W.	Willis, Ella M.
" , Joseph D.	Tomas, Bettie	Wicks, -----	Wilson, John W.
" , Sam'l	Toy, George	" , Carrie	Winder, -----
Sterling, -----	Travis, Charlotte	" , James Sr.	" , Georgianna
Stevens, -----	Trower, -----	Widgen, -----	" , Maggie G.
" , Raymond	" , -----	" , Fannie	" , Maria
Stewart, Herbert	Tyler, John A.	Wilkins, Emily	Wise, -----
Stoakley, Alfred	Upshur, Caleb	" , Fred	Wright, J. C.
Stoakley, Alfred	" , Geo.	" , Thos.	" , William
Stockey, Henry	" , John M.	Williams, Jesse	Wyatt, Thos. H.

(224)

1894 Deaths

Addison, -----	Fisher, Hennie	Mears, Sarah A.	Sunkett, Mack
Ames, Florida	" , James A.	Melson, Pearl	Tankard, -----
" , Lola	" , Jane	Mills, England	" , Mary G.
" , Mollie	Fitchett, Emiline	Morris, Martha	" , Roland
" , Sallie	" , Isaac	Neilass, -----	Taylor, Elizabeth B.
" , Wm. C	" , Thos. J.	Nickerson, John W.	" , Harry
Andrews, Polly	Floyd, Russell	Nottingham, Jacob T.	Tazwell, John
Ashby, Kesiah	Francis, Jacob	" , Robt. L.	Thom, Annie P.
Bayly, Marie	Frost, Frank	" , S. T.	Thomas, -----
" , Sarah	Garrison, Mary	Parker, Susan	Turner, Isaac
" , Sarah E.	Griffith, Jacob	Pitts, Oliver	" , Sarah
" , " " .	" , Thos. E.	Read, Alfred	Tyler, -----
Bell, Mary	Grimmer, Walter H.	Richardson, -----	Upshur, Addie
Bowden, Geo.	Gunter, Sallie A.	" , R. B.	" , Leah
Brickhouse, -----	Hallett, Leonard Jr.	Roberson, Virginia	" , Nellie
" , Emma	Harman, Dolly	Roberts, Arthur M.	" , Sarah
Brown, Margaret	" , Geo.	Robins, Abraham J.	" , William Jr.
Bull, James	" , Nim	" , Charles	Vincent, Laura
Carpenter, Marion	Heath, Wm. H.	" , Lafe	Waddy, Priscilla
" , Mary An	Howard, Henry J.	Robinson, Estelle	Walker, Annie
Chambers, Lizzie J.	Iliff, Hattie	Rooks, -----	Wallace, -----
Chandler, E. Willis	Jacob, Geo.	" , Oliver P.	Ward, Edgar
Charnock, Julian	" , Joseph M.	Sample, -----	" , Sam'l D.
Church, Atta	James, Helen P.	Satchell, Leonard	Watson, -----
" , James	Johnson, Nancy	Sears, Fairfield	West, Daniel
Collins, Leonard	Jones, Mary C.	Sedgewick, Florence	Wilkins, Geo. W.
Costin, Jerry	Kellam, Alfred	Sharpley, Bettie	Williams, Sarah
Custis, Rose	" , Jacob	Sheppard, -----	" , Wm. J.
Cutler, Sam'l	" , Rosa B.	Six, Sallie	Wilson, -----
Delano, Richard	Kelley, -----	Smaw, -----	" , Ellen
Doughty, Alonzo	" , Kitty	" , Spencer	" , Mary
" , Chas. B.	Kendall, Susan W.	Smith, Alfred	Wise, -----
" , John L.	Ketcham, Nathan A.	" , Alfred	" , -----
" , Mary	Mallett, Isaac	" , Elton B.	" , James
Downes, -----	Manning, A. J.	" , Toby	" , W. H.
Drennan, William	Mapp, -----	Spady, Ella	" , William
Dunne, H. W.	Matthews, Nillie	Stevenson, Ella	
East, -----	McGuire, Henry	Strausburg, C. H.	

(150)

1895 Deaths

Addison, -----	Fisher, Henrietta	Mapp, R. W. Jr.	Savage, Ella
Ames, H. W.	Fitchett, L. A.	", R. W. Sr.	", Robt.
", James S.	", Mary	Matthews, James	", T. P.
", W. C.	Floyd, G. Fred Jr.	McKown, Wm.	Shackleford, LeCato
Banister, -----	", Mary	Miles, John W. Jr.	Sheppard, Mary E.
Baxter, Robt.	Giddings, -----	Moore, Sam'l	Shivers, John
Bayly, -----	", Ella	Morris, -----	Sisco, Louisa
", Erline	Gladson, -----	", -----	Smith, -----
", Sarah	Godwin, Jacob Sr.	", Cornelius	", Mary
Beckett, Ada	Goody, Wm. T.	", Marian	Spady, Leolin
", William	Griffith, Severn	Moses, Levin	Stevens, -----
Belote, Maggie	Grimmer, Frank	Nottingham, -----	Stewart, -----
Berry, Geo. W.	", Walter	", -----	Tankard, Sophie E.
Borom, Wm. T.	Grinnalds, Mary A.	Offer, Martha E.	Trower, -----
Bowdoin, Elizabeth	Gunter, Jane	Only, Manie	Turner, -----
Brickhouse, Carson	Hamilton, W. J.	Outten, Elizabeth	Upshur, Abraham
", Geo.	Hargis, Mary A.	Palmer, Mary E.	", Levin
", Lloyd	Harman, Austin	Parks, -----	", Sallie
", Maggie	", Mary	Perkins, Mollie	", Sam'l
Brown, James	Hastings, -----	Phillips, Aaron	Ward, Nettie
Chandler, Ben. J.	Henderson, Wm. N. P	", Custis	", Ruth S.
", Margaret	Hunt, Monie	Powell, -----	Watson, Daniel
Church, Jacob	Ireland, Arlene	Prince, Albert	Wescott, Wm. B.
Collins, Jas. L.	Jacobs, -----	Read, Alfred	Wesley, Estelle
Costin, John	", Caroline	", Smith	White, John
Cottingham, W. H.	", Lloyd	Robbins, Geo. M.	Whitehead, Fannie
Cox, Peter	James, John	", W. F., Rev.	Whitman, Mary E.
Cutler, Maria	Jefferson, -----	Robinson, Wm. K.	Widgen, Mary
Cypress, Sallie	Johnson, Amy	Rolly, -----	Wilson, Fannie
Dalby, Margaret	", Dallas	Sample, Eliza	", Sam'l
Davy, Levin	", Joseph	Satchel, -----	Winder, Jno.
Dix, Asa Sr.	Jubilee, -----	", Carrie	", Joseph
Doughty, E. B.	Kellam, -----	", Southey	Wise, William
Downes, Thos. H.	Knight, -----	Saunders, Arthur	Wright, Fred
Drummond, Ada	Lambertson, Essie M.	Savage, -----	
Elliott, -----	LeCato, -----	", -----	
", Rosa	Lindsay, Emma	", Edward	

(145)

1896 Deaths

Addison, -----	East, Edward	Lingo, Susan	Smith, Severn
Allen, -----	Elliott, John W.	Marsh, Manie	Spady, -----
" , Leah	Elsner, Robert	Mason, Elizabeth	" , -----
Ashby, Margaret	Ennis, J. J.	" , Mary L.	" , -----
Baptist, James	" , John W.	Matthews, Adah	Stevens, -----
Bayly, -----	Evans, Ben	McKown, Blanch	" , -----
" , Seth N.	Fatherly, Henry F.	Mears, Henry S.	" , John
Beckett, -----	Fisher, Florence	Miles, Esther D.	" , Josephine
Bell, -----	" , Harriet	Moore, Willie	" , Lavinia
" , -----	Fitchett, Emily L.	Morris, Edna L.	Stevenson, Blanche
" , Harry	" , Ibbie	Nottingham, Leah	Stratton, -----
Beloat, John S.	" , Mary	" , Sophie	" , -----
" , Robert	" , Robert	" , W. R.	Sturgis, -----
Bird, -----	Floyd, Emily	Palmer, Sam	Taylor, Wesley
Bool, Mary E.	Fowler, Polly F.	Parker, Emiline	Toliver, John H.
Bowdoin, Rose	Francis, H. T.	Phillips, George C.	Trower, Alfred
Boytt, -----	" , Mary H.	Pitts, John	" , "
" , -----	Gibb, Emma J.	Pool, -----	" , Annie L.
Bradford, -----	Griffith, -----	Powell, -----	Turner, Julia
" , Fisher	Guy, Bettie	Roberts, John L.	Upshur, -----
Brickhouse, Rebecca	Harmon, Luke	Rolley, Wm. S.	" , Liddie
" , Severn	Hopkins, Henry	Sample, David	" , Mary E.
Brooks, -----	Humphreys, -----	Satchell, -----	Waddy, Mary E.
Burr, Henry B.	Jacob, Maggie	Savage, -----	Warren, M. Sarah
Carpenter, -----	" , Sarah V.	Savage, -----	Watson, Ben
Carroll, Patrick	James, -----	Savage, -----	" , John C.
Causey, L. P.	" , Lucy	Savage, Liddie	Wescott, Margaret
Collins, Adah	" , Mary	Scarboro, Emeline	West, Comfort
" , Martha S.	Jarvis, Mary G.	Scarboro, William	White, John M.
" , Rachel	Johnson, Susan	Scisco, Russell	Wilkins, -----
Custis, -----	Joynes, -----	Scott, Annie	Williams, E. J.
" , Preston S.	Kellam, Marion	" , Seth G.	Winder, Edith
Dalby, George R.	" , Tom	Seymour, Abe	" , William
" , James B.	Kelly, Arthur F.	Skinner, William	Wise, -----
Doughty , Sarah	Lane, -----	Smith, -----	" , -----
Downes, Thomas A.	Lawson, Abraham	" , Ed	" , Arintha S.
Downing, Joseph	Leatherbury, -----	" , George	Wyatt, Robert
Dunton, Thomas R.	Lewis, Charles	" , Leah	" , Wm. E.

(152)

The following pages contain Deaths 1884-96 in Chronological order

1884 Deaths "Chronological"

Nottingham, -------	Jan. 12	Scott, H. Hy	June 15	Rose, -------	Oct. 6
Downing, Luen	Jan. 13	Willett, -------	June 15	Mapp, Geo.	Oct. 15
Stoakley, Thos. A.	Feb. 24	Scott, -------	June 17	Kellam, Southey	Oct. 23
Fitchett, -------	Feb. 27	Wescoat, Sarah	June 23	Upshur, Sarah P.	Oct. 26
Morris, -------	Mar. '84	Chandler, -------	July '84	Joynes, Garnet	Nov. '84
Hargis, -------	Mar. 5	Gladson, Vernon	July 1	Nottingham, Thos. H.	Nov. 12
Griffith, Sallie	Mar. 9	Harcus/Hargis, -----	July 1	Baker, Sallie	Nov. 20
Dixon, Mary Susan	Mar. 25	Kelly, Annie	Aug. 1	Nottingham, -------	Nov. 25
Goffigon, Nath'l S.	Mar. 30	Roberts, -------	Aug. 2	Giddings, Robert	Nov. 29
Ames, Peggy	Apr. 20	Wilkins, -------	Aug. 7	Warren, Lukie	Dec. '84
Dunton, Mrs. Mary	Apr. 20	Hickman, -------	Aug. 15	Trower, Daisy	Dec. 1
Nottingham, Mary	Apr. 27	Wise, -------	Aug. 15	Hamby, Elizabeth	Dec. 10
Laupheimer, Jacob	May '84	Trower, Jesse	Sept. 1	Mears, Esther S.	Dec. 17
Ashby, Mary A.	May 1	Burton, Eva	Sept. 16	Trower, Clement	Dec. 20
Metcalf, Wm. T.	May 12	Parker, -------	Oct. 3	Skidmore, -------	Dec. 23

(45)

1885 Deaths "Chronological"

Satchell, -------	Jan. 15	Wilson, Ricca	Apr. 23	Fitchett, Walter T.	Aug. 22
Banks, -------	Jan. 24	Wilson, Michael	May 10	Sturgis, Lillian L.	Aug. 23
Hemings, Viola	Feb. '85	Bloxom, -------	June '85	Nottingham, -------	Sept. 11
Bagwell, Susanna	Feb. 1	Sunket, -------	June '85	Turner, Major	Sept. 18
James, Jno.	Feb. 8	Warren, Rebecca	June '85	Sturgis, Vianna	Sept. 20
Parker, Tantha	Feb. 13	Wilson, Ricca	June 5	Nottingham, -------	Sept. 25
Sample, Octava	Feb. 25	Scott, Willie H.	June 7	Only, Margt.	Oct. 2
Morris, -------	Feb. 28	Smith, -------	June 8	Church, Laura Ellen	Oct. 15
White, Annie	Mar. 4	Floyd, Ruth	June 20	Nottingham, Sallie	Oct. 17
Johnson, Jno. M. H.	Mar. 10	Dunton, Dana A.	June 22	LaPeters, Lloyd	Nov. '85
Ames, -------	Mar. 17	Thompson, -------	June 29	Scisco, Etha L.	Nov. '85
Savage, Isaac	Mar. 20	West, Mary A.	June 29	Wyatt, Virginia E.*	Nov. '85
Williams, Jno. H.	Mar. 22	James, Hez. P.	July 5	Jarvis, Wm. S.	Nov. 28
Jacob, C. W.	Mar. 26	Watson, Joseph	July 7	Collins, -------	Dec. '85
Wilson, Hennie	Mar. 30	Holland, N. L.	July 9	Johnson, Sydney	Dec. '85
Spady, Thos.	Apr. '85	Cobb, Nathan E.	Aug. 3	Sheppard, Lloyd	Dec. 1
Nottingham, Jno. E. Sr.	Apr. 1	Bell, Lottie E.	Aug. 12		
Barrott, Tabitha	Apr. 20	Wescott, Comfort	Aug. 15		52

*Wyatt, Virginia E. Oct. 10 on Miles files

1886 Missing

xxiv

1887 Deaths "Chronological"

Hickman, -------	1887	Scott, -------	June 3	Scarborough, -------	Aug. 14
Savage, William	Jan. 1	Nottingham, Southey	June 12	Winder, Wesley	Aug. 14
Simpkins, -------	Jan. 3	Drummond, Robert A.	June 13	Upshur, Elizabeth	Aug. 25
Parsons, Emily L.	Jan. 4	Dixon, -------	June 14	Cisco/Brown, Isaac	Sept. 6
Nottingham, Alonzo	Jan. 8	Carter, John	June 15	Nock, -------	Sept. 13
Stevens, Robert	Jan. 25	Lawson, Edwin	June 15	Wescoat, Rose	Sept. 13
Sturgis, -------	Feb. 2	Warren, Mary	June 15	Spady, Susan	Sept. 30
Miles, Eliza	Feb. 3	Spady, -------	June 29	Sturgis, William	Oct. 4
Giddings, -------	Feb. 4	Spady, George	June 30	Goodie, Margaret	Oct. 5
Hunt, Jane	Feb. 29	Trehern, -------	June 30	Spady, -------	Oct. 8
Scisco, Annie	Mar. 2	Nelson, Laura	July 1	Goffigon, Edward	Oct. 14
Doughty, Annie	Mar. 13	Dunton, Littleton	July 9	Goffigon, Jennie	Oct. 15
Jones, Whittingham	Mar. 14	Fisher, Wilmer W.	July 9	Becket, -------	Nov. 1
Scisco, Annie	Mar. 21	Beloate, -------	July 14	Johnson, Jacob	Nov. 1
Brisco, Susan	Mar. 30	James, Arthur	July 15	Ames, -------	Nov. 18
Giddings, -------	Apr. 1	Moore, Roland B.	July 18	Collins, George	Nov. 19
Tankard, Maria	Apr. 1	Bayly, -------	July 20	Wilson, Annie	Nov. 21
Carter, Priscilla	Apr. 3	Morris, -------	July 20	Warrington, Wissie May	Nov. 29
Dunton, James	Apr. 5	Thomas, -------	Aug. 1	Widgen, Alfred	Dec. 2
Wise, Horace	Apr. 11	Upshur, Caroline	Aug. 2	Walston, Thos. C.	Dec. 6
Savage, -------	May 3	Ames, James P.	Aug. 3	Fisher, Elizabeth	Dec. 14
Melson, William	May 4	Brickhouse, Ether	Aug. 3	Badger, -------	Dec. 15
Sample, -------	May 4	Williams, George	Aug. 4	Bott, Jas. S.	Dec. 18
Wilkins, Jafus	May 4	Scott, -------	Aug. 5	Taylor, -------	Dec. 18
Webb, Rosa	May 6	Winder, William	Aug. 6	Fitchett, Jane	Dec. 25
Joynes, Arthur	May 18	Abbott, Charles B.	Aug. 10	Douglass, Frederick	Dec. 28
Nottingham, Arintha	May 28	Goffigon, Arthur	Aug. 11	Holt, -------	Dec. 28
Eates, Fritz	June 3	Moore, -------	Aug. 11	Collins, Susan	Dec. 30
Hayes, Emma	June 3	Baker, E. Sarah	Aug. 14	86	

85 + 1 (Hickman,------- 1887) from 1888 records

1888
contains no Month or Day only year thereby omitted

1889 & 1890
Missing

1891 Deaths "Chronological"

Name	Date	Name	Date	Name	Date
Hargis, Lovey	1891	Hack, W. T.	June 91	East, Mollie	Sept. 4
Thomas, Sophia	1891	Harman, Susan	June 91	Lane, Mary	Sept. 4
Wilson, Mary E.	Jan. 2	Pitts, -------	June 91	Costen, Mary F.	Sept. 8
LeCato, Sallie L.	Jan. 3	Trower, Joseph	June 91	Andrews, Jacob	Sept. 14
Giddings, -------	Jan. 16	Doughty, Edith	June 2	Fitchett, Fred	Sept. 14
Johnson, Maria	Jan. 28	Trower, Alfred	June 4	Wilson, Fannie	Sept. 14
Giddings, Smith	Feb. 91	Doughty, Sheppard	June 6	Lingo, F. T.	Sept. 17
Kelly, Obed *	Feb. 91	Stratton, Jennie	June 6	Bell, Ellen	Oct. 91
Lambertson, Jessie	Feb. 91	Hurtt, G. K.	June 8	Mapp, Victor	Oct. 91
Copes, Elizabeth	Feb. 3	Burton, Annie	June 10	Upshur, -------	Oct. 2
Richardson, -------	Feb. 10	Read, John W.	June 17	Travis, Madaline	Oct. 4
Rippon, Peggie	Feb. 12	Upshur, Patience	June 21	Sample, -------	Oct. 8
Richardson, Sarah	Feb. 18	Kellam, Cora	June 25	Dalby, Kate	Oct. 10
Doughty, -------	Feb. 21	Ames, Ambro	July 91	Mariner, Ruth	Oct. 17
Thomas, Geo.	Mar. 91	Jacobs, Susie	July 91	Doughty, -------	Oct. 19
Turner, -------	Mar. 91	Webb, Jno. J.	July 91	Hargis, Alice R.	Oct. 24
Milby, James	Mar. 2	Wise, -------	July 2	Rolley, C. P	Oct. 28
Carpenter, John P.	Mar. 10	Davis, E. E.	July 4	Beckett, -------	Nov. 91
Savage, Peter	Mar. 12	Henderson, Jacob	July 4	Walston, Maggie	Nov. 91
Custis, Jas. S.	Mar. 15	James, Toby	July 4	Winder, John B.	Nov. 3
LeCato, E. F.	Mar. 15	Roberts, -------	July 4	Willis, Harriet	Nov. 10
Smith, Virginia	Mar. 15	Pead, Mary	July 7	Wilson, Ellen	Nov. 11
Wise, -------	Mar. 15	Turner, Julia	July 7	Killmon, Polly	Nov. 14
Lee, Ella W.	Mar. 17	Upshur, Paul	July 8	Saunders, Jas. T.	Nov. 14
Scott, James B.	Mar. 17	Lawson, Isaac	July 9	Foreman, -------	Nov. 17
Brickhouse, Mary	Mar. 18	Pitts, Annie J.	July 11	Isdell, Sam'l R.	Nov. 23
Nottingham, Sallie P.	Mar. 28	Read, Mary	July 12	Jarvis, Virginia	Nov. 23
Godwin, Maria	Mar. 31	Harmon, Jane	July 16	Bivans, Eliza	Nov. 25
Brickhouse, Robt. **	Apr. 91	Johnson, J. C. Jr.	July 16	Satchell, Geo. Jr.	Dec. 91
Thomas, Luke	Apr. 91	Mapp, Trower	July 18	Stevens, -------	Dec. 91
Washington, Geo.	Apr. 91	Carpenter, James ***	Aug. 91	Travis, -------	Dec. 91
Bullman, Virginia	Apr. 3	Pead, Georgeanna	Aug. 91	Bayly, Missouri	Dec. 2
Mapp, Tabbie	Apr. 6	Taylor, Mary	Aug. 91	Collins, Delia	Dec. 10
Starchey, -------	Apr. 7	Gordy, -------	Aug. 4	Rhea, Rebecca H.	Dec. 14
Ames, Nora	Apr. 15	Stewart, Thos.	Aug. 12	LeCato, -------	Dec. 15
Fitchett, Henry I.	Apr. 18	Thompson, -------	Aug. 16	Wyatt, Estelle P.	Dec. 16
Dunton, Susan A.	Apr. 28	Spady, -------	Aug. 19	James, Benjamin	Dec. 18
White, Annie E.	May 8	Abrams, John W.	Aug. 20	Trehurne, -------	Dec. 28
Johnson, Berry	May 10	Kellam, Jas. C.	Aug. 23	Council, Virginia S.	Dec. 30
Savage, -------	May 10	Gibb, Ann W.	Sept. 91	Mapp, M. S.	Dec. 30
Sheppard, Agnes	May 18	Stevens, -------	Sept. 91		
Hunt, Ruth T.	May 31	Scott, Mrs. V.A.	Sept. 2	124	

*Kelly, Obed 2/8/91 on Ancestry   **Brickhouse, Robt. 4/1/91 on Ancestry

***Carpenter, James 7/16/91 on Ancestry

1892 Deaths "Chronological"

Wilson, Geo.	Jan. 4	Powell, Holland	Apr. 16	Mears, -------	July 7		
Goffigon, Arintha S.	Jan. 5	Wright, James	Apr. 16	Doughty, James S.	July 12		
Johnson, Edward B.	Jan. 8	Webb, D. R.	Apr. 17	Scott, Ellen	July 12		
Addison, -------	Jan. 9	Liliston, E. C.	Apr. 23	Abott, -------	July 15		
Fisher, Geo.	Jan. 9	Stewart, Mary	Apr. 23	Nottingham, W. R.	July 21		
Powell, -------	Jan. 10	Downing, Martha S.	Apr. 27	Ashby, Maggie	July 29		
Stoakley, Milley	Jan. 10	Only, Frank	Apr. 28	Whitehead, Wm.	Aug. 3		
Sisco, Henry	Jan. 12	Wicks, Mattie	May 3	Bell, Richard	Aug. 4		
Stoakley, Henry	Jan. 12	Tankard, Ezekiel	May 6	Taylor, Mary	Aug. 4		
Johnson, Berry	Jan. 16	Lingo, Ben F.	May 7	Johnson, Isabella	Aug. 12		
Allen, Moses	Jan. 16	Rogers, -------	May 14	Stevens, Geo.	Aug. 13		
James, Hezekiah	Jan. 18	Sterling, L. R.	May 15	Ashby, Harold	Aug. 14		
Upshur, Mary E.	Jan. 20	Satchel, Julia	May 16	Read, Geo. H.	Aug. 16		
Wilkins, Anna B.	Jan. 22	Williams, Nannie B.	May 23	Taylor, Adelaide	Aug. 16		
Nottingham, Wm. K.	Jan. 24	Bool, Willie	May 26	Dix, Martha S.	Aug. 19		
Smith, Edward	Jan. 31	Bool, Sallie	May 30	Badger, Elizabeth	Aug. 20		
Davis, Elijah	Feb. 3	Burrows, Eva	June 4	Kerr, Dr. Geo. W.	Aug. 22		
Read, L. S.	Feb. 5	Dix, John H.	June 4	Carpenter, Rinie D.	Aug. 26		
Spady, Patience	Feb. 6	Robins, -------	June 5	Winder, E. L.	Sept. 3		
Whitehead, Edgar	Feb. 6	Giddings, -------	June 6	Brickhouse, Maggie	Sept. 4		
Carpenter, Stephen	Feb. 10	Jarvis, Jesse N.	June 7	Wilson, Martha	Sept. 4		
Boggs, E. T.	Feb. 11	Taylor, Peter	June 8	Beckett, Patience	Sept. 5		
Heath, Caroline	Feb. 15	Ephraim, -------	June 10	Hallett, Lee	Sept. 6		
Lewis, Adah	Feb. 16	Nottingham, Ruth V.	June 10	Luker, -------	Sept. 7		
Hall, Jacob	Feb. 18	Fitchett, -------	June 12	Giddings, Millie	Sept. 10		
Richardson, Mary E.	Feb. 22	Fitchett, W. P.	June 12	Goody, James S.	Sept. 10		
Stevens, -------	Feb. 22	Mears, Lizzie	June 12	Brown, Norris L.	Sept. 11		
Beckett, Linie	Feb. 24	Upshur, Arthur	June 12	Johnson, Maria E.	Sept. 13		
Smith, J. W.	Feb. 24	Johnson, John C.	June 14	Thompson, Ella	Sept. 15		
Read, Dr. Wm. P.	Mar. 2	Powell, Bennett	June 14	Sturgis, Leonard	Sept. 16		
Brown, Major	Mar. 4	Brady, Frank	June 16	Harmon, John	Sept. 19		
Sample, Lloyd	Mar. 4	Stewart, -------	June 16	Lingo, Mary	Sept. 19		
Winder, Alice	Mar. 4	Custis, Cordelia	June 18	Johnson, W. L.	Sept. 20		
Satchel, -------	Mar. 13	Fitchett, Priscilla	June 24	Colona, Willie	Oct. 3		
Collins, -------	Mar. 15	Hamilton, Lena	June 25	Scott, Wesley U.	Oct. 3		
Bayly, John	Mar. 16	Fitchett, Edith	June 27	Mapp, Harry W.	Oct. 4		
Stevens, -------	Mar. 25	Bagwell, Emily	July 2	Rayfield, Wm. H.	Oct. 4		
Baker, J. R.	Mar. 29	Harmon, Jane	July 2	Major, Clara	Oct. 10		
Satchel, Leah	Apr. 4	Ashby, Edward	July 3	Brickhouse, -------	Oct. 11		
Scott, Geo. W.	Apr. 4	Nelson, Rosa	July 4	Major, May	Oct. 13		
Francis, Demorey L.	Apr. 6	Willis, Lola	July 4	Belote, Fannie	Oct. 16		
Ball, Sam'l	Apr. 11	Wright, Isaac	July 4	Heath, Julius C.	Oct. 16		
Scott, Lucile	Apr. 14	Massey, J. W.	July 6	Kellam, Zed	Oct. 19		
Bayly, Geo.	Apr. 16	Smaw, Edward	July 6	Marriner, -------	Oct. 19		

1892 Deaths "Chronological" cont'd

Nottingham, Virginia F.	Oct. 24	Rogers, -------	Nov. 17	Sutton, Hennie	Dec. 12
Doughty, -------	Nov. 92	Dix, Carrie	Nov. 26	Ames, Willie F.	Dec. 13
Dunton, -------	Nov. 6	Andrews, W. W.	Dec. 4	Nottingham, Sallie A.	Dec. 15
Melson, Mary	Nov. 8	Belote, Amanda C.	Dec. 5	Rhea, Rebecca	Dec. 15
Taylor, Jas. W.	Nov. 10	Riley, Peter	Dec. 5	Dennis, James	Dec. 22
Upshur, William	Nov. 14	Mallett, Elizabeth	Dec. 8	Palmer, Ellen	Dec. 25

1893 Deaths "Chronological"

Name	Date	Name	Date	Name	Date
Upshur, Geo.	Jan. 4	Tomas, Bettie	Mar. 6	Moore, Geo.	May 14
Downing, John H.	Jan. 5	Downing, S. B.	Mar. 8	Brown, -------	May 16
Widgen, -------	Jan. 7	Stoakley, Alfred	Mar. 9	Hodges, -------	May 18
Nottingham, Wm. J.	Jan. 9	Dixon, Lillie	Mar. 10	Scott, Victoria J.	May 26
Costin, Henry	Jan. 10	Williams, Lloyd W.	Mar. 10	Mears, -------	May 31
Hallett, Hebrew	Jan. 10	Winder, Maggie G.	Mar. 10	Doughty, Martin	June 1
Allen, Moses	Jan. 14	Satchell, Juliet	Mar. 12	Brown, Thos.	June 4
Brown, -------	Jan. 14	Stoakley, Alfred	Mar. 14	Lankford, B. S.	June 4
Gaskins, Mary	Jan. 14	Wright, William	Mar. 14	Shackelford	June 4
Lindsay, Imogene	Jan. 14	Bloxom, W. F.	Mar. 15	Perkins, Patience	June 8
Upshur, Wm. B.	Jan. 14	Pearson, Emma M.	Mar. 15	Belote, Fanny	June 10
Kellam, -------	Jan. 15	Doughty, John W.	Mar. 16	Nottingham, Robt.	June 10
Wicks, -------	Jan. 16	Hamilton, -------	Mar. 16	Anderson, -------	June 13
Wise, -------	Jan. 16	Milligan, Robt.	Mar. 16	Smith, -------	June 14
Phillips, Maude C.	Jan. 19	Phillips, Zoro.	Mar. 16	Fisher, Julius	June 15
Scott, Ibbie	Jan. 20	Collins, -------	Mar. 19	Drier, Geo.	June 16
Dunton, Peter	Jan. 22	Dix, Wm. T. Sr.	Mar. 19	Griffith, Severn Sr.	June 16
Costin, Robt. S.	Jan. 23	Booker, Lee	Mar. 20	Savage, Mary	June 18
Floyd, James B.	Jan. 23	Dixon, -------	Mar. 20	Travis, Charlotte	June 18
Upshur, Caleb	Jan. 23	Williams, Mrs. Maria P. H.	Mar. 24	Fiitchett, -------	June 19
Stevens, -------	Jan. 26	Dixon, Bell	Mar. 25	Jacob, Sallie	June 20
Read, Isaac	Feb. 2	Spady, Sam'l	Mar. 27	Nottingham, Roberta	June 20
Wicks, Carrie	Feb. 2	Stewart, Herbert	Apr. 2	Redden, Dolly M.	June 27
Wilkins, Fred	Feb. 2	Spady, -------	Apr. 6	Wright, J. C.	June 30
Griffin, Patsy	Feb. 10	Harman, Frank	Apr. 10	Ames, F. Willis	July 2
Bell, Smith	Feb. 12	Mapp, Bettie H.	Apr. 10	Lewis, -------	July 3
Charnock, Mary E.	Feb. 14	Taylor, Levin	Apr. 10	Powell, -------	July 3
Johnson, William	Feb. 14	Roberts, E. T.	Apr. 12	Wilson, John W.	July 3
Upshur, Julia A.	Feb. 15	Ward, Sam'l N.	Apr. 12	Bingham, Charlotte	July 4
Guy, James	Feb. 16	Ashby, Wilhemina	Apr. 13	Stevens, Raymond	July 4
Morris, Wm.	Feb. 16	Spady, Joseph D.	Apr. 13	Tankard, Calno	July 4
Morris, Wm. Sr.	Feb. 16	Williams, Levin	Apr. 15	Bell, Alfred T. Jr.	July 5
Wicks, James Sr.	Feb. 17	Mapp, John C.	Apr. 16	Copes, Lizzie	July 6
Spady, Grace	Feb. 19	Roberts, Grace M.	Apr. 17	Marriner, -------	July 6
Mapp, J. A.	Feb. 20	Doughty, Betsey	Apr. 18	Jefferson, -------	July 10
Winder, -------	Feb. 24	Brown, Mattie	Apr. 20	Savage, Geo. W.	July 10
Baker, Nancy C.	Feb. 27	Satchell, Thos. J.	Apr. 27	Savage, Walker	July 11
Powell, John	Feb. 28	Moore, Geo. W.	May 5	Willis, Ella M.	July 11
Williams, Jesse	Mar. 1	Hatany, Arintha	May 6	Doughty, Mary	July 12
Bell, -------	Mar. 3	Savage, Ann	May 10	Harman, -------	July 12
Bayly, Thos. M.	Mar. 4	Spady, Betsy	May 10	Hayes, Emma	July 12
Kellam, Sam'l	Mar. 5	Trower, -------	May 12	Henry, Alex.	July 13
Bayly, Mary	Mar. 6	Winder, Georgianna	May 12	Douglass, Lummie	July 15
Parker, Joseph	Mar. 6	Goffigon, Mildred E.	May 14	Fenderson, Thos.	July 17

1893 Deaths "Chronological" cont'd

Griffith, Severn	July 20	Bayly, John	Sept. 10	Johnson, Nancy	Oct. 30
Hamilton, Geo. W.	July 20	Thompson, Geo.	Sept. 11	Goffigon, Mary A.	Nov. 1
Sheppard, James	July 21	Kendall, Lucius	Sept. 12	Charnock, Mary	Nov. 4
Jackson, Ibbie	July 22	Sterling, -------	Sept. 12	Toy, George	Nov. 10
Mapp, Frank B.	July 25	Bailey, Maria	Sept. 14	Wilkins, Emily	Nov. 10
Pruden, Mamie	July 27	Jones, William	Sept. 14	Kishpaugh, W. D.	Nov. 13
Nottingham, Hattie	July 29	Kellam, Sarah	Sept. 14	Mapp, Bessie	Nov. 14
Ames, Florida	July 31	Horsey, Luther N.	Sept. 15	Mapp, Sarah J.	Nov. 14
White, John W.	July 31	Winder, Maria	Sept. 16	Griffin, Jacob H.	Nov. 15
Nottingham, Thos. H.	Aug. 2	Nottingham, -------	Sept. 19	Saunders, Effie	Nov. 15
Brown, W. C.	Aug. 4	Brickhouse, -------	Sept. 22	Dix, Mary	Nov. 16
Ferby, Milton	Aug. 4	Savage, Kate	Sept. 24	Ashby, Easter	Nov. 18
Brown, I. J.	Aug. 10	Colona, Ethel	Sept. 27	Riddick, -------	Nov. 21
Hallett, Comfort	Aug. 10	Guy, Lillie M.	Sept. 30	Hodges, Edith	Nov. 27
Trower, -------	Aug. 10	Scott, -------	Oct. 1	Stepney, Badger	Nov. 29
Burruss, Mary E.	Aug. 12	Bivans, -------	Oct. 2	Ashby, Lizzie	Dec. 2
Harman, Dolph	Aug. 14	Smith, -------	Oct. 2	Heath, Rachel	Dec. 2
Mapp, Severn	Aug. 15	Spady, Ella	Oct. 2	Nelson, David	Dec. 4
Johnson, Ruth	Aug. 16	Wyatt, Thos. H.	Oct. 2	Green, John	Dec. 15
Powell, Bennett	Aug. 16	Wilkins, Thos.	Oct. 5	Rogers, John	Dec. 15
Upshur, John M.	Aug. 16	Bool, Wm. F.	Oct. 9	Randolph, Geo.	Dec. 16
Moore, Levin	Aug. 25	Goffigon, Spencer	Oct. 9	Stockley, Henry	Dec. 16
Parramore, Mary	Aug. 30	Henderson, -------	Oct. 9	Godwin, Harriet B.	Dec. 18
Bayly, Lillie E.	Sept. 1	Sharpley, James E.	Oct. 9	Finney, Chas.	Dec. 20
Scott, S. H.	Sept. 1	Dennis, Littleton	Oct. 10	Tyler, John A.	Dec. 20
Thomas, Solomon	Sept. 2	Johnson, Sudie M.	Oct. 10	Moody, -------	Dec. 21
Bell, -------	Sept. 3	Miles, Mary	Oct. 11	Doughty, Mary A.	Dec. 24
Savage, Thos.	Sept. 3	Sisco, Leonard	Oct. 12	Johnson, Annie	Dec. 24
Dunton, Peter	Sept. 4	Fitchett, Isaac	Oct. 15	Widgen, Fannie	Dec. 28
Dunton, Juliet	Sept. 7	Mason, Edward	Oct. 15	Heath, Wm. H.	Dec. 29
Burton, James	Sept. 9	Messick, Sallie A.	Oct. 28	224	

1894 Deaths "Chronological"

Name	Date	Name	Date	Name	Date
Nickerson, John W.	Jan. 1	Gunter, Sallie A.	Apr. 15	Richardson, -------	July 27
Sharpley, Bettie	Jan. 8	Iliff, Hatie	Apr. 19	Nottingham, Robt. L.	July 28
Thom, Annie P.	Jan. 9	Tankard, Roland	Apr. 20	Ames, Florida	July 30
Vincent, Laura	Jan. 11	Rooks, -------	Apr. 22	Church, James	Aug. 2
Ashby, Kesiah	Jan. 14	Fisher, James A.	Apr. 26	Sheppard, -------	Aug. 2
Wise, -------	Jan. 15	Read, Alfred	May 4	Ames, Mollie	Aug. 12
Bayly, Sarah	Jan. 16	Manning, A. J.	May 7	Pitts, Oliver	Aug. 12
Cutler, Sam'l	Jan. 20	Kendall, Susan W.	May 10	Rooks, Oliver P.	Aug. 12
Neilass, -------	Feb. '94	Mills, England	May 12	Wallace, -------	Aug. 12
Wilkins, Geo. W.	Feb. '94	Nottingham, S. T.	May 12	Garrison, Mary	Aug. 13
Wilson, -------	Feb. 8	Custis, Rose	May 15	Chandler, E. Willis	Aug. 14
Wise, William	Feb. 10	Carpenter, Marion	May 16	Tankard, Mary G.	Aug. 14
Harman, Nim	Feb. 12	Fisher, Jane	May 16	Mapp, -------	Aug. 15
Kellam, Alfred	Feb. 12	Wilson, Ellen	May 25	Roberson, Virginia	Aug. 15
Turner, Isaac	Feb. 13	Kellam, Rosa B.	May 26	Addison, -------	Aug. 16
Taylor, Elizabeth B.	Feb. 15	Bell, Mary	June 2	Ames, Wm. C.	Aug. 16
Bayly, Marie	Feb. 16	Bull, James	June 2	Doughty, Chas. B.	Aug. 16
Walker, Annie	Feb. 20	Harman, Dolly	June 2	Watson, -------	Aug. 16
Morris, Martha	Feb. 23	Mallett, Isaac	June 2	Ames, Lola	Aug. 29
Upshur, Addie	Feb. 29	Church, Atta	June 4	Dunne, H. W.	Sept. '94
Upshur, Sarah	Feb. 29	Costin, Jerry	June 4	Doughty, John L.	Sept. 2
Ketcham, Nathan A.	Mar. 1	Jacob, Geo.	June 4	Spady, Ella	Sept. 2
Bowdoin, Geo.	Mar. 2	Upshur, William J.	June 4	Stevenson, Ella	Sept. 2
Sears, Fairfield	Mar. 4	East, -------	June 10	Collins, Leonard	Sept. 3
Williams, Sarah	Mar. 4	Hallett, Leonard Jr.	June 10	Kelley, Kitty	Sept. 3
Fitchett, Isaac	Mar. 5	Jones, Mary C.	June 14	Drennan, William	Sept. 4
Robins, Lafe	Mar. 5	Waddy, Priscilla	June 16	Bayly, Sarah E.	Sept. 5
Tazwell, John	Mar. 6	Wilson, Mary	June 23	Jacob, Joseph M.	Sept. 5
James, Helen P.	Mar. 16	McGuire, Henry	June 25	Upshur, Nellie	Sept. 6
Kelly, -------	Mar. 16	Griffith, Jacob	July 4	Doughty, Alonzo	Sept. 10
Robins, Charles	Mar. 20	Smaw, -------	July 4	Fitchett, thos. J.	Sept. 10
Robins, Abraham J.	Mar. 21	Tankard, -------	July 4	Fitchett, Emiline	Sept. 11
Sunkett, Mack	Mar. 22	Wise, James	July 4	Nottingham, Jacob T.	Sept. 11
Grimmer, Walter H.	Mar. 28	Carpenter, Mary An	July 5	Strausbury, C. H.	Sept. 12
Thomas, -------	Mar. 29	Downes, -------	July 6	Charnock, Julian	Sept. 14
Griffith, Thos. E.	Apr. 2	Sedgewick, Florence	July 10	Turner, Sarah	Sept. 14
Satchell, Leonard	Apr. 2	Wise, -------	July 11	Upshur, Leah	Sept. 14
Smith, Alfred	Apr. 2	Six, Sallie	July 12	Kellam, Jacob	Sept. 15
Smith, Elton B.	Apr. 6	Roberts, Arthur M.	July 14	Robinson, Estella	Sept. 16
Fisher, Hennie	Apr. 7	Bayly, Sarah E.	July 16	Ward, Edgar	Sept. 28
Melson, Pearl	Apr. 9	Floyd, Russell	July 16	Smaw, Spencer	Oct. 2
Francis, Jacob	Apr. 10	Smith, Toby	July 16	Delano, Richard	Oct. 3
Harman, Geo.	Apr. 12	Richardson, R. B.	July 17	Wise, W. H.	Oct. 8
Brickhouse, -------	Apr. 15	Chambers, Lizzie J.	July 20	Mears, Sarah A.	Oct. 12

1894 Deaths "Chronological" cont'd

Williams, Wm. J.	Oct. 13	West, Daniel	Nov. 15	Brickhouse, Emma	Dec. 5
Ames, Sallie	Oct. 15	Smith, Alfred	Nov. 21	Heath, Wm. H.	Dec. 15
Taylor, Harry	Oct. 16	Doughty, Mary	Nov. 28	Parker, Susan	Dec. 23
Sample, -------	Nov. 1	Andrews, Polly	Dec. 2	Frost, Frank	Dec. 25
Howard, Henry J.	Nov. 5	Tyler, -------	Dec. 2	Matthews, Nellie	Dec. 28
Johnson, Nancy	Nov. 13	Brown, Margaret	Dec. 3	Ward, Sam'l D.	Dec. 28

(150)

1895 Deaths "Chronological"

Henderson, Dr. N. P.	Jan. 4	Borom, Wm. T.	May 16	Shivers, John	Aug. 2
Hamilton, W. Jr.	Jan. 5	Brickhouse, Lloyd	May 16	Collins, Jas. L.	Aug. 3
Read, Alfred	Jan. 12	Johnson, Dallas	May 20	LeCato, -------	Aug. 3
Cox, Peter	Jan. 14	Beckett, William	June 1	Elliott, -------	Aug. 7
Upshur Levin	Jan. 16	Satchel, Carrie	June 1	Moses, Levin	Aug. 7
Gunter, Jane	Jan. 23	Bowdoin, Elizabeth	June 2	Grinnalds, Mary A.	Aug. 8
Berry, Geo. W.	Feb. 2	Harman, Mary	June 2	Read, Smith	Aug. 8
Goody, Wm. T.	Feb. 2	Mapp, R. W. Jr.	June 2	Ward, Nettie	Aug. 8
Mapp, R. W. Sr.	Feb. 2	Rolly, -------	June 2	Doughty, E. B.	Aug. 12
Savage, T. P.	Feb. 2	Savage, -------	June 2	Jefferson, -------	Aug. 14
White, John	Feb. 2	James, John	June 3	McKown, Wm.	Aug. 15
Kellam, -------	Feb. 4	Watson, Daniel	June 4	Matthews, James	Aug. 17
Robbins, Geo. M.	Feb. 4	Jacobs, Caroline	June 6	Hargis, Mary A.	Aug. 18
Bayly, Sarah	Feb. 10	Savage, -------	June 8	Wesley, Estelle	Aug. 28
Stewart, -------	Feb. 10	Brickhouse, Maggie	June 11	Tankard, Sophie E.	Aug. 29
Sample, Eliza	Feb. 14	Jacobs, -------	June 12	Bayly, -------	Sept. 1
Robinson, Wm. K.	Feb. 16	Savage, Robt.	June 12	Prince, Albert	Sept. 1
Fisher, Henrietta	Feb. 27	Whitman, Mary E.	June 12	Baxter, Robt.	Sept. 2
Wilson, Sam'l	Mar. 2	Offer, Martha E.	June 13	Dix, Asa Sr.	Sept. 2
Stevens, -------	Mar. 4	Morris, -------	June 14	Giddings, Ella	Sept. 2
Robbins, W. F. Rev.	Mar. 6	Godwin, Jacob Jr.	June 15	Morris, Cornelius	Sept. 2
Trower, -------	Mar. 13	Ward, Ruth S.	June 15	Only, Manie	Sept. 2
Downes, Thos. H.	Mar. 15	Harman, Austin	July 1	Upshur, Sam'l	Sept. 2
Nottingham, -------	Mar. 15	Fitchett, L. A.	July 3	Brickhouse, Geo.	Sept. 7
Powell, -------	Mar. 15	Gladson, -------	July 3	Costin, John	Sept. 8
Morris, -------	Mar. 19	Satchel, -------	July 4	Giddings, -------	Sept. 10
Spady, Leolin	Mar. 21	Johnson, Joseph	July 6	Beckett, Ada	Sept. 11
Grimmer, Walter	Mar. 26	Moore, Sam'l	July 6	Cutler, Maria	Sept. 28
Hunt, Monie	Mar. 30	Floyd, Mary	July 7	Lambertson, Essie M.	Oct. 2
Sheppard, Mary E.	Apr. 2	Miles, John W. Jr.	July 10	Savage, Ella	Oct. 2
Wise, William	Apr. 2	Morris, Marion	July 10	Grimmer, Frank	Oct. 10
Widgen, Mary	Apr. 3	Savage, Edward	July 10	Winder, Joseph	Oct. 10
Nottingham, -------	Apr. 7	Jubilee, -------	July 12	Ireland, Arlene	Oct. 12
Smith, -------	Apr. 7	Shackleford, LeCato	July 12	Knight, -------	Oct. 12
Brickhouse, Carson	Apr. 8	Smith, Mary	July 12	Cottingham, W. H.	Oct. 15
Davy, Levin	Apr. 12	Cypress, Sallie	July 13	Sisco, Louisa	Oct. 15
Griffith, Severn	Apr. 12	Floyd, G. Fred Jr.	July 13	Whitehead, Fannie	Oct. 20
Wilson, Fannie	Apr. 12	Upshur, Sallie	July 14	Banister, -------	Nov. 1
Addison, -------	Apr. 18	Wright, Fred	July 14	Ames, H. W.	Nov. 3
Elliott, Rosa	Apr. 19	Turner, -------	July 25	Phillips, Custis	Nov. 13
Drummond, Ada	Apr. 30	Hastings, -------	July 28	Upshur, Abraham	Nov. 13
Ames, James S.	May 2	Church, Jacob	Aug. 1	Chandler, Margaret	Nov. 14
Outten, Elizabeth	May 2	Palmer, Mary E.	Aug. 2	Saunders, Arthur	Nov. 25
Fitchett, Mary	May 15	Phillips, Aaron	Aug. 2	Bayly, Erline	Nov. 28

1895 Deaths "Chronologically" cont'd

Johnson, Amy	Dec. 1	Jacobs, Lloyd	Dec. 15	Satchel, Southey	Dec. 22
Perkins, Mollie	Dec. 4	Parks, -------	Dec. 15	Wescott, Wm. B.	Dec. 24
Brown, James	Dec. 8	Ames, W. C.	Dec. 17	Winder, Jno.	Dec. 27
Dalby, Margaret	Dec. 12	Belote, Maggie W.	Dec. 17		
Chandler, Ben. J.	Dec. 15	Lindsay, Emma	Dec. 22	145	

1896 Deaths "Chronologically"

Elsner, Robert	Jan. 1	Rolley, Wm. S.	May 9	Parker, Emiline	Aug. 10
Skinner, William	Jan. 2	Johnson, Susan	May 10	Upshur, -------	Aug. 10
Fatherly, Henry, F.	Jan. 10	Mears, Henry S.	May 10	Guy, Bettie	Aug. 11
Carroll, Patrick	Jan. 12	Wilkins, -------	May 10	Stevens, John	Aug. 12
Fitchett, Ibbie	Jan. 15	Addison, -------	May 11	Trower, Annie L.	Aug. 12
Taylor, Wesley	Jan. 20	Savage, Liddie	May 12	Lawson, Abraham	Aug. 14
Stratton, -------	Jan. 25	McKown, Blanch	May 16	Harmon, Luke	Aug. 15
Francis, Mary H.	Jan. 29	Beloat, Robert	May 17	Jacob, Sarah V.	Aug. 15
Spady, -------	Jan. 30	Lane, -------	May 20	Leatherbury, -------	Aug. 15
Stevens, -------	Jan. 30	Waddy, Mary E.	May 21	Evans, Ben	Aug. 20
Stevens, Lavinia	Feb. 2	Scarboro, Emeline	May 25	Wise, -------	Aug. 27
Bell, -------	Feb. 7	Trower, -------	June 2	Dunton, Thomas R.	Sept. '96
Bradford, Fisher	Feb. 7	Allen, Leah	June 4	Joynes, -------	Sept. 1
Watson, Ben	Feb. 8	West, Comfort	June 6	Fitchett, Mary	Sept. 2
Custis, -------	Feb. 13	Wise, Arinthia S.	June 8	Ashby, Margaret	Sept. 6
Miles, Esther D.	Feb. 16	Toliver, John H.	June 9	Roberts, John L.	Sept. 10
Stevens, -------	Feb. 25	Elliott, John W.	June 10	Nottingham, W. R.	Sept. 12
Bayly, -------	Mar. 3	Hopkins, Henry	June 10	Powell, -------	Sept. 14
Jacob, Maggie	Mar. 3	Burr, Henry B.	June 16	East, Edward	Sept. 15
Beckett, -------	Mar. 5	Gibb, Emma J.	June 17	Baptist, James	Sept. 24
Downes, Thomas A.	Mar. 6	James, Lucy	June 21	Fitchett, Emily L.	Sept. 27
Moore, Willie	Mar. 10	Satchell, -------	June 23	Phillips, George	Oct. 2
Brickhouse, Severn	Mar. 14	Dalby, George R.	July '96	Trower, Alfred	Oct. 2
Doughty, Sarah	Mar. 15	Humphreys, -------	July 3	Nottingham, Leah	Oct. 3
Bayly, Seth N.	Mar. 16	Allen, -------	July 6	Sample, David	Oct. 4
Boytt, -------	Mar. 18	Wyatt, Wm. E.	July 7	Smith, Ed	Oct. 9
Lingo, Susan	Mar. 24	Winger, Edith	July 8	Downing, Joseph	Oct. 10
Ennis, J. J.	Mar. 26	Francis, H. T.	July 9	Dalby, James B.	Oct. 15
Kellam, Marion	Apr. 2	Stevenson, Blanche	July 13	Fisher, Harriet	Oct. 17
Kellam, Tom	Apr. 2	Sturgis, -------	July 15	Warren, M. Sarah	Oct. 20
Ennis, John W.	Apr. 3	Spady, -------	July 16	Smith, -------	Oct. 21
Williams, E. J.	Apr. 4	Marsh, Manie	July 17	Smith, Leah	Oct. 22
Kelly, Arthur F.	Apr. 6	Stratton, -------	July 20	Mason, Mary L.	Oct. 25
Seymour, Abe	Apr. 6	Bird, -------	July 27	Scisco, Russell	Oct. 25
Smith, Severn	Apr. 16	Bradford, --------	July 29	Nottingham, Sophie	Oct. 31
Turner, Julia	Apr. 17	Brooks, -------	Aug. 2	Pitts, John	Nov. 1
Wescott, Margaret	Apr. 18	James, Mary	Aug. 2	Brickhouse, Rebecca	Nov. 2
Wyatt, Robert	Apr. 23	Savage, -------	Aug. 2	James, -------	Nov. 2
Boytt, -------	Apr. 25	Upshur, Liddie	Aug. 2	Fowler, Polly F.	Nov. 3
Wise, -------	Apr. 28	Winder, William	Aug. 2	Mason, Elizabeth	Nov. 7
Causey, L. P.	May '96	Spady, -------	Aug. 6	Custis, Preston S.	Nov. 10
White, John M.	May '96	Palmer, Sam	Aug. 8	Bell, -------	Nov. 12
Floyd, Emily	May 5	Bell, Harry	Aug. 10	Collins, Adah	Nov. 15
Smith, George	May 5	Bowdoin, Rose	Aug. 10	Scarboro, William	Nov. 15

1896 Deaths "Chronologically" cont'd

Matthews, Adah	Nov. 16	Morris, Edna L.	Dec. 11	Griffith, -------	Dec. 16
Bool, Mary E.	Nov. 21	Beloat, John S.	Dec. 12	Scott, Seth G.	Dec. 16
Jarvis, Mary G.	Nov. 29	Collins, Raechel	Dec. 12	Pool, -------	Dec. 20
Carpenter, -------	Nov. 30	Fisher, Florence	Dec. 13	Upshur, Mary E.	Dec. 20
Savage, -------	Dec. 2	Stevens, Josephine	Dec. 13	Watson, John C.	Dec. 21
Savage, -------	Dec. 2	Scott, Annie	Dec. 14	Fitchett, Robert	Dec. 24
Collins, Martha S.	Dec. 6	Lewis, Charles	Dec. 15	152	

Causes of Deaths
1871 - 1883

	1871	1872	1873	1874	1875	1876	1877	1878	1882	1883
Asthma	.	.	.	.	.	1	.	.	.	2
Bilious	2	.	.	.	.	.	.	.	.	.
Bilious Diarrhea	.	.	1	.	.	.	.	1	.	.
Bilious Dysentery	.	.	1	.	.	.	.	.	.	.
Bilious Fever	1	3	7	.	.	5	4	6	.	1
Biuret	.	1	.	.	.	.	.	.	.	.
Born Dead	2	.	.	.	.	.	.	.	.	.
Bowels, Congestive	.	.	.	.	.	.	.	1	.	.
Bowels, Inflammation of	1	1	1	.	.	3	.	.	.	.
Brain, Congestion of	.	.	.	.	.	1	.	.	.	.
Brain, Disease of the	.	.	.	.	.	.	.	1	.	1
Brain Fever	3	1	.	.	.	1	.	.	2	2
Brain, Inflammation of	.	1	.	.	.	.	.	.	.	.
Brain, Softening of	.	.	1	.	.	1	.	.	.	.
Bright's Disease	.	.	.	1	.	.	.	.	.	1
Burned	.	.	.	1	.	2	1	1	1	.
Burned to Death	.	.	.	.	.	.	1	.	.	.
Cancer	.	1	.	.	.	1	.	1	.	.
Child Birth	1	4	1	.	3	1	1	1	2	.
Cholera, Bilious	.	.	.	.	.	1				
Cholera Infantum	1	2	.	4	.	.	2	.	.	2
Choleramorbus	.	.	.	.	.	1	.	.	.	.
Cold	.	.	.	.	.	1	.	.	.	.
Congestion	5	.	2	1	1	.	.	.	.	.
Congestive	.	.	.	.	.	.	3	1	.	.
Congestive Chill	.	1	.	2	.	.	2	3	1	.
Congestive Fever	1	1	1	.	.	2	.	.	.	.
Consumption	7	12	4	9	13	7	6	7	6	6
Convulsions	2	.	.	.	.	.	.	.	.	.
Croup	2	2	.	.	1	2	.	1*	.	2
Crying Fits	8	13	7	2	1	9	3	6	.	1
Debility	.	.	.	.	.	2	.	.	.	.
Delerium Tremens	.	.	.	.	.	.	1	.	.	.
Diarrhea	1	.	.	.	.	3	1	2	.	.
Diphtheria	14	8	8	.	.	5	.	.	.	.
Dissipation	.	.	.	.	2	.	.	.	.	.
Dropsy	2	3	4	2	3	3	2	1	6	2
Drowned	.	.	2	1	.	1	.	7	.	2
Drunkeness	.	.	.	.	.	.	.	1	.	.
Dysentery	4	2	4	1	2	2	.	.	1	1
Epileptic fits	.	.	1	.	.	.	.	.	.	.
Erysipelas	.	.	.	1	.	.	.	.	.	.
Eusipilus	1	1	.	.	.	.	.	.	.	.
Exposure	.	1	.	.	.	.	.	.	.	.
Fall	.	.	.	.	.	.	.	1	.	.
Fall, Killed by Tree	.	.	.	.	.	.	1	.	.	.

*Cramp Colic

Causes of Deaths "cont'd"
1871 - 1883

	1871	1872	1873	1874	1875	1876	1877	1878	1882	1883
Falling from/of Tree	.	.	.	1	.	.	.	1	.	.
Fever	.	.	.	.	1	.	.	.	1	1
Fits*	.	.	.	.	1	.	.	.	.	.
Gangrene	.	.	.	.	.	1	.	.	.	.
Gastro Entertis	.	.	.	.	.	1	.	.	.	.
Head, Big	.	.	.	.	.	.	1	2	.	1
Heart Disease/Failure	1	1	3	4	2	4	3	1	2	1
Heart, Neuralgia of	.	.	.	.	.	1	.	.	.	.
Heart, Rheumatism of	.	.	.	.	.	1	.	.	.	.
Infantile	5	21	21	8	.	2	18	10	.	.
Inflammation	.	.	.	.	.	.	1	2	.	1
Insane								1	.	
Jaundice, Yellow	.	.	.	.	.	1	.	.	.	.
Lockjaw	.	1	2	.	.	.	.	.	.	.
Lungs, Congestive	.	.	.	.	.	.	1	.	.	.
Lung Fever	.	.	.	.	.	1	.	.	.	.
Lungs, Hemorrhage of	.	.	1	.	.	.	.	.	.	.
Measles	.	.	3	.	.	.	7	4	.	.
Meningitis	.	.	.	1	.	.	.	.	.	.
Murdered	.	.	1	.	.	.	.	.	.	.
Neglect	.	1	.	.	.	.	.	.	.	.
Nerves, Broken down	.	.	1	.	.	.	2	.	.	.
Old Age	.	5	5	1	5	7	4	6	.	4
Paralysis	1	.	.	.	.	2	.	.	.	1?
Puerperal Fever	.	.	.	.	.	.	.	.	.	1
Pleurisy	.	.	2	1	.	5	.	.	.	.
Pneumonia	3	7	4	1	2	8	.	5	5	
Quinsey	.	1	1	.	.	.	.	1	.	.
Rheumatism	.	.	.	.	.	.	.	.	.	1?
Shot	.	.	1	.	.	.	1	.	1	.
Small Pox	.	1	4	.	.	.	.	.	.	.
Smothered	.	.	.	.	.	.	.	1	.	.
Sore Throat	.	.	.	.	.	2	.	.	.	.
Spasms	.	.	.	.	.	1	.	.	.	.
Stomach Inflammation	.	.	1	.	.	.	.	.	.	.
Summer Disease	.	.	.	.	.	2	.	.	.	.
Thrush	.	.	.	1	.	.	.	.	.	.
Tumor	.	.	.	.	.	.	.	.	.	1
Typhoid Fever	5	6	1	4	2	6	13	2	.	4
Typhoid Pneumonia	.	.	1	.	.	.	.	.	3	.
Unkn., Cause	6	7	19	16	53	53	5	21	10	9
Whooping Cough	1	.	.	1	3	1	.	5	.	.
Womb, cancer of the	.	.	1	.	.	1	.	.	.	.
Worms	3	2	.	2	.	.	.	4	.	.
Totals	82	111	117	66	95	156	84	109	41	48

1871 – 1 Born Dead - cause Infantile, in both categories, *1875 Fits individual was 18, different from Crying Fits

Causes of Deaths
1884 - 1896

	1884	1885	1887	1888	1891	1892	1893	1894	1895	1896
Abscess	.	.	1	.	.	.	.	.	.	.
Accident	.	.	.	.	1	.	.	.	.	1
Accident, Gun Shot	.	.	.	.	1	.	.	.	2	.
Accident, Knife wound	.	.	.	.	.	.	.	.	1	.
Accident, R. R.	.	.	.	.	.	.	.	1	.	.
Ague	.	.	1	.	.	.	.	.	.	.
Appoplaxy	.	.	.	1	.	.	.	.	1	.
Asthma	.	1	.	.	.	1	2	.	2	.
Bilious Fever	.	.	2	.	.	.	.	.	.	.
Birth, Premature	.	.	.	2	.	.	.	.	.	.
Bladder Disease	.	.	.	.	1	.	.	.	.	.
Bled to Death	.	.	.	.	1	.	.	.	.	1
Blood Cancer	.	.	.	.	1	.	.	.	.	.
Born Dead	1	.	.	1	.	.	.	.	.	.
Brain, Congestion of	.	1	1	2	1	.	3	.	1	.
Brain, Enlargement	.	.	.	.	.	.	1	.	.	.
Brain Fever	.	.	.	.	.	.	2	2	2	1
Brain, Paralysis of	.	.	.	.	.	.	1	.	.	.
Brain Stroke	.	.	.	.	.	1	.	.	.	.
Bright's Disease	.	.	1	.	1	.	.	.	1	1
Bronchitis	.	.	1	.	.	2	1	2	1	1
Burn	.	2	1	.	1	.	7	3	.	2
Burned to Death	1	.	.	1	.	2	1	.	1	.
Cancer	1	.	1	.	.	1	2	2	1	3
Catarrh	.	.	.	.	.	.	1	.	.	1
Child Birth	.	1	2	.	3	4	.	1	2	3
Cholera Infantum	5	6	1	.	8	8	12	8	14	7
Congestion	.	.	1	.	.	.	.	.	.	.
Congestive Chill	.	1	4	2	1	1	1	1	1	.
Consumption	1	4	6	3	16	21	29	14	9	12
Croup	1	.	1	1	9	4	6	2	5	3
Crying Fits	2	2	8	4	1	.	2	2	2	.
Debility, General	.	.	1	1	.	.	.	4	1	1
Diabetes	.	.	.	.	.	.	.	1	3	.
Diarrhea	.	.	.	.	1	.	1	2	3	2
Diphtheria	.	2	.	.	.	3	.	.	.	.
Dropsy	1	2	6	1	7	3	4	7	6	8
Drowned	2	.	1	.	1	3	2	1	3	1
Dysentery	1	1	6	1	2	5	15	2	11	1
Dyspepsia	.	.	.	.	1	1	1	2	.	1
Eczema	.	.	.	.	.	.	1	.	.	.
Encephalitis(Encyphalus)	1	.	.	.	.	.	.	.	.	.
Erysipelas	.	.	.	.	.	.	1	1	.	.
Fever	.	.	.	.	2	.	.	.	.	.
Froze to Death	.	.	.	.	.	.	1	.	.	.

Causes of Deaths "cont'd"
1884 - 1896

	1884	1885	1887	1888	1891	1892	1893	1894	1895	1896
Gravel	.	.	.	.	.	1	.	.	.	.
Grief	.	.	.	.	1	.	.	.	.	.
Gripps/Grippee	.	.	.	.	.	4	.	1	1	.
Hanged for Murder	.	.	.	.	.	.	1	.	.	.
Head, Big	.	.	.	.	.	.	.	1	.	.
Head, Gathering in	.	.	.	1	.	.	.	.	.	.
Heart, Congestive	.	.	.	.	.	1	.	.	.	.
Heart Disease/Failure	2	2	2	1	4	2	6	5	8	3
Heart, Neuralgia of	.	.	.	.	1	.	.	.	.	.
Hemorrhage	.	.	.	.	1	.	.	.	.	.
Hydrophopia	.	.	.	.	.	.	1	.	.	.
Infirmity	.	.	1	.	.	.	.	.	.	.
Inflammation of Bowels	.	1	.	1	3	.	1	1	.	.
Injuries from fall	.	.	.	.	1	.	.	.	.	.
Insanity	.	.	.	.	1	.	2	1	.	.
Kidney Disease	.	.	.	.	1	.	2	2	.	1
LaGrippe	.	.	.	.	2	.	.	.	.	.
Liver, Abscess/Disease	.	.	.	1	.	.	.	.	1	.
Lockjaw	.	.	1	.	.	.	.	.	.	.
Lung, Abscess	.	.	.	.	.	1	.	.	.	.
Lung, Congestive	.	.	.	.	.	.	1	.	.	.
Malaria	.	.	.	2*	.	.	.	3	3	1
Measles	.	.	.	.	.	12	3	.	.	.
Meningitis	.	.	.	.	.	.	.	.	.	1
Neck, Broke	.	.	.	.	.	.	2	.	.	.
Old Age	3	2	5	5	7	3	11	7	6	9
Overdose/Laudanum	.	.	.	.	.	.	.	1	.	.
Paralysis	.	.	.	1	1	.	5	1	3	3
Peritonitis	.	.	.	.	.	.	.	1	.	1
Pleurisy	.	1	.	.	.	1	1	.	.	.
Pneumonia	2	3	2	3	8	14	12	17	13	18
Poison/Blood	.	.	1	.	.	1	1	2	.	1
Quinzy	1	.	.	.	.	.	.	.	.	1
Rheumatic Fever	.	.	1	.	.	.	.	.	.	.
Rheumatism at Heart	.	.	.	.	.	1	2	1	1	2
Run over/ Cart	.	.	.	.	.	.	1	.	.	.
Scarlet Fever	.	.	.	.	1	.	.	.	.	.
Scofula	.	.	.	1	1	.	.	.	.	.
Septicaemia	.	.	.	.	.	.	.	.	1	.
Spasms	.	.	.	.	.	.	1	.	.	2
Spinal Meningitis	.	.	.	.	.	.	3	.	.	.
Spine Disease	.	.	.	.	1	.	.	.	.	.
Stomach Inflammation	.	.	1	.	.	.	.	.	.	.
Stomach, Neuralgia	.	1	.	.	.	.	.	.	.	.
Stomach pain	.	.	.	1	.	.	.	.	.	.

Causes of Deaths "cont'd"
1884 - 1896

	1884	1885	1887	1888	1891	1892	1893	1894	1895	1896
Stroke	.	1	.	.	.	.	.	.	.	.
Suicide	.	.	.	.	.	.	.	.	1	2
Summer Sickness	.	.	1	.	.	.	.	.	.	.
Tetanus	.	.	.	.	.	.	1	.	.	.
Thrush	.	.	.	.	1	.	1	1	3	.
Tumor	.	.	.	.	.	.	.	.	.	1
Typhoid Fever	.	1	3	2	3	20	5	19	6	3
Unkn., Cause	20	17	21	14	25	28	62	28	25	46
Wart of Palate	.	.	.	.	.	.	1	.	.	.
Whooping Cough	.	.	.	1	.	1	.	.	.	6
Womb Disease	.	.	.	.	1	.	1	.	.	.
Yellow Jaundice	.	.	.	.	.	.	.	.	.	1
Total	45	52	86	54	124	150	224	150	145	152

*1888 written Melarial

Age at Death
1884 – 1896

		1884	1885	1887	1888	1891	1892	1893	1894	1895	1896	Totals
Day	1 - 7	13	7	14	7	13	9	18	9	12	16	118
	8 - 14	3	4	4	7	6	4	9	7	3	11	58
	15 - 21	0	0	2	0	0	0	2	1	1	2	8
	22 - 30	0	0	0	0	1	0	2	0	0	0	3
Month	1 - 2	3	4	5	3	2	8	17	7	10	8	67
	3 - 4	1	3	4	2	10	6	6	7	9	3	51
	5 - 6	1	0	3	4	1	6	6	2	4	7	34
	7 - 8	1	1	0	2	5	2	9	4	3	5	32
	9 - 10	1	0	0	0	3	4	7	2	3	1	21
	11	1	2	0	0	0	0	0	2	0	1	6
Year	1 - 4	7	6	11	7	8	15	18	14	14	12	112
	5 - 9	1	4	2	1	4	2	5	6	7	4	36
	10 - 19	0	3	8	3	12	10	11	8	8	10	73
	20 - 29	3	5	2	6	10	18	20	12	11	5	92
	30 - 39	1	3	7	0	10	15	9	12	10	11	78
	40 - 49	0	1	3	2	10	16	26	16	15	16	105
	50 - 59	2	2	10	3	5	16	10	10	10	9	77
	60 - 69	3	3	1	1	13	12	25	13	13	12	96
	70 - 79	2	4	4	3	8	5	13	13	7	10	69
	80 - 89	1	0	4	2	2	1	6	5	5	7	33
	90 up	1	0	1	1	1	1	5	0	0	2	12
	Total	45	52	85	54	124	150	224	150	145	152	1181
Oldest		90	(3)76	95	93	91	96	101	86	85	105	

1886, 1889-90 records missing

Oldest 95 & above

1887 – Cisco/Brown, Isaac – 95
1892 – Sam'l Ball – 96
1893 – Betsey Doughty – 101
1896 – Luke Harmon – 99
        Comfort West – 105

Largest age groups

1st – Day 1 – 7   (118)
2nd – Year 1 - 4   (112)
3rd – Year 40 – 49 (105)

ACKNOWLEDGEMENTS

I would like to thank the E.S.P.L. for use of their view scan to save these historic documents on flash drive. I would also like to thank Dr. Miles Barnes for his help in transcribing the names, causes of death and other information to make this document accurate.

Table of Contents

Northampton County, VA, Deaths from Death Register and Wills, 1871-1896

-------, **Infant** CF Jan. 10, 1872, Northampton, Crying Fits, 8 days, Molly & Travis, Northampton, Single, Physician source

-------, **Infant** CM Dec. 25, 1872, Northampton, Crying Fits, 5 days, Easther & Caleb, Northampton, Single, Caleb, Father source [Laborer?] Surname possibly Collins

ABBOTT, Charles B. WM Aug. 10, 1887, Northampton, Cause Unkn., 7 days, David H. & Emily, [Farmer?], Northampton, Single, David Abbott, Father source

ABOTT, ------- WF July 15, 1892, Northampton, Cause Unkn., 6 months, Sam'l & Lelia, Northampton, Single, Sam'l Abott, Father source

ABRAMS, John W. WM Aug. 20, 1891, Northampton, Diarrhea, 4 months, Jno. T. & Maggie J., Northampton, Single, Jno. T. Abrams, Father source

ADAMS, Viola BF Mar. 1880, Northampton, Cause Unkn., 35, Parents Unkn., Va., Va., Va., Keeping House, Married, source unkn.

ADDISON, ------- CF Apr. 18, 1895, Northampton, Cause Unkn., 2 days, Richard & Sarah, Northampton, Single, Sarah Addison, Mother source

ADDISON, ------- CF Aug. 16, 1894, Northampton, Cause Unkn., 2 days, Richard & Sarah, Northampton, Single, Sarah Addison, Mother source

ADDISON, ------- CF June 1875, Northampton, Cause Unkn., 7 days, Mathew & Sarah, Northampton, Single, Mathew Addison, Father source

ADDISON, ------- CM Jan. 9, 1892, Northampton, Cause Unkn., 5 days, Rich'd & Sarah, Northampton, Single, Rich'd Addison, Father source

ADDISON, ------- CM May 11, 1896, Northampton, Cause Unkn., 11 days, Richd. & Sarah, Northampton, Single, Richard Addison, Father source

ADDISON, ------- CM Oct. 12, 1877, Northampton, Infantile, 10 days, Jacob & Emily, Northampton, Single, Jacob Addison, Father source

ADDISON, Henry WM May 10, 1876, Northampton, Consumption, 28, John & Ann, Northampton, Single, Ann E. Addison, Mother source

ADDISON, Infant WF Aug. 1879, Northampton, Cholic, 1 day, Parents Unkn., Birthplace Unkn., at Home, Single, source unkn.

ADDISON, John Sr. WM Dec. 2, 1873, Northampton, Consumption, 57, John & Margaret, Northampton, Farmer, Ann E. Wife, Jas. U. Fisher, Brother-in-Law source

ADDISON, John W. WM May 7, 1877, Northampton, Congestive, 4 months, Thomas & Virginia, Northampton, Single, Thomas Addison, Father source

ALLEN, ------- CM July 6, 1896, Northampton, Cause Unkn., 3 months, Wm. H. & Leah, Northampton, Single, Wm. H. Allen, Father source

ALLEN, Jno. CM July 1871, Northampton, Consumption, 12, Wm. & Mary, Northampton, Single, Wm. G. Smith, Physician source

ALLEN, Leah CF June 4, 1896, Northampton, Diarrhea, 32, Ames & Esther Ker, Northampton, Married, Wm. H. Allen, Husband source

ALLEN, Moses CM Jan. 14, 1893, Northampton, Old Age, 80, Parents Unkn., Northampton, Laborer, Single, Laura Collins, Friend source

Northampton County, VA, Deaths from Death Register and Wills, 1871-1896

ALLEN, Moses CM Jan. 16, 1892, Northampton, Cause Unkn., 2 months, Wm. H. & Mary, Northampton, Single, Wm. H. Allen, Father source

ALLEN, Polly CF Aug. 22, 1876, Northampton, Consumption, 24, Abel & Sarah Spady, Northampton, Seamstress, Married, Harriet (Hammit) Allen, Husband source

AMES, ------- CM Nov. 18, 1887, Northampton, Crying Fits, 3 months, John & Mary, [Laborer?], Northampton, Single, Mary Ames, Mother source

AMES, ------- WF Mar. 17, 1885, Northampton, Cause Unkn., 0, Benj. & Susan, Northampton, Single, Benj. T. Ames, Head of Family source

AMES, ------- WM July 1875, Northampton, Cause Unkn., 3 months, Elijah Ames & Vandelia, Northampton, Single, Elijah Ames, Father source

AMES, Ambro CM July 1891, Northampton, Fever, 2, Thos. & Cherry, Northampton, Single, Thos. Ames, Father source

AMES, F. Willis WM July 2, 1893, Northampton, Croup, 7, J. R. & Laura, Northampton, Single, J. R. Ames, Father source

AMES, Florida CF July 30, 1894, Northampton, Typhoid Fever, 2, William & Mary, Northampton, Single, Wm. Ames, Father source

AMES, Florida CF July 31, 1893, Northampton, Brain Fever, 1 yr. 6 mos., Wm. & Mary, Northampton, Single, Wm. Ames, Father source

AMES, H. W. WM Nov. 3, 1895, Northampton, Typhoid Fever, 32, John & Laura, Acco., Co., Liveryman, Married, G. P. Moore, Physician source

AMES, James P. WM Aug. 3, 1887, Northampton, Dysentery, 34, Jas. & Susan, Northampton, Farmer, Married, James Ames, Father source

AMES, James S. WM May 2, 1895, Northampton, Pneumonia, 63, James & Susan, Acco. Co., Farmer, Married, Geo. W. Nottingham, Son-in-Law source

AMES, Juletta BF June 1879, Northampton, Bilious Fever, 2, Thomas & Cherry, Va., Va., Va., Single, Dr. William W. Wilkins, Physician source

AMES, Lola WF Aug. 29, 1894, Northampton, Typhoid Fever, 15, E. C. & Lee D., Acco. Co., Single, Frank Shield, Uncle source

AMES, Mollie WF Aug. 12, 1894, Northampton, Typhoid Fever, 18, E. C. & Lee D., Northampton, Single, Frank Shield, Uncle source

AMES, Nora CF Apr. 15, 1891, Northampton, Fever, 9, Thos. & Cherry, Northampton, Single, Thos. Ames, Father source

AMES, Peggy CF Apr. 20, 1884, Northampton, Heart Disease, 30, Jas. & Mary Sheppard, Northampton, Laborer, Jas. Ames, Father source

AMES, Sallie WF Oct. 15, 1894, Northampton, Dysentery, 4 months, M. T. & Nellie, Northampton, Single, M. T. Ames, Father source

AMES, W. C. WM Dec. 17, 1895, Northampton, Diabetes, 39, W. C. & Elizabeth, Northampton, Farmer, Single, J. W. Chandler, Nephew source

AMES, Willie F. WM Dec. 13, 1892, Northampton, Croup, 7 months, John R. & Laura, Northampton, Single, John R. Ames, Father source

AMES, Wm. C. WM Aug. 16, 1894, Northampton, Typhoid Fever, 42, R. B. & Lovey C. Ames, Northampton Sailor, Married, L. T. Ames, Brother source

ANDERSON, ------- CF June 13, 1893, Northampton, Cause Unkn., 1 day, Neely &

Northampton County, VA, Deaths from Death Register and Wills, 1871-1896

Henrietta, Northampton, Single, Neely Anderson, Father source

ANDERSON, ------- CM Jan. 1873, Northampton, Infantile, 1 day, Mary Anderson, Northampton, Single, source unkn.

ANDERSON, ------- CM Oct. 1873, Northampton, Infantile, 1 day, Asia Anderson, Northampton, Single, Geo. Savage, Friend source

ANDERSON, Sarah WF Mar. 10, 1876, Northampton, Cause Unkn., 65, George & ---- Young, Northampton, Widow, Edwd. W. Anderson, Son source

ANDREWS, ------- WF Mar. 13, 1875, Northampton, Cause Unkn., 1 day, Wm. A. & Mary, Northampton, Single, Wm. A. Andrews, Father source

ANDREWS, ------- WM Oct. 14, 1877, Northampton, Cholera Infantum, 18 days, William & Margaret, Northampton, Single, William Andrews, Father source

ANDREWS, Custis BM May 1880, Northampton, Diarrhea, 2, Jesse & Harriet, Va., Va., Va., Single, Dr. Geo. W. Smith, Physician source

ANDREWS, Geo. CM July 6, 1876, Northampton, Diarrhea, 1 yr. 1 day, James & Edith, Northampton, Single, Jim Andrews, Father source

ANDREWS, Jacob CM Sept. 14, 1891, Northampton, Consumption, 75, Parents Unkn., Northampton, Laborer, Married, J. W. Fox, Neighbor source

ANDREWS, Margaret S. WF May 12, 1876, Northampton, Paralysis, 63, John & ---- Doughty, Hog Island, Widow, Ida Andrews, Daughter source

ANDREWS, Polly WF Dec. 2, 1894, Northampton, Gen. Debility, 60, Wm. & Sallie

Parsons, Northampton, Married, S. H. Parsons, Brother source

ANDREWS, W. W. WM Dec. 4, 1892, Northampton, Diphtheria, 10, W. D. & Ida E., Northampton, Single, W. D. Andrews, Father source

ANDREWS, William W. WM Oct. 9, 1876, Northampton, Spasms, 6 days, William D. & Ida, Northampton, Single, Ida Andrews, Mother source

ANDREWS, Wm. W. WM May 13, 1873, Northampton, Cause Unkn., 63 yrs., 5 mos., 10 days, Wm. W. & Drucilla, Northampton, Carpenter, Margaret S. Wife, Geo. A. Stoakley, Friend source

ANTNEY, ------- CF Dec. 1875, Northampton, Cause Unkn., 1 month, ----- & Lizzy, Northampton, Single, Lizzie Antney, Mother source

ASHBY, ------- WF Aug. 1872, Northampton, Infantile, 1 month, Wm. T. & Sarah, Birth Unkn., Single, W. T. Ashby, Father source

ASHBY, ------- WM June 25, 1883, Northampton, Disease of the Brain, 5 days, Jas. K. & Eliza Badger, Birth Unkn., Jas. K. Badger, Father source

ASHBY, Charles CM Feb. 10, 1882, Northampton, Cause Unkn., 3, Charles & Ellen, Northampton, Single, Ellen Ashby, Mother source

ASHBY, Darky CF Oct. 9, 1877, Northampton, Typhoid Fever, 30, Unkn. & Mary Ashby, Northampton, Laborer, Single, William Ashby, Friend source

ASHBY, Easter CF Nov. 18, 1893, Northampton, Womb Disease, 65, Isaac & Mary Nottingham, Accomac, Married, Sarah Savage, Niece source

ASHBY, Edward WM July 3, 1892, Northampton, Typhoid, 14, S. T. & Mary, Northampton, Single, Rich'd Warrington, Friend source

ASHBY, Harold WM Aug. 14, 1892, Northampton, Typhoid, 16 months, J. H. & Ida L., Northampton, Single, J. H. Ashby, Father source

ASHBY, James F. WM April 1872, Northampton, Heart Disease, 36, Benj. Ashby, Accomac, Farmer, Susan Ashby, Wife source unkn.

ASHBY, Jno. H. WM Apr. 1874, Northampton, Infantile, 3 months, Wm. T. & Sarah, Northampton, Single, W. T. Ashby, Father source

ASHBY, Kesiah CF Jan. 14, 1894, Northampton, Old Age, 72, Parents Unkn., Acco., Co., Married, Jas. Smith, Undertaker source

ASHBY, Lizzie CF Dec. 2, 1893, Northampton, Consumption, 49, Tony & Lizzie Church, Northampton, Married, Isaac Ashby, Husband source

ASHBY, Maggie WF July 29, 1892, Northampton, Typhoid, 17, R. C. & Nervilla, Acco., Co., Single, R. C. Ashby, Father source

ASHBY, Margaret WF Sept. 6, 1896, Northampton, Rheumatism at Heart, 72, Jno. C. & Druetta Smith, Northampton, Married, Geo. L. Roberts, Son source

ASHBY, Mary WF Feb. 22, 1878, Northampton, Infantile, 1 mo. 10 days, Severn T. & Mary, Northampton, Single, Henry B. Stewart, Friend source

ASHBY, Mary A. WF May 1, 1884, Northampton, Cholera Infantum, 11 months, Soren & Mary, Northampton, Soren T. Ashby, Father source

ASHBY, Mary E. WF Aug. 4, 1883, Northampton, Pen. Fever, 38 yrs. 2 mos., Arthur E. & Margt. Roberts, Northampton, House Keeper, Soren Ashby, Husband source

ASHBY, Navillia E. WF Nov. 8, 1883, Northampton, Cause Unkn., Age Unkn., Parents Unkn., House Keeper, Robt. C. Ashby, Husband source

ASHBY, Saly E. WF Mar. 8, 1878, Northampton, Congestive Chill, 2 months, Wm. T. & Sarah E., Northampton, Single, Wm. T. Ashby, Father source

ASHBY, Sarah E. WF Mar. 1877, Northampton, Child Birth, 35, Hezakiah & Margt. Beloat, Northampton, William Ashby, Husband source

ASHBY, Wilhemina WF Apr. 13, 1893, Northampton, Measles, 28, Thos. & Mary Nottingham, Northampton, Married, R. C. Ashby, Husband source

BADGER, ------- WM Dec. 15, 1887, Northampton, Inflammation of Stomach, 15 days, Jas. & Elizabeth, Northampton, Single, James Badger, Father source

BADGER, Edmond WM Aug. 1879, Northampton, Congestion, 1, James H. & Elizabeth, Va., Va., Va., Single, Dr. Wm. Stoakley, Physician source

BADGER, Elizabeth WF Aug. 20, 1892, Northampton, Cause Unkn., 35, Jas. & Mary Carpenter, Northampton, Married, Jas. H. Badger, Husband source

BADGER, Mary F. WF June 1871, Fredericksburg, Bowels, 27, Jno. W. & Susan Tankard, Northampton, Married, Jno. W. Badger, Husband source

BADGER, Sarah CF 1888, Northampton, Cause Unkn., 1, Geo. & Nancy, Northampton, Single, Nancy Badger Mother, source

BADGER, Stepney CM Nov. 29, 1893, Northampton, Old Age, 92, Parents Unkn., Northampton, Married, John Badger, Son source

BAGWELL, Comfort CF Sept. 1872, Northampton, Old Age, 75, Parents Unkn., Birth Unkn., Isma Wyatt, source

BAGWELL, Emily CF July 2, 1892, Northampton, Dysentery, 42, Major & Tinny Tankard, Northampton, Laborer, Married, Levi Bagwell, Husband source

BAGWELL, Susanna WF Feb. 1, 1885, Northampton, Child Birth, 24, Arelius & Susan Henderson, Northampton, Married, L. T. Johnson, source

BAILEY, Infant BM Sept. 1879, Northampton, Diphtheria, 2 days, Edith Baily, Va., Va., Va., Single, Dr. R. H. Parker, Physician source

BAILEY, Maria CF Sept. 14, 1893, Northampton, Dropsy, 80, Parents Unkn., Northampton, Single, J. R. Tankard, Neighbor source

BAILEY, Sarah BF Oct. 1879, Northampton, Cause Unkn., 1 month, Phillip & Frances, Va., Va., Va., source unkn.

BAILY, ------- WM July 20, 1887, Northampton, Dysentery, 4 days, Seth & Emily, Northampton, Single, Seth Baily, Father source

BAKER, ------- CF June 30, 1876, Northampton, Crying Fits, 20 days, Thos. S. & Edith, Northampton, Single, Thos. S. Baker, Father source

BAKER, ------- CM May 1875, Northampton, Cause Unkn., 10 days, Shadrack & Edy, Northampton, Single, Edy Baker, Mother source

BAKER, E. Sarah CF Aug. 14, 1887, Northampton, Cause Unkn., 10, George & Sarah, Northampton, Single, George Baker, Father source

BAKER, J. R. WM Mar. 29, 1892, Northampton, Typhoid, 21, Peter & Nancy, Acco. Co., Laborer, Single, Julia Bradford, Sister source

BAKER, Nancy C. WF Feb. 27, 1893, Northampton, Consumption, 60, Parents Unkn., Delaware, Single, O. H. Badger, Neighbor source

BAKER, Sallie CF Nov. 20, 1884, Northampton, Burned to Death, 26, Dan'l & Sarah Watson, Northampton, Laborer, Hez. James, source

BALL, Isaac BM Aug. 1879, Northampton, Drowning, 30, Parents Unkn., Va., Sailor, Va., Married, Wm. J. Scott, source (PR)

BALL, Sam'l CM Apr. 11, 1892, Northampton, Old Age, 96, Parents Unkn., Northampton, Laborer, Married, Lettie Ball, Wife source

BANISTER, ------- CM Nov. 1, 1895, Northampton, Crying Fits, 9 months, Wm. & Nannie, Northampton, Annie Banister, Mother source

BANKS, ------- CM Jan. 24, 1885, Northampton, Cause Unkn., 9 days, Shelly & Unkn., Northampton, Single, Shelly Banks, Father source

BAPTIST, James CM Sept. 24, 1896, Northampton, Pneumonia, 60, Jim & Caddy, Newport News, Va., Married, Jacob Babtist, Son source

BARCRAFT, Fanny WF Feb. 11, 1874, Northampton, Heart Disease, 45, Andrew & Sallie Hambleton, Northampton, House Keeper, Jno. Barcraft, Husband source

BARCRAFT, Patsy WF July 1875, Northampton, Typhoid, 35, Parents Unkn., Northampton, Jno. Barcraft, Husband source

BARROTT, Tabitha WF Apr. 20, 1885, Northampton, Neuralgia of the Stomach, 36, Thos. & Unkn., Northampton, Married, Thos. Barrott, Father source

BARROTT, William WM Apr. 1880, Northampton, Typhoid Fever, 37, Parents Unkn., Va., Va., Va., Carpenter, Single, source unkn.

BAXTER. Robt. WM Sept. 2, 1895, Northampton, Cholera E., 3 months, Isaac W. & Bettie, Northampton, Single, Isaac W. Baxter, Father source

BAYLY, ------- CF Sept. 1, 1895, Northampton, Cause Unkn., 4 days, John A. & Georgie, Northampton, John A. Bayly, Father source

BAYLY, ------- CM Feb. 1873, Northampton, Infantile, 3 days, Jackson & Fanny, Northampton, Single, source unkn.

BAYLY, ------- CM July 16, 1873, Northampton, Crying Fits, 1 day, Henry & Edy, Northampton, Single, Henry Bayly, Father source

BAYLY, ------- CM Mar. 3, 1896, Northampton, Croup, 2 months, Harry & Esther, Northampton, Single, Esther Bayly, Mother source

BAYLY, ------- CF Dec. 1872, Northampton, Infantile, 10 days, Jackson & Mary, Northampton, Single, Gennie Stephens, Friend source

BAYLY, Ann CF Feb. 13, 1883, Northampton, Dropsy, 31, Bowdoin & Lucy Chandler, Birth Unkn., Hy "Henry" Bayly, Husband source

BAYLY, Betty CF Mar. 8, 1873, Northampton, Bilious Fever, 6 yrs. 1 mo., Zed Baly & Eliza Nottingham, Northampton, Single, Eliza Nottingham, Mother source

BAYLY, Edward P. WM Apr. 2, 1873, Northampton, Consumption, 39, Edward & Pamelia, Northampton, Dy. Coll. Custorus, Sally Bayly, Widow source

BAYLY, Elizabeth CF June 8, 1876, Northampton, Congestive Fever, 14, ------- & Elizabeth Bayly, Northampton, Single, Elizabeth Bayly, Mother source

BAYLY, Erline WF Nov. 28, 1895, Northampton, Consumption, 24, R. E. & Esther D. Miles, Northampton, R. E. Miles, Father source

BAYLY, Fanny CF Sept. 1875, Northampton, Dropsy, 60, Parents Unkn., Northampton, Thomas Bayly, Husband source

BAYLY, Geo. CM Apr. 16, 1892, Northampton, Cause Unkn., 43, Parents Unkn., Northampton, Laborer, Married, Betsy Bayly, Wife source

BAYLY, John CM Mar. 16, 1892, Northampton, Drowned, 46, Parents Unkn., Northampton, Laborer, Single, Newspaper report source

BAYLY, John CM Sept. 10, 1893, Northampton, Cause Unkn., 45, Parents Unkn., Northampton, Laborer, Single, John Read, Neighbor source

BAYLY, Lillie E. WF Sept. 1, 1893, Northampton, Cholera Infantum, 8 Months, Seth M. & Elizabeth, Northampton, Single, Seth M. Bayly, Father source

BAYLY, Maria CF June 6, 1876, Northampton, Cause Unkn., 5, Jane Bayly, Northampton, Single, Jane Bayly, Mother source

BAYLY, Marie CF Feb. 16, 1894, Northampton, Cause Unkn., 2, Harry & Esther, Northampton, Single, Harry Bayly, Father source

BAYLY, Mary CF Mar. 6, 1893, Northampton, Dysentery, 1, James & Fannie, Northampton, Single, James Bayly, Father source

BAYLY, Mary D. CF Dec. 12, 1877, Northampton, Infantile, 4 days, Thomas & Emily, Northampton, Single, Thomas Bayly, Father source

BAYLY, Missouri, WF Dec. 2, 1891, Northampton, Cholera Infantum, 1 month, J. B. & L. A., Northampton, Single, J. B. Bayly, Father source

BAYLY, Sarah CF Feb. 10, 1895, Northampton, Child Birth, 32, John & Hannah Heath, Northampton, Married, James Bayly, Husband source

BAYLY, Sarah CF Jan 16, 1894,Northampton, Old Age, 78, Parents Unkn., Northampton, Married, Hamilton Waddy, Friend source

BAYLY, Sarah E. WF July 16, 1894, Northampton, Typhoid Fever, 70, Arthur & Julia Robbins, Northampton, Married, Arthur R. Bayly, Son source

BAYLY, Sarah E. WF Sept. 5, 1894, Northampton, Cholera Intantum, 20 days, M. J. & Ida, Northampton, Single, M. J. Bayly, Father source

BAYLY, Seth N. WM Mar. 16, 1896, Northampton, Pneumonia, 35, Parents Unkn, Princess Anne, Va. Farmer, Married, R. E. Miles, Father-in-law source

BAYLY, Thomas W. WM Jan. 9, 1877, Northampton, Heart Disease, 60, Thomas & Mary, Northampton, Farmer, Louisa Wife, Arthur Bayly, Son source

BAYLY, Thos. M. WM Mar. 4, 1893, Northampton, Kidney Disease, 42, Thos. & Sarah, Acco. Co., Clerk, Single, Arthur Bayly, Brother source

BEAVINS, Shadrack CM Jan. 10, 1872, Northampton, Dropsy, 78, Parents Unkn., Acco. Co., Laborer, Single, Wm. Satchell, where died source

BECKET, ------- CM May 18, 1877, Northampton, Crying Fits, Age Unkn., James & Emily, Northampton, Single, Emily Becket, Mother source

BECKET, ------- CM Nov. 1, 1887, Northampton, Cause Unkn., 15 days, William & Alice, Northampton, Single, Alice Becket, Mother source

BECKET, Kessiah CF Sept. 8, 1873, Northampton, Hemorrhage Lungs, 60, Abram & Kessiah, Northampton, Single, S. Bingham, Friend source

BECKET, Mary CF Apr. 18, 1882, Northampton, Pneumonia, 30, Jacob & Susan Weeks, Northampton, Single, Cook, Husband source

BECKET, Sarah CF May 28, 1875, Northampton, Cause Unkn., 45, Parents Unkn., Birth Unkn., Neighbor source

BECKETT, ------- CM Mar. 5, 1896, Northampton, Cause Unkn., 3 days, Arthur & Maggie, Northampton, Single, Rose Giddings, Aunt source

BECKETT, ------- CM Nov. 1891, Northampton, Cholera Infantum, 4 days, S. B. & Maria, Northampton, Single, S. B. Beckett, Father source

BECKETT, Ada CF Sept. 11, 1895, Northampton, Malaria, 12, James & Virginia, Northampton, Single, Virginia Beckett, Mother source

BECKETT, Linie CF Feb. 24, 1892, Northampton, Child Birth, 21, Chas. & Martha Savage, Acco. Co., Laborer, Married, Geo. Beckett, Father-in-Law source

BECKETT, Patience CF Sept. 5, 1892, Northampton, Child Birth, 35, Parents Unkn., North Carolina, Laborer, Married, Arthur Booker, Friend source

BECKETT, William CM June 1, 1895, Northampton, Old Age, 82, Parents Unkn., Acco. Co., Laborer, Single, John H. Kellam, Son-in-Law source

BELL, ------- CM Mar. 3, 1893, Northampton, Crying Fits, 2 days, Peter & Tabbie, Northampton, Single, Peter Bell, Father source

Northampton County, VA, Deaths from Death Register and Wills, 1871-1896

BELL, ------- WF Apr. 4, 1871, Northampton, Infantile, 1 day, Edwd. & Ellen, Northampton, Edwd. Bell, Father source

BELL, ------- WF Sept.3, 1893, Northampton, Cholera Infantum, 3 months, H. N. & Peggie, Northampton, Single, H. N. Bell, Father source

BELL, ------- WM Feb. 7, 1896, Northampton, Cause Unkn., 2 days, M. M. & Elizabeth, Northampton, Single, M. M. Bell, Father source

BELL, ------- WM Nov. 12, 1896, Northampton, Cause Unkn., 2 days, M. M. & Elizabeth, Northampton, Single, M. M. Bell, Father source

BELL, ------- WM Oct. 7, 1874, Alms' House, Cause Unkn., 16 days, Maria Bell, Alms' House Northampton, Single, N. W. Wyatt, source

BELL, Alfred T. Jr. WM July 5, 1893, Northampton, Cause Unkn., 1 month, A. T. & Alice, Northampton, Single, A. T. Bell, Father source

BELL, Edward CM Aug. 1873, Northampton, Bilious Fever, 6 yrs., 2 mos., Eliza Bell, Northampton, Single, N. H. Fisher, Friend source

BELL, Ellen WF Oct. 1891, Northampton, Cause Unkn., 6 months, H. A. & Susan, Northampton, Single, H. A. Bell, Father source

BELL, Ezekiel CM Oct. 1875, Northampton, Old Age, 90, Parents Unkn., Northampton, Neighbor source

BELL, Harriet CF June 1, 1876, Northampton, Cause Unkn., 65, Peter & Harriet, Northampton, Cook, Widow, George James, Son source

BELL, Harry WM Aug. 10, 1896, Northampton, Peritonites, 18, H. A. & Susan, Northampton, Single, H. A. Bell, Father source

BELL, Jane WF Apr. 1872, Northampton, Consumption, 45, Nelson & -------, Northampton, Jno. F. Bell, Husband source unkn.

BELL, John H. CM Mar. 30, 1876, Northampton, Cause Unkn., 1 yr. 8 mos., John & Olivia, Northampton, Single, John H. Bell, Father source

BELL, Levin CM Mar. 25, 1876, Northampton, Inflammation Bowels, 67, Parents Unkn., Accomack, Laborer, Single, John Bell, Neighbor source

BELL, Lottie E. WF Aug. 12, 1885, Northampton, Consumption, 27, James S. & Lottie, Accomack, Married, Jas. B. Bell, Head of Family source

BELL, Maggie _F 1882, Northampton, Consumption, 61, Geo. Jarvis, Northampton, Single, Mrs. Edmonds, source

BELL, Major CM Jan. 25, 1882, Northampton, Congestive Chill, 65, Geo. & Hettie Bell, Northampton, Farmer, Son source

BELL, Mary CF June 2, 1894, Northampton, La Grippes, 32, Chas. & Eliza Parks, Northampton, Married, Eliza Parks, Mother source

BELL, Mrs. Allen WF Apr. 1, 1875, Northampton, Consumption, 40, Parents Unkn., Northampton, Edwd. Bell Husband source

BELL, Richard CM Aug. 4, 1892, Northampton, Cause Unkn., 26, James & Jane, Northampton, Laborer, Married, Jas. Moses Friend source

BELL, Smith WM Feb. 12, 1893, Northampton, Old Age, 92, Parents Unkn., Northampton, Single, John Bell, Son source

BELL, William T. WM June 1879, Northampton, Diarrhea, 5 months, Robert W. & Margaret A., Va., Va., Va., Single, Dr. William W. Wilkins, Physician source

BELOAT,------- WF May 9, 1877, Northampton, Infantile, 3 days, Laban J. & Amanda, Northampton, Single, Laban J. Beloat, Father source

BELOAT, John S. WM Dec. 12, 1896, Northampton, Pneumonia, 19, Laban & Fannie, Northampton, Single, Laban Beloat, Father source

BELOAT, Robert WM May 17, 1896, Northampton, Cause Unkn., 1 month, Tom & Maggie, Northampton, Single, R. W. Bell, Grandfather source

BELOATE, ------- WM July 14, 1887, Northampton, Cause Unkn., 1 yr. 4 mos., Laban J. Belote, [Farmer?], Northampton, Single, Laban J. Beloate, Father source

BELOTE, Amanda C. WF Dec. 5, 1892, Northampton, Grippee, 45, J. B. & Elizabeth Dalby, Northampton, Married, L. J. Belote, Husband source

BELOTE, Fannie WF Oct. 16, 1892, Northampton, Croup, 3 months, P. S. & Fannie, Northampton, Single, L. J. Belote, Friend source

BELOTE, Fanny WF June 10, 1893, Northampton, Diarrhea, 7 months, G. T. & Lizzie, Northampton, Single, G. T. Belote, Father source

BELOTE, John WM Mar. 30, 1876, Northampton, Croup, 10 days, Laban & Victoria, Northampton, Single, Laban A. Belote, Father source

BELOTE, Maggie W. WF Dec. 17, 1895, Northampton, Child Birth, 37, Jacob & Susan Nottingham, Northampton, Married, Susan Nottingham, Mother source

BENSON, Edward Jr. WM May 1875, Northampton, Consumption, 34, Edward & Sally, Northampton, Farmer, Edward Benson, Father source

BERRY, Geo. W. WM Feb. 2, 1895, Northampton, Bright's Dis., 37, Geo. H. & Margaret, Maryland, R. R. Service, R. H. Berry, Brother source

BEVANS, ------- CM June 14, 1876, Northampton, Cause Unkn., 15 days, Edith Bevans, Northampton, Single, Saml. Bevans, Grandfather source

BINGHAM, Charlotte CF July 4, 1893, Northampton, Cause Unkn., 8 months, Mary Bingham, Northampton, Single, Maria Bingham, Grandmother source

BINGHAM, James W. CM Nov. 1874, Eastville Township, Cholera Infantum, 2 months, Southey & Louisa, Eastville Township, Southey Bingham, Father source

BIRD, ------- WM July 27, 1896, Northampton, Cause Unkn., 7 days, Jas. L. & Mary, Northampton, Single, J. L. Watson, Father source

BIVANS, ------- CF Oct. 2, 1893, Northampton, Cause Unkn, 4 days, Lit & Emma, Northampton, Single, Emma Bivans, Mother source

BIVANS, Eliza CF Nov. 25, 1891, Northampton, Old Age, 71, Charity Becket, Acco. Co., Laborer, Single, Jas. Braxton, Friend source

BIVVINS, Samuel Sr. BM June 1879, Northampton, Aneurism, 68, Parents Unkn., Va., Va., Va., Farmer, Matilda Wife, Wm. A. Thom source (see Will Book deaths)

BLOXOM, ------- WF June 1885, Northampton, Cholera Infantum, 3 months, E. Bloxom, Northampton, Single, E. Bloxom, Father source

BLOXOM, W. F. WM Mar. 15, 1893, Northampton, Cause Unkn., 41, Parents Unkn., Acco. Co., Oysterman, Single, J. R. Read, Neighbor source

BOGGS, E. T. WM Feb. 11, 1892, Northampton, Consumption, 25, J. E. & N. G., Acco. Co., Sailor, Single, J. E. Boggs, Father source

BONWELL, Alice WF Oct. 1871, Northampton, Diphtheria, 18, Chas. & Jane Bonwell, Northampton, Single, Jno. W. Read, Friend source

BOOKER, Henry CM July 10, 1872, Northampton, Billious Fever, 1 yr. 6 mos., Harriet Booker, Northampton, Single, Jno. Becket, Friend where died source

BOOKER, Lee CM Mar. 20, 1893, Northampton, Heart Disease, 19, Fontaine & Sophia, Laborer, Single, Fontaine Booker, Father source

BOOL, Mary E. WF Nov. 21, 1896, Northampton, Pneumonia, 1, J. D. & Rosa A., Northampton, Single, J. D. Bool, Father source

BOOL, Sallie WF May 30, 1892, Northampton, Measles, 1, Wm. F. & Janie, Northampton, Single, C. A. Burton, Friend source

BOOL, Willie WM May 26, 1892, Northampton, Measles, 3, Wm. F. & Janie, Northampton, Single, C. A. Burton, Friend source

BOOL, Wm. F. WM Oct. 9, 1893, Northampton, Drowned, 43, David & Sarah, Northampton, Waterman, Married, P. H. Bool, Brother source

BOROM, Wm. T. WM May 16, 1895, Northampton, Pneumonia, 24, Parents Unkn., Maryland, Barber, Single, R. H. Berry, Neighbor source

BOTT, Jas. S. WM Dec. 18, 1887, Northampton, Cause Unkn., 10 days, Jas. & Georgie, Northampton, Single, G. Fred Floyd, Physician source

BOWDOIN, ------- CF Nov. 1875, Northampton, Cause Unkn., 7 days, Unkn. & Easter Bowdoin, Northampton, Single, Easter Bowdoin, Mother source

BOWDOIN, Elizabeth CF June 2, 1895, Northampton, Malaria Fever, 8, Edie Bowdoin, Northampton, Single, Ellison Harmanson, Friend source

BOWDOIN, Geo. CM Mar. 2, 1894, Northampton, Dropsy, 42, Parents Unkn., Northampton, Laborer, Single, Henry Jackson, Friend source

BOWDOIN, Peter S. WM June 1875, Northampton, Old Age, 80, Parents Unkn., Northampton, Mrs. E. U. Smith, Sister source

BOWDOIN, Rose CF Aug. 10, 1896, Northampton, Paralysis, 67, Juliet Brickhouse, Northampton, Widow, Ed Bowdoin, Son source

BOYTT, ------- WM Apr. 25, 1896, Northampton, Cause Unkn., 1 month 7 days, J. T. & Annie, Northampton, Single, Jno. R. Read, Neighbor source

BOYTT, ------- WM Mar. 18, 1896, Northampton, Cause Unkn., 3 days, J. T. & Annie, Northampton, Single, Jno. R. Read, Neighbor source

BRADFORD, ------- CF July 29, 1896, Northampton, Cause Unkn., 21 days, Amanda Bradford, Northampton, Single, Amanda Bradford, Mother source

BRADFORD, Anna WF Nov. 16, 1876, Northampton, Cuddue, 5, Geo. & Joana, Northampton, Single, Geo. W. Bradford, Father source

BRADFORD, Fisher WM Feb. 7, 1896, Northampton, Old Age, 85, Parents Unkn., Northampton, Farmer, Married, Jas. A. Smith, Friend source

BRADFORD, Jim CM Feb. 10, 1872, Northampton, Inflammation of Bowels, 17, Parents Unkn., Acco. Co., Laborer, Single, Hezh. P. Wescoat, where died source

Northampton County, VA, Deaths from Death Register and Wills, 1871-1896

BRADFORD, Joana WF Oct. 18, 1876, Northampton, Typhoid Fever, 32, Abel & Margaret Stott, Northampton, Married, Geo. W. Bradford, Husband source

BRADFORD, John WM Jan. 9, 1876, Northampton, Bilious Fever, 45, William & Nancy, Northampton, Married, Edwd. V. Gunter, Neighbor source

BRADFORD, Mary WF July 12, 1872, Northampton, Consumption, 57, Chas. & Betsy Dillion, Northampton, Married, Wm. W. Bradford, Husband source

BRADFORD, William WM Dec. 16, 1873, Northampton, Bilious Diarrhea, 55, Abel & Mary, Northampton, Farmer, Angeline Wife, Abel Bradford, Son source

BRADY, Frank WM June 16, 1892, Northampton, Measles, 1, Frank & Emma, Northampton, Single, John H. Doughty, Neighbor source

BRAGG, Severn CM Apr. 10, 1878, Northampton, Measles, 4, Charles & Susan, Northampton, Single, Charles Bragg, Father source

BRAXTON, Leonard BM Nov. 1879, Northampton, Croup, 1, Thomas & Priscilla., Va., Va., Va., Single, Source unkn.

BRAXTON, Richard CM Sept. 1, 1882, Northampton, Consumption, 1 yr. 6 mos., Thos. & P., Northampton, S. H. K., Single, Thos. Braxton, Father source

BRICKHOUSE, ------- BM Apr. 1880, Northampton, Debility, 2 days, Parents Unkn., Va., Va., Va., Single, Source unkn.

BRICKHOUSE, ------- CF 1888, Northampton, Cause Unkn., 1 day, Hugh & Comfort, [Laborer?], Northampton, Single, Hugh Brickhouse, Father source

BRICKHOUSE, ------- CF Apr. 15, 1894, Northampton, Crying Fits, 10 days, John & Leah, Northampton, Single, John Brickhouse, Father source

BRICKHOUSE, ------- CM Oct. 11, 1892, Northampton, Cause Unkn., 3 days, Susan, Northampton, Single, Susan Brickhouse, Mother source

BRICKHOUSE, ------- CM Sept. 22, 1893, Northampton, Cause Unkn. 12 days, John & Jennie, Northampton, Single, John E. Brickhouse, Grandfather source

BRICKHOUSE, Ben Sr. CM Aug. 14, 1878, Northampton, Old Age, 87, Ben & Polly, Northampton, Farmer, Liza Wife, Ben Brickhouse, Son source

BRICKHOUSE, Carrie CF June 18, 1882, Northampton, Fever, 8 mos., Wm. & Janie, Northampton, Single, Wm. Brickhouse, Father source

BRICKHOUSE, Carrie WF Aug. 18, 1877, Northampton, Typhoid Fever, 18, James M. & Virginia, Northampton, Single, James M. Brickhouse, Father source

BRICKHOUSE, Carson CM Apr. 8, 1895, Northampton, Consumption, 7, John L. & Georgeanna, Acco. Co., Single, John L. Brickhouse, Father source

BRICKHOUSE, Cora CF June 1875, Northampton, Cause Unkn., 1, Ben & Mary, Northampton, Single, Mary Brickhouse, Mother source

BRICKHOUSE, Eadmond CM Aug. 9, 1877, Northampton, Old Age, 78, Unkn. & Sallie, Northampton, Laborer, Single, William Brickhouse, Neighbor source

BRICKHOUSE, Elizabeth M. WF Sept. 6, 1873, Northampton, Heart Disease, 72 yrs., 2 mos., 4 days, Benjamin & Sally Scott, Northampton, House Keeper, Thomas E. Brickhouse, Husband source

BRICKHOUSE, Emily CF Dec. 19, 1877, Northampton, Crying Fits, 12 days, Jacob & Susan, Northampton, Single, Jacob Brickhouse, Father source

BRICKHOUSE, Emma WF Dec. 5, 1894, Acco. Co., Heart Failure, 13, Thos. E. & Mary E., Northampton, Single, John H. Doughty, Father-in-Law source

BRICKHOUSE, Ether CF Aug. 3, 1887, Northampton, Cause Unkn.,12, Jack & Emily, Northampton, Single, Jack Brickhouse, Father source

BRICKHOUSE, Geo. CM Sept. 7, 1895, Northampton, Heart Disease, 72, Leah Brickhouse, Northampton, Laborer, Married, John H. Kellam, Nephew source

BRICKHOUSE, Geo. WM May 12, 1877, Northampton, Old Age, 88, Geo. & Ann, Northampton, Farmer, Single, William Brickhouse, Son source

BRICKHOUSE, James M. WM Apr. 13, 1877, Northampton, Heart Disease, 50, Geo. & Ann, Northampton, Clerk of Court, Virginia Wife, George Brickhouse, Son source

BRICKHOUSE, Lloyd CM May 16, 1895, Northampton, Pneumonia, 72, Parents Unkn., Farmer, Married, Wm. Stratton, Friend source

BRICKHOUSE, Maggie CF June 11, 1895, Northampton, Dropsy, 3, John L. & Georgeanna, Northampton, Single, John L. Brickhouse, Father source

BRICKHOUSE, Maggie CF Sept. 4, 1892, Northampton, Typhoid, 19, Johnson & Juliet, Northampton, Single, Johnson Brickhouse, Father source

BRICKHOUSE, Mary CF Mar. 18, 1891, Northampton, Scrofula, 18, Robt. & Eveline, Northampton, Laborer, Married, J. M. Stuartt, Neighbor source

BRICKHOUSE, Polly CF Feb. 20, 1876, Northampton, Pneumonia, 35, Wm. & Fanny, Northampton, Cook, Single, Fanny Brickhouse, Mother source

BRICKHOUSE, Polly WF June 10, 1878, Northampton, Old Age, 98, Parents Unkn., Northampton, Single, Richard Taylor, Friend source

BRICKHOUSE, Rebecca CF Nov. 2, 1896, Northampton, Pneumonia, 7 months, W. H. & Jane, Northampton, Single, W. H. Brickhouse, Father source

BRICKHOUSE, Robt. CM Apr. 1891, Northampton, Consumption, 56, Parents Unkn., Northampton, Laborer, Single, J.M. Stuartt, Neighbor source

BRICKHOUSE, Severn CM Mar. 14, 1896, Northampton, Dropsy, 40, Severn & Mary, Northampton, Farmer, Married, Peter Custis, Neighbor source

BRICKHOUSE, Smith CM Oct. 10, 1878, Northampton, Heart Disease, 60, Parents Unkn., Northampton, Farmer, Emeline Brickhouse, Wife source

BRICKHOUSE, William CM June 10, 1878, Northampton, Bilious Fever, 9 months, Wm. & Polly, Northampton, Single, Wm. Brickhouse, Father source

BRISCO, Susan CF Mar. 30, 1887, Northampton, Dropsy, 5, Parents Unkn., [Servant?], Northampton, Single, George Church, Neighbor source

BRITTINGHAM, Elijah WM Apr. 14, Northampton, Typhoid Fever, 70, Elijah & Susan, Northampton, Postmaster, Single, Polly Underhill, Friend source

BRITTINGHAM, Joseph B. WM 1876, Northampton, Fever of Brain,55, Elijah & Peggy, Northampton, Farmer, Married, Elijah Brittingham, Brother source

BROOKS, ------- WM Aug. 2, 1896, Northampton, Cause Unkn., 6 months, Pat & Annie, Northampton, Single, A. Saunders, Neighbor source

BROOKS, Adline CF Feb. 1, 1882, Northampton, Pneumonia, 39, Morris Carpenter, Northampton, House Keeper, Married, V. Small, source

BROOKS, John CM Oct. 10, 1878, Northampton, Worms, 3, Augustus & Lucy, Northampton, Single, Augustus Brooks, Father source

BROOKS, Lucy E. BF Apr. 1880, Northampton, Pleurisy, 34, Parents Unkn., Va., Va., Va., Keeping House, Augustus Husband, Dr. William J. Scott, Physician source

BROWN, ------- CF Jan. 14, 1893, Northampton, Cause Unkn., 1, Runie Brown, Northampton, Single, Levin Smith, Friend source

BROWN, ------- CF May 16, 1893, Northampton, Cause Unkn., 4 days, Lewis & Leah, Northampton, Single, Wm. Fitchett, Neighbor source

BROWN, ------- CM Sept. 1875, Northampton, Crying Fits, 1 month, Horace & Sophia, Northampton, Single, Horace Brown, Father source

BROWN, Caroline CF Aug. 1875, Northampton, Congestion, 4, Horace & Sophia, Northampton, Single, Horace Brown, Father source

BROWN, I. J. WM Aug.10, 1893, Northampton, Dysentery, 7 months, W. A. & Annie, Northampton, Single, W. A. Brown, Father source

BROWN, James CM Dec. 8, 1895, Northampton, Old Age, 80, Parents Unkn., Culpepper, Va., Laborer, Alex Brown, Friend source

BROWN, Major CM Mar. 4, 1892, Northampton, Typhoid, 50, Parents Unkn., Northampton, Laborer, Single, John Webb, Friend source

BROWN, Margaret WF Dec. 3, 1894, Northampton, Cause Unkn., 47, Parents Unkn., Norfolk, Va., Housekeeper, Married, E. S. Herald County paper source

BROWN, Mattie CF Apr. 20, 1893, Northampton, Consumption, 23, P. H. & Priscilla Fitchett, Northampton, Single, Sydney Fitchett, Brother source

BROWN, Norris L. Sept. 11, 1892, Northampton, Typhoid, 37, Wm. A. & J. E., New Jersey, Farmer, Married, Mary W. Brown, Wife source

BROWN, Thos. CM June 4, 1893, Northampton, Dysentery, 2, Thos. & Mary, Northampton, Single, Thos. Brown, Father source

BROWN, W. C. WM July 4, 1893, Northampton, Cause Unkn., 6 mo. 1 day, W. A. & Annie, Northampton, Single, W. A. Brown, Father source

BULL, Anna CF May 20, 1873, Northampton, Bilious Fever, 10, John & Eliza Stevens, Northampton, Single, Eliza Stevens, Mother source

BULL, James CM June 2, 1894, Northampton, Consumption, 40, Parents Unkn., Northampton, Laborer, Married, Lewis James, Friend source

BULL, Leah WF July 24, 1882, Northampton, Consumption, 61, Wm. & Betsy Littleton, Accomack Co., Housekeeper, Mrs. Edmonds, source

BULL, Major WM Mar. 1880, Northampton, Congestive Chill, 58, Parents Unkn., Va., Va., Va., Widower, William Reid, source

BULL, Mary F. WF Mar. 20, 1876, Northampton, Consumption, 28, Parents Unkn., Accomack, Single, Roland Bull, Brother source

BULLMAN, Virginia WF Apr. 3, 1891, Northampton, Pneumonia, 7 months, R. C. & Virginia, Northampton, Single, R. C. Bullman, Father source

BUNTING, ------- CM Aug. 2, 1878, Northampton, Infantile, 11 days, Unkn. & Mary Bunting, Northampton, Single, Mary Bunting, Mother source

BUNTING, Alice CF Sept. 1872, Northampton, Worms, 5, Sam & Bethanie Bayly, Northampton, Single, source unkn.

BURBRIDGE, Infant WF Aug. 1879, Northampton, Enteritis, 9 months, Henry & Elizabeth, Md., Md., Md., Single, Dr. William W. Wilkins, Physician source

BURR, Henry B. WM June 16, 1896, Northampton, Typhoid, 19, Warren & Ella, Northampton, Single, Warren Burr, Father source

BURRIS, Caleb CM July 6, 1874, Eastville Township, Heart Disease, 50, Parents Unkn., Northampton, Minister, Eugenie Burris, Wife source

BURROUGHS, Mary WF Jan. 11, 1878, Northampton, Cause Unkn., 65, Parents Unkn., Northampton, Laborer, Single, Patrick Fitchett, Friends source

BURROWN, Caleb W. J. CM 1888, Philadelphia, Pa., Congestion of Brain, 21, Caleb & Mary E., Northampton, Laborer, Geo. P. Burrown, source

BURROWS, Eva CF June 4, 1892, Northampton, Cholera Infantum, 3, Geo. P. & Mary E., Northampton, Single, Geo. P. Burrows, Father source

BURRUSS, Mary E. CF Aug. 12, 1893, Northampton, Cholera Infantum, 5 months, Geo. & Mary, Northampton, Single, Geo. Burruss, Father source

BURTIN, ------- CM Oct. 9, 1877, Northampton, Infantile, Age Unkn., James & Mary, Northampton, Single, Mary Burtin, Mother source

BURTIN, Adah CF Oct. 14, 1878, Northampton, Consumption, 31, James & Mariah, Northampton, Laborer, Single, James Burtin, Father source

BURTIN, James CM Aug. 15, 1875, Northampton, Old Age, 70, Parents Unkn., Northampton, Laborer, Neighbor source

BURTIN, Walter CM Aug. 12, 1878, Northampton, Congestive Bowels, 8, James & Sarah, Northampton, Laborer, Single, James Burtin, Father source

BURTON, Annie WF June 10, 1891, Northampton, Cause Unkn., 60, Garrison & Mary, Acco. Co., Married, John R. Nottingham, Friend source

BURTON, Eva CF Sept. 16, 1884, Northampton, Cholera Infantum, 2, Lit & Hennie, Northampton, Lit Burton, Father source

Northampton County, VA, Deaths from Death Register and Wills, 1871-1896

BURTON, James CM Sept. 9, 1893, Northampton, Cause Unkn., 58, Robin & Adah, Northampton, Laborer, Single, Jim Bailey, Friend source

BURTON, John W. WF Apr. 22, 1876, Northampton, Consumption, 58, Parents Unkn., Accomack, Married, Dr. Sev. F. Nottingham, Physician source

BYRD, ------- WF Feb. 11, 1876, Northampton, Crying Fits, 2 months, Lloyd & Betsy, Northampton, Single, Betsy Byrd, Mother source

CARPENTER, ------- C(?) Born Dead Sept. 1871, Northampton, Born Dead, Stephen & Mary, Northampton, Single, Stephen Carpenter, Father source

CARPENTER, ------- WF Nov. 30, 1896, Northampton, Whooping Cough, 2 months, Jas. R. & Nellie, Northampton, Single, Nellie Carpenter, Mother source

CARPENTER, Adah CF July 10, 1878, Northampton, Old Age, 80, Jacob & Kate, Northampton, Laborer, Single, Smith Wyatt, Friend source

CARPENTER, Alfred CM June 1875, Northampton, Pneumonia, 9 months, Jacob & Alexine, Birth Unkn., Single, Physician source

CARPENTER, Anna CF Dec. 1, 1873, Northampton, Small Pox, 5, Richard & Leah, Northampton, Single, Leah Carpenter, Mother source

CARPENTER, Becca CF Dec. 3, 1873, Northampton, Small Pox, 3, Richard & Leah, Northampton, Single, Leah Carpenter, Mother source

CARPENTER, Geo. WM Jan. 28, 1872, Northampton, Pneumonia, 23, Jas. S. & Arlene, Northampton, Sailor, Single, Jas. S. Carpenter, Father source

CARPENTER, Henry CM Sept. 1872, Northampton, Cause Unkn., 3, Stephen & Mary, Northampton, Single, Gennie Stephens, source

CARPENTER, James WM Aug. 1891, Northampton, Old Age, 91, Parents Unkn., Northampton, Farmer, Married, W. G. Bell, Friend source

CARPENTER, Jas. CM July 1872, Northampton, Old Age, 70, Parents Unkn., Northampton, Isma Wyatt, source

CARPENTER, John P. WM Mar. 10, 1891, Northampton, Heart Disease, 62, Jno. P. & Mary, Northampton, Sailor, Married, G. V. Carpenter, Son source

CARPENTER, Marion WF May 16, 1894, Northampton, Cholera Infantum, 8 months, A. C. & Henrietta, Northampton, Single, A. C. Carpenter, Father source

CARPENTER, Mary An CF July 5, 1894, Northampton, Old Age, 80, Parents Unkn., Northampton, Married, Mary A. Thomas, Daughter source

CARPENTER, Nim CM Oct. 12, 1878, Northampton, Consumption, 35, Unkn. & Dinah, Northampton, Married, Farmer, Caroline Wife, Dinah Carpenter, Mother source

CARPENTER, Rinie D. WF Aug. 26, 1892, Northampton, Typhoid, 31, L. D. & Elizabeth Copes, Northampton, Married, T. F. Carpenter, Husband source

CARPENTER, Sarah CF July 1872, Northampton, Consumption, 25, Jas. Carpenter, Northampton, source unkn.

CARPENTER, Stephen CM Feb. 10, 1892, Northampton, Consumption, 52, Parents Unkn., Northampton, Laborer, Married, Newspaper report source

CARROLL, Patrick WM Jan. 12, 1896, Northampton, Consumption, 65, Parents Unkn, Ireland, Farmer, Married, L. H. Johnson Neighbor source

CARTER, ------- CM July 4, 1876, Northampton, Cause Unkn., 15 days, Lizzy Carter, Northampton, Single, Lizzy Carter, Mother source

CARTER, ------- WM Apr. 1880, Northampton, Inanition, 1 day, Parents Unkn., Va., Va., Va., Single, source unkn.

CARTER, Geo. CM May 10, 1877, Northampton, Congestive Lungs, 9 months, Peter & Eliza, Northampton, Single, Peter Carter, Father source

CARTER, Henretta CF Sept. 18, 1878, Northampton, Quinsy, 20, Unkn. & Silla Carter, Northampton, Laborer, Single, Silla Carter, Mother source

CARTER, Infant CF Jan. 10, 1873, Northampton, Infantile, 5 days, Alfred & Tamer, Northampton, Single, Alfred Carter, Father source

CARTER, James H. CM Feb. 6, 1876, Northampton, Typhoid Fever, 2 yrs. 25 days, Eliza Carter, Northampton, Single, Eliza Carter, Mother source

CARTER, Jesse CM Feb. 10, 1873, Northampton, Small Pox, 27, Abel & Eliza, Northampton, Laborer, Single, Geo. Carter, Friend source

CARTER, John CM June 15, 1887, Northampton, Consumption, 35, Victor & Jane, Northampton, Teacher, John Robins, Friend source

CARTER, Peggie CF May 2, 1883, Northampton, Asthma, 65, Job & Malinda Jacob, Birth Unkn., Peter J. Carter, source

CARTER, Priscilla CF Apr. 3, 1887, Northampton, Pneumonia, 63, Parents Unkn., Northampton, Servant, Widow, George Simpkins, Friend source

CARTER, Tamer BF Apr. 1880, Northampton, Ovarian Dropsy, 60, Parents Unkn., Va., Va., Va., Washerwoman, Widow, Spencer Weeks Husband, Dr. Geo. W. Smith, Physician source

CAUSEY, L. P. WM May 1896, Northampton, Cause Unkn., 58, Parents Unkn., Delaware, Mechanic, Single, Herbert Nottingham, Tenant source

CHAMBERS, Lizzie J. WF July 20, 1894, Northampton, Typhoid Fever, 20, David & Georgia, Acco. Co., Laborer, Single, David Chambers, Father source

CHANDLER, ------- WF July 1884, Northampton, Born Dead, 0, Jos. W. & Maggie, Northampton, Single, Jos. W. Chandler, Father source

CHANDLER, ------- WM Apr. 1875, Northampton, Cause Unkn., 20 days, Louis & Missouri, Northampton, Single, Louis Chandler, Father source

CHANDLER, Ben J. WM Dec. 15, 1895, Northampton, Gun Shot wound accident, 25, Joseph & Maggie, Northampton, Farmer, Single, Joseph C. Chandler, Father source

CHANDLER, E. Willis WM Aug. 14, 1894, Northampton, Typhoid Fever, 21, John & Margaret, Northampton, Clerk, Single, John Chandler, Father source

CHANDLER, Jas. WM Mar. 4, 1883, Northampton, Cause Unkn., 7 yrs. 9 mos., Jno. J. & Margt., Birth Unkn., Jno. J. Chandler, Father source

CHANDLER, Margaret WF Nov. 14, 1895, Northampton, Pneumonia, 46, Joseph & Emma Gibb, Northampton, Married, Joseph C. Chandler, Husband source

CHARNICK, Leah WF May 14, 1874, Northampton, Typhoid Fever, 74 yrs. 5 mos. 1 day, Jno. & Severn Williams, Northampton, Jno. T. Husband, Jno. Charnick, Son source

CHARNOCK, ------- WF Sept. 1871, Northampton, Cause Unkn., 1, Wm. Charnock, Northampton, Single, Wm. Charnock, Father source

CHARNOCK, ------- WM Mar. 1872, Northampton, Infantile, 1 month, Wm. & Charlotte, Birth Unkn., Single, Wm. Charnock, Father source

CHARNOCK, Alec WM June 1872, Northampton, Consumption, 37, Parents Unkn., Northampton, source unkn.

CHARNOCK, Fanny WF Oct. 1871, Northampton, Convulsions, 1, Jas. & Ann, Northampton, Single, Jas. Charnock, Father source

CHARNOCK, Julian WM Sept. 14, 1894, Northampton, Pneumonia, 11 months, W. T. & Mary V., Northampton, Single, W. T. Charnock Father source

CHARNOCK, Mary WF Nov. 4, 1893, Northampton, Insanity, 45, Major & Sallie Colona, Acco. Co., Married, Lafayette Charnock, Husband source

CHARNOCK, Mary E. WF Feb. 14, 1893, Northampton, Cause Unkn., 68, Joshua & Margaret Nottingham, Northampton, Married, W. J. Charnock, Husband source

CHRISTIAN, Amanda BF Aug. 1879, Northampton, Drowned, 9, Parents Unkn., Va., Va., Va., Single, source unkn.

CHRISTIAN, Maria CF Apr. 20, 1883, Northampton, Heart Disease, Age Unkn., Arthur & Mary Susan, Birth Unkn., Arthur Christian Father source

CHURCH, ------- CM Jan. 1873, Northampton, Infantile, 2 days, Abe & Margt., Northampton, Single, source unkn.

CHURCH, Arthur CM Oct. 10, 1878, Northampton, Cause Unkn., 14 yrs. 4 mos., James & Susan, Northampton, Laborer, Single, James Church, Father source

CHURCH, Atta CF June 4, 1894, Northampton, Consumption, 7, Jas. & Mary, Northampton, Single, Major Sample, Uncle source

CHURCH, Charles CM Feb. 1874, Northampton, Cause Unkn., 6, Geo. & Eliza, Northampton, Single, Geo. Church, Father source

CHURCH, Georgiana CF May 9, 1876, Northampton, Cause Unkn., 1 month, John & Ada, Accomack, Single, John Church, Father source

CHURCH, Jacob CM Aug. 1, 1895, Northampton, Old Age, 76, C. N. & Bethany, Northampton, Laborer, Single, John H. Kellam, Nephew source

CHURCH, James CM Aug. 2, 1894, Northampton, Consumption, 30, Lizzie Bivans, Northampton, Farmer, Married, Edmond James, Friend source

CHURCH, James CM Dec. 1872, Northampton, Old Age, 70, Parents Unkn., Northampton, M. A. Savage, Neighbor source

CHURCH, James CM Dec. 1873, Northampton, Old Age, 80, Parents Unkn., Northampton, Laborer, Ellen Savage, Friend source

CHURCH, John CM Apr. 15, 1872, Northampton, Billious Fever, 1 yr. 4 mos., Ann Church, Northampton, Single, Hezh. P. Wescoat, where died source

Northampton County, VA, Deaths from Death Register and Wills, 1871-1896

CHURCH, Laura Ellen CF Oct. 15, 1885, Northampton, Burned, 6, Abe & Margt., Northampton, Single, Abe Church, Father source

CHURCH, Mary Esther CF March 1875, Northampton, Cause Unkn., 3, Geo. & Alexine, Single, Geo. Church, Father source

CHURCH, Sissy CF Apr. 1875, Northampton, Cause Unkn., 3, Geo. & Alexine, Birth Unkn., Single, Geo. Church, Father source

CHURCH, Tony BM July 1879, Northampton, Asthma, 80, Anthony & Bettie, Va., Va., Va., Married, source unkn.

CHURN, ------- CF Feb. 11, 1878, Northampton, Infantile, 3 days, Walter & Peggie, Northampton, Single, Walter Churn, Father source

CHURN, Eliza WF June 1874, Northampton, Heart Disease, 60, Parents Unkn., Birth Unkn., Jno. Husband, Jas. K. Savage, Son-in-Law source

CHURN, Jno. WM Dec. 1872, Northampton, Old Age, 70, Parents Unkn., Northampton, source unkn.

CHURN, Peggy CF Jan. 10, 1876, Northampton, Dysentery, 5 months, John & Peggy, Northampton, Single, Peggy Churn, Mother source

CHURN, Sally WF Oct. 1871, Northampton, Diphtheria, 6 months, Sev. B. & Essie, Northampton, Single, Sev. B. Churn, Father source

CHURN, William WM Sept. 1873, Northampton, Cause Unkn., 65, Parents Unkn., Northampton, Farmer, source unkn.

CISCO, Emma BF Aug. 1879, Northampton, Whooping Cough, 2, George & Mary, Va., Va., Va., Single, Dr. Wm. A. Thom, Physician source

CISCO, Henry CM Apr. 4, 1882, Northampton, Consumption, 65, Bettie Cisco, Northampton, Laborer, Married, Wife source

CISCO/BROWN, Isaac CM Sept. 6, 1887, Northampton, Old Age, 95, Parents Unkn., Northampton, Laborer, Married, George Reed, Friend source

COBB, Mary WF Aug. 1879, Northampton, Cause Unkn., 8 days, Warren & Emily, Va., Mass., Va., Single, source unkn.

COBB, Nathan E. WM Aug. 3, 1885, Northampton, Cholera Infantum, 7 mos. 10 days, Warren & Emily, Northampton, Single, Warren Cobb, Father source

COBOURN, Jno. C. WM 1888, Northampton, Old Age, 88, Parents Unkn., Northampton, Laborer, Single, W. B. Stewart, Neighbor source

COFFER, ------- CF Sept. 5, 1873, Northampton, Crying Fits, 10 days, Patrick & Fanny, Northampton, Single, Patrick Coffer, Father source

COLAWAY, Ida WF Sept. 25, 1878, Northampton, Cause Unkn., 14, A. B. & Susan, Northampton, Laborer, A. B. Colaway, Father source

COLEMAN, Richard CM Oct. 14, 1877, Northampton, Bilious Fever, 14, Unkn. & Jane, Northampton, Laborer, Single, Jane Coleman, Mother source

COLEMAN, Sallie BF Aug. 1879, Northampton, Bilious Fever, 1, Parents Unkn., Va., Va., Va., Single, source unkn.

COLES, ------- CF July 19, 1873, Northampton, Cause Unkn., Age Unkn., Elen Wilkins & Jno. Coles, Northampton, Single, Jno. Coles, Father source

COLES, Ellen L. CF Dec. 22, 1876, Northampton, Diphtheria, 7 months, Colbert & Mary, Northampton, Single, Mary A. Coles, Mother source

COLES, Infant C. Sex Unkn., Feb. 27, 1873, Northampton, Infantile, 4 days, Colbert & Mary, Northampton, Single, Mary Coles, Mother source

COLEY, Samuel CM 1888, Northampton, Old Age, 74, Samuel Coley, Northampton, Laborer, Samuel Coley, Head of Family source

COLLINS, ------- CF Nov. 1875, Northampton, Cause Unkn., 1 month, Henry & Lizzie, Birth Unkn., Single, Lizzie Collins, Mother source

COLLINS, ------- CM 1888, Northampton, Crying Fits, 10 days, Geo. Collins, [Laborer?], Northampton, Single, Geo. Collins, Head of Family source

COLLINS, ------- CM Mar. 15, 1892, Northampton, Measles, 5 days, Horace & Tobitha, Northampton, Single, Horace Collins, Father source

COLLINS, ------- CM Mar. 19, 1893, Northampton, Cause Unkn., 3 days, Garnett & Melvina, Northampton, Single, Garnett Collins, Father source

COLLINS, ------- WM Dec. 1885, Northampton, Cause Unkn., 0 days, Ellison & Maggie, Northampton, Single, Ellison Collins, Father source

COLLINS, Adah CF Nov. 15, 1896, Northampton, Typhoid Fever, 61, John & Adah, Northampton, Single, Elizabeth Custis, Friend source

COLLINS, Ann CF May 1, 1878, Northampton, Pneumonia, 41, Parents Unkn., Northampton, Laborer, Single, Jacob James, Friend source

COLLINS, Ann CF May 1, 1882, Northampton, Typhoid Pneumonia, 65, Bettie Collins, Northampton, Laborer, James Collins, source

COLLINS, Annie CF Sept. 1875, Northampton, Child Birth, 30, Parents Unkn., Northampton, Horace Collins, Husband source

COLLINS, Arby CM June 1875, Northampton, Cause Unkn., 17, Griffith & Amy, Birth Unkn., Griffith Collins, Father source

COLLINS, Caleb P. CM Oct. 1873, Northampton, Typhoid Pneumonia, 35, Ralph & Rachel, Northampton, Laborer, Single, Jas. Collins, Neighbor source

COLLINS, Delia CF Dec. 10, 1891, Northampton, Consumption, 31, Arthur & Lizzie Harmon, Northampton, Married, Geo. Collins, Brother source

COLLINS, George CM Nov. 19, 1887, Northampton, Consumption, 16, Victor & Elizabeth, Northampton, Laborer, Lizzie Collins, Aunt source

COLLINS, Henry CM May 3, 1882, Northampton, Cause Unkn., 1 yr. 4 mos., Mary Collins, Northampton, Single, Jas. Perkins, Sailor source

COLLINS, Infant WM June 18, 1872, Northampton, Crying Fits, 2 days, Susan & William, Northampton, Physician source William Father [Farmer?]

COLLINS, Jacob BM Jan. 1880, Northampton, Pneumonia, 22, Smith & Susan, Va., Va., Va., Farm Laborer, Single, Dr. Geo. Kerr, Physician source

COLLINS, Jacob Henry CM Jan. 16, 1882, Northampton, Pneumonia, 22 yrs. 6 mos, Smith & Susan, Northampton, Laborer, Susan Collins, Mother source

COLLINS, James CM Oct. 16, 1872, Northampton, Quinsey, 10, Amy & Griffin, Northampton, Laborer, Single, Griffin Collins, Father source

COLLINS, James CM Sept. 11, 1882, Northampton, Cause Unkn., 21 yr. 6 mos., Griffin & Mary, Northampton, Griffin Collins, Father source

COLLINS, Jas. L. CM Aug. 3, 1895, Northampton, Pneumonia, 25, Parents Unkn., Northampton, Laborer, Single, Custis Wright, Neighbor source

COLLINS, Jim CM Mar. 3, 1874, Eastville Township, Consumption, 28, Griffin & -----, Eastville Township, Farmer, Sol. Nottingham, source

COLLINS, John CM Apr. 17, 1877, Northampton, Cause Unkn., 63, Unkn. & Adah, Northampton, Laborer, Adah Wife, O. N. Badger, Friend source

COLLINS, Leonard CM Sept. 3, 1894, Northampton, Consumption, 42, Welcher & Mary, Northampton, Farmer, Married, S. S. Wilkins, Neighbor source

COLLINS, Lizzy WF Mar. 1875, Northampton, Child Birth, 34, Parents Unkn., Birth Unkn., Jno. Collins, Husband source

COLLINS, Major CM June 9, 1876, Northampton, Asthma, 61,Stephen & Sarah, Northampton, Laborer, Single, Wm. Collins, Neighbor source

COLLINS, Martha S. CF Dec. 6, 1896, Northampton, Col. Infantum, 2, Jas. & Margaret A., Northampton, Single, Sallie Mapp, Grandmother source

COLLINS, Mary CF May 7, 1876, Northampton, Pleurisy, 9, Wilsher & Susan, Northampton, Single, Susan Collins, Mother source

COLLINS, Noah CM Dec. 9, 1876, Northampton, Cause Unkn., 7 days, Noah & Mary, Northampton, Single, Noah Collins, Father source

COLLINS, Raechel CF Dec. 12, 1896, Northampton, Cause Unkn., 72, Peter & Lauretta, Northampton, Single, George Collins, Brother source

COLLINS, Rosie E. CF Mar. 12, 1878, Northampton, Infantile, 5 days, Caleb & Rose, Northampton, Single, Caleb Collins, Father source

COLLINS, Sallie CF May 9, 1882, Northampton, Cause Unkn., 4, Smith & Susan, Northampton, Single, Smith Collins, Father source

COLLINS, Susan CF 1888, Northampton, Dropsy, 57, Smith Collins, Northampton, Laborer, Smith Collins, Head of Family source

COLLINS, Susan CF Dec. 30, 1887, Northampton, Dropsy, 57, Parents Unkn., Northampton, Laborer, Married, Smith Collins, Husband source

COLLINS, Victor CM July 27, 1873, Northampton, Inflammation Stomach, 27 yrs. 7 mos., Griffin & Betsy, Northampton, Laborer, Single, Griffin Collins, Father source

COLLINS, Wilcher CM Jan. 11, 1873, Northampton, Murdered by Jake Roberts, 43 yrs. 6 mos., Luke Dunton & Adah Collins, Northampton, Laborer, Mary Collins, Widow source

COLLINS, William WM June 17, 1872, Northampton, Dysentery, 2, Susan & Wm. Collins, Northampton, Wm. Collins, source [Waterman?]

COLONA, Ethel WF Sept. 27, 1893, Northampton, Cholera Infantum, 9 months, W. T. & Virginia, Northampton, Single, W. T. Colona, Father source

Northampton County, VA, Deaths from Death Register and Wills, 1871-1896

COLONA, Willie WM Oct. 3, 1892, Northampton, Croup, 3 months, Geo. H. & Alice, Northampton, Single, Geo. H. Colona, Father source

COLONNA, Ella WF Oct. 10, 1883, Northampton, Consumption, 17, Wm. E. Colonna, Birth Unkn., Wm. E. Colonna, Father source

COLONY, Cincinatus U. WM Sept. 1871, Northampton, Whooping Cough, 1 yr. 6 mos., Wm. F. & Marg't A., Northampton, Single, Wm. F. Colony, Father source

CONNER, Lloyd CM Oct. 4, 1883, Northampton, Drowned, 10, C. H. & Tabitha, Birth Unkn., C. H. Conner, Father source

CONNER, Parker CM Oct. 4, 1883, Northampton, Drowned, 7, C. H. & Tabitha, Birth Unkn., C. H. Conner, Father source

CONWAY, Matilda WF Sept. 10, 1878, Northampton, Pneumonia, 30, Jacob & Dillia Sparrow, Maryland, Eli Husband, Mariah Godwin, Friend source

COOK, Wm. Snr. CM Nov. 1874, Northampton, Consumption, 40, Parents Unkn., Northampton, Laborer, Martha Cook, wife source

COPES, Elizabeth WF Feb. 3, 1891, Northampton, Neuralgia of Heart, 48, Henry & Betsy Cottingham, Northampton, Married, Margaret Copes, Sister source

COPES, Lizzie WF July 6, 1893, Northampton, Cause Unkn., 1 month, J. L. & Susan, Northampton, Single, J. L. Copes?, Father source

CORNELL, Ben WM Aug. 1875, Northampton, Cause Unkn., 5, Ben & Sally, Birth Unkn., Sally Cornell, Mother source

COSTEN, Mary F. WF Sept. 8, 1891, Northampton, Child Birth, 22, W. H. & Josephine Allen, Northampton, Married, Seth Costin, Husband source

COSTIN, ------- CM Dec. 1875, Northampton, Cause Unkn., 10 days, Severn & Margt., Birth Unkn., Single, Neighbor source

COSTIN, ------- CM Mar. 16, 1876, Northampton, Cause Unkn., 6 days, George & Maria, Northampton, Single, Maria Costin, Mother source

COSTIN,------- WF Jan. 1875, Northampton, Cause Unkn., 7 days, Sam'l & Margt. Costin, Birth Unkn., Single, Sam'l Costin, Father source

COSTIN, Cordellia CF Sept. 2, 1878, Northampton, Burned, 6 months, Unkn. & Sarah Costin, Northampton, Single, Sarah Costin, Mother source

COSTIN, Henry CM Jan. 10, 1893, Northampton, Froze to Death, 40, Wesley & Maria, Northampton, Laborer, Married, Maria Costin, Mother source

COSTIN, Infant CM Apr. 6, 1872, Northampton, Crying Fits, 3 days, Madora & John, Northampton, John Costin, Father source [Laborer?]

COSTIN, Infant WF Feb. 1880, Northampton, Cholera Infantum, 1 day, Samuel J. & Mary E., Va., Va., Va., Single, Dr. R. H. Parker, Physician source

COSTIN, James CM Dec. 10, 1876, Northampton, Burned, 40, Parents Unkn., Northampton, Laborer, Single, John Williams, Supt. of Poor source

COSTIN, James H. WM May 27, 1876, Northampton, Heart Disease, 73 yrs. 1 mon., Wm. & Lucretia, Northampton, Widower, Ellison L. Costin, Son source

COSTIN, Jerry CM June 4, 1894, Northampton, Cause Unkn., 8, John & Emma, Northampton, Single, John Costin, Father source

COSTIN, John WM Sept. 8, 1895, Northampton, Cholera E., 1, Eldred & Ella, Northampton, Single, Eldred Costin, Father source

COSTIN, Joseph WM Dec. 15, 1872, Northampton, Typhoid Fever, 15, Mary & Samuel, Northampton, Single, Samuel Costin, Father source [Laborer?]

COSTIN, Margt. WF Jan 1875, Northampton, Consumption, 34, Parents Unkn., Birth Unkn., Sarah Costin, Neighbor source

COSTIN, Mary E. CF May 10, 1876, Northampton, Burned up, 3, Caleb & Juliet, Accomack, Single, Juliet Costin, Mother source

COSTIN, Nat. WM Jan. 22, 1882, Northampton, Pneumonia, 28, Cove & Mary, Northampton, Farmer, Single, J. Richardson, source

COSTIN, Nathaniel BM Jan. 1880, Northampton, Pneumonia, 30, Parents Unkn., Va., Va., Va., Farm Laborer, Single, Dr. William J. Scott, Physician source

COSTIN, Robt. S. WM Jan. 23, 1893, Northampton, Paralysis, 65, James & Lucy, Northampton, Farmer, Married, Wm. F. Costin, Son source

COSTIN, Susan WF June 1875, Northampton, Dropsy, 23, Parents Unkn., Birth Unkn., Thos. H. Costin, Husband source

COSTON, Joseph CM Jan. 28, 1876, Northampton, Dysentery, Age Unkn., Wm. Coston & Mary Stevens, Northampton, Single, Mary Stevens, Mother source

COTTINGHAM, W. H. WM Oct. 15, 1895, Northampton, Rheumatism, 65, Henry & Mollie, Farmer, Married, John R. Read, Friend source

COUNCIL, Virginia S. WF Dec. 30, 1891, Northampton, La Grippe, 52, W. J. & H. S. Goffigon, Northampton, John H. Goffigon, Brother source

COX, Peter CM Jan. 14, 1895, Northampton, Pneumonia, 51, Parents Unkn., Northampton, Laborer, Custis Wright, Neighbor source

CROSBY, Thomas CM Feb. 10, 1878, Northampton, Typhoid Fever, 9, Thomas & Ella, Northampton, Laborer, Single, Thomas Crosby, Father source

CROW, William CM Oct. 10, 1874, Northampton, Burned, 3 yrs. 9 mos. 1 day, James & Mariah, Northampton, Single, Julious Parsons, Friend source

CUSTIS, ------- CF Feb. 13, 1896, Northampton, Cause Unkn., 2 days, Peter & Georgianna, Northampton, Single, Peter Custis, Father source

CUSTIS, ------- CM 1888, Northampton, Cause Unkn., 7 days, Philip Custis, [Laborer?], Northampton, Single, Philip Custis, Head of Family source

CUSTIS, Cordelia CF June 18, 1892, Northampton, Measles, 10 months, Andrew & Elizabeth, Northampton, Single, Andrew Custis, Father source

CUSTIS, Edward BM May 1880, Northampton, Measles, 9 months, Henry & Emily, Va., Va., Va., Single, source unkn.

CUSTIS, James BM Sept. 1879, Northampton, Consumption, 10, Henry & Emily, Va., Va., Va., Single, Dr. Wm. A. Thom, Physician source

CUSTIS, James CM Sept. 1, 1882, Northampton, Consumption, 9 yrs. 8 mos., Henry & Emily, Northampton, Single, Henry Custis, Father source

CUSTIS, Jas. S. CM Mar. 15, 1891, Northampton, Cause Unkn., 8, Andrew & Eliza, Northampton, Single, Andrew Custis, Father source

Northampton County, VA, Deaths from Death Register and Wills, 1871-1896

CUSTIS, Preston S. CM Nov. 10, 1896, Northampton, Whooping Cough, 2, C. S. & Sallie, Northampton, Single, Elizabeth Custis, Grandmother source

CUSTIS, Rose CF May 15, 1894, Northampton, Insanity, 25, Ben & Patience, Northampton, Single, Ben Custis, Father source

CUTLER, ------- CM Apr. 18, 1878, Northampton, Crying Fits, 7 days, Luke & Ada, Northampton, Single, Luke Cutler, Father source

CUTLER, Maria CF Sept. 28, 1895, Northampton, Typhoid Fever, 11, Ed & Sue, Northampton, Single, Henry Trower, Friend source

CUTLER, Sam'l CM Jan. 20, 1894, Northampton, Pneumonia, 65, Parents Unkn., Acco. Co., Farmer, Married, Ed Cutler, Son source

CYPRESS, Sallie CF July 13, 1895, Northampton, Consumption, 58, Abe & Fannie Fitchett, Northampton, Married, Henry Cypress, Husband source

DALBY, ------- WM Dec. 1875, Northampton, Cause Unkn., 3 months, Geo. R. & Maria, Birth Unkn., Single, Geo. R. Dalby, Father source

DALBY, ------- WM Nov. 1874, Eastville Township, Whooping Cough, 2 months, G. R. & Maria, Eastville Township, Single, G. R. Dalby, Father source

DALBY, ------- WM Oct. 23, 1877, Northampton, Infantile, 3 days, Isaac & Susan, Northampton, Single, Isaac Dalby, Father source

DALBY, Alberta WF Feb. 13, 1871, Northampton, Croup, 4 yrs. 4 mos., Jno. L. & Emma D., Northampton, Single, Jno. L. Dalby, Father source

DALBY, Emma D. WF July 8, 1871, Northampton, Eusipilus, 28 yrs. 2 mos., Luther & Emeline Nottingham, Northampton, Married Jno. L. Dalby, Husband source

DALBY, George R. WM July 1896, Northampton, Dropsy, 53, Nathaniel & Ellen, Northampton, Farmer, Married, Lelia Wilkins, Daughter source

DALBY, James B. WM Oct. 15, 1896, Northampton, Cause Unkn., 75, Parents Unkn, Northampton, Farmer, Married, C. C. Read, Neighbor source

DALBY, Kate WF Oct. 10, 1891, Northampton, Cholera Infantum, 3 months, H. & Margaret, Northampton, Single, H. Dalby, Father source

DALBY, Margaret WF Dec. 12, 1895, Northampton, Croup, 3 months, Hezzie & Margaret, Northampton, Single, Margaret Dalby, Mother source

DALBY, Mary A. WF Sept. 7, 1874, Eastville Township, Dropsy, 62, Parents Unkn., Northampton, Thos. Dalby Husband (dead), Geo. Robertson, source

DALBY, Tabitha CF July 6, 1871, Northampton, Dysentery, 2, Jacob & Eliza, Northampton, Single, Jacob Dalby, Father source [Laborer?]

DALBY, Thomas WM Apr. 1874, Eastville Township, Pneumonia, 56, Parents Unkn., Northampton, Farrmer, Mary A. Wife (dead), Isaac Dalby, source

DARBY or PETERSON, William CM Dec. 18, 1873, Northampton, Cause Unkn., 70 yrs. 5 mos., Peter & Nelly Darby, Northampton, Single, Rich. Costin, Neighbor source

DAVIS, E. E. WM July 4, 1891, Northampton, Cause Unkn., 35, Jno. & Mary, Maryland, Laborer, Married, L. T. Carpenter, Brother-in-Law source

DAVIS, Elijah WM Feb. 3, 1892, Northampton, Cause Unkn., 44, Parents Unkn., Delaware, Laborer, Married, L. T. Carpenter, Neighbor source

DAVIS, Sarah BF Aug. 1879, Northampton, Dysentery, 1 month, Robert & Mary J., Va. Va., Va., source unkn.

DAVY, Levin WM Apr. 12, 1895, Northampton, Apoplexy, 41, Parents Unkn., Birth Unkn., Laborer, Single, Dr. G. P. Moore, Physician source

DELANO, Richard WM Oct. 3, 1894, Northampton, Over dose Laudanum, 40, Parents Unkn., Long Is. N.Y. Waterman, Single, M. E. Dunton, Friend source

DENNIS, James WM Dec, 22, 1892, Northampton, Old Age, 69, Archie & Mary, Northampton, Married, J. M. Godwin, Friend source

DENNIS, John WM Oct. 1879, Northampton, Malarial Fever, 22, Parents Unkn., Teamster, Va., Ire., Ire., Single, W. W. Wilkins, source (PR)

DENNIS, Littleton CM Oct. 10, 1893, Northampton, Consumption, 18, Frank & Adah, Northampton, Laborer, Single, Frank Dennis, Father source

DENNIS, Sallie A. WF Nov. 15, 1883, Northampton, Tumor, 39, Tr. & Sallie Selby, Maryland, R. G. Dennis, Head of Family source

DENNIS, Stephen WM Sept. 1879, Northampton, Malarial Fever, 19, Parents Unkn., Teamster, Va., Ire., Ire., Single, W. W. Wilkins, source (PR)

DEXTER, Sadie CF May 14, 1878, Northampton, Bilious Fever, 19, Unkn. & Emily Dexter, Birth Unkn., Laborer, Single, Emily Dexter, Mother source

DILLIARD, Richard CM May 12, 1878, Northampton, Bilious Fever, 9, Unkn. & Susan Dilliard, Birth Unkn., Laborer, Susan Dilliard, Mother source

DIX, ------- CF Feb. 6, 1872, Northampton, Infantile, 1 day, Asa & Emily, Northampton, Single, Fred Waddy, where died source

DIX, Asa Sr. CM Sept. 2, 1895, Northampton, Diabetes, 54, Parents Unkn., Northampton, Farmer, Married, Asa Dix Jr., Son source

DIX, Carrie WF Nov. 26, 1892, Northampton, Measles, 1, John H. & Mary, Northampton, Single, Arthur Dix, Uncle source

DIX, John H. WM June 4, 1892, Northampton, Typhoid, 27, John & Martha S., Northampton, Farmer, Married, Arthur Dix, Brother source

DIX, Martha S. WF Aug. 19, 1892, Northampton, Typhoid, 60, Parents Unkn., Northampton, Married, Arthur Dix, Son source

DIX, Mary WF Nov. 16, 1893, Northampton, Dysentery, 59, Parents Unkn., Northampton, Married, Wm. T. Dix Jr., Son source

DIX, Peggy WF Aug. 27, 1873, Northampton, Bilious Fever, 8 yrs. 3 mos., Wm. & Martha, Northampton, Single, Wm. Dix, Father source

DIX, Wm. T. Sr. WM Mar. 19, 1893, Northampton, Heart Disease, 62, Parents Unkn., Northampton, Farmer, Married, Wm. T. Dix Jr., Son source

DIXON, ------- CF Mar. 20, 1893, Northampton, Eczema, 10, Wm. & Bell, Northampton, Single, Lavenia Trower, Friend source

DIXON, ------- WF June 14, 1887, Northampton, Dysentery, 13 days, Thomas & Mary, [Farmer?], Northampton, Single, Thomas Dixon, Father source

DIXON, Bell CF Mar. 25, 1893, Northampton, Burned, 40, Jacob & Lavenia, Northampton, Laborer, Married, Smith Spady, Brother source

DIXON, Infant CF Oct. 28, 1871, Northampton, Crying Fits, 3 days, Madora, Northampton, Single, Madora Dixon, Mother source

DIXON, James CM May 9, 1877, Northampton, Cause Unkn., 3, James & Lucy, Northampton, Single, Mary Dixon, Mother source

DIXON, John C. CM Aug. 10, 1876, Northampton, Bilious Fever, 9 months, Henry & Ginny, Northampton, Single, Henry Dixon, Father source

DIXON, Lillie CF Mar. 10, 1893, Northampton, Burned, 5, Wm. & Bell, Northampton, Single, Lavenia Trower, Friend source

DIXON, Mary CF May 12, 1877, Northampton, Typhoid Fever, 22, Unkn. & Mary, Northampton, Laborer, Single, John Read, Friend source

DIXON, Mary Susan CF Mar. 25, 1884, Northampton, Cause Unkn., 1 yr. 6 mos., Wm. & Belle, Northampton, Single, Wm. Dixon, Father source

DIXON, Samuel CM Aug. 16, 1871, Northampton, Worms, 1 Yr. 9 months, Samuel & Ginnie, Northampton, Single, Samuel Dixon, Father source [Laborer?]

DIXON, Wesley CM Aug. 10, 1872, Northampton, Biuret, 3, Ginnie & Henry, Northampton, Single, Henry Dixon, Father source [Laborer?]

DOUGHTY, ------- WF Feb. 21, 1891, Northampton, Cause Unkn., 5 days, E. J. & W. Doughty, Northampton, Single, E. J. Doughty, Father source

DOUGHTY, ------- WF Oct. 12, 1878, Northampton, Cause Unkn., 2 days, Geo. L. & Peggie, Birth Unkn., Single, Geo. L. Doughty, Father source

DOUGHTY, ------- WM Nov. 1892, Northampton, Cause Unkn., 4 months, Ben U. & Jane, Northampton, Single, B. U. Doughty, Father source

DOUGHTY, ------- WM Oct. 19, 1891, Northampton, Cause Unkn., 9 days, Wm. & Amanda, Northampton, Single, Wm. Doughty, Father source

DOUGHTY, Albert L. WM 1888, Baltimore, Md., Cause Unkn., 16, S. A. Doughty, [Farmer?], Northampton, Farmer, S. A. Doughty, Head of Family source

DOUGHTY, Alonzo WM Sept. 10, 1894, Northampton, Typhoid Fever, 18, Geo. W. & Annie, Northampton, Waterman, Single, Eli Doughty, Friend source

DOUGHTY, Annie CF Mar. 13, 1887, Northampton, Bilious Fever, 3, Peter & Mary, [Laborer?], Northampton, Single, Peter Doughty, Father source

DOUGHTY, Archibald WM Apr. 1880, Northampton, Cancer on Leg, 61, Parents Unkn., Va., Va., Va., Fisherman, Married, source unkn.

DOUGHTY, Arthur WM Dec. 23, 1875, Northampton, Whooping Cough, 4 months, Ben & Jane, Birth Unkn., Single, Ben Doughty, Father source

DOUGHTY, Betsey WF Apr. 18, 1893, Northampton, Old Age 101, Parents Unkn., Birth Unkn., Married, G. W. Carpenter, Grandson source

DOUGHTY, Chas. B. WM Aug. 16, 1894, Northampton, Peritonitis, 25, B. U. & Jane, Northampton, Mechanic, Married, B. U. Doughty, Father source

DOUGHTY, E. B. WM Aug. 12, 1895, Northampton, Suicide by shooting, 66, Parents Unkn., Northampton, Overseer of Poor, T. P. Bell, Brother-in-Law source

DOUGHTY, Edith CF June 2, 1891, Northampton, Consumption, 60, Parents Unkn., Accomac, Laborer, Single, J. A. Eichelberger, Employer source

DOUGHTY, Geo. T. WM 1888, Northampton, Consumption, 23, Geo. T. Doughty, Northampton, Laborer, Geo. T. Doughty, Head of Family source

DOUGHTY, Harriett WF Sept. 17, 1883, Northampton, Hog Island, Consumption, 72, Jno. & Eliz. Cottrell, Birth Unkn., Wm. J. Doughty, Husband source

DOUGHTY, James S. WM July 12, 1892, Northampton, Cholera Infantum, 7 months, John H. & Mary, Northampton, Single, John H. Doughty, Father source

DOUGHTY, John L. WM Sept. 2, 1894, Northampton, Typhoid Fever, 24, Eli & Lizzie, Northampton, Mail Carrier, Married, Eli Doughty, Father source

DOUGHTY, John W. WM Mar. 16, 1893, Northampton, Cancer, 58, John & Mollie, Acco. Co., Mechanic, Single, J. C. Doughty, Son source

DOUGHTY, Lloyd CM 1888, Northampton, Cause Unkn., 6 months, Peter Doughty, [Laborer?], Northampton, Single, Peter Doughty, Head of Family source

DOUGHTY, Martin WM June 1, 1893, Northampton, Cause Unkn., 72, Eli & Jane, Northampton, Waterman, Married, Eli Doughty, Son source

DOUGHTY, Mary WF July 12, 1893, Northampton, Cause Unkn., 40, Tully & Mary Snead, Acco. Co., Married, J. H. Doughty, Husband source

DOUGHTY, Mary WF Mar. 1880, Northampton, Epilepsy, 30, Parents Unkn., Va., Va., Va., At Home, Single, source unkn.

DOUGHTY, Mary WF Nov. 28, 1894, Northampton, Cause Unkn., 18 months, Sorin & Mary, Northampton, Single, Sorin Doughty, Father source

DOUGHTY, Mary A. WF Dec. 24, 1893, Northampton, Consumption, 60, Archie & Mary Kelly, Northampton, John H. Robins, Neighbor source

DOUGHTY, Mary E. WF May 14, 1872, Northampton, Pneumonia, 25, Wm. C. Ames, Accomac, Jno. W. Doughty, Husband source

DOUGHTY, Peggie WF Oct. 10, 1878, Northampton, Child Birth, 30, Albert & Lellia Ward, Northampton, Millinery, Geo. L. Doughty, Husband source

DOUGHTY, Sarah CF Mar. 15, 1896, Northampton, Burn, 2, Peter & Sallie, Northampton, Single, Peter Doughty, Father source

DOUGHTY, Sheppard WM June 6, 1891, Northampton, Old Age, 76, Eli & Nancy D., Northampton, Waterman, Married, Jno. W. Doughty, Friend source

DOUGHTY, Susan WF Jan. 1871, Northampton, Paralysis, 60, Parents Unkn., Northampton, Married, Husband James, Geo. H. Thomas, Friend source

DOUGLASS, ------- CF Dec. 20, 1877, Northampton, Infantile, 7 days, Unkn. & Sallie, Northampton, Single, Sallie Douglass, Mother source

DOUGLASS, Frederick CM Dec. 28, 1887, Northampton, Heart Disease, 12, James & Kate, Northampton, Laborer, Single, James Douglas, Father source

DOUGLASS, Lummie CF July 15, 1893, Northampton, Cause Unkn., 2 months, James & Madora, Northampton, Single, Sarah Douglass, Mother source

DOUGLASS, Madora CF Sept. 4, 1878, Northampton, Crying Fits, 8 days, James & Madora, Birth Unkn., Single, James Douglass, Father source

DOWNES, ------- CF July 6, 1894, Northampton, Typhoid Fever, 7 months, Guy & Jane, Northampton, Single, Guy Downes, Father source

DOWNES, Thomas A. WM Mar. 6. 1896, Northampton, Heart Disease, 75, Thos. & Mary, Northampton, Oyster Inspector, Widower, J. B. Wise, Son-in-law source

DOWNES, Thos. H. WM Mar. 15, 1895, Northampton, Congestive chill, 54, Nathaniel & Diana, Farmer, Married, John R. Read, Friend source

DOWNING, ------- CF Dec. 1875, Northampton, Cause Unkn., 7 days, Henry & Margt., Birth Unkn., Single, Margt. Downing, Mother source

DOWNING, ------- CM Dec. 1873, Northampton, Infantile, 5 days, Jos. & Lizzie, Northampton, Single, James Jacob, Father-in-Law source

DOWNING, ------- CM Feb. 1872, Northampton, Infantile, Age Unkn., Zor. & Lizzie, Birth Unkn., Single, source unkn.

DOWNING, Hubert WM Sept. 1872, Northampton, Diphtheria, 3, S. B. & Milla, Northampton, Single, Physician, source unkn.

DOWNING, John H. WM Jan. 5, 1893, Northampton, Broken Neck, 2, John C. & Martha, Northampton, Single, John C. Downing, Father source

DOWNING, Joseph CM Oct. 10, 1896, Northampton, Pneumonia, 61, Joseph & Lucy, Northampton, Laborer, Single, Lucy Wise, Friend source

DOWNING, Lina BF May 1880, Northampton, Malarial Fever, 9, William & Maria, Va., Va., Va., Single, S. P. Nottingham, source

DOWNING, Luen CM Jan. 13, 1884, Northampton, Pneumonia, 90, Parents Unkn., Northampton, Dr. A. W. Downing, Physician source

DOWNING, Maria BF Apr. 1880, Northampton, Typhoid Fever, 11, Parents Unkn., Va., Nurse, Single, Jas. M. McNutt source (PR)

DOWNING, Maria WF Sept. 1872, Northampton, Diphtheria, 11, S. B. & Milla, Northampton, Single, Physician, source unkn.

DOWNING, Martha S. WF Apr. 27, 1892, Northampton, Measles, 28, John & Susan Mears, Northampton, Married, John C. Downing, Husband source

DOWNING, S. B. WM Mar. 8, 1893, Northampton, Cause Unkn., 68, Edmond & Mary, Northampton, Physician, Married, E. W. Downing, Son source

DOWNING, Sissie WF Sept. 1872, Northampton, Diphtheria, 8, S. B. & Milla, Northampton, Single, Physician, source unkn.

DOWNS, Allice CF May 11, 1874, Northampton, Consumption, 29, Spencer & Virginia Blew, Northampton, Single, Benjamin Trower, Friend source

DOWNS, Ed. P. WM Nov. 21, 1874, Northampton, Bright's Disease of K., 28 yrs. 3 mos., Nath. G. & Anna, Northampton, Farmer, Single, Albert Downs, Brother source

DOWNS, Nellie CF Jan. 8, 1882, Northampton, Child Birth, 30, Sarah Griffin, Northampton, House Keeper, Married, Sister source

Northampton County, VA, Deaths from Death Register and Wills, 1871-1896

DRENNAN, William WM Sept. 4, 1894, Erysipelas, 2 months, Wm. & Sarah, Northampton, Single, William Drennan, Father source

DRIER, Geo. WM June 16, 1893, Northampton, Hanged for Murder, 26, Parents Unkn., Germany, Laborer, Single, S. A. Jarvis, Sheriff source

DRUMMOND, Ada WF Apr. 30, 1895, Northampton, Cause Unkn., 5, G. W. & Mary, Acco. Co., Single, G. W. Drummond, Father source

DRUMMOND, Robert A. WM June 13, 1887, Northampton, Remittent Fever, 45, Parents Unkn., Northampton, Laborer, Married, H. C. Miles, Friend source

DUNNE, H. W. WM Sept. 1894, Northampton, Typhoid Fever, 38, H. W. & Sarah, Phil., Pa., Supt. N. Y. P. & N. R. R., Married, P. W. Savage, Friend source

DUNTON, ------- CM Sept. 9, 1878, Northampton, Cause Unkn., 3 days, Peter & Lucy, Birth Unkn., Single, Peter Dunton, Father source

DUNTON, ------- WF Nov. 6, 1892, Northampton, Pneumonia, 2 months, John R. & Sarah, Northampton, Single, John R. Dunton, Father source

DUNTON, Adaline WF May 18, 1878, Northampton, Pneumonia, 44, James & Vianna Sturgis, Northampton, K. Dunton Wife, John Dunton, Brother-in-Law source

DUNTON, Adeline WF May 1880, Northampton, Pneumonia, Inflammation of Uterus, 40, Parents Unkn., Va., Va., Va., Keeping House, Married, Stratton B. Downing, source

DUNTON, Dana A. WM June 22, 1885, Northampton, Consumption, 60, Jas. & Unkn., Northampton, Farmer, Jacob B. Dunton, Senr. Source

DUNTON, Devericks WM July 1872, Northampton, Worms, 3, Wm. T. & Em, Northampton, Single, source unkn.

DUNTON, Ellison CM Jan. 12, 1876, Northampton, Cause Unkn., 35, Peter & Mary, Northampton, Single, Peter Dunton, Father source

DUNTON, Geo. U. WM Sept. 1, 1871, Northampton, Heart Disease, 63, Isaac & Hanna L., Accomac, Farmer, Married, Arinthia Wife, Lloyd A. Mapp, Son-in-Law source

DUNTON, Henry R. WM May 1875, Northampton, Consumption, 27, Parents Unkn., Birth Unkn., Physician source

DUNTON, James CM Apr. 5, 1887, Northampton, Heart Disease, 37, Parents Unkn., Northampton, Laborer, Married, W. A. Downing, Physician source

DUNTON, Jos. L. WM Mar. 1883, Northampton, Inflammation, 16, Jos. B. & Ellen S., Birth Unkn., Jos. B. F. Dunton, Father source

DUNTON, Juliet CF Sept. 7, 1893, Northampton, Old Age, 82, Parents Unkn., Northampton, Married, Geo. White, Friend source

DUNTON, Littleton WM July 9, 1887, Northampton, Bright's Disease, 33, Custis & Annie, Northampton, Clerk, James A. Smith, Friend source

DUNTON, Mrs. Mary WF Apr. 20, 1884, Northampton, Cancer, 60, Parents Unkn., Northampton, Jno. T. Rogers, source

DUNTON, Peter CM Jan. 22, 1893, Northampton, Erysipelas, 74, Peter & Patsy, Northampton, Laborer, Married, Em Dunton, Wife source

DUNTON, Peter CM Sept. 4, 1893, Northampton, Cause Unkn. 5 months, Mike & Mary, Northampton, Single, Mike Dunton, Father source

DUNTON, Susan A. WF Apr. 28, 1891, Northampton, Injuries from a Fall, 70, W. J. & Elizabeth Fitchett, Northampton, Married, S. F. Dunton, Son source

DUNTON, Thomas R. WM Sept. 1896, Northampton, Heart Disease, 56, Parents Unkn., Northampton, Farmer, Married, Sarah Dunton, Wife source

DUNTON, Thos. R. WM Dec. 1872, Northampton, Pneumonia, 37, Jno. R. & Emeline, Northampton, Farmer, Caroline Dunton, source

EAST, ------- WF June 10, 1894, Northampton, Cholera Infantum, 3 months, Edward R. & Mary, Northampton, Single, J. E. Prior, Uncle source

EAST, ------- WM Sept. 19, 1878, Northampton, Cause Unkn., 2 months, Edward T. & Kitty, Birth Unkn., Single, Edward East, Father source

EAST, Edward WM Sept. 15, 1896, Northampton, Dropsy, 50, Parents Unkn, Northampton, Waterman, Married, Maggie East, Wife source

EAST, Mollie WF Sept. 4, 1891, Northampton, Scarlet Fever, 28, Jno. & Mary Gordon, Richmond, Va., Married, Ed East, Husband source

EASTER, Mary CF Dec. 9, 1882, Northampton, Cause Unkn., 1 yr. 2 mos., Mary Scott, Northampton, Single, Mary Scott, Mother source

EASTON, ------- CF Dec. 10, 1876, Northampton, Crying Fits, 7 days, Pat & Lorana, Accomack, Single, Lorana Easton, Mother source

EATES, Fritz WM June 3, 1887, Northampton, Congestive Chill, 4, Fritz & Catherine, Germany, Single, A. W. Wise, Neighbor source

EICHELBURGER, Mary WF 1888, Northampton, Typhoid Fever, 6, Jno. A. Eichelburger, [Farmer?], Northampton, Single, Jno. A, Eichelburger, Head of Family source

ELLIOTT, ------- WM Aug. 7, 1895, Northampton, Cause Unkn., 3 days, H. W. & Ellen, Northampton, Single, H. W. Elliott, Father source

ELLIOTT, John W. WM June 10, 1896, Northampton, Pneumonia, 69, Parents Unkn., Northampton, Mechanic, Single, W. D. Elliott, Nephew source

ELLIOTT, Rosa WF Apr. 19, 1895, Northampton, Paralysis, 72, Jerry & Rachel, Maryland, Single, S. S. Parsons, Son-in-Law source

ELLIOTT, Thomas WM Oct. 6, 1872, Northampton, Consumption, 60, Sallie & Thos. Elliott, Northampton, Laborer, Married, Physician source

ELSNER, Robert WM Jan. 1, 1896, Northampton, Bright's Disease, 14, Martin & Lizzie, Germany, Single, Martin Elsner, Father source

ENNIS, J. J. WM Mar. 26, 1896, Northampton, Paralysis, 74, E. E. & Mary, Worcester Co., Md., Farmer, Married, Joseph Ennis, Son source

ENNIS, John W. WM Apr. 3, 1896, Northampton, Cause Unkn., 8 days, Joseph & Mary, Northampton, Single, Joseph Ennis, Father source

EPHRAIM, ------- CM June 10, 1892, Northampton, Cause Unkn., 8 days, Jacob & Sarah, Northampton, Single, Jacob Ephraim, Father source

EPHRAIM, James CM Oct. 14, 1877, Northampton, Cause Unkn., 5 months, James & Susan, Northampton, Single, James Ephraim, Father source

EPHRAIM, John CM Dec. 9,1877, Northampton, Inflammation, 9 mos. 3 days, Jacob & Emily, Northampton, Single, Jacob Ephraim, Father source

ESHOM, Katie B. WF Mar. 1880, Northampton, Softness of the Brain, 51, Parents Unkn., Va., Va., Va., Keeping House, Widow, Dr. P. A. Fitz Hugh, Physician source

EVANS, Ben CM Aug. 20, 1896, Northampton, Old Age, 86, Died at Alms House, Northampton, Laborer, Single, Wm. G. Bell, Overseer of Poor source

EVANS, Isaac CM May 5, 1876, Northampton, Debility, 40, Parents Unkn., Accomack, Laborer, Married, George Bell, Neighbor source

EVANS, Lambert WM Aug. 10, 1878, Northampton, Drowned, 45, Parents Unkn., New York, Sea Capt., John M. Stewart, Friend source

EXALL, George CM Aug. 22, 1878, Northampton, Inflammation, 13 yrs. 4 mos., Geo. Exall & Sallie Bell, Northampton, Laborer, Geo. Exall, Father source

FATHERLY, ------- CM Nov. 12, 1883, Northampton, Cause Unkn. , 2 days, Levin & Comfort Floyd, Birth Unkn., Levin Floyd, source

FATHERLY, Ellen CF July 1875, Northampton, Consumption, 17, Parents Unkn., Birth Unkn., Neighbor source

FATHERLY, Henry F. WM Jan. 10, 1896, Northampton, Suicide, 35, Wm. J. & Patsy F., Northampton, Farmer, Single, Geo. J. Fatherly, Brother source

FATHERLY, Major CM 1888, Northampton, Pneumonia & Complications, 17, Nathaniel Fitchett, Northampton, Farmer, Married, Nathaniel Fitchett, Parent source

FATHERLY, Wm. J. WM Mar. 10, 1883, Northampton, Bright's Disease, 65, Parents Unkn., Northampton, Farmer, Patsy Fatherly, Wife source

FENDERSON, Rosie CF 1888, Northampton, Stomach Pain, 46, M. F. Fenderson, [Farmer?], Northampton, Jas. F. Fenderson, Husband source

FENDERSON, Thos. CM July 17, 1893, Northampton, Dysentery, 1, James & Adelaide, Northampton, Single, Adelaide Fenderson, Mother source

FERBY, Milton CM Aug. 4, 1893, Northampton, Consumption, 7 months, Ed & Mary, Northampton, Single, Mary Ferby, Mother source

FEREBY, Newman CM Sept. 7, 1883, Northampton, Big Head, 2, Americas & Maria, Birth Unkn., Americas Ferby, Father source

FINNEY, Chas. CM Dec. 20, 1893, Northampton, Heart Disease, 74, Isaac & Henny, Acco. Co., Laborer, Married, Geo. E. Finney, Son source

FINNEY, Edna F. CF 1888, Northampton, Pneumonia, 2 months, Geo. & Nora, [Merchant?], Northampton, Single, Benj. Bowen, Head of Family source

FISHER, ------- CF Dec. 1872, Northampton, Infantile, 1, Nena Fisher, Birth Unkn. Single, source unkn.

FISHER, ------- CM Dec. 1875, Northampton, Cause Unkn., 15 days, Wallace & Amy, Birth Unkn., Single, Amy Fisher, Mother source

Northampton County, VA, Deaths from Death Register and Wills, 1871-1896

FISHER, ------- CM May 1872, Northampton, Infantile, 1 month, Geo. & Esther, Northampton, Single, Gennie Stephens, Friend source

FISHER, ------- CM 1872, Northampton, Infantile, 15 days, Sam & Leah, Birth Unkn., Single, Gennie Stephens, Friend source

FISHER, Charles BM Oct. 1879, Northampton, Acute Dysentery, 20, Parents Unkn., Va. Va., Va., Single, P. F. Scott, source

FISHER, Elizabeth WF Dec. 14, 1887, Northampton, Drowned, 14, George Fisher, Northampton, Laborer, Single, George Fisher, Father source

FISHER, Ellyson D. WM Oct. 1873, Northampton, Diphtheria, 23, Saml. P & Mary, Northampton, Merchant, Single, source unkn.

FISHER, Florence CF Dec. 13, 1896, Northampton, Croup, 10, Joseph & Eliza, Northampton, Single, Joseph Fisher, Father source

FISHER, Geo. CM Jan. 9, 1892, Northampton, Consumption, 42, Parents Unkn., Northampton, Laborer, Single, James Fisher, Brother source

FISHER, Harriet CF Oct. 17, 1896, Northampton, Suicide, 73, Abe & Selma, Northampton, Single, Alfred Bell, Brother source

FISHER, Hennie CF Apr. 7, 1894, Northampton, Heart Disease, 40, Lucinda Harmon, Northampton, Married, Wallace Fisher, Husband source

FISHER, Henrietta CF Feb. 27, 1895, Northampton, Heart Disease, 40, Lucinda Harmon, Northampton, Married, Walker Fisher, Husband source

FISHER, James A. WM Apr. 26, 1894, Northampton, Dyspepsia, 61, John & Sallie, Northampton, Farmer, Married, John A. Fisher, Son source

FISHER, Jane CF May 16, 1894, Northampton, Heart Disease, 55, Agnes Thomas, Northampton, Married, Charlotte Gunter, Friend source

FISHER, Julius CM June 15, 1893, Northampton, Cholera Infantum, 9 months, Joseph & Eliza, Northampton, Single, Joseph Fisher, Father source

FISHER, Mary Race Unkn. F Sept. 1873, Northampton, Measles, 45, Parents Unkn., Northampton, Saml. P. Fisher, Husband, source unkn.

FISHER, Thomas H. BM May 1880, Northampton, Consumption, 18, Thomas & Maria, Va., Va., Va., Laborer, Single, Dr. William W. Wilkins, Physician source

FISHER, W. Miers WM June 18, 1873, Northampton, Softening of the Brain, 67, George & Susan, Northampton, Lawyer, Single, U. N. Fisher, Son source

FISHER, Wilmer W. WM July 9, 1887, Accomac Co. Va., Typhoid Fever, 41, George & Mary, Accomac Co., Va., Farmer, Married, William James, Neighbor source

FITCHETT, ------- CF Apr. 10, 1876, Northampton, Crying Fits, 6 days, Patrick & Prisey, Northampton, Single, Patrick Fitchett, Father source

FITCHETT, ------- CF Feb. 27, 1884, Northampton, Crying Fits, 6 days, Spencer & Dora, Northampton, Single, Spencer Fitchett, Father source

FITCHETT, ------- CF Feb. 8, 1876, Northampton, Cause Unkn., 2 mos. 15 days, Parents Unkn., Northampton, Single, Source unkn.

FITCHETT, ------- CF May 1875, Northampton, Cause Unkn., 1 month, Dan'l & Melvina, Birth Unkn.,Single, Neighbor source

FITCHETT, ------- CM Jan. 26, 1876, Northampton, Cause Unkn., 1 yr. 8 mos., Cordelia Fitchett, Birth Unkn., Single, Ann Roberts, Neighbor source

FITCHETT, ------- CM June 19, 1893, Northampton, Cause Unkn., 6 days, Geo. & Laura, Northampton, Single, Geo. Fitchett, Father source

FITCHETT, ------- WF June 12, 1892, Northampton, Cause Unkn., 10 days, B. T. & Margaret, Northampton, Single, B. T. Fitchett, Father source

FITCHETT, ------- WM 1888, Northampton, Cause Unkn., 3 days, B. T. & Maria, [Laborer?], Northampton, Single, B. T. Fitchett, Parent source

FITCHETT, ------- WM June 1875, Northampton, Cause Unkn., 3 days, Geo. & Rachel, Birth Unkn., Single, Neighbor source

FITCHETT, Bennet CM Jan. 10, 1874, Northampton, Cause Unkn., 60, Geo. & Betsey, Northampton, Mariah wife, Fred E. Nottingham, Friend source

FITCHETT, Charles WM Sept. 1875, Northampton, Dysentery, 2, Leon'd T. & Maggie, Birth Unkn., Single, Leon'd T. Fitchett, Father source

FITCHETT, Edith WF June 27, 1892, Northampton, Typhoid, 18, Horace & Mary W. Heath, Northampton, Married, Parker Fitchett, Husband source

FITCHETT, Emiline WF Sept. 11, 1894, Northampton, Typhoid Fever, 42, B. T. & Mary Nottingham, Northampton, Married, J. H. Roberts, Friend source

FITCHETT, Emily L. CF Sept. 27, 1896, Northampton, Consumption, 13, Mary Fitchett, Northampton, Single, Lloyd Trehurne, Friend source

FITCHETT, Francis CF Jan. 9, 1877, Northampton, Congestive, 14 yrs. 1 mo., Lewis & Margaret, Northampton, Laborer, Single, Lewis Fitchett, Father source

FITCHETT, Fred WM Sept. 14, 1891, Northampton, Consumption, 24, Jacob & Elizabeth, Northampton, Farmer, Single, Parker Fitchett, Brother source

FITCHETT, Georgie S. WF Feb. 10, 1871, Northampton, Croup, 3 yrs. 8 mos., Wm. J. & Georgie, Northampton, Single, Wm. J. Fitchett, Father source

FITCHETT, Henry I. WM Apr. 18, 1891, Northampton, Bladder Disease, 30, Jacob & Elizabeth, Northampton, Farmer, Single, Parker Fitchett, Brother source

FITCHETT, Ibbie CF Jan. 15, 1896, Northampton, Chol. Infantum, 1 month 10 days, Isaac & Lelia, Northampton, Single, Isaac Fitchett, Father source

FITCHETT, Infant CF Sept. 15, 1872, Northampton, Crying Fits, 4 days, Mariah & Leon, Northampton, Leon Fitchett, Father source [Laborer?]

FITCHETT, Isaac CM Mar. 5, 1894, Northampton, Paralysis, 84, Parents Unkn., Laborer, Married, John Wilson, Friend source

FITCHETT, Isaac CM Oct. 15, 1893, Northampton, Cause Unkn., 60, Lew & Caroline, Northampton, Married, W. L. Hanby, Neighbor source

FITCHETT, Jane WF Dec. 25, 1887, Northampton, Cancer, 52, George Fitchett, Northampton, Laborer, Sam'l Fitchett, Husband source

FITCHETT, John Senr. CM July 5, 1876, Northampton, Drowned, 49, Sam & Lucinda, Northampton, Laborer, Married, Lucinda Fitchett, Widow source

FITCHETT, Joseph CM Apr. 7, 1876, Northampton, Diarrhea, 7, Abram & Susan, Northampton, Single, Susan Fitchett, Mother source

FITCHETT, Julia CF Oct. 30, 1876, Northampton, Summer Disease, 4 mos. 10 days, Alfred & Julia, Northampton, Single, Julia Fitchett, Mother source

FITCHETT, Kessie CF Nov. 16, 1883, Northampton, Old Age, 70, Nelson & Hannah, Birth Unkn., Abram Smith, source

FITCHETT, L. A. WM July 3, 1895, Northampton, Cholera E., 3 months, W. T. & Maggie, Northampton, Single, W. T. Fitchett, Father source

FITCHETT, Maggie WF Apr. 7, 1876, Northampton, Heart Disease, Age Unkn., Robins & Peggy Mapp, Northampton, Wm. P. Fitchett, Husband source

FITCHETT, Margariet S. WF Feb. 11, 1873, Northampton, Cancer of Womb, 47 yrs., 9 mos., 10 days, Perry & Sally Leatherbury, Acco. Co., Housekeeping, Dennard Fitchett, Husband source

FITCHETT, Maria CF Sept. 8, 1872, Northampton, Child Birth, 28, Parents Unkn., Northampton, Married, Husband source

FITCHETT, Mary CF 1888, Northampton, Cause Unkn., 14 days, Frank & Mary, [Farmer?], Northampton, Frank Fitchett, Parent source

FITCHETT, Mary CF May 15, 1895, Northampton, Cause Unkn., 55, Levin & Sallie Fox, Northampton, S. W. Nottingham, Neighbor source

FITCHETT, Mary CF Sept. 2, 1896, Northampton, Consumption, 50, Esther White, Northampton, Married, Lloyd Trehurne, Son-in-Law source

FITCHETT, Priscilla CF June 24, 1892, Northampton, Pneumonia, 46, Hary & Mary Burruss, Northampton, Married, Patrick Fitchett, Husband source

FITCHETT, Robert CM Dec. 24, 1896, Northampton, Pneumonia, 30, John & Lucinda, Northampton, Farmer, Married, Alfred Riley, Friend source

FITCHETT, Susan CF 1888, Northampton, Dysentery, 2 yrs. 2 mos., Isaac Fitchett, [Farmer?], Northampton, Single, Isaac Fitchett, Head of Family source

FITCHETT, Thos. J. WM Sept. 10, 1894, Northampton, Dropsy, 59, Nathaniel & Sallie, Northampton, Farmer, Married, N. P. Fitchett, Son source

FITCHETT, Violett CF June 15, 1871, Northampton, Consumption, 80, Parents Unkn., Northampton, Physician source

FITCHETT, W. P. WM June 12, 1892, Northampton, Pneumonia, 52, W. P. & Elizabeth, Northampton, Married, W. P. J. Fitchett, Son source

FITCHETT, Walter T. WM Aug. 22, 1885, Northampton, Cholera Infantum, 2 mos. 5 days, B. T. & Mammie, Northampton, Single, B. T. Fitchett, Father source

FITCHETT, Wilson CM June 6, 1872, Northampton, Consumption, 22, Minnie Fitchett, Northampton, Laborer, Single, Jno. Becket, Friend where died source

Northampton County, VA, Deaths from Death Register and Wills, 1871-1896

FLETCHER, James WM Jan. 27, 1872, Northampton, Pneumonia, 22, Thos. & Sally, Northampton, Sailor, Single, Jas. S. Carpenter, Friend Neighbor source

FLOYD, ------- CM Jan. 10, 1876, Northampton, Cause Unkn., 3 months, John & Lydia, Northampton, Single, John Floyd, Father source

FLOYD, Edmund CM Sept. 11, 1878, Northampton, Whooping Cough, 3, Levin & Philus, Northampton, Single, Levin Floyd, Father source

FLOYD, Emily CF May 5, 1896, Northampton, Cancer, 47, Wm. & Violette Wicks, Northampton, Married, Thomas Floyd, Husband source

FLOYD, G. Fred Jr. WM July 13, 1895, Northampton, Dysentery, 2, G. Fred & Mary, Northampton, Single, G. Fred Floyd, Dr. Father source

FLOYD, Henrietta CF Mar. 2, 1876, Northampton, Old Age, 70, Parents Unkn., Northampton, Laborer, Single, John Williams, Supt. Of Poor source

FLOYD, James B. WM Jan. 23, 1893, Northampton, Pneumonia, 63, Geo. & Susan, Acco. Co., Shoemaker, Married , John E. Floyd, Son source

FLOYD, Jane CF July 5, 1876, Northampton, Dropsy, 68, Parents Unkn., Northampton, Laborer, Single, John Williams, Supt. Of Poor source

FLOYD, John WM Sept. 10, 1872, Northampton, Congestive Chill, 4, Jno. & Fluvanna, Northampton, Single, Jno. Floyd, Father source

FLOYD, John M. WM Apr. 3, 1882, Northampton, Consumption, Age Unkn., Martha & Nancy Floyd, Northampton, Farmer, Married, Son source

FLOYD, John W. WM Apr. 1880, Northampton, Consumption, 57, Parents Unkn., Va., Va., Va., Carpenter, Widower, F. P. Wife, Dr. William J. Scott, Physician source

FLOYD, Maria BF May 1880, Northampton, Cause Unkn., 7 days, Thomas & Emily, Va., Va., Va., Single, Source unkn.

FLOYD, Mary WF July 7, 1895, Northampton, Dysentery, 30, E. B. & A. E. Swanger, Acco. Co., Married, G. Fred Floyd, Dr. Husband source

FLOYD, Mary F. WF 1888, Northampton, Liver Disease, 25, Wm. E. Floyd, [Farmer?], Northampton, Wm. E. Floyd, Parent source

FLOYD, Rachiel WF Feb. 18, 1878, Northampton, Measles, 9, John & Mary, Northampton, Single, John Floyd, Father source

FLOYD, Russell WM July 16, 1894, Northampton, Inflamation of bowels, 4 months, R. E. & Lucille, Northampton, Single, R. E. Floyd, Father source

FLOYD, Ruth CF June 20, 1885, Northampton, Cause Unkn., 1 mo. 10 days, Jim & Emily, Northampton, Single, Jim Floyd, Father source

FOREMAN, ------- CM Nov. 17, 1891, Northampton, Fits, 7 days, Lemuel & Laura, Northampton, Single, Lemuel Foreman, Father source

FORTUNE, ------- CF July 10, 1878, Northampton, Infantile, 8 days, Lewis & Peggie, Northampton, Single, Lewis Fortune, Father source

FOWLER, Polly F. WF Nov. 3, 1896, Northampton, Pneumonia, 68, Edward & Margaret Turner, Northampton, Widow, John E. Fowler, Son source

FOX, James CM Dec. 2, 1871, Northampton, Worms, 2, William & Betsy, Northampton, Single, William Fox, Father source [Laborer?]

FRANCES, Sabra CF 1871, Northampton, Diphtheria, 3, Abel & Bridget, Northampton, Single, Gennie Stephens, Friend source

FRANCIS, Demorey L. CF Apr. 6, 1892, Northampton, Burned to Death, 6, Horace T. & Maggie S., Northampton, Single, Horace T. Francis, Father source

FRANCIS, H. T. CM July 9, 1896, Northampton, Consumption, 34, Horace & Hennie, Northampton, Farmer, Married, Horace Francis, Father source

FRANCIS, Jacob CM Apr. 10, 1894, Northampton, Dysentery, 4 months, Thos. & Mary, Northampton, Single, Thos. Francis, Father source

FRANCIS, Jeremiah BM June 1879, Northampton, Dentition, 2, Thomas & Mary, Va., Va., Va., Single, source unkn.

FRANCIS, Jerry CM June 10, 1878, Northampton, Congestive, 2, Thomas & Mary Francis, Northampton, Single, Thomas Francis, Father source

FRANCIS, Mary H. CF Jan. 29, 1896, Northampton, Pneumonia, 11 months, George L. & Georgianna, Northampton, Single, Geo. L. Francis, Father source

FRANCIS, William CM Oct. 9, 1878, Northampton, Infantile, 10 days, Horace & Emily, Northampton, Single, Horace Francis, Father source

FROST, Frank WM Dec. 25, 1894, Northampton, Gen. Debility, 76, Parents Unkn., Northampton, Shoe Maker, Married, John Frost, Son source

FRY, Joseph BM July 1879, Northampton, Lock Jaw, 21, James H. & Winney K., Va., Va., Va., Farm Laborer, Single, Wm. A. Thom, source

FRY, Joseph BM June 1879, Northampton, Traumatic Tetanus, 24, Parents Unkn., Va., Laborer, Single, Dr. W. W. Wilkins, Physician source (PR)

GARRETT, Lucian WM Aug. 1874, Eastville Township, Cholera Infantum, 1, Wm. & Mary A., Eastville Township, Single, Wm. T. Garrett, Father source

GARRISON, Laura BF Nov. 1879, Northampton, Inflammation of Brain, 21, Parents Unkn., Va., Va., Va., Laborer, Married, source unkn.

GARRISON, Mary CF Aug. 13, 1894, Northampton, Brain Fever, 58, Parents Unkn., Northampton, Married, J. F. Garrison, Son source

GASKINS, Mary WF Jan. 14, 1893, Northampton, Typhoid & Via. Pneumonia, 21, G. S. & Lettitia, Acco. Co., Single, G. S. Gaskins, Father source

GAYLE, Lucy WF Dec. 14, 1877, Northampton, Old Age, 76 yrs. 3 mos. 21 days, Christopher & Lucy, Northampton, C. C. Gayle, Brother source

GIBB, Ann W. WF Sept. 1891, Northampton, Typhoid Fever, 16, Frank & Julia, Northampton, Single, Frank Gibb, Father source

GIBB, Emma J. WF June 17, 1896, Northampton, Bronchitis, 70, John & Comfort Hosier?, Northampton, Married, Jno. E. Gibb, Son source

GIBBINS, Isaac CM May 18, 1877, Northampton, Consumption, 78, Parents Unkn., Maryland, Farmer, Eliza Wife, Robert Richardson, Friend source

GIDDINGS, ------- CF Apr. 1, 1887, Northampton, Cause Unkn., 4 days, George & Hester, Northampton, Single, George Giddings, Father source

GIDDINGS, ------- CF June 6, 1892, Northampton, Cause Unkn., 1 day, Sam'l & Maggie, Northampton, Single, Geo. Beckett, Grandfather source

GIDDINGS, ------- CF Sept. 10, 1895, Northampton, Cause Unkn., 1 month, Saml. & Maggie, Northampton, Single, Maggie Giddings, Mother source

GIDDINGS, ------- CM Feb. 4, 1887, Northampton, Cause Unkn., 4 months, Aaron & Mary, [Laborer?], Northampton, Single, Aaron Giddings, Father source

GIDDINGS, ------- CM Jan. 16, 1891, Northampton, Cause Unkn., 1 day, James & Sarah, Accomac, Single, James Giddings, Father source

GIDDINGS, Abram CM Nov. 25, 1872, Northampton, Dropsy, 21, Ann Jackson, Northampton, Laborer, Single, Geo. Becket, Brother source

GIDDINGS, Colbert CF Oct. 14, 1878, Northampton, Cause Unkn., 90, Parents Unkn., Northampton, Polly Jacob, Friend source

GIDDINGS, Ella CF Sept. 2, 1895, Northampton, Cholera E., 2, Saml. & Maggie, Northampton, Single, Maggie Giddings, Mother source

GIDDINGS, Joshua BM Feb. 1880, Northampton, Pulmonary Consumption, 31, Parents Unkn., Va., Va., Va., Laborer, Married, William E. Brickhouse, source

GIDDINGS, Millie CF Sept. 10, 1892, Northampton, Diphtheria, 3, Ellison & Maria, Northampton, Single, Ellison Giddings, Father source

GIDDINGS, Robert CF Nov. 29, 1884, Northampton, Croup, 3 months, Alfred & Rena, Northampton, Single, Alfred Giddings, Father source

GIDDINGS, Smith CM Feb. 1891, Northampton, Pneumonia, 85, Parents Unkn., Northampton, Laborer, Married, Geo. Giddings, Nephew source

GIDDINS, Infant CM Dec. 20, 1873, Northampton, Crying Fits, 10 days, Jim Giddins, Northampton, Single, Mahala Giddins, Friend source

GIDDINS, Isaac CM May 11, 1876, Northampton, Old Age, 83, Parents Unkn., Accomack, Laborer, Widower, Friend source

GLADDEN, Ellen CF 1888, Northampton, Gathering in Head, 2 yrs. 15 days, Jas. F. Gladden, [Mechanic?], Northampton, Single, Jas. T. Gladden, Parent source

GLADDEN, Moses W. WM Mar. 28, 1876, Place of Death Unkn., Consumption, 60, Edwd. & Eliz, Maryland, Merchant, Single, Susan Gladden, Sister source

GLADSON, ------- WM July 3, 1895, Northampton, Cholera E., 2 months, J. E. & Henrietta, Northampton, Single, J. E. Gladson, Father source

GLADSON, Annie T. WF Nov. 1879, Northampton, Congestive Chill, 5, Edward E. & Margaret E., Va., Va., Va., Single, Dr. N. P. Henderson, Physician source

GLADSON, Annie T. WF Nov. 5, 1882, Northampton, Consumption, 21 yrs. 6 mos., Edward Gladson, Northampton, Single, Edward Gladson, Father source

GLADSON, Sally WF May 1872, Northampton, Cause Unkn., 50, Parents Unkn., Northampton, Wm. Gladson Husband, source unkn.

GLADSON, Vernon WM July 1, 1884, Northampton, Cholera Infantum, 8 months, Jno. J. & Emily, Northampton, Single, Jno. J. Gladson, Father source

GLADSTONE, ------- WF May 9, 1877, Northampton, Infantile, 3 days, John & Bettie, Northampton, Single, William Gladstone, Grandfather source

GODWIN, Harriet B. WF Dec. 18, 1893, Northampton, Consumption, 59, Edwin & Julia, Nansemond Co., Va., Single, E. S. Jacob, Nephew source

GODWIN, Jacob Jr. CM June 15, 1895, Northampton, Typhoid Fever, 66, Parents Unkn., Northampton, Laborer, Married, Daniel Spady, Neighbor source

GODWIN, Maria WF Mar. 31, 1891, Northampton, Heart Disease, 79, Southey & Sallie J. Nelson, Northampton, Married, Jno. H. Floyd, Son-in-Law source

GODWIN, Mary CF Mar. 16, 1876, Northampton, Typhoid Fever, Age Unkn., Louis & Agnes Read, Northampton, Cook, Married, Robin Godwin, Husband source

GODWIN, Nicy CF Mar. 22, 1876, Northampton, Congestive Fever, 55, Parents Unkn., Northampton, Washerwoman, Married, Robert Godwin, Husband source

GODWIN, Rosie A. P. WF 1888, Northampton, General Debility, 74, Parents Unkn., Northampton, Laborer, Elton B. Husband, Alex. G. Godwin, son source

GODWIN, William WM Apr. 11, 1876, Northampton, Rheumatism Heart, 50, Edmd. & Rosa, Northampton, Farmer, Single, Alex Godwin, Brother source

GOFFIGON, ------- CF May 7, 1877, Northampton, Infantile, 9 days, Spencer & Sallie, Northampton, Single, Spencer Goffigon, Father source

GOFFIGON, ------- CM June 4, 1878, Northampton, Cause Unkn., 4 days, Obed & Sallie, Northampton, Single, Sallie Goffigon, Mother source

GOFFIGON, Arintha S. WF Jan. 5, 1892, Northampton, Consumption, 35, John & Arintha, Northampton, Single, John H. Goffigon, Brother source

GOFFIGON, Arthur CM Aug. 11, 1887, Northampton, Bronchitis, 57, Parents Unkn., Northampton, Laborer, Married, James Smith, Neighbor source

GOFFIGON, Arthur CM May 10, 1873, Northampton, Drowning, 19 yrs., 11 mos., Arthur & Ibby, Northampton, Laborer, Single, Arthur Goffigon, Father source

GOFFIGON, Ben CM Nov. 11, 1876, Place of Death Unkn., Old Age, 81, Haven Bell, Northampton, Laborer, Widower, Wm. Wright, Friend source

GOFFIGON, Edward CM Oct. 14, 1887, Northampton, Cause Unkn., 17, Luther & Laura, Northampton, Farmer, Luther Goffigon, Father source

GOFFIGON, Jennie CF Oct. 15, 1887, Northampton, Cause Unkn., 27, Luther & Laura, Northampton, Farmer, Luther Goffigon, Father source

GOFFIGON, Mary A. CF Nov. 1, 1893, Northampton, Consumption, 27, Major & Mary Wicks, Northampton, Married, Matilda Young, Friend source

GOFFIGON, Mildred E. WF May 14, 1893, Northampton, Pneumonia, 5, L. H. & Mary B., Northampton, Single, L. H. Goffigon, Father source

GOFFIGON, Nath'l S. WM Mar. 30, 1884, Northampton, Old Age, 76, Parents Unkn., Northampton, Mrs. Arintha Goffigon, Sister-in-Law source

GOFFIGON, Obediah WM Dec. 13, 1872, Northampton, Consumption, 68, Polly & William, Northampton, Farmer, Married, Physician source

GOFFIGON, Severn CM June 10, 1873, Northampton, Crying Fits, 13 days, Severn & Mary, Northampton, Single, Sev. Goffigon, Father source

GOFFIGON, Solomon CM Dec. 28, 1883, Northampton, Asthma, 24, Arthur & Ibby, Birth Unkn., Arthur Goffigon, Father source

GOFFIGON, Spencer CM Oct.9, 1893, Northampton, Old Age, 80, Parents Unkn., Northampton, Laborer, Single, Spencer Smith, Nephew source

GOFFIGON, Susan WF June 8, 1878, Northampton, Bilious Fever, 14 yrs. 6 mos., Fred G. & Lucy, Northampton, Lucy Goffigon, Mother source

GOODIE, Margaret WF Oct. 5, 1887, Northampton, Child Birth 17, Parents Unkn., Northampton, Married, W. H. Spady, Friend source

GOODY, James S. WM Sept. 10, 1892, Northampton, Drowned 22, Wm. T. & Louisa, Northampton, Laborer, Single, Wm. H. Spady, Brother-in-Law source

GOODY, Wm. T. WM Feb. 2, 1895, Northampton, Drowned, 22, Wm. & Louisa, Northampton, Laborer, Single, Henry Kellam, Friend source

GORDY, ------- WM Aug. 4, 1891, Northampton, Acco. Co., Inflammation of Bowels, 6 days, L. C. & M. E., Northampton, Single, L. C. Goody, Father source

GREEN, John CM Dec. 15, 1893, Northampton, Hydrophobia, 23, James & Margaret, Somerset Co., Md., Laborer, Single, T. W. Turner, Neighbor source

GRIFFIN, ------- CM Dec. 10, 1878, Northampton, Cause Unkn., 2 days, Unkn. & Lucy Griffin, Birth Unkn. , Single, Lucy Griffin, Mother source

GRIFFIN, Jacob H. CM Nov, 15, 1893, Northampton, Paralysis of Brain, 3, Jacob & Annie, Northampton, Single, Edward Griffin, Brother source

GRIFFIN, Patsy CF Feb. 10, 1893, Northampton, Croup, 6 mos. 7 days, Solomon & Bettie, Northampton, Single, Solomon Griffin, Father source

GRIFFIN, Tabby CF 1888, Northmpton, Cause Unkn., 70, Parents Unkn., Northampton, Single, Laborer, Jno. Bell, Neighbor source

GRIFFITH, ------- CF Dec. 15, 1874, Northampton, Cause Unkn., 5 days, Levin & Lucey, Northampton, Single, Thos. W. Costin, Friend source

GRIFFITH, ------- CF Dec. 16, 1896, Northampton, Whooping Cough, 4 months, James & Henrietta, Northampton, Single, James Griffith, Father source

GRIFFITH, ------- WF Jan. 1875, Northampton, Cause Unkn., 13 days, Jno. & Missouri, Birth Unkn., Single, Jno. Griffith, Father source

GRIFFITH, Alexandrew WM Aug. 21, 1874, Northampton, Consumption, 40 yrs. 1 day, Benj. & Sallie, Northampton, Sailor, Single, Jno. F. Floyd, Friend source

GRIFFITH, Elizabeth WF Mar. 30, 1876, Northampton, Consumption, 63, Wm. Griffith, Northampton, Widow, Jno. B. Wilkins, Son-in-Law source

GRIFFITH, Infant BM Apr. 1880, Northampton, Inanition, 1 day, Levin & Lucy, Va., Va., Va., Single, source unkn.

GRIFFITH, Infant Dec. 13, 1871, Northampton, Crying Fits, 1 day, John & Missouri, Northampton, Single, John Griffith, Father source [Farmer?]

GRIFFITH, Infant WF Apr. 1880, Northampton, Cause Unkn., 18 days, William M. & Lelia A., Va. Va., Va., Single, source unkn.

GRIFFITH, Jacob CM July 4, 1894, Northampton, Brain Fever, 4, Jacob & Anna, Northampton, Single, Walter Griffith, Brother source

GRIFFITH, James CM June 11, 1871, Northampton, Dysentery, 2, Luke & Mary, Northampton, Single, Luke Griffith, Father source [Laborer?]

GRIFFITH, James WM June 10, 1872, Northampton, Dysentery, 20 days, Missouri & Jno., Northampton, Single, Jno. Griffith, source [Farmer?]

GRIFFITH, Moses WM Mar. 10, 1872, Northampton, Consumption, 23, Sallie & Benj., Northampton, Farmer, Married, Physician source

GRIFFITH, Nathan CM Oct. 14, 1877, Northampton, Typhoid Fever, 19, Severn & Emily, Northampton, Laborer, Single, Severn Griffith, Father source

GRIFFITH, Sallie WF Mar. 9, 1884, Northampton, Old Age, 82, Unkn. & Sallie, Northampton, Nathan Griffith, source

GRIFFITH, Severn CM Apr. 12, 1895, Northampton, Cause Unkn., 42, Parents Unkn., Northampton, Farmer, Married, Geo. Wilson, Friend source

GRIFFITH, Severn CM July 20, 1893, Northampton, Typhoid Fever, 59, Parents Unkn., Northampton, Farmer, Single, C. H. Savage, Neighbor source

GRIFFITH, Severn Sr. CM June 16, 1893, Northampton, Consumption, 70, Parents Unkn., Northampton, Laborer, Married, Thos. Brown, Friend source

GRIFFITH, Thos. E. WM Apr. 2, 1894, Northampton, Pneumonia, 49, Parents Unkn., Northampton, Farmer, Married, E. S. Herald, County paper source

GRIMMER, Frank WM Oct. 10, 1895, Northampton, Cholera Infection, 1, Conrad & Fannie, Northampton, Single, Conrad Grimmer, Father source

GRIMMER, Walter WM Mar. 26, 1895, Northampton, Gripps, 3, Conrad & Fannie, Northampton, Single, Conrad Grimmer, Father source

GRIMMER, Walter H. Mar. 28, 1894, Northampton, Cause Unkn., 3, Conrad & Fannie, Northampton, Single, Conrad Grimmer, Father source

GRINNALDS, Mary A. WF Aug. 8, 1895, Northampton, Old Age, 85, Jno. & Mary Colbourn, Acco. Co., Married, Bagwell Bull, Son-in-Law source

GUNTER, Charles CM Aug. 9, 1882, Northampton, Cause Unkn., 20, John & Sukey, Northampton, Mother/Father source

GUNTER, Isabella WF Dec. 1872, Northampton, Cause Unkn., 58, Parents Unkn., Northampton, Laban I. Gunter, Husband source unkn.

GUNTER, Jane CF Jan. 23, 1895, Northampton, Pneumonia, 45, Chas. & Ann Finney, Acco. Co., Married, Geo. Gunter, Son-in-Law source

GUNTER, Jno. CM Dec. 1872, Northampton, Infantile, Age Unkn., Jno. Gunter, Northampton, source unkn.

GUNTER, Missouri WF Sept. 1872, Northampton, Child Birth, 25, E. T. White, Northampton, Jas. L. Gunter Husband, source unkn.

GUNTER, Philip B. WM Jan. 22, 1876, Northampton, Pneumonia, 24, Wesley & Sally, Northampton, Farmer, Married, Edwd. L. Gunter, Brother source

GUNTER, Sallie A. WF Apr. 15, 1894, Northampton, Old Age, 80, Wm. R. & Peggie Johnson, Northampton, Married, E. V. Gunter, Son source

GUNTER, William WM Apr. 24, 1873, Northampton, Pneumonia, 24 yrs. 6 mos., Wesley & Sally, Northampton, Farmer, Married, Virginia wife, G. N. Jarvis, Friend source

GUY, ------- CM May 10, 1876, Northampton, Cause Unkn., 2 mos. 15 days, Edward & Mary, Northampton, Single, Edwd. J. Guy, Father source

GUY, Bettie CF Aug. 11, 1896, Northampton, Child Birth, 33, Major & Caroline Dunton, Northampton, Married, Peter Guy, Husband source

GUY, James CM Feb. 16, 1893, Northampton, Pneumonia, 18 months, Peter & Bettie, Northampton, Single, Peter Guy, Father source

GUY, Lillie M. WF Sept. 30, 1893, Northampton, Wart of Palete, 13 days, John W. & Alice, Northampton, Single, John W. Guy, Father source

HACK, Alfred CM May 1873, Northampton, Pleurisy, 43, Jacob Hack, Accomack Co., Laborer, Single, Jno. Hack, Friend source

HACK, Thomas H. CM June 23, 1876, Northampton, Cause Unkn., 68, Parents Unkn., Accomack, Laborer, Married, John H. Hack Brother source

HACK, W. T. CM June 1891, Accomac, Dropsy, 14, Thos. & Willonna, Northampton, Laborer, Single, An. H. Mapp, Neighbor source

HALEY, ------- CM July 24, 1872, Northampton, Infantile, 6 days, Mary A. Haley, Northampton, Single, Edwd. O. Gladson, where died source

HALL, Jacob CM Feb. 18, 1892, Northampton, Pleurisy, 42, Parents Unkn., Northampton, Laborer, Single, W. H. Heath, neighbor source

HALLETT, ------- CF Aug. 9, 1878, Northampton, Cause Unkn., 9 days, Spencer & Emily, Northampton, Single, Spencer Hallett, Father source

HALLETT, ------- CF Dec. 29, 1873, Northampton, Crying Fits, 3 days, Caleb & Esther, Northampton, Single, Caleb Hallett, Father source

HALLETT, ------- CM Jan. 1875, Northampton, Cause Unkn., 3 days, Caleb & Easter, Birth Unkn., Single, Easter Hallett, Mother source

HALLETT, ------- CM Jan. 23, 1876, Northampton, Crying Fits, 8 days, Caleb & Esther, Northampton, Single, Esther Hallett, Mother source

HALLETT, ------- CM Jan. 6, 1874, Northampton, Crying Fits, 6 days, Caleb & Esther, Northampton, Single, Esther Hallett, Mother source

HALLETT, Comfort CM Aug. 10, 1893, Northampton, Old Age, 70, Ezekiel & Rachel Young, Northampton, Married, John Allen, Grandson source

HALLETT, Ed. M. WM June 21, 1873, Northampton, Dysentery, 5 mos., 21 days, Ed. M. & Sabra Hallett, Northampton, Single, Ed. M. Hallett, Father source

HALLETT, Eliza CF Nov. 6, 1871, Northampton, Pneumonia, 21, Abe & Tamar, Northampton, Laborer, Single, Friend, Physician source [Laborer?]

HALLETT, Elizabeth WF Sept. 11, 1874, Northampton, Consumption, 45 yrs. 9 days, Jno. & Nancy Griffith, Northampton, Robt. I. Hallett, Husband source

HALLETT, Hebrew CM Jan. 10, 1893, Northampton, Enlargement of Brain, 2 months, Elias & Emma, Northampton, Single, Jennie Byrd, Aunt source

HALLETT, Ibby CF Feb. 24, 1876, Northampton, Cancer Womb, 35 yrs. 6 mos., Bennett & Adah Griffin, Northampton, Laborer, Abel Hallett, Husband source

HALLETT, Infant WF Jan. 18, 1872, Northampton, Crying Fits, 3 days, Elizabeth & Robt., Northampton, Robt. Hallett, Father source [Farmer?]

HALLETT, Laura CF July 8, 1876, Northampton, Heart Disease, 40, Abel & Maria, Northampton, Single, Abel Hallett, Father source

HALLETT, Lee CM Sept. 6, 1892, Northampton, Measles, 1, Len & Ella, Northampton, Single, Len Hallett, Father source

HALLETT, Leonard Jr. CM June 10, 1894, Northampton, Typhoid Fever, 2, Leonard & Ellen, Northampton, Single, Leonard Hallett, Father source

HALLETT, Sabra WF June 1, 1873, Northampton, Bilious Dysentery, 33 yrs., 11 mos., 21 days, Wm. W. & Mary P. Dixon, Northampton, Housekeeping, Edward M. Hallett, Husband source

HALLETT, Tamar WF Feb. 1875, Northampton, Consumption, 78, Parents Unkn., Birth Unkn., Son source

HAMBY, Elizabeth WF Dec. 10, 1884, Northampton, Encylhalus, 67, Edmd. & Elizabeth Wescoat, Northampton, Wm. L. Hanby, Husband source

HAMILTON, ------- WF Mar. 16, 1893, Northampton, Cholera Infantum, 2 months, L. J. & Mary, Northampton, Single, Mary Hamilton, Mother source

HAMILTON, Geo. W. WM July 20, 1893, Northampton, Rheumatism, 19, W. J. & Virginia, Northampton, Farmer, Single, W. J. Hamilton, Father source

HAMILTON, John WM Sept. 14, 1871, Northampton, Consumption, 55, Parents Unkn., Birth Unkn., Farmer, Married, Friend Physician source

HAMILTON, Lena WF June 25, 1892, Northampton, Cholera Infantum, 2 months, John S. & Patsie, Northampton, Single, Patsie Hamilton, Mother source

HAMILTON, W. Jr. WM Jan. 5, 1895, Northampton, Pneumonia, 55, Parents Unkn., Northampton, Farmer, John R. Read, Friend source

HANBY, ------- WF Apr. 19, 1876, Northampton, Diphtheria, 9 days, Wm. & Nancy, Northampton, Single, Wm. L. Hanby, Father source

HANBY, William T. WM June 1879, Northampton, Cause Unkn., 11 months, William L. & Nannie T., Va., Va., Va., Single, Dr. William W. Wilkins, Physician source

HARCUS/HARGIS, ------- WM July 1, 1884, Northampton, Cause Unkn., 7 days, Thos. & Ella, Northampton, Single, Thos. J. Harcus/Hargis, Father source

HARGIS, ------- CM Apr. 20, 1876, Northampton, Cause Unkn., 1 day, Nancy Hargis, York County, Single, Robt. Hallett, Neighbor source

HARGIS, ------- CF Apr. 20, 1876, Northampton, Cause Unkn., 1 day, Nancy Hargis, York County, Single, Robt. Hallett, Neighbor source

HARGIS, ------- CF Apr. 20, 1876, Northampton, Cause Unkn., Age Unkn., Nancy Hargis, York County, Single, Robt. Hallett, Neighbor source

HARGIS, ------- WF Mar. 5, 1884, Northampton, Cause Unkn., 7 days, Jno. W. & Margt., Northampton, Single, Jno. W. Hargis, Father source

HARGIS, Alice R. WF Oct. 24, 1891, Williamsburg, Va., Insanity, 28, L. T. & Mary A., Acco. Co., Single, L. S. Hargis, Brother source

HARGIS, Lovey WF 1891, Northampton, Cause Unkn., 8 days, J. W. & Maggie, Northampton, Single, Maggie Hargis, Mother source

HARGIS, Mary A. Aug. 18, 1895, Northampton, Heart Disease, 66, John & Mary Fosque, Northampton, C. H. Hargis, Son source

HARMAN, ------- C Sex Unkn. Feb. 1873, Northampton, Infantile, 1 day, Amey Harman, Northampton, Single, source unkn.

HARMAN, ------- CM July 12, 1893, Northampton, Cause Unkn., 1 day, Leon & Lucy, Northampton, Single, Leon Harman, Father source

HARMAN, Amy CF Feb. 1873, Northampton, Child Birth, 21, Geo. & Charlotte, Birth Unkn. Geo. Harman, Father source

HARMAN, Arthur CM Dec. 1871, Northampton, Cause Unkn., 1, Nim Harman, Northampton, Single, source blank

HARMAN, Austin WM July 1, 1895, Northampton, Dysentery, 5 months, Martin & Nervilla, Northampton, Single, Martin Harman, Father source

HARMAN, Dolly CF June 2, 1894, Northampton, Gen. Debility, 69, Parents Unkn., Northampton, Married, Jas. Smith, Undertaker source

HARMAN, Dolph CM Aug. 14, 1893, Northampton, Cause Unkn., 7 months, Isaac & Harriet, Northampton, Single, Isaac Harman, Father source

HARMAN, Frank CM Apr. 10, 1893, Northampton, Pneumonia, 3, John & Annie, Northampton, Single, Chas. Kellam, Neighbor source

HARMAN, Geo. CM Apr. 12, 1894, Northampton, Pneumonia, 66, Parents Unkn., Northampton, Farmer, Married, Jas. Smith, Undertaker source

HARMAN, Henry CM Feb. 1872, Northampton, Cause Unkn., Age Unkn., Nim Harman, Northampton, source unkn.

HARMAN, Mary CF June 2, 1895, Northampton, Consumption, 23, Isaac & Harriet, Northampton, Single, Isaac Harman, Father source

HARMAN, Nim CM Feb. 12, 1894, Northampton, Pneumonia, 65, Dublin & Mary, Northampton, Farmer, Married, Custis Harman, Son source

HARMAN, Rosey CF Sept. 1873, Northampton, Diphtheria, 5, Jas. & Laura, Northampton, Single, Jas. Harman, Father source

HARMAN, Susan CF June 1891, Northampton, Cause Unkn., 46, James & Susan, Northampton, Laborer, Single, Jas. Harman, Brother source

HARMANSON, William WM Nov. 12, 1876, Northampton, Typhoid Fever, 84, Henry & Eliz., Northampton, Farmer, Married, A. T. Leatherbury, Grandson source

HARMON, ------- WM Nov. 6, 1878, Northampton, Whooping Cough, 4, John & Jane, Northampton, Single, John Harmon, Father source

HARMON, Jane CF July 16, 1891, Northampton, Womb Disease, 45, Tenny Wright, Northampton, Laborer, Married, Arthur Harmon, Husband source

HARMON, Jane CF July 2, 1892, Northampton, Consumption, 60, Parents Unkn., Northampton, Laborer, Married, Arthur Harmon, Husband source

HARMON, John CM Sept. 19, 1892, Camden, N. J., Brain Stroke, 5 months, Edward & Tobitha, Camden, N. J., Single, Edward Harmon, Father source

HARMON, Lloyd CM June 1883, Northampton, Cause Unkn., 1 day, Lloyd & Phillis, Birth Unkn., Lloyd Harmon, Father source

HARMON, Luke CM Aug. 15, 1896, Northampton, Old Age, 99, Parents Unkn., Acco. Co., Married, Ben Harmon, G. Nephew, source

HARRISON, Margt. WF Aug. 12, 1883, Northampton, Consumption, Age Unkn., Wm. & Margt. Sterling, Birth Unkn., Jno. T. Harrison, Husband/Head of Family source

HARRISON, William WM May 9, 1876, Northampton, Pneumonia, 4, Wm. & Fanny, Northampton, Single, Wm. Harrison, Father source

HASTINGS, ------- WM July 28, 1895, Northampton, Crying Fits, 2 days, E. M. & Liddie, Northampton, Single, E. M. Hastings, Father source

HASTINGS, Renatus R. WM June 1874, Northampton, Congestion, 9 months, Ano. & Martha, Northampton, Single, Ano. Hastings, Father source

HATANY, Arintha CF May 6, 1893, Northampton, Consumption, 20, James & Ann, Northampton, Single, Jas. Hatany, Father source

HAYES, Emma CF July 12, 1893, Northampton, Cholera Infantum, 2 months, Chas. & Susan, Northampton, Single, Chas. Hayes, Father source

HAYES, Emma CF June 3, 1887, Northampton, Summer Sickness, 1, Charles & Mary, [Farmer?], Northampton, Single, Charles Hayes, Father source

HEATH, ------- CM Oct. 1875, Northampton, Cause Unkn., 1 month, Jno. & Lucinda, Birth Unkn., Single, Neighbor source

HEATH, Augustus C. WM May 1880, Northampton, Cause Unkn., 43, Parents Unkn., Va., Va., Va., Farmer, Married, source unkn.

HEATH, Augustus WM Sept. 1871, Northampton, Congestion, 3, Julius C. & Virginia, Northampton, Single, Julius C. Heath, Father source

HEATH, Caroline WF Feb. 15, 1892, Northampton, Blood Poison, 45, Parents Unkn., Dinwiddie Co., Va., Married, 2, W. H. Heath, Son source

HEATH, Horace M. WM Apr. 12, 1877, Northampton, Congestive Chill, 48, Augustus & Esther, Northampton, Physician, Virginia Wife, James M. Dunton, Step Father source

HEATH, Jasper CM Jan. 10, 1876, Northampton, Pleurisy, 1 yr. 2 mos., Jasper & Sarah, Northampton, Single, Jasper Heath, Father source

HEATH, Jno. Arthur CM Sept. 1873, Northampton, Diphtheria, 5, Jno. & Louisa, Northampton, Single, Jno. Heath, Father source

HEATH, John CM Nov. 20, 1873, Northampton, Infantile, 6 days, John & Ruth, Northampton, Single, Ruth Heath, Mother source

HEATH, Julius C. WM Oct. 16, 1892, Northampton, Heart Disease, 57, Jas. & Mary, Northampton, Merchant, Married, J. S. Heath, Son source

HEATH, Rachel CF Dec. 2, 1893, Northampton, Rheumatism, 76, Jas. & Susan Church, Northampton, Married, Jas. Heath, Husband source

HEATH, Wm. H. WM Dec. 15, 1894, Northampton, Pneumonia, 35, Parents Unkn., Northampton, Farmer, Married, E. S. Herald County paper source

HEATH, Wm. H. WM Dec. 29, 1893, Northampton, Catarrh, 35, Parents Unkn., North Carolina, Farmer, Married, Kitty Heath, Wife source

HEMINGS, Viola CF Feb. 1885, North Carolina, Burnt, 11 months, J. W. & Matilda, Northampton, Single, J. W. Hemings, Father source

HENDERSON, ------- WM Oct. 9, 1893, Northampton, Cause Unkn., 1 day, A. D. & Margaret, Northampton, Single, A. D. Henderson, Father source

HENDERSON, Dr. N. P. WM Jan. 4, 1895, Northampton, Heart Failure, 56, J. M. & Louisa, Northampton, Physician, Married, J. M. Henderson, Brother source

HENDERSON, Jacob CM July 4, 1891, Northampton, Cause Unkn., 40, Jno. & Mary, Northampton, Laborer, Married, Jack Henderson, Friend source

HENRY, Alex. CM July 13, 1893, Northampton, Cause Unkn., 5 days, James & Annie, Northampton, Single, Annie Henry, Mother source

HENRY, James BM Aug. 1879, Northampton, Brain Fever, 6 months, Parents Unkn., Va., Va., Va., Single, source unkn.

HICKMAN, ------- CF Aug. 15, 1884, Northampton, Crying Fits, 10 days, Geo. & Lila, Northampton, Single, Geo. Hickman, Father source

HICKMAN, ------- CM 1887, Northampton, Cause Unkn., 8 days, Severn Hickman, Northampton, N. S. & S. Service, Single, Severn Hickman, Parent source

HICKMAN, ------- WM July 1875, Northampton, Cause Unkn., 7 days, Jno. & Mary, Birth Unkn., Single, Jno. Hickman, Father source

HICKMAN, John BM Dec. 1879, Northampton, Croup, 9 months, John & Mary, Va., Va., Va., Single, source unkn.

HODGES, ------- CM May 18, 1893, Northampton, Cause Unkn., 8 days, Joseph & Edith, Northampton, Single, Jos. Hodges, Father source

HODGES, Edith CF Nov, 27, 1893, Northampton, Consumption, 34, Geo. & Sophia Burton, Northampton, Married, Jos. Hodges, Husband source

HOLLAND, N. L. WM July 9, 1885, Northampton, Cholera Infantum, 1, N. L. & Juliet, Northampton, Single, N. L. Holland, Father source

HOLT, ------- CF Dec. 28, 1887, Northampton, Cause Unkn., 4 days, George & Susan, [Farmer?], Northampton, Single, George Holt, Father source

HOLT, Ginny CF Sept. 10, 1873, Northampton, Infantile, 4 days, George & Susan, Northampton, Single, Geo. Holt, Father source

HOLT, Joseph CM Feb. 12, 1876, Northampton, Pneumonia, 3, George & Susan, Northampton, Single, George Holt, Father source

HOLT, Lucy CF Dec. 8, 1876, Northampton, Bilious Cholera, Age Unkn., Joseph & Edith Upshur, Northampton, Edith Upshur, Mother source

HOPKINS, Henry CM June 10, 1896, Northampton, Old Age, 82, Henry & Jennie, Northampton, Laborer, Single, Mary Hopkins, Niece source

HOPKINS, Peter CM Sept. 20, 1883, Northampton, Brain Fever, 1 yr. 6 mos., Peter & Sarah, Birth Unkn., Peter Hopkins, Father source

~~**HOPKINS, Tinnie** BF June 1879, Northampton, Red Fever, 20, Peter & Harriet, Va., Va., Va., Keeping House, Wright Husband, Dr. Thomas Mapp, Physician source~~

HORSEY, Luther N. WM Sept. 15, 1893, Northampton, Spinal Meningitis, 2 months, L. J. & T. G., Northampton, Single, L. J. Horsey, Father source

HOUSE, ------- CF Sept. 10, 1873, Northampton, Crying Fits, 5 days, George & Mary, Northampton, Single, George House, Father source

HOWARD, Henry J. WM Nov. 5, 1894, Northampton, Cause Unkn., 42, Parents Unkn., Birth Unkn., R. R. Service, Single, E. S. Herald County paper source

HUMPHREYS, ------- WM July 3, 1896, Northampton, Chol. Infantum, 6 months, Thomas & Meta, Northampton, Thos. Humphreys, Father source

HUNT, Belfert F. WM Oct. 10, 1878, Northampton, Brain [Fever?] Wm. M. & Peggie, Northampton, Carpenter, Single, Wm. M. Hunt, Father source

HUNT, Isaac WM June 1879, Northampton, Gastritis, 70, Parents Unkn., Va., Va., Va., Farm Laborer, Married, source unkn.

HUNT, Jane CF Feb. 29, 1887, Northampton, Crying Fits, 7 days, Jane Hunt, Northampton, Single, W. D. Wise, Employer source

HUNT, Mary E. WF May 1, 1876, Northampton, Gastro Enteritis, Age Unkn., John & Mary, Nansemond, Single, Wm. Taylor, Brother-in-Law source

HUNT, Monie CF Mar. 30, 1895, Northampton, Cause Unkn., 8 months, Jesse & Nannie, Northampton, Single, Jos. Weston, Grandfather source

HUNT, Ruth T. WF May 31, 1891, Northampton, Cause Unkn., 10 days, Henry & Ida, Northampton, Single, Henry Hunt, Father source

HUNT, Virginnia CF Sept. 4, 1878, Northampton, Bilious Fever, 20, Parents Unkn., Northampton, Laborer, Single, Thomas W. Spady, Friend source

HUNT, Washington WM July 3, 1874, Northampton, Falling from Tree, 5 yrs. 10 days, Washington Hunt, Northampton, Single, Washington Hunt, Father source

HURTT, G. K. WM June 8, 1891, Northampton, Heart Disease, 4 days, W. G. & C. H., Northampton, Single, Wm. G. Hurtt, Father source

HYSLOP, ------- CF June 4, 1876, Northampton, Lung Fever, 10 days, James & Lottie, Northampton, Single, Jas. Hyslop, Father source

ILIFF, Hattie WF Apr. 19, 1894, Northampton, Typhoid Fever, 29, L. T. & Eliza Trader, Stockton, Md., Married, John W. Iliff, Husband source

IRELAND, Arlene WF Oct. 12, 1895, Northampton, Dysentery, 42, Wilson & Susan Smallwood, Matthews Co., Va., Married, E. B. Ireland, Husband source

ISDELL, John WM Jan. 17, 1872, Northampton, Pneumonia, 28, Jas. & Lovey, Northampton, Farmer, Mary Wife, Jas. S. Carpenter, Friend Neighbor source

ISDELL, Sally WF Jan. 27, 1872, Northampton, Pneumonia, 35, Parents Unkn., Northampton, Single, Jas. S. Carpenter, Friend Neighbor source

ISDELL, Sam'l R. WM Nov. 23, 1891, Northampton, Cause Unkn., 24, S. P. & Fannie, Northampton, Laborer, Single, Geo. Isdell, Brother source

ISDELL, Wm. E. WM Jan. 26, 1872, Northampton, Pneumonia, 41, Jas. & Lovey, Northampton, Married, Sally Wife, Jas. S. Carpenter Friend Neighbor source

IVINS, Robert CM Oct. 4, 1877, Northampton, Cause Unkn., 60, Parents Unkn., Birth Unkn., Laborer, Single, Sol Church, Friend source

JACKSON, Ibbie CF July 22, 1893, Northampton, Dysentery, 84, Parents Unkn., Northampton, Married, Mary A. Fitchett, Daughter source

JACKSON, Rachel CF Aug. 1871, Northampton, Dropsy, 80, Parents Unkn., Northampton, Single, Robt. B. Taylor, when died source

JACOB, ------- CF Sept. 1873, Northampton, Infantile, 3 days, Jas. & Betsy, Northampton, Single, James Jacob, Father source

JACOB, C. W. WF Mar. 26, 1885, Northampton, Consumption, 36, R. W. & Margt. Dorsey, Northampton, Married, Edwin S. Jacob, Head of Family source

JACOB, Ella CF May 4, 1878, Northampton, Whooping Cough, 11 months, Geo. & Rachiel, Northampton, Single, Geo. Jacob, Father source

JACOB, Geo. CM June 4, 1894, Northampton, Dropsy, 62, Parents Unkn., Northampton, Farmer, Married, Mary Jacob, Wife source

JACOB, James CM May 9, 1877, Northampton, Typhoid Fever, 48, Lloyd & Susan, Northampton, Farmer, Single, Lloyd Jacob, Father source

JACOB, Joseph M. CM Sept. 5, 1894, Northampton, Cholera Infantum, 1, Solomon & Maggie, Northampton, Single, Sol. Jacob, Father source

JACOB, Maggie CF Mar. 3, 1896, Northampton, Child Birth, 27, Louis & Eliza Jarvis, Northampton, Married, Caroline James, Friend source

JACOB, Marg't S. WF June 30, 1871, Northampton, Consumption, 58, Robt. & Eliz. Wilkins, Northampton, Married, Robt. C. Husband, Geo. R. Jacob, Son source

JACOB, Robert C. WM May 12, 1877, Northampton, Broken down Nerves, 65, Hancock & Ann, Northampton, Farmer, Single, Jno. R. Mapp, Step Son source

JACOB, Sallie WF June 20, 1893, Northampton, Heart Disease, 46, Nat & Sallie Fitchett, Northampton, Married, T. A. Jacob, Son source

JACOB, Sarah V. CF Aug. 15, 1896, Northampton, Cause Unkn., 1 day, Sol & Maggie, Northampton, Single, Maggie Jacob, Mother source

Northampton County, VA, Deaths from Death Register and Wills, 1871-1896

JACOB, Susan CF May 10, 1873, Northampton, Measles, 12, Mary Jacob, Northampton, Single, Mary Jacob, Mother source

JACOB, Wm. T. WM May 9, 1878, Northampton, Whooping Cough, 8 months, Wm. T & Sallie A., Northampton, Single, Wm. T. Jacob, Father source

JACOBS, ------- CF June 12, 1895, Northampton, Cause Unkn., 1 month, Lloyd & Caroline, Northampton, Single, Adah Moses, Grandmother source

JACOBS, Caroline CF June 6, 1895, Northampton, Dropsy, 45, Henry & Adah Moses, Northampton, Married, Adah Moses, Mother source

JACOBS, Lloyd CM Dec. 15, 1895, Northampton, Dropsy, 60, Jas. & Emeline, Northampton, Laborer, Married, Adah Moses, Sister-in-Law source

JACOBS, Susie CF July 1891, Northampton, Dropsy, 1, Lloyd & Caroline, Northampton, Single, Lloyd Jacob, Father source

JAMES, ------- CF Feb. 15, 1876, Northampton, Infantile, Age Unkn., Isaac & Lydia, Northampton, Isaac James, Father source

JAMES, ------- CM Dec. 25, 1877, Northampton, Infantile, 6 days, George & Emily, Northampton, Single, George James, Father source

JAMES, ------- CM Nov. 2, 1896, Northampton, Cause Unkn., 1 month, Charles & Cordie, Northampton, Single, Chas. James, Father source

JAMES, Arthur CM July 15, 1887, Northampton, Dropsy, 2, Murray & Susan, Northampton, Single, Murray James, Father source [Laborer?]

JAMES, Benjamin CM Dec. 18, 1891, Northampton, Shot by Accident, 18, Parents Unkn., Northampton, Laborer, Single, R. B. Handy, Reporter source

JAMES, Helen P. WF Mar. 16, 1894, Northampton, Pneumonia, 5, H. P. & Sarah C., Northampton, Single, H. P. James, Father source

JAMES, Hez. P. WM July 5, 1885, Northampton, Dysentery, 76, Wm. & Sallie, Northampton, Farmer, Married, Hez. P. James Jr., Son source

JAMES, Hezekiah WM Jan. 18, 1892, Northampton, Pneumonia, 70, Parents Unkn., Northampton, Merchant, Single, Newspaper report source

JAMES, Isaac BM Aug. 1879, Northampton, Drowned, 45, Parents Unkn., Va., Va., Va., Sailor, Dianna Wife, source unkn.

JAMES, Jno. CM Feb. 8, 1885, Northampton, Consumption, 35, Jno. & Rachael, Northampton, Married, Louis James, Head of Family source

JAMES, John CM June 3, 1895, Northampton, Heart Failure, 37, Parents Unkn., Northampton, Laborer, Married, Asa Dix Jr., Friend source

JAMES, Lucy CF June 21, 1896, Northampton, Diarrhea, 34, Isaac & Julia Satchell, Northampton, Married, Henry James, Husband source

JAMES, Margt. WF Oct. 20, 1883, Northampton, Consumption, 32, Jno. & Eliza Thompson, Birth Unkn., House keeper, Jno. James, Father source

JAMES, Mary WF Aug. 2, 1896, Northampton, Cause Unkn., 48, Alfred & Laura Mapp, Northampton, Married, S. M. James, Husband source

JAMES, Napolean CM Dec. 24. 1871, Northampton, Consumption, 56, Parents Unkn., Northampton, Laborer, Single, Jno. U. Gunter, when died source

JAMES, Toby CM July 4, 1891, Northampton, Congestion Brain, 3, Ellis & Patience, Northampton, Single, Rich'd Milby, Friend source

JARVIS, ------- CF Dec. 28, 1877, Northampton, Infantile, 3 days, George & Mary, Northampton, Single, George Jarvis, Father source

JARVIS, Geo. T. WM Apr. 13, 1874, Eastville Township, Erysipelas, 56, Wm. & Elizabeth, Northampton, Farmer, Single, Saml. A. Jarvis, source

JARVIS, Jesse N. WM June 7, 1892, Northampton, Pneumonia, 62, Wm. & Sarah, Northampton, Sheriff, Married, Sam'l A. Jarvis, Son source

JARVIS, Joshua CM Dec. 17, 1871, Northampton, Pneumonia, 50, Parents Unkn., Northampton, Carpenter, Married, Wife source

JARVIS, Maggie WF Sept. 18, 1878, Northampton, Congestive Chill, 22, Jessie N. & Virginnia, Northampton, Single, Jessie N. Jarvis, Father source

JARVIS, Margaret S. WF Sept. 1879, Northampton, Malarial Fever Congestive Chill, 23, Jessie N. & Virginia, Va., Va., Va., Single, Dr. N. Henderson, Physician source

JARVIS, Mary G. WF Nov. 29, 1896, Northampton, Cholera Infantum, 6 months, Geo. T. & Emily, Northampton, Single, Geo. T. Jarvis, Father source

JARVIS, Sam'l CM Oct. 18, 1882, Northampton, Scarlet Fever, 5 yrs. 6 mos., Geo. & Virginia Jarvis, Northampton, Single, Geo. Jarvis, Father source

JARVIS, Samuel BM Oct. 1879, Northampton, Croup, 3, George & Jane, Va., Va., Va., Single, source unkn.

JARVIS, Thomas CM Sept. 1872, Northampton, Cause Unkn., 7, Harriet Jarvis, Northampton, Single, source unkn.

JARVIS, Thos. B. WM July 21, 1872, Acco. Co., Consumption, 59, Wm. & Peggie, Northampton, Farmer, Married, Mary Wife, Jas. A. Jarvis, source

JARVIS, Virginia CF Oct. 10, 1872, Northampton, Diphtheria, 4 yrs. 6 mos., Severn & Caroline, Northampton, Single, Severn Jarvis, Father source

JARVIS, Virginia WF Nov. 23, 1891, Northampton, Consumption, 60, Benj. & Mary Dalby, Northampton, Married, J. N. Jarvis, Husband source

JARVIS, William WM Oct. 15, 1871, Northampton, Typhoid Fever, 20 yrs. 9 mos., Jesse N. & Virginia A., Northampton, Farmer, Single, Jesse N. Jarvis, Father source

JARVIS, William S. WM Oct. 20, 1871, Northampton, Cholera Infantum, 40, William & Betsy, Northampton, Farmer, Married, Wife & Physician source

JARVIS, Wm. S. Wm Nov. 28, 1885, Northampton, Diphtheria, 8 yrs. 6 mos., Sam'l A. & Bettie, Northampton, Single, Sam'l A. Jarvis, Father source

JEFFERSON, ------- CF Aug. 14, 1895, Northampton, Cause Unkn., 5 months, J. D. & Martha, Northampton, Single, J. D. Jefferson, Father source

JEFFERSON, ------- CF July 10, 1893, Northampton, Spinal Meningitis, 3 months, T. D. & Mary S., Northampton, Single, T. D. Jefferson, Father source

JEFFERSON, Ellen CF Oct. 10, 1876, Northampton, Cause Unkn. 9 Months, Mary Jefferson, Northampton, Single, Charles Smith, Neighbor source

JOHNSON, ------- WF Oct. 1872, Northampton, Infantile, 10 days, Jno. C. & Mary, Birth Unkn., Single, J. C. Johnson, Father source

JOHNSON, Amy CF Dec. 1, 1895, Northampton, Asthma, 59, Parents Unkn., Northampton, Daniel Spady, Neighbor source

JOHNSON, Annie CF Dec. 24, 1893, Northampton, Spasm, 7 months, Alfred & Eliza, Northampton, Single, Alfred Johnson, Father source

JOHNSON, Berry CM Jan. 16, 1892, Northampton, Pneumonia, 69, Parents Unkn., Northampton, Laborer, Married, Henry Bayly, Son-in-Law source

JOHNSON, Berry CM May 10, 1891, Northampton, Consumption, 60, Parents Unkn., Northampton, Laborer, Married, Henry Bailey, Friend source

JOHNSON, Dallas CM May 20, 1895, Northampton, Pneumonia, 49, Fannie Johnson, Northampton, Farmer, Married, Jeff Johnson, Brother source

JOHNSON, Edward B. WM Jan. 8, 1892, Northampton, Pneumonia, 77, Laban & Rosa, Northampton, Farmer, Married, J. H. Johnson, Son source

JOHNSON, Edward L. WM June 1876, Northampton, Cold, 2, Littleton & Maggie, Northampton, Single, Littleton Johnson, Father source

JOHNSON, Eliza WF Sept. 1873, Northampton, Dropsy, 36, Mich'l & Ann Douty, Northampton, L. T. Johnson, Husband, source unkn.

JOHNSON, Esther CF Oct. 5, 1876, Northampton, Pneumonia, 60, Ibby Costin, Northampton, Laborer, Widow, Mary Wilkins, Neighbor source

JOHNSON, Geo. E. WM Sept. 18, 1883, Northampton, Typhoid Fever, 20, Jno. E. M., Birth Unkn., Jno. Ed Johnson, Father source

JOHNSON, Grace BF Dec. 1879, Northampton, Old Age, 75, Parents Unkn., Va., Va., Va., Domestic Servt., Widow, George Ker, source

JOHNSON, Isabella CF Aug. 12, 1892, Northampton, Consumption, 19, John & Ellen, Northampton, Single, John H. Johnson, Father source

JOHNSON, J. C. Jr. WM July 16, 1891, Northampton, Inflammation of Bowels, 23, J. C. Sr. & M. E., Northampton, Farmer, Married, J. C. Johnson, Sr. Father source

JOHNSON, Jacob CM Nov. 1, 1887, Northampton, Lockjaw, 55, Parents Unkn., Northampton, Laborer, Married, Belford Francis, Neighbor source

JOHNSON, Jno. M. H. WM Mar. 10, 1885, Northampton, Cause Unkn., 17 months, S. T. & Susan A., Northampton, Single, L. T. Johnson, source

JOHNSON, Jno. Y. WM Sept. 1871, Northampton, Congestion, 2, Jas. F. & Delitha, Northampton, Single, Jas. F. Johnson, Father source

JOHNSON, John C. WM June 14, 1892, Northampton, Consumption, 53, John T. & Mary, Northampton, Farmer, Married, Lizzie Johnson, Wife source

JOHNSON, Joseph CM July 6, 1895, Northampton, Dysentery, 3, Jas. R. & Louisa, Northampton, Single, William Ames, Neighbor source

Northampton County, VA, Deaths from Death Register and Wills, 1871-1896

JOHNSON, Maria CF Jan. 28, 1891, Northampton, Child Birth, 30, Henry & Clorissa Mapp, Northampton, Laborer, Married, Dallas Johnson, Husband sourse

JOHNSON, Maria E. CF Sept. 13, 1892, Northampton, Measles, 16 months, John & Ellen, Northampton, Single, John H. Johnson, Father source

JOHNSON, Nancy CF Nov. 13, 1894, Northampton, Consumption, 20, John H. & Ellen, Northampton, Single, John H. Johnson, Father source

JOHNSON, Nancy CF Oct. 30, 1893, Northampton, Consumption, 19, John H. & Ellen, Northampton, Single, John H. Johnson, Father source

JOHNSON, Obedience WM Sept. 1875, Northampton, Cause Unkn., 2 months, Wm. F. & Sally, Birth Unkn., Single, Wm. F. Johnson, Father source

JOHNSON, Ruth WF Aug. 16, 1893, Northampton, Dysentery, 9 months, Wm. T. & Sudie M., Northampton, Single, W. T. Johnson, Father source

JOHNSON, Sudie M. WF Oct. 10, 1893, Northampton, Blood Poison, 39, Geo. M. & Rosa Wescott, Northampton, Married, W. T. Johnson, Husband source

JOHNSON, Susan CF May 10, 1896, Northampton, Dropsy, 70, Parents Unkn., Died at Alms House, Northampton, Single, Wm. G. Bell, Overseer of Poor source

JOHNSON, Sydney WM Dec. 1885, Northampton, Dropsy of the Heart, 26, Sydney & Martha, Northampton, Laborer, Single, A. T. Turner, source

JOHNSON, W. L. WM Sept. 20, 1892, Northampton, Typhoid, 18, L. W. & Maggie V., Northampton, Farmer, Single, L. W. Johnson, Father source

JOHNSON, William WM Feb. 14, 1893, Northampton, Cause Unkn., 46, Parents Unkn., Northampton, Laborer, Single, John R. Read, Friend source

JOHNSON, Wm. WM Sept. 1871, Northampton, Congestion, 4, Jas. F. & Delitha, Northampton, Single, Jas. F. Johnson, Father source

JOHNSON, Wm. G. WM Nov. 1875, Northampton, Typhoid, 63, Parents Unkn., Birth Unkn., Farmer, Son-in-Law source

JONES, Geo. T. CM Oct. 12, 1878, Northampton, Drowned, 45, Parents Unkn. Accomac, Farmer, Emily Wife, Jas B. Floyd, Friend source

JONES, Hebrew CM Oct. 14, 1877, Northampton, Typhoid Fever, 12, George & Emily, Northampton, Laborer, Single, George Jones, Father source

JONES, Hessie M. WF Oct. 30, 1883, Northampton, Fever, 1, G. B. Jones, Birth Unkn., Single, Gorton Jones, Father source

JONES, Jacob CM Oct. 12, 1878, Northampton, Drowned, 18, Geo. T. & Emily, Northampton, Laborer, Single, Jas. B. Floyd, Friend source

JONES, Mary C. WF June 14, 1894, Northampton, Cause Unkn., 3 months, H. E. & Elizabeth, Northampton, Single, H. E. Jones, Father source

JONES, Whittington WM Mar. 14, 1887, Northampton, Old Age, 78, George & Sarah, Maryland, Farmer, Married, Horace C. Jones, Son source

Northampton County, VA, Deaths from Death Register and Wills, 1871-1896

JONES, William CM Sept. 14, 1893, Northampton, Consumption, 46, Parents Unkn., Northampton, Laborer, Married, John R. Read, Neighbor source

JONES, Wm. CM Oct. 12, 1878, Northampton, Drowned, 20, Geo. T. & Emily, Northampton, Laborer, Single, Jas. B. Floyd, Friend source

JOYNES, ------- CF Oct. 31, 1876, Northampton, Cause Unkn., 14 days, Wm. P. & Cath, Northampton, Single, Wm. P. Joynes, Father source

JOYNES, ------- CM Dec. 1875, Northampton, Cause Unkn., 1 month, Jesse & Louisa, Birth Unkn., Single, Neighbor source

JOYNES, ------- CM Sept. 1, 1896, Northampton, Cause Unkn., 3 days, Jno. H. & Eleanora, Northampton, Single, Mary Bayly, Grandmother source

JOYNES, Arthur CM May 18, 1887, Northampton, Old Age, 80, Parents Unkn., Northampton, Laborer, Married, Thomas Arthur, Friend source

JOYNES, E. G. WF 1888, Northampton, Approplexy, 4, R. C. & B. L., [Mechanic?], Northampton, Single, R. C. Joynes, Parent source

JOYNES, Garnet WM Nov. 1884, Northampton, Quinsy, 4, Wm. & Unkn., Northampton, Single, W. W. Joynes, source

JOYNES, Infant CM Dec. 15, 1872, Northampton, Crying Fits, 2 days, Emily Joynes, Northampton, Single, Physician source

JOYNES, Major CM Feb. 12, 1876, Northampton, Cause Unkn., 68, Edwd. & Julia, Northampton, Laborer, Julia Fitchett, Mother source

JOYNES, Margt. WF Aug. 2, 1875, Northampton, Cause Unkn., 68, Parents Unkn., Birth Unkn., Physician source

JOYNES, Tobitha CF 1888, Northampton, Whooping Cough, 1, Hez. Joynes, [Laborer?], Northampton, Single, Hez. Joynes, Parent source

JUBILEE, ------- CF July 12, 1895, Acco. Co., Cause Unkn., 2 months, Wm. H. & Harriet, Acco. Co., Single, Wm. H. Jubilee, Father source

JUSTICE, Jane WF July 4, 1877, Northampton, Consumption, 36, Smith & Margt. Bell, Northampton, Thomas Justice, Husband source

KELLAM, ------- WF Jan. 15, 1893, Northampton, Cause Unkn., 3 months, J. E. & Sarah, Northampton, Single, J. E. Kellam, Father source

KELLAM, ------- WM Feb. 4, 1895, Northampton, Dysentery, 3 months, John H. & Sadie, Northampton, Single, John H. Kellam, Father source

KELLAM, Alfred CM Feb. 12, 1894, Northampton, Kidney Disease, 48, Abel & Sarah, Northampton, Farmer, Married, Mary Scott, Mother-in-Law source

KELLAM, Cora CF June 25, 1891, Northampton, Consumption, 9 months, Harry & Esther, Northampton, Single, Harry Kellam, Father source

KELLAM, Edward WM May 1872, Northampton, Cause Unkn., 53, Parents Unkn., Northampton, source unkn.

KELLAM, Jacob CM Sept. 15, 1894, Phil., Penn., Heart Disease, 30, John & Sallie, Northampton, Hotel waiter, Married, Sadie Kellam, source

KELLAM, Jas. C. WM Aug. 23, 1891, Northampton, Cholera Infantum, 9 months, A. W. & Sarah, Northampton, Single, A. W. Kellam, Father source

KELLAM, Kitty CF June 10, 1876, Northampton, Diarrhea, 1 yr. 2 mos., Thomas & Peggy, Northampton, Single, Thos. Kellam, Father source

KELLAM, Marion CF Apr. 2, 1896, Northampton, Whooping Cough, 2, Levi & Raechel, Northampton, Single, Levi Kellam, Father source

KELLAM, Nim T. WM Sept. 1, 1874, Northampton, Worms, 4 yrs. 2 days, Nim & Emely, Northampton, Single, Nim T. Kellam, Father source

KELLAM, Rosa B. CF May 26, 1894, Northampton, Pneumonia, 41, Thos. & Mary Scott, Northampton, Married, Mary Scott, Mother source

KELLAM, Sam'l CM Mar. 5, 1893, Northampton, Broke Neck by fall, 52, Sam'l & Mary, Northampton, Laborer, Single, Newspaper Report

KELLAM, Sam'l E. D. WM Oct. 12, 1882, Northampton, Dysentery, 52, S. E. D. Kellam, Northampton, Farmer, Dr. Scott, Physician source

KELLAM, Samuel E. D. WM Oct. 1879, Northampton, Chronic Dysentery, 51, Parents Unkn., Va., Va., Va., Farmer, Married, Peter F. Scott, source

KELLAM, Sarah WF Sept. 14, 1893, Northampton, Consumption, 23, Eli & Susan Doughty, Northampton, Married, Eli Doughty, Father source

KELLAM, Southey WM Oct. 23, 1884, Northampton, Cause Unkn., 5 days, Frank & Mary, Northampton, Single, Frank Kellam, Father source

KELLAM, Thomas CM Dec. 30, 1876, Northampton, Bilious Fever, 3 mos. 20 days, Thomas & Peggy, Northampton, Single, Thos. Kellam, Father source

KELLAM, Tom CM Apr. 2, 1896, Northampton, Cause Unkn., 6, Harry & Esther, Northampton, Single, G. H. Thomas, Neighbor source

KELLAM, Zed CM Oct. 19, 1892, Northampton, Cause Unkn., 68, Parents Unkn., Northampton, Laborer, Married, Arthur Colona, Neighbor source

KELLEY, ------- CM Mar. 16, 1894, Northampton, Cause Unkn., 1 month, James & Annie, Northampton, Single, Jas. Kelley, Father source

KELLEY, Kitty WF Sept. 3, 1894, Northampton, Rheumatism, 65, Wm. & Tama Churn, Northampton, Married, Edward Kelley, Son source

KELLEY, Mary Susan WF Aug. 1871, Northampton, Diphtheria, 1 yr. 2 mos., Obed & Virginia U., Accomac, Single, Obed Kelley, Father source

KELLY, ------- CF Oct. 1873, Northampton, Infantile, 3 days, Geo. & Alice, Northampton, Single, source unkn.

KELLY, ------- WF Aug. 1871, Northampton, Diphtheria, 6 months, O. & Virginia Kelly, Northampton, Single, source blank

KELLY, Annie WF Aug. 1, 1884, Northampton, Cholera Infantum, 9 months, Obed & Virginia, Northampton, Single, Obed Kelly, Father source

KELLY, Arthur F. WM Apr. 6, 1896, Northampton, Cancer, 46, Timothy & Mary E., Northampton, Farmer, Married, Geo. E. Kelly, Brother source

KELLY, Charles WM May 1880, Northampton, Cause Unkn., 100, Parents Unkn., Va., Va., Va., Widower, source unkn.

KELLY, Lizzie WF Oct. 1871, Northampton, Cause Unkn., 50, Parents Unkn., Northampton, Timothy Kelly, Husband source

KELLY, Obed WM Feb. 1891, Northampton, Bright's Disease, 50, Obed & Mary, Northampton, Farmer, Married, S. S. Wilkins, Friend source

KENDALL, Infant WM Aug. 20, 1872, Northampton, Crying Fits, 10 days, Hannah & William, Northampton, William Kendall, Father source [Farmer?]

KENDALL, Lucius CM Sept. 12, 1893, Northampton, Pleurisy, 43, John & Mary, Northampton, Laborer, Married, John R. Read, Neighbor source

KENDALL, Mary CF Dec. 10, 1876, Northampton, Diphtheria, Age Unkn., Lucius & Lucretia, Northampton, Lucius Kendall, Father source

KENDALL, Susan W. WF May 10, 1894, Northampton, Cancer, 75, J. N. & Catherine C. Brickhouse, Northampton, Married, G. S. Kendall, Son source

KENNERLY, William A. WM July 1873, Northampton, Dysentery, 60, Parents Unkn., Maryland, Miller, Married, source unkn.

KERR, Dr. Geo. W. WM Aug. 22, 1892, Northampton, Cause Unkn., 67, Hugh & Margaret, Northampton, Physician, Married, Mrs. Kerr, Wife source

KETCHAM, Nathan A. WM Mar. 1, 1894, Northampton, Old Age, 86, Nathan & Mary, Conn., Gentleman, Married, John W. Ketcham, Son source

KILLMON, Polly WF Nov. 14, 1891, Northampton, Heart Disease, 66, Isoriah & Juliet, Northampton, Married, S. V. Killmon, Son source

KISHPAUGH, W. D. WM Nov. 13, 1893, Northampton, Consumption, 64, Anthony & Martha, New Jersey, Farmer, Married, Mrs. Kishpaugh, Wife source

KNIGHT, ------- CM Oct. 12, 1895, Northampton, Croup, 1 month, Wm. & Mary E., Northampton, Single, Mary Knight, Mother source

LaFORGE, John R. WM Jan. 1876, Northampton, Pneumonia, 65, Ellen LaForge, New York, Lawyer, Single, Louis B. Taylor Friend source

LaPETERS, Lloyd WM Nov. 1885, Northampton, Cause Unkn., 9 days, Jacob & Ella, Northampton, Single, Jacob La Peters, Father source

LAMBERTSON, Essie M. WF Oct. 2, 1895, Northampton, Septicemia (Blood Poison), 29, Archie & Mary Gooch?, Maryland, Married, Dr. G. P. Moore, Physician source

LAMBERTSON, Jessie WF Feb. 1891, Northampton, Pneumonia, 2, Wm. H. & Essie, Northampton, Single, W. H. Lambertson, Father source

LANE, ------- CF May 20, 1896, Northampton, Spasms, 10 days, Kittie, Northampton, Single, John Lane, Grandfather source

LANE, Mary CF Sept. 4, 1891, Northampton, Cause Unkn., 36, Patsy Richardson, Northampton, Laborer, Married, L. W. Nottingham, Neighbor source

LANKFORD, B. S. WM June 4, 1893, Northampton, Heart Disease, 35, Parents Unkn., Maryland, Tailor, Single, Geo. G. Savage, Friend source

LAUPHEIMER, Jacob WM May 1884, Northampton, Old Age, 72, Parents Unkn., Germany, J. Ambler Jarvis, source

Northampton County, VA, Deaths from Death Register and Wills, 1871-1896

LAWSON, Abraham WM Aug. 14, 1896, Northampton, Chol. Infantum, 2 months, A. D. & Martha, Northampton, Single, A. D. Lawson, Father source

LAWSON, Edwin WM June 15, 1887, Northampton, Cause Unkn., 2 months, Edwin & Mary, Northampton, Single, Edwin Lawson, Father source

LAWSON, Isaac WM July 9, 1891, Northampton, Cholera Infantum, 8 months, A. D. & Sarah, Northampton, Single, A. D. Lawson, Father source

LEATHERBURY, ------- CM Aug. 15, 1896, Northampton, Pneumonia, 1, Nancy Leatherbury, Northampton, Single, Litt Leatherbury, Brother source

LEATHERBURY, Chas. CM May 1875, Northampton, Old Age, 80, Parents Unkn., Birth Unkn., Laborer, Neighbor source

LEATHERBURY, George CM May, 10, 1876, Northampton, Old Age, 70, Matthew & Vianes, Northampton, Single, T. E. Leatherbury, Friend source

LeCATO, ------- CF Aug. 3, 1895, Northampton, Croup, 4 months, Jennie LeCato, Northampton, Single, Joseph Widgen, Neighbor source

LeCATO, ------- CM Dec. 15, 1891, Northampton, La Grippe, 24 days, L. T & Susan, Northampton, Single, L. T. LeCato, Father source

LeCATO, E. F. WM Mar. 15, 1891, Chicago, Ill., Inflammation of Bowels, 30, L. T. & Cordelia, Acco. Co., Clerk, Married, L. T. LeCato, Father source

LeCATO, Sallie L. WF Jan. 3, 1891, Northampton, Pneumonia, 40, Wm. & Susan Tilton, N. C., Single, L. T. LeCato, Father source

LEE, Ella W. CF Mar. 17, 1891, Northampton, Burned, 11, Isaac & Josephine, Northampton, Single, Isaac Lee, Father source

LEWIS, ------- July 3, 1893, Northampton, Cause Unkn., 10 days, Chas. & Mattie, Northampton, Single, Mattie Lewis, Mother source

LEWIS, Adah CF Feb. 16, 1892, Northampton, Consumption, 45, Parents Unkn., Northampton, Laborer, Married, Geo. Beach, Friend source

LEWIS, Charles CM Dec. 15, 1896, Northampton, Accident, 30, Charles & Louisa, Northampton, Laborer, Married, L. N. Sturgis, Friend source

LEWIS, Littleton W. WM Feb. 20, 1873, Northampton, Infantile, 6 days, John R. & Rachel, Northampton, Single, Jno. R. Lewis, Father source

LEWIS, Margaret E. WF Apr. 1, 1876, Northampton, Pleurisy, 30, William & Mary, Northampton, Laban T. Lewis, Husband source

LILISTON, E. C. WM Apr. 23, 1892, Northampton, Grippee, 42, E. C. & Mahala, Acco. Co., Farmer, Married, Mrs. Liliston, Wife source

LINDSAY, Emma CF Dec. 22, 1895, Northampton, Drowned, 15 months, Frank & Susan, Northampton, Single, Seymour Lindsay, Sister source

LINDSAY, Imogene WF Jan. 14, 1893, Northampton, Tetanus, 17 days, W. C. & Mattie B., Northampton, Single, Rev. W. C. Lindsay, Father source

LINGO, ------- WM May 17, 1876, Northampton, Cause Unkn., 1 month, James & Susan, Northampton, Single, Susan Lingo, Mother source

LINGO, Ben. F. WM May 7, 1892, Northampton, Consumption, 50, Robt. & Maria, Northampton, Carpenter, Married, Mary Lingo, Wife source

LINGO, F. T. WM Sept. 17, 1891, Northampton, Blood Cancer, 14, J. E. & Susan, Northampton, Farmer, Single, J. E. Lingo, Father source

LINGO, Mary WF Sept. 19, 1892, Northampton, Croup, 9 months, Ben F. & Mary, Northampton, Single, Mary Lingo, Mother source

LINGO, Susan WF Mar. 24, 1896, Northampton, Tumor, 50, Ed & Eliza Lewis, Northampton, Married, J. E. Lingo, Husband source

LIPSCOME, Charles CM Apr. 20, 1874, Northampton, Pleurisy, 70, Chas. & Lucey, King William Co., Va., Single, Thos. J. Fitchett, Friend source

LITTLE, George BM Mar. 1880, Northampton, Trismus Nascent, 10 days, David L. & Mary S., Va. Va., Va., source unkn.

LITTLE, Robert BM May 1880, Northampton, Cholera Infantum, 1, Parents Unkn., Va., Single, Jas. M. McNutt, source (PR)

LOTHAND, Garrett WM Nov. 1875, Northampton, Cause Unkn., 21 days, Wm. T. & Mary, Birth Unkn., Single, Wm. T. Lothand, Father source

LUKER, ------- CM Sept. 7, 1892, Northampton, Diphtheria, 2, Geo. & Cordie, Northampton, Single, Geo. Luker, Father source

MADDOX, Francis WM July 1873, Northampton, Cause Unkn., 45, Parents Unkn., Birth Unkn., Farmer, source unkn.

MAJOR, ------- WF Apr. 1880, Northampton, Stillborn, 0 days, Parents Unkn., Va., Va., Va., at home, Single, source unkn.

MAJOR, ------- WM Aug. 4, 1878, Northampton, Infantile, 4 months, James C. & Olevia, Northampton, Single, James Major, Father source

MAJOR, Clara WF Oct. 10, 1892, Northampton, Dysentery, 26, Robt. W. & Mary, Northampton, Married, S. Downing, Husband source

MAJOR, Matilda WF Oct. 1879, Northampton, Dropsy, 32, Parents Unkn., Va., Va., Va., Keeping House, Married, source unkn.

MAJOR, May WF Oct. 13, 1892, Northampton, Dysentery, 5 months, S. Downing & Clara, Northampton, Single, S. Downing, Father source

MAJOR, Olevia WF Aug. 28, 1878, Northampton, Consumption, 30, Severn E. & Bridget Nottingham, Northampton, James C. Husband, Severn E. Nottingham, Father source

MALLETT, Elizabeth WF Dec. 8, 1892, Northampton, Cholera Infantum, 3 months, J. T. & Mamie, Northampton, Single, J. T. Mallett, Father source

MALLETT, Isaac WM June 2, 1894, Northampton, Bronchitis, 6, J. T. & Nannie, Northampton, Mrs. E. T. Turner, Friend source

MANNING, A. J. WM May 7, 1894, Northampton, Blood Poison, 63, Wm. & Fannie, Norfolk, Va., Hotel Keeper, Married, Mrs. Geo. W. Chea, Daughter source

MAPP, ------- CF Aug. 15, 1894, Northampton, Cause Unkn., 8 days, Thos. & Mary, Northampton, Single, Thos. Mapp, Father source

MAPP, ------- CF Dec. 29, 1877, Northampton, Infantile, 2 days, George & Hellen, Northampton, Single, Hellen Mapp, Mother source

MAPP, ------- CF Mar. 10, 1876, Northampton, Cause Unkn., 4 months, Severn & Adah, Northampton, Single, Severn Mapp, Father source

MAPP, ------- WF Feb. 14, 1876, Northampton, Cause Unkn., 3 days, Edwd. & Esther, Northampton, Single, Esther Mapp, Mother source

MAPP, Annie CF Sept. 10, 1878, Northampton, Consumption, 19, Sam & Adah, Northampton, Laborer, Single, Sam Mapp, Father source

MAPP, Bessie CF Nov. 14, 1893, Northampton, Burned, 2 months, John H. & Sarah J.. Northampton, Single, Isaac Lee, Grandfather source

MAPP, Bettie H. WF Apr. 10, 1893, Northampton, Burned to Death, 25, Jas. H. & S. M. Belote, Northampton, Married, J. C. Mapp, Husband source

MAPP, E. D. WM 1888, Northampton, Congestion of Brain, 22, V. A. Mapp, [Farmer?], Northampton, F. A. Mapp, Parent source

MAPP, Elizabeth WF Oct. 1873, Northampton, Consumption, 58 yrs. 1 mon., George & Elizabeth Scott, Northampton, Single, Victor A. Mapp, Son source

MAPP, Frank B. WM July 25, 1893, Northampton, Dysentery, 62, F. B. & Margaret, Northampton, Farmer, Married, F. P. Mapp, Son source

MAPP, Geo. WM Oct. 15, 1884, Northampton, Dropsy, 1 yr. 6 mos., Fred & Sally, Northampton, Single, L. T. Johnson, source

MAPP, Harriett WF Nov. 27, 1871, Northampton, Typhoid Fever, 38, Chas. & Leah Fitchett, Married, Husband source [Farmer?]

MAPP, Harry B. WM July 13, 1883, Northampton, Cholera Infantum, 4 months, Jno. A. & Margt., Birth Unkn., M. Sue Mapp, source

MAPP, Harry W. WM Oct. 4, 1892, Northampton, Typhoid, 31, Alfred & Sarah, Northampton, Merchant, Married, Wm. T. Johnson, Father-in-Law source

MAPP, J. A. CM Feb. 20, 1893, Northampton, Pneumonia, 3 yrs. 9 mos., Severn & Emily, Northampton, Single, Severn Mapp, Father source

MAPP, John C. WM Apr. 16, 1893, Northampton, Dysentery, 25, R. W. & Mary, Northampton, Merchant, Single, R. W. Mapp, Father source

MAPP, Kate WF Aug. 1872, Northampton, Child Birth, 35, Louis & Sarah Roberts, Northampton, E. W. Mapp, Husband source

MAPP, M. S. WF Dec. 30, 1891, Northampton, Child Birth, 39, H. P. & Margaret James, Northampton, Married, W. J. Mapp Jr., Husband source

MAPP, Marg't. WF Sept. 1871, Northampton, Congestion, 7, A. N. H. & Laura, Northampton, Single, A. N. H. Mapp, Father source

MAPP, Peter CM May 1871, Northampton, Cause Unkn., 20, Parents Unkn., Northampton, Laborer, Single, Virginia Stephens, Friend source

MAPP, R. W. Jr. WM June 2, 1895, Northampton, Diabetes, 65, William & Mary, Northampton, Merchant, Married, Dr. G. P. Moore, Physician source

MAPP, R. W. Sr. WM Feb. 2, 1895, Northampton, Paralysis, 67, William & Betsy, Northampton, Merchant, Married, R. H. Berry, Neighbor source

MAPP, Robin WM Aug. 1873, Northampton, Bill Fever, 78, Robin & Peggy, Northampton, Farmer, Peggy Wife, Jno. R. Mapp, Son source

MAPP, Sally WF Nov. 30, 1883, Northampton, Typhoid Fever, 27, Arleus & Susan Henderson, Birth Unkn., F. G. Mapp, Husband source

MAPP, Sarah J. CF Nov. 14, 1893, Northampton, Burned, 21 yrs. 2 mos. 17 days, Isaac & Josephine Lee, Richmond, Va., Married, Isaac Lee, Father source

MAPP, Severn CM Aug. 15, 1893, Northampton, Consumption, 22, James & Sarah, Northampton, Sailor, Single, Jas. Mapp, Father source

MAPP, Tabbie CF Apr. 6, 1891, Northampton, Old Age, 84, Parents Unkn., Northampton, Laborer, Married, Lewis Winder, Friend source

MAPP, Thomas WM July 1872, Northampton, Typhoid, 14, Wm. W. & Marg't T., Northampton, Single, source unkn.

MAPP, Trower WM July 18, 1891, Accomac, Cholera Infantum, 9 months, A. N. H. & Natilia, Accomac, Single, A. N. H. Mapp, Father source

MAPP, Victor WM Oct. 1891, Northampton, Croup, 5, Geo. R. & Ellen, Northampton, Single, Geo. R. Mapp, Father source

MAPP, William BM Aug. 1879, Northampton, Consumption, 24, Parents Unkn., Va., Va., Va., Laborer, Single, Dr. Thomas Mapp, Physician source

MARINER, Ruth WF Oct. 17, 1891, Northampton, Dysentery, 7 months, Jno. T. & M. L., Northampton, Single, J. T. Mariner, Father source

MARRINER, ------- WF Oct. 19, 1892, Northampton, Dysentery, 4 months, John T. & Sallie, Northampton, Single, John T. Marriner, Father source

MARRINER, ------- WM July 6, 1893, Northampton, Brain Fever, 4 months, John T. & Maria L., Northampton, Single, John T. Marriner, Father source

MARSH, Manie WF July 17, 1896, Northampton, Pneumonia, 4, Fred & Maggie, Northampton, Single, Fred Marsh, Father source

MARTIN, Rose WF Sept. 17, 1883, Northampton, Old Age, 84, Major & Ann Clegg, Birth Unkn., Edwd. B. Johnson, source

MASON, ------- WM 1888, Northampton, Pneumonia, 8 months, Wm. T. Mason, [Merchant?], Northampton, Single, Jas. T. Mason, Parent source

MASON, Edward WM Oct. 15, 1893, Northampton, Dysentery, 8 mos. 5 days, John E. & Maggie, Northampton, Single, John E. Mason, Father source

MASON, Elizabeth CF Nov. 7, 1896, Northampton, Consumption, 40, Severn & Marg. Collins, Northampton, Married, Jas. Mason, Husband source

MASON, John CM July 20, 1878, Northampton, Cause Unkn., 48, Parents Unkn., Northampton, Laborer, Single, John T. Bell, Friend source

MASON, Mary L. Oct. 25, 1896, Northampton, Whooping Cough, 1, W. H. & Emma, Northampton, Single, Emma Mason, Mother source

MASON, Wm. A. CM 1888, Northampton, Scrofula, 4 months, Jas. Mason, [Laborer?], Northampton, Single, Jas. Mason, Parent source

MASSEY, Ellen WF 1888, Northampton, Burned to Death, 3, Jas. W. Massey, [Farmer?], Northampton, Single, Jas. W. Massey, Parent source

MASSEY, J. W. WM July 6, 1892, Northampton, Consumption, 36, Parents Unkn., Maryland, Farmer, Married, R. E. Floyd, Neighbor source

MATHEWS, Mary CF July 1875, Northampton, Heart Disease, 61, Parents Unkn., Birth Unkn., Neighbor source

MATTHEWS, Adah CF Nov. 16, 1896, Northampton, Consumption, 65, Robt. & Peggie, Northampton, Married, Geo. J. Matthews, Husband source

MATTHEWS, James CM Aug. 17, 1895, Northampton, Cholera E., 9 months, Thos. & Maria, Northampton, Single, Maria Matthews, Father source

MATTHEWS, Levi CM Mar. 1874, Eastville Township, Cause Unkn., 70, Parents Unkn., Northampton, Laborer, L. J. Goffigon, source

MATTHEWS, Nellie CF Dec. 28, 1894, Northampton, Croup, 2 months, William & Delia, Northampton, Single, Wm. Matthews, Father source

McGUIRE, Henry CM June 25, 1894, Acco. Co., Big Head, 6 months, Anderson & Martha, Acco. Co., Single, Anderson McGuire, Father source

McKANDESS?, ------- (2) CM Feb. 1873, Northampton, Infantile, 1 day, Wm. & Martha, Northampton, Single, Ellen Savage, Friend source

McKOWN, Ann WF Nov. 20, 1874, Northampton, Heart Disease, 68, Sev. & Betsey Nottingham, Northampton, House Keeper, Single, Washington Hunt, Friend source

McKOWN, Blanch WF May 16, 1896, Northampton, Croup, 8 months, Herbert & Annie, Northampton, Single, Herbert McKown, Father source

McKOWN, Infant WM Mar. 1880, Northampton, Cause Unkn., 20 days, Unkn. & Sallie McKown, Va. Va., Va., Single, source unkn.

McKOWN, Wm. WM Aug. 15, 1895, Northampton, Drowned, 34, Parents Unkn., Maryland, Sea Capt., Married, G. P. Moore, Neighbor source

McMATH, Samuel WM Dec. 13, 1877, Northampton, Congestive Chill, 58, Samuel & Virginia, Delaware, Farmer, Susan Wife, John McMath, Son source

McPHEARSON, ------- WF Sept. 1879, Northampton, Child Birth, 39, Parents Unkn., Va., Va., Va., Keeping Home, Married, source unkn.

MEARS, ------- CM July 7, 1892, Northampton, Cause Unkn., 1 month, Geo. & Lizzie, Northampton, Single, Geo. Mears, Father source

MEARS, ------- WF May 31, 1893, Northampton, Cause Unkn., 21 days, Geo. & Emily, Northampton, Single, Emily Mears, Mother source

MEARS, Annie WF Oct. 1879, Northampton, Malarial Fever, 8 months, Parents Unkn., Va., Single, Dr. S. P. Nottingham, Physician source (PR)

MEARS, Esther S. WF Dec. 17, 1884, Northampton, Pneumonia, 68, Shadrick & [Jemima?] Northampton, A. G. Godwin, source

MEARS, Henry S. WM May 10, 1896, Northampton, Kidney Disease, 8, W. T. & Margie, Northampton, Single, W. T. Mears, Father source

MEARS, Lizzie CF June 12, 1892, Northampton, Child Birth, 37, Levi & Rachel Turlington, Acco. Co., Laborer, Married, Geo. Mears, Husband source

MEARS, Samuel WM 1888, Northampton, Crying Fits, 10 days, Jas. T. Mears, [Mechanic?], Northampton, Single. Jas. T. Mears, Parent source

MEARS, Sarah A. CF Oct. 12, 1894, Northampton, Pneumonia, 8, Geo. & Mary, Northampton, Single, Geo. Mears, Father source

Northampton County, VA, Deaths from Death Register and Wills, 1871-1896

MEARS, Wm. J. WM Aug. 1879, Northampton, Congestion of Brain, 2, Parents Unkn., Va., Single, Dr. S. P. Nottingham, Physician source (PR)

MELSON, Mary WF Nov. 8, 1892, Northampton, Pneumonia, 66, John & Mary Taylor, Northampton, Married, J. T. Melson, Husband source

MELSON, Pearl WF Apr. 9, 1894, Northampton, Diarrhea, 1 month, W. I. & Maggie, Northampton, Single, W. I. Nelson, Father source

MELSON, William WM May 4, 1887, Northampton, Pneumonia, 75, Parents Unkn., Northampton, Farmer, Annie Melson, Wife source

MENICA, Laura BF Jan. 1880, Northampton, Consumption, 19, Parents Unkn., Va., Va., Va., Single, source unkn.

MESSICK, Sallie A. WF Oct. 28, 1893, Northampton, Congestion of Brain, 47, Joshua B. & Sallie Turner, Northampton, Married, J. T. Messick, Husband source

METCALF, Wm. T. WM May 12, 1884, Northampton, Drowned, 7, Thos. & Lucy, Northampton, Single, Thos. Metcalf, Father source

MILBY, James CM Mar. 2, 1891, Northampton, Pneumonia, 18, R. & Rebecca, Northampton, Laborer, Single, Geo. Garrison, Uncle source

MILES, Eliza WF Feb. 3, 1887, Northampton, Old Age, 72, Richard & Mary, Northampton, Laborer, Widow, A. B. Doughty, Friend source

MILES, Esther D. WF Feb. 16, 1896, Northampton, Consumption, 44, Jas. & Tabitha Ward, Northampton, Married, R. E. Miles, Husband source

MILES, John W. Jr. WM July 10, 1895, Northampton, Heart Disease, 23, John W. & Mary, Acco. Co., Single, John W. Miles Sr., Father source

MILES, Mary WF Oct. 11, 1893, Northampton, Typhoid Fever, 14, R. E. & Esther, Northampton, Single, R. E. Miles, Father source

MILLIGAN, Robt. WM Mar. 16, 1893, Northampton, Congestive Chill, 14, J. H. & Ida, Northampton, Clerk, Single, Clerk, J. H. Milligan Father source

MILLS, England CM May 12, 1894, Northampton, Cause Unkn., 2 days, England & Emory, Northampton, Single, England Mills Father source

MINGO, ------- C Born Dead Mar. 1871, Northampton, Infantile, Born Dead, Emeline Mingo, Northampton, Single, Emeline Mingo, Mother source

MINGO, James CM July 1872, Northampton, Infantile, 1 month, Jas. & Amy, Northampton, Single, source unkn.

MOODY, ------- CM Dec. 21, 1893, Northampton, Cause Unkn., 1 day, Henry & Florence, Northampton, Single, Florence Moody, Mother source

MOORE, -------- C Sex Unkn., Dec. 11, 1876, Northampton, Cause Unkn., 8 months, Jane Moore, Northampton, Single, Jane Moore, Mother source

MOORE, ------- CM Aug. 11, 1887, Northampton, Crying Fits, 6 days, John & Mary, Northampton, Single, John Moore, Father source

MOORE, ------- WM Aug. 23, 1876, Northampton, Summer Disease, 6 months, Abraham & Hennie, Northampton, Single, Abram Moore, Father source

Northampton County, VA, Deaths from Death Register and Wills, 1871-1896

MOORE, Arameah WF Aug. 24, 1876, Smith Island, Dropsy, 50, Parents Unkn., Ohio, Wife of Lt. House keeper, Married, Robert B. Moore, Husband source

MOORE, Arthur WM Dec. 4, 1878, Northampton, Bilious Fever, 7, Severn & Mary, Northampton, Single, Mary Moore, Mother source

MOORE, Catherine WF Aug. 10, 1876, Northampton, Cause Unkn., 4 mos. 6 days, Wm. H. & Matilda, Northampton, Single, Wm. H. Moore, Father source

MOORE, Fanny L. WF Mar. 10, 1876, Northampton, Cause Unkn., 3 days, Wash. & Hennie, Northampton, Single, Hennie Moore, Mother source

MOORE, Geo. CM May 14, 1893, Northampton, Consumption, 38, Parents Unkn., Northampton, Married, Mack Robinson, Friend source

MOORE, Geo. W. CM May 5, 1893, Northampton, Cause Unkn., 11, James & Lottie, Northampton, Laborer, Single, James Moore, Father source

MOORE, Ginny CF Dec. 20, 1876, Northampton, Cause Unkn., Age Unkn., Adain & Mary, Northampton, Single, Mary Moore, Mother source

MOORE, Grace WF Jan. 10, 1872, Northampton, Typhoid Fever, 40, Parents Unkn., Northampton, Married, Husband source

MOORE, John W. WM May 1, 1873, Northampton, Dropsy, 50 yrs. 3 mos., Abram & Betsy, Northampton, Fisherman, Single, Mack Moore, Uncle source

MOORE, Leonard WM Oct. 10, 1872, Northampton, Lockjaw, 16, Geo U. & Emily, Northampton, Single, Geo. U. Moore, Father source

MOORE, Levin WM Aug. 25, 1893, Northampton, Croup, 1 month, Isaac T. & Bettie L., Northampton, Single, Isaac T. Moore, Father source

MOORE, Lloyd WM Apr. 4, 1877, Northampton, Heart Disease, 50, Mathew & Betsy, Northampton, Minister, Sarah Moore, Wife source

MOORE, Mary CF 1888, Northampton, Cause Unkn., 4 months, Major & Susan Moses, [Farmer?], Northampton, Single, Major Moses, Parent source

MOORE, Pop WF Oct. 5, 1873, Northampton, Quinsey, 3 yrs. 4 mos. 2 days, William & Peggy, Northampton, Single, Mack Moore, Grandfather source

MOORE, Richard WM Dec. 1879, Northampton, Dropsy, 57, Abraham & Betsy, Va., Va., Va., Farmer, Harriet Wife, Dr. William Scott, Physician source

MOORE, Roland B. WM July 18, 1887, Northampton, Congestion of Brain, 2, Jesse & Mary, Northampton, Single, Jesse Moore, Father source

MOORE, Sam'l WM July 6, 1895, Northampton, Pneumonia, 62, Matthew & Mary, Northampton, Farmer, Married, J. E. Moore, Friend source

MOORE, William WM Mar. 1880, Northampton, Colic, 6 months, John N. & Margaret, Va., Va., Va., Single, S. P. Nottingham, source

MOORE, William. P. Jr. WM July 26, 1873, Northampton, Inflammation of Bowels, 26, William P. & Mary, Accomack, Co., Farmer, Single, Jno. C. P. Kellam, Brother-in-Law source

Northampton County, VA, Deaths from Death Register and Wills, 1871-1896

MOORE, Willie WM Mar. 10, 1896, Northampton, Pneumonia, 18, L. W. & Hennie, Northampton, Farmer, Single, L. W. Moore, Father source

MOORE, Zack P. WM Apr. 7, 1872, New York, Small Pox, 25, Thos. & Drucilla, Northampton, Sailor, Single, Drucilla Moore, Mother source

MORRIS, ------- CF Mar. 1884, Northampton, Cause Unkn., 9 days, Geo. & Sarah, Northampton, Single, Geo. Morris, Father source

MORRIS, ------- CM Feb. 28, 1885, Northampton, Cause Unkn., 0 days, Geo. & Sarah, Northampton, Single, Geo. Morris, Father source

MORRIS, ------- CM June 14, 1895, Northampton, Cause Unkn., 9 days, Cornelius & Mollie, Northampton, Single, Mollie Morris, Sister source

MORRIS, ------- CM Mar. 19, 1895, Northampton, Cause Unkn., 5 days, W. H. & Virgie, Northampton, Single, Ed Burton, Friend source

MORRIS, ------- CM Nov. 9, 1877, Northampton, Infantile, 11 days, Henry & Sallie, Northampton, Single, Henry Morris, Father source

MORRIS, ------- WF July 20, 1887, Northampton, Crying Fits, 4 days, Jacob & Susan, Northampton, Single, Jacob Morris, Father source

MORRIS, Alfred BM Mar. 1880, Northampton, Meningitis, 4, Unkn. & Henrietta, Va., Va., Va., Single, source unkn.

MORRIS, Cornelius CM Sept. 2, 1895, Northampton, Cholera E., 3 months, Cornelius & Mollie, Northampton, Single, Mollie Morris, Sister source

MORRIS, Edna L. CF Dec. 11, 1896, Northampton, Chol. Infantum, 6 months, Nat & Lucy, Northampton, Single, Lucy Morris, Mother source

MORRIS, Infant BM May 1880, Northampton, Convulsions, 8 days, Unkn. & Lucy Morris, Va., Va., Va., Single, source unkn.

MORRIS, Infant CF Sept. 10, 1872, Northampton, Crying Fits, 5 days, Ellen & Luke, Northampton, Luke Morris, Father source [Laborer?]

MORRIS, Infant Mar. 10, 1871, Northampton, Crying Fits, 2 days, Luke & Ellen, Northampton, Single, Luke Morris, Father source [Laborer?]

MORRIS, Jack CM June 1876, Northampton, Croup, 4, Caleb Morris, Northampton, Single, Caleb Morris, Father source

MORRIS, Luke CM May 9, 1883, Northampton, Phen. 70, Parents Unkn., Birth Unkn., Cornelius Morris, source

MORRIS, Marion CF July 10, 1895, Northampton, Diarrhea, 3, James & Rosa, Northampton, Single, Rosa Morris, Mother source

MORRIS, Martha CF Feb. 23, 1894, Northampton, Cholera Infantum, 1, Geo. & Martha, Northampton, Single, Geo. Morris, Father source

MORRIS, Nat CM Apr. 28, 1882, Northampton, Typhoid Pneumonia, 70, Sillie Morriss, Northampton, Farmer, Married, Wife source

MORRIS, Nathaniel BM Apr. 1880, Northampton, Typhoid Pneumonia, 68, Parents Unkn., Va., Va., Va., Farmer, Single, Dr. William J. Scott, Physician source

MORRIS, Sallie CF Feb. 19, 1877, Northampton, Bilious Fever, 9 yrs. 2 days, Caleb & Jane, Northampton, Laborer, Single, Caleb Morris, Father source

MORRIS, Wm. CM Feb. 16, 1893, Northampton, Congestion of Brain, 72, Parents Unkn., Acco. Co., Laborer, Married, James Morris, Son source

MORRIS, Wm. Sr. CM Feb. 16, 1893, Northampton, Cause Unkn., 62, Parents Unkn., Northampton, Laborer, Single, Sam'l Morris, Brother source

MOSES, ------- CM Nov. 14, 1878, Northampton, Crying Fits, 6 days, Nat & Catharine, Northampton, Laborer, Single, Nat Moses, Father source

MOSES, George CM Sept. 15, 1876, Northampton, Cause Unkn., 6, Cyrus & Francis, Northampton, Single, Cyrus Moses, Father source

MOSES, Levin CM Aug. 7, 1895, Northampton, Asthma, 72, Levin & Fannie, Northampton, S. W. Nottingham, Neighbor source

NEAL, Ruth WF Mar. 8, 1878, Northampton, Cause Unkn., 7 months, Hamilton S. & Elizabeth B., Northampton, Single, H. S, Neal, Father source

NEILASS, ------- WF Feb. 1894, Northampton, Cause Unkn., 2 months, John & Mary, Northampton, Single, E. S. Herald County Paper source

NELSON, Amanda CF May 1873, Northampton, Congestive Fever, 7, Jim & Mary, Northampton, Single, Mary Nelson, Mother source

NELSON, David CM Dec. 4, 1893, Northampton, Consumption, 77, Parents Unkn., Macon, Ga., Laborer, Married, Geo. E. Finney, Neighbor source

NELSON, Laura CF July 1, 1887, Northampton, Bilious Fever, 6 months, Parents Unkn., Northampton, Single, James Nelson, Friend source

NELSON, Lucy BF May 1880, Northampton, Pneumonia, 50, Parents Unkn., Va., Cook, Shadrack Baldwin Husband, Dr. S. P. Nottingham, Physician source (PR)

NELSON, Rosa CF Jan. 1873, Northampton, Pneumonia, 60, Wesley & Ruth, Accomac Co., Single, Ruth Nelson, Mother source

NELSON, Rosa CF July 4, 1892, Northampton, Cause Unkn., 1, David & Susan, Northampton, Single, David Nelson, Father source

NELSON, Sallie CF Feb. 24, 1878, Northampton, Measles, 18 months, Unkn. & Mary, Northampton, Single, Mary Nelson, Mother source

NICKERSON, John W. WM Jan. 1, 1894, Northampton, Dropsy, 3, Handy & Dora, Northampton, Single, Handy Nickerson, Father source

NOCK, ------- WM Sept. 13, 1887, Northampton, Cause Unkn., 4 months, William & Mary, Northampton, Single, William Nock, Father source

NOTTINGHAM, ------- Sept. 30, 1872, Northampton, Infantile, 12 days, Candis Nottingham, Single, Thos. H. Nottingham, where died source

NOTTINGHAM, ------- CM 1888, Northampton, Crying Fits, 8 days, Samuel & Susan, [Farmer?], Northampton, Single, Sam Nottingham, Parent source

NOTTINGHAM, ------- CM Apr. 15, 1874, Northampton, Cause Unkn., 10 days, Nelson & Sarah, Northampton, Single, Ed. W. Nottingham, Friend source

NOTTINGHAM, ------- CM Apr. 7, 1895, Northampton, Cause Unkn., 7 days, Robt. & Agnes, Northampton, Single, Agnes Nottingham, Mother source

NOTTINGHAM, ------- CM Feb. 10, 1878, Northampton, Cause Unkn., 4 days, Unkn. & Jane Nottingham, Northampton, Jane Nottingham, Mother source

NOTTINGHAM, ------- CM Sept. 1882, Northampton, Cause Unkn. , 4 days, Jno. Nottingham, Northampton, Single, Jno. Nottingham, Father source

NOTTINGHAM, ------- WF Feb. 1875, Northampton, Cause Unkn., 7 days, Severn E. & Lucretia, Birth Unkn., Single, Severn E. Nottingham, Father source

NOTTINGHAM, ------- WF July 1875, Northampton, Cause Unkn., 7 days, Cary F. & Mary, Birth Unkn., Single, Cary F. Nottingham, Father source

NOTTINGHAM, ------- WF Mar. 15, 1895, Northampton, Cause Unkn., 1 day, Wm. & Mary, Northampton, Single, Agnes Nottingham, Friend source

NOTTINGHAM, ------- WF May 18, 1877, Northampton, Infantile, 1 mo. 4 days, Lloyd & Sallie, Northampton, Single, Lloyd Nottingham, Father source

NOTTINGHAM, ------- WF 1882 Northampton, Pneumonia, 6 days, Jno. Nottingham, Northampton, Single, Mother source

NOTTINGHAM, ------- WF Sept. 2, 1873, Northampton, Cause Unkn., 10 days, Richard V. & Julia, Northampton, Single, B. V. Nottingham, Father source

NOTTINGHAM, ------- WM Jan. 12, 1884, Northampton, Cause Unkn., 7 days, Geo. U. & Ellena, Northampton, Single, Geo. U. Nottingham, Father source

NOTTINGHAM, ------- WM Jan. 21, 1873, Northampton, Cause Unkn., 21 days, William Th. & Mary, Northampton, Single, Wm. Thos. Nottingham, Father source

NOTTINGHAM, ------- WM July 1874, Eastville Township, Cause Unkn., Age Unkn., R. V. & Juliet, Eastville Township, R. V. Nottingham, Father source

NOTTINGHAM, ------- WM May 10, 1877, Northampton, Infantile, 2 days, John R. & Isadora, Northampton, Single, John R. Nottingham, Father source

NOTTINGHAM, ------- WM Nov. 25, 1884, Northampton, Cause Unkn., 2 months, Sam & Emily, Northampton, Single, Sam Nottingham, Father source

NOTTINGHAM, ------- WM Sept. 11, 1885, Northampton, Cause Unkn., 0, Jno. E. & Mary C., Northampton, Single, Jno. Edwd. Nottingham, Father source

NOTTINGHAM, ------- WF Sept. 25, 1885, Northampton, Cause Unkn., 10 days, Cary F. & Mary, Northampton, Single, Cary F. Nottingham, Father source

NOTTINGHAM, ------- WM Sept. 19, 1893, Northampton, Cause Unkn., 2 days, Wm. & Bettie, Northampton, Single, Wm. Nottingham, Father source

NOTTINGHAM, Alonzo WM Jan. 8, 1887, Northampton, Croup, 1 month, Cary & Mary, Northampton, Single, Cary Nottingham, Father source

NOTTINGHAM, Annie WF Oct. 15, 1872, Northampton, Croup, 10, Sallie & Henry, Northampton, Single, Henry Nottingham, Father source [Farmer?]

NOTTINGHAM, Arintha WF May 28, 1887, Northampton, Typhoid Fever, 58, John & Leah Fitchett, Northampton, Clay Nottingham, Husband source

NOTTINGHAM, Chas. WM Aug. 10, 1872, Northampton, Billious Fever, 3, Sue & Jacob, Northampton, Single, Jacob Nottingham, Father source [Farmer?]

NOTINGHAM, E. H. WM July 1879, Northampton, Water on the Brain, 1, John R. & Isadora A. J.., Va., Va., Va., Single, Scott & Wilkins, source

NOTTINGHAM, Edgar WM Mar. 25, 1877, Northampton, Large Head, 3, John R. & Isadora, Northampton, Single, John R. Nottingham, Father source

NOTTINGHAM, Elizabeth WF May 7, 1871, Northampton, Worms, 9 months, Severn &, Lucretia, Northampton, Single, Severn Nottingham, Father source [Farmer?]

NOTTINGHAM, Ella CF June 10, 1878, Northampton, Worms, 4, Abram & Silla, Northampton, Single, Silla Nottingham, Mother source

NOTTINGHAM, Ella K. WF Mar. 20, 1883, Northampton, Parae, 1 yr. 7 mos. 18 days, Sev. T. & Emmy, Birth Unkn., Sev. T. Notthingham, Father source

NOTTINGHAM, Ellen CF Dec. 10, 1872, Northampton, Diptheria, 30, Bennet & Sarah, Northampton, Seamstress, Single, Geo. Beckett, Brother source

NOTTINGHAM, Fanny CF Aug. 1871, Northampton, Consumption, 20, Adam Nottingham, Northampton, Single, Jas. A. Smith, Neighbor Friend source

NOTTINGHAM, Florence CF Mar. 23, 1873, Northampton, Small Pox, 3 yrs. 3 mos., Unkn. & Laura Taylor, Northampton, Single, Laura Taylor, Mother source

NOTTINGHAM, Hattie, WF July 29, 1893, Northampton, Typhoid Fever, 13, Wm. & Bettie, Northampton, Single, Wm. Nottingham, Father source

NOTTINGHAM, Henry BM Sept. 1879, Northampton, Paralysis, 73, Parents Unkn., Va, Va., Va., Farm Laborer, Single, source unkn.

NOTTINGHAM, Henry CM July 1871, Northampton, Diarrhea, 55, Parents Unkn., Northampton, Carpenter, Single, source blank

NOTTINGHAM, Hezakiah WM May 18, 1878, Northampton, Congestive Chill, 21 days, Wm. T. & Lizzie, Northampton, Wm. T. Nottingham, Father source

NOTTINGHAM, Hezekiah WM Oct. 10, 1877, Northampton, Measles, 2, William & Elizabeth, Northampton, Single, William Nottingham, Father source

NOTTINGHAM, Ida CF Oct. 24, 1878, Northampton, Typhoid Fever, 4, Sol & Annie, Northampton, Single, Sol Nottingham, Father source

NOTTINGHAM, Infant BM Sept. 1879, Northampton, Debility, 4 days, John & Fannie, Va., Va., Va., Single, source unkn.

NOTTINGHAM, Infant WM Oct. 24, 1872, Northampton, Crying Fits, 6 days, Bettie & Henry, Northampton, Single, Henry Nottingham, Father source [Farmer?]

NOTTINGHAM, Infant WM Sept. 8, 1872, Northampton, Crying Fits, 2 days, Rinie & T. E., Northampton, Single, T. E. Nottingham, Father source [Merchant?]

NOTTINGHAM, Jacob T. WM Sept. 11, 1894, Northampton, Cancer, 59, Jacob & Rosa, Northampton, Farmer, Married, Henry Nottingham, Son source

NOTTINGHAM, James CM Nov. 20, 1872, Northampton, Neglect, 2, Annie & Josh, Northampton, Single, Physician source, Josh Father [Laborer?]

NOTTINGHAM, James B. WM Jan. 8, 1873, Northampton, Heart Disease, 69 Yrs., 3 mos., Sev. & Betsey, Northampton, Farmer, Ann Wife, John A. Nottingham, Son source

NOTTINGHAM, Jas. S. WM June 10, 1872, Northampton, Cholera Infantum, 8 mos., Cary & Mary, Northampton, Single, Cary Nottingham, Father source

NOTTINGHAM, Jno. E. Sr. WM Apr. 1, 1885, Northampton, Old Age, 76, Severn & Betsy, Northampton, Married, Lucius S. Nottingham, source

NOTTINGHAM, Jno. W. WM Oct. 1875, Northampton, Dissipation, 40, Parents Unkn., Birth Unkn., R. Nottingham, source

NOTTINGHAM, John WM May 1880, Northampton, Crying Fits, 7 days, John R. & Isadora A. J., Va., Va., Va., Single, source unkn.

NOTTINGHAM, John C. WM Aug. 19, 1876, Northampton, Cause Unkn., 5 mos. 28 days, Francis & Vandalia, Northampton, Single, Francis Nottingham, Father source

NOTTINGHAM, Joseph D. WM Sept. 1, 1873, Northampton, Old Age, 73, Joseph & Mary, Northampton, Farmer, Single, Wm. Dix, Son-in-Law source

NOTTINGHAM, Leah CF Oct. 3, 1896, Northampton, Quinzy, 2, Bennett & Sallie, Northampton, Single, Sallie Nottingham, Mother source

NOTTINGHAM, Leah WF May 26, 1876, Northampton, Heart Disease, 72, John & Lucy Carpenter, Northampton, Lady, Widow, Rob. Nottingham, Son-in-Law source

NOTTINGHAM, Leonard B. WM Feb. 16, 1877, Northampton, Broken down Nerves, 72, Jacob & Sallie, Northampton, Merchant, Emily Wife, L. J. Nottingham, Son source

NOTTINGHAM, Leta CM Jan. 9, 1876, Northampton, Pleurisy, 80, Parents Unkn., Northampton, Laborer, Luther L. Nottingham, Neighbor source

NOTTINGHAM, Lilie WF Oct.8, 1871, Northampton, Diphtheria, 4, Jno. & Gennie, Northampton, Jno. Nottingham, Father source [Farmer?]

NOTTINGHAM, Maria WF Apr. 8, 1876, Northampton, Dropsy, Age Unkn., Thos. W. & Sarah Wilkins, Northampton, Married, Fred E. Nottingham, Husband source

NOTTINGHAM, Maria WF Jan. 9, 1875, Northampton, Whooping Cough, 10 months, L. J. & Ellen, Birth Unkn., Single, L. J. Nottingham, Father source

NOTTINGHAM, Mary CF Oct. 9, 1878, Northampton, Cause Unkn., 50, Parents Unkn., Northampton, Laborer, Single, Geo. Stephens, Friend source

NOTTINGHAM, Mary WF Apr. 27, 1884, Northampton, Dysentery, 23, Thos. & Sally Spady, Northampton, Wm. Thos. Nottingham, source

NOTTINGHAM, R. W. WM Dec. 1879, Northampton, Acute Tuberculosis, 42, Parents Unkn., Va., Merchant, Married, W. W. Wilkins, source (PR)

NOTTINGHAM, Roberta WF June 20, 1893, Northampton, Cause Unkn., 9 months, Robt. & Lizzie, Northampton, Single, Fannie Widgen, Friend source

NOTTINGHAM, Robt. WM June 10, 1893, Northampton, Cause Unkn., 28, W. C. & Lizzie, Northampton, Farmer, Married, J. T. Widgen, Friend source

NOTTINGHAM, Robt. L. WM July 28, 1894, Northampton, Pneumonia, 32, W. T. & Elizabeth, Northampton, Farmer, Married, Elizabeth Nottingham, Mother source

NOTTINGHAM, Ruth V. WF June 10, 1892, Northampton, Cholera Infantum, 6 months, Zeb & Mary A., Northampton, Single, Zeb Nottingham, Father source

NOTTINGHAM, S. T. WM May 12, 1894, Northampton, Dropsy, 57, Thos. & Mary A., Northampton, Mechanic, Married, John E. Nottingham, Brother source

NOTTINGHAM, Sallie CF Oct. 17, 1885, Northampton, Diphtheria, 5, Sam & Emily, Northampton, Single, Sam Nottingham, Father source

NOTTINGHAM, Sallie WF July 8, 1877, Northampton, Cholera Infantum, 6 months, William T. & Sallie, Northampton, Single, Sallie Nottingham, Mother source

NOTTINGHAM, Sallie A. WF Dec. 15, 1892, Northampton, Pneumonia, 56, John & Maria Godwin, Northampton, Married, Wm. T. Nottingham, Husband source

NOTTINGHAM, Sallie P. WF Mar. 28, 1891, Northampton, Kidney Affection, 42, Wm. & Sarah Parker, Northampton, Married, L. W. Nottingham, Husband source

NOTTINGHAM, Samuel Y. WM June 28, 1873, Northampton, Broken down Nerves, 69, William & Peggy, Northampton, Farmer, Leah Wife, Wm. P. Nottingham, Brother source

NOTTINGHAM, Sophie WF Oct. 31, 1896, Northampton, Heart Failure, 53, J. W. & Sophia E. Thomas, Northampton, Married, B. F. Nottingham, Husband source

NOTTINGHAM, Southey CM June 12, 1887, Northampton, Infirmity, 83, Parents Unkn., Northampton, Laborer, Married, William Smith, Friend source

NOTTINGHAM, Susan A. WF Dec. 23, 1871, Northampton, Brain Fever, 43 yrs. 6 mos., Wm. & Ann Cutler, Northampton, Married, Jno. R. Nottingham, Husband source

NOTTINGHAM, Thos. H. WM Aug. 2, 1893, Northampton, Pneumonia, 45, Thos. & Mary, Northampton, Farmer, Married, Geo. Nottingham, Friend source

NOTTINGHAM, Thos. H. WM Nov. 12, 1884, Northampton, Cause Unkn., 5 mos. 12 days, Lev. T. & Emory, Northampton, Single, Sev. T. Nottingham, source

NOTTINGHAM, Virginia F. WF Oct. 24, 1892, Northampton, Cancer, 54, Sam'l & Eliz. Face, Norfolk, Va., Married, John A. Nottingham, Husband source

NOTTINGHAM, W. R. WM July 21, 1892, Northampton, Consumption, 28, W. R. & Sallie, Northampton, Farmer, Married, Mrs. Widgen, Sister-in-Law source

NOTTINGHAM, W. R. WM Sept. 12, 1896, Northampton, Cholera Infantum, 4 months, Southey & Nora, Northampton, Single, Southey Nottingham, Father source

NOTTINGHAM, William WM May 6, 1871, Northampton, Dropsy, 21, Joseph & Fannie, Northampton, Fannie Nottingham, Mother source, Joseph [Farmer?]

Northampton County, VA, Deaths from Death Register and Wills, 1871-1896

NOTTINGHAM, William WM Oct. 25, 1872, Northampton, Croup, 8, Sallie & Henry, Northampton, Single, Henry Nottingham, Father source [Farmer?]

NOTTINGHAM, Wm. J. WM Jan. 9, 1893, Northampton, Paralysis, 81, Wm. & Susie, Northampton, Married, Geo. Nottingham, Son source

NOTTINGHAM, Wm. K. Jan. 24, 1892, Congestive Chill, 26, John E. & Mary, Northampton, Co. Surveyor, Single, John E. Nottingham, Father source

NOTTINGHAM, Wm. P. WM Dec. 16, 1876, Northampton, Neuralgia of Heart, 70 yrs. 6 mos. 28 days, Wm. & Margt., Northampton, Farmer, Widower, Comfort Nottingham, Daughter source

OFFER, Martha E. CF June 13, 1895, Northampton, Paralysis, 65, Rhodie Sisco, Maryland, Married, Richard Satchel, Son-in-Law source

ONLY, Esther WF Apr. 12, 1876, Northampton, Cause Unkn., 4, Jno. & Esther, Northampton, Single, John Only, Father source

ONLY, Frank WM Apr. 28, 1892, Northampton, Bronchitis, 56, John & Lovey, Acco. Co., Laborer, Single, John H. Only, Brother source

ONLY, Isaac CM Dec. 1874, Northampton, Consumption, 28, Parents Unkn., Birth Unkn., Single, A. Thomas, Friend source

ONLY, Isaac CM Feb. 1875, Northampton, Consumption, 35, Parents Unkn., Birth Unkn., Neighbor source

ONLY, Manie CF Sept. 2, 1895, Northampton, Cholera E., 3 months, Frank & Margaret, Northampton, Single, Frank Only, Father source

ONLY, Margt. WF Oct. 2, 1885, Northampton,, Cause Unkn., 2 yrs. 6 mos., Jno. & Mary, Northampton, Single, Jno. Only, Father source

OUTEN, Infant WF Aug. 18, 1871, Northampton, Crying Fits, 2 days, Isaac & Annie, Northampton, Single, Isaac Outen, Father source [Farmer?]

OUTTEN, Elizabeth WF May 2, 1895, Northampton, Croup, 6, W. D. & Mary, Northampton, Single, W. D. Outten, Father source

PALMER/PARMER, Catharine CF 1888, Northampton, Typhoid Fever, 51, Peter Parmer, [Farmer?], Northampton, Peter Parmer, Parent source

PALMER, Ellen BF Sept. 1879, Northampton, Diphtheria, 35, Parents Unkn., Va., Va., Va., Keeping House, Married, Dr. W. A. Thom, Physician source

PALMER, Ellen CF Dec. 25, 1892, Northampton, Cause Unkn., 6 months, Henry & Mary, Northampton, Single, Mary Palmer, Mother source

PALMER, Mary E. CF Aug. 2, 1895, Northampton, Cancer, 26, Sarah Simpkins, Northampton, Geo. Beckett, Brother source

PALMER, Missouri CF Mar. 1, 1873, Northampton, Typhoid Fever, 30, Jim & Maria Spady, Northampton, Jim Spady, Father source

PALMER, Nim BM Mar. 1880, Northampton, Old Age, 85, Parents Unkn., Va., Va., Va., Farmer, Married, source unkn.

~~PALMER, Rachel A. BF June 1879, Northampton, Cause Unkn., 1, Joseph & Bethanie, Va., Va., Va., Single, Dr. Thomas Mapp, Physician source~~

PALMER, Sam CM Aug. 8, 1896, Northampton, Spasms, 12, Henry & Mary, Northampton, Laborer, Single, Henry Palmer, Father source

PARAMORE, Raymond CM Sept. 10, 1878, Northampton, Old Age, 88, Parents Unkn., Hampton, Va., Laborer, Single, C. L. Wyatt, Friend source

PAREMORE, Raymond CM Oct. 9, 1877, Northampton, Old Age, 78, Parents Unkn., Northampton, Laborer, Single, Fannie Johnson, Friend source

PARKER, ------- WF Oct. 3, 1884, Northampton, Cause Unkn., 1 day, Hy "Henry" G. & Susan R., Northampton, Single, Hy "Henry" G. Parker, Father source

PARKER, Ann G. WF May 28, 1883, Northampton, Old Age, 88, Jno. & Lucy Stratton, Birth Unkn., Alfred Parker, source

PARKER, Anna WF May 18, 1883, Northampton, Cause Unkn., 24, Wm. & Ann Nottingham, Birth Unkn., Jno. J. Parker, Husband source

PARKER, Emiline CF Aug. 10, 1896, Northampton, Gen. Debility, 69, George & Mary Kelly, Northampton, Laborer, Married, Henry Roberts, Friend source

PARKER, Joseph WM Mar. 6, 1893, Northampton, Cause Unkn., 36, Parents Unkn., Northampton, Laborer, Single, John R. Read, Friend source

PARKER, Susan CF Dec. 23, 1894, Northampton, Consumption, 50, John & Millie Ward, Acco. Co., Married, Sev. Parker, Husband source

PARKER, Tantha WF Feb. 13, 1885, Northampton, Heart Disease, 59, Parents Unkn., Married, Jno. J. Parker, source

PARKER, Wm. CM Feb. 14, 1878, Northampton, Old Age, 91, Parents Unkn., Norfolk Co. Va., Preacher, Single, L. J. Goffigon, Friend source

PARKS, ------- WF Dec. 15, 1895, Northampton, Cause Unkn., 2 months, J. P. & Marietta, Northampton, Single, J. P. Parks, Father source

PARRAMORE, Mary CF Aug. 30, 1893, Northampton, Dysentery, 2 mos. 12 days, James & Rosa, Northampton, Single, Jas. Parramore, Father source

PARSONS, Emily L. WF Jan. 4, 1887, Northampton, Cause Unkn., 6 months, John & Mary, Northampton, Single, John Parsons, Father source

PARSONS, Susan WF June 1875, Northampton, Dropsy, 24, Frank & Rosey, Birth Unkn., Frank Parsons, Father source

PEAD, Georgeanna CF Aug. 1891, Northampton, Typhoid Fever, 20, Mitchel & Mary, Northampton, Laborer, Married, Isaac Peed, Father-in-Law source

PEAD, Mary CF July 7, 1891, Northampton, Typhoid Fever, 30, Geo. & Mary Jacob, Northampton, Laborer, Married, Isaac Peed, Father-in-Law source

PEARSON, Emma M. WF Mar. 15, 1893, Northampton, Cancer, 50, Parents Unkn., Northampton, Single, John Hargis, Son-in-Law source

PEARSON, Maria WF 1888, Northampton, Old Age, 93, Zac. Pearson, Northampton, Married, Zac. Pearson source

PEARSON, Stoakley WM June 16, 1875, Northampton, Consumption, 45, Parents Unkn., Birth Unkn., Son source

PEED, ------- CM Aug. 1, 1876, Northampton, Sore Throat, 6, Cordelia Peed, Northampton, Single, Cordelia Peed, Mother source

PEED, Fanny CF Feb. 5, 1876, Northampton, Pneumonia, 55, Severn & Elisha, Northampton, Laborer, Single, Elisha Peed, Mother source

Northampton County, VA, Deaths from Death Register and Wills, 1871-1896

PEED, Isaac CM June 19, 1876, Northampton, Cause Unkn., 10 days, Isaac & Mary, Northampton, Single, Isaac Peed, Father source

PEED, Mary CF 1888, Northampton, Old Age, 80, Isaac Peed, Northampton, Married, Isaac Peed, Parent source

PERKINS, Emily CF Oct. 20, 1878, Northampton, Worms, 6 months, Henry & Emily, Northampton, Single, Emily Perkins, Mother source

PERKINS, Mary CF Jan. 10, 1878, Northampton, Smothered, 1 day, Unkn. & Mary, Northampton, Single, Mary Perkins, Mother source

PERKINS, Mollie CF Dec. 4, 1895, Northampton, Bronchitis, 2 months, Henry & Clara, Northampton, Single, Henry Perkins, Father source

PERKINS, Patience CF June 8, 1893, Northampton, Congestion of Brain, 61, Major & Ibby Collins, Northampton, Married, Mattie Lewis, Daughter source

PETERSON or DARBY, William CM Dec. 18, 1873, Northampton, Cause Unkn., 70 yrs. 5 mos., Peter & Nelly Darby, Northampton, Single, Rich. Costin, Neighbor source

PHILIPS, Evans WM Nov. 30, 1876, Northampton, Gangrene, 45, Abel R. & Margt., Accomack, Married, Patsy Philips, Widow source

PHILLIPS, Aaron CM Aug. 2, 1895, Northampton, Dysentery, 7 months, Custis & Celia, Northampton, Single, Celia Phillips, Mother source

PHILLIPS, Custis CM Nov. 13, 1895, Northampton, Consumption, 45, Mary Peed, Northampton, Farmer, Married, Celia Phillips, Wife source

PHILLIPS, George WM Jan. 1880, Northampton, Convulsions, 6 months, Parents Unkn., Va., Single, G. W. Smith, source (PR)

PHILLIPS, George C. WM Oct. 2, 1896, Northampton, Pneumonia, 69, George C. & Catharine, Acco. Co., Farmer, Widower, Geo. R. Phillips, Son source

PHILLIPS, Maude C. WF Jan. 19, 1893, Northampton, Burned, 9, Geo. R. & Sadie A., Acco. Co., Single, Geo. R. Phillips, Father source

PHILLIPS, Zoro. WM Mar. 16, 1893, Northampton, Cause Unkn., 75, Parents Unkn., Northampton, Merchant, Married, Mrs. Phillips, Wife source

PITTS, ------- CM June 1891, Northampton, Croup, 4 months, Wm. & Sarah, Northampton, Single, Nat Churn, Neighbor source

PITTS, ------- CM Mar. 27, 1883, Northampton, Cause Unkn. 26 days, Wm. & Sarah Pitts, Birth Unkn., Wm. Pitts, Father source

PITTS, Annie J. CF July 11, 1891, Northampton, Cause Unkn., 7 months, Geo. & Annie, Northampton, Single, Nat Churn, Neighbor source

PITTS, John CM Nov. 1, 1896, Northampton, Dyspepsia, 54, Jno. & Peggie, Northampton, Laborer, Married, Sallie Mapp, Sister source

PITTS, Major WM Sept. 1872, Northampton, Cause Unkn., 60, Parents Unkn., Northampton, Asa Savage, son source

PITTS, Nellie CF May 10, 1878, Northampton, Worms, 1, John & Nellie, Northampton, Single, John Pitts, Father source

PITTS, Oliver CM Aug. 12, 1894, Northampton, Cholera Infantum, 10 months, Wm. & Rebecca, Northampton, Single, Sallie Pitts, Grandmother source

Northampton County, VA, Deaths from Death Register and Wills, 1871-1896

PITTS, Parker CM Apr. 10, 1877, Northampton, Consumption, 61, Parents Unkn., Northampton, Farmer, Susan Pitts, Wife source

PITTS, Parker H. CM Apr. 10, 1878, Northampton, Consumption, 56, Parker & Peggie, Northampton, Farmer, Margaret Wife, Geo. M. Wescoat, Neighbor source

PITTS, Sarah CF Apr. 12, 1876, Northampton, Cause Unkn., 12, Jno. & Leah, Northampton, Single, Leah Pitts, Mother source

PITTS, Sydney WM Apr. 14, 1877, Northampton, Shot by A. P. Thom, 21 yrs. 9 mos., Edward & Margaret, Northampton, No Job, Single, Patrick Savage, Friend source

PITTS, William CM Feb. 1874, Northampton, Consumption, 35, Parker Pitts, Northampton, Single, A. Thomas, Friend source

PLATT, Capt. WM Aug. 1879, Northampton, Drowning, 50, Parents Unkn., Va., Sailor, Married, Wm. J. Scott, source (PR)

PLATT, Jobe WM Aug. 19, 1878, Northampton, Drowned, 60, Parents Unkn., New Jersey, Sea Capt., Single, Geo. M. Robbins, Undertaker source

PLATT, Wm. WM Aug. 19, 1878, Northampton, Drowned, 28, Parents Unkn., New Jersey, Sailor, Single, Geo. M. Robbins, Undertaker source

POOL, ------- CM Dec. 20, 1896, Northampton, Bled to Death, 4 days, Wm. & Margaret, Northampton, Single, Margaret Pool, Mother source

POOL, ------- CM Oct. 1874, Northampton, Infantile, 1 day, Sally Pool, Northampton, Ha Tankard, Neighbor source

POWELL, ------- CF Jan. 10, 1892, Northampton, Cause Unkn., 9 days, Isaac & Nervella, Northampton, Single, Isaac Powell, Father source

POWELL, ------- WF July 3, 1893, Northampton, Cholera Infantum, 30 days, Geo. H. & Lynnie, Northampton, Single, Geo. H. Powell, Father source

POWELL, ------- WF Mar. 15, 1895, Northampton, Cause Unkn., 2 days, C. D. & Claudie, Northampton, Single, C. D. Powell, Father source

POWELL, ------- WF Sept. 14, 1896, Northampton, Cause Unkn., 9 months, G. H. & Arintha, Northampton, Single, V. A. Mapp, Grand Father source

POWELL, Bennett CM Aug. 16, 1893, Northampton, Consumption, 42, Ben & Susan, Northampton, Laborer, Single, John R. Read, Neighbor source

POWELL, Bennett CM June 14, 1892, Northampton, Gravel, 74, Parents Unkn., Northampton, Laborer, Married, Richard Powell, Son source

POWELL, Handy CM June 25, 1873, Northampton, Lockjaw, 18 yrs., 9 mos., 2 days, Bennett & Eady, Northampton, Laborer, Single, Bennett Powell, Father source

POWELL, Holland CM Apr. 16, 1892, Northampton, Dyspepsia, 2, Richard & Hannah, Northampton, Single, Richard Powell, Father source

POWELL, Jackson B. WM Apr. 14, 1877, Northampton, Delirium Tremens, 70, John & Sallie, Northampton, Merchant, Single, Frank Powell, Nephew source

POWELL, John CM Feb. 28, 1893, Northampton, Cause Unkn., 42, Parents Unkn., Northampton, Laborer, Single, John R. Read, Neighbor source

POWELL, Levin CM Jan. 12, 1878, Northampton, Cause Unkn., 2, Unkn. & Adah, Northampton, Single, Adah Powell, Mother source

PRESS, ------- CF Oct. 12, 1878, Northampton, Cause Unkn., 7 days, Edmund & Sarah, Northampton, Single, Sarah Press, Mother source

PRINCE, Albert CM Sept. 1, 1895, Northampton, Pneumonia, 17, Albert & Juliet, Northampton, Laborer, Single, Henry Collins, Friend source

PRUDEN, Mamie CF July 27, 1893, Northampton, Dyspepsia, 22, Isaac & Eliza Riley, Northampton, Married, Willamina Moore, Sister source

PURNELL, Levin CM May 1871, Northampton, Brain Fever, 60, Parents Unkn., Northampton, Laborer, Single, Nat Schroeder, when died source

PYLE, ------- WM Oct. 1875, Northampton, Cause Unkn., 1 day, Isaac & Julia Pyle, Birth Unkn., Single, Isaac Pyle, Father source

PYLE, ------- WM Sept. 1, 1883, Northampton, Cause Unkn., 7 days, Isaac & Julia, Birth Unkn., Single, Isaac Pyle, Father source

PYLE, Wm. T. WM Oct. 7, 1874, Eastville Township, Cholera Infantum, 9 months, Isaac S. & Juliet, Eastville Township, Single, Isaac Pyle, Father source

RANDAL, Alfred BM June 1879, Northampton, Cause Unkn., 1 day, George & Fanny, Va., Va., Va., Single, source unkn.

RANDOLPH, Geo. CM Dec. 16, 1893, Northampton, Cholera Infantum, 2 months, James & Elizabeth, Northampton, Single, Elizabeth Williams, Grandmother source

RAYFIELD, ------- WM Oct. 10, 1876, Northampton, Cause Unkn., 2 months, Leon'd & Cath., Northampton, Single, Leon'd Rayfield, Father source

RAYFIELD, Fannie S. WF Jan. 6, 1872, Northampton, Diptheria, 4, Wesley & Lettie, Northampton, Single, Wesley Rayfield, Father source

RAYFIELD, Fanny S. WF Jan. 10, 1873, Northampton, Pleurisy, 6, Wesley & Letty, Northampton, Single, Wesley Rayfield, Father source

RAYFIELD, Minnie WF 1888, Northampton, Cause Unkn., 1 day, Wm. A. Rayfield, [Farmer?], Northampton, Single, Wm. A. Rayfield, Parent source

RAYFIELD, Wm. H. WM Oct. 4, 1892, Northampton, Typhoid, 37, Wesley & Lettie, Northampton, Farmer, Married, Henry S. Rayfield, Brother source

READ, ------- WM Sept. 1875, Northampton, Cause Unkn., 3 days, Jno. & Jane Read, Birth Unkn., Single, Neighbor source

READ, Alfred CM Jan. 12, 1895, Northampton, Congestion of Brain, 32, Smith & Mary, Northampton, Laborer, Single, Geo. Read, Brother source

READ, Alfred CM May 4, 1894, Northampton, Heart Disease, 75, Wm. & Esther, Northampton, Laborer, Married, Peggie Stephens, Daughter source

READ, Dr. Wm. P. WM Mar. 2, 1892, Northampton, Congestion of Heart?, 51, Enoch & Anna T., Acco. Co., Physician, Married, I. S. Ennis, Son-in-Law source

READ, Edward WM Dec. 15, 1876, Northampton, Infantile, 6 days, Parents Unkn., Accomack, Physician, Single, source unkn.

READ, Geo. H. WM Aug. 16, 1892, Northampton, Typhoid, 48, L. S. & Mary, Northampton, Merchant, Married, J. T. B. Hyslop, Physician source

READ, Isaac CM Feb. 2, 1893, Northampton, Cause Unkn., 42, Parents Unkn., Northampton, Laborer, Married, Sam'l Morris, Friend source

READ, John W. WM June 17, 1891, Northampton, Consumption, 67, Jno. T. & Mary, Birth Unkn., Painter, Married, Mrs. Jno. W. Reid, Wife source

READ, L. S. WM Feb. 5, 1892, Northampton, Heart Failure, 67, John & Lucy, Northampton, Life Ins. Agent, Married, J. T. B. Hyslop, Physician source

READ, Lucy CF Jan. 12, 1877, Northampton, Typhoid Fever, 11 yrs. 8 mos., Severn & Mary, Northampton, Laborer, Single, Mary Read, Mother source

READ, Margt. L. WF Sept. 26, 1872, Northampton, Consumption, 76, Litt. & Eliz., Savage, Northampton, Single, Dr. Jas. B. Floyd, Physician source

READ, Maria CF Apr. 9, 1876, Northampton, Cause Unkn., 1 month, Maria Read, Northampton, Single, Maria Read, Mother source

READ, Maria J. WF May 14, 1877, Northampton, Burned to Death, 60, Luther & Mary, Northampton, Single, Polly Underhill, Friend source

READ, Mary CF July 12, 1891, Northampton, Old Age, 79, Parents Unkn., Northampton, Laborer, Single, Geo. House, Friend source

READ, Peggy CF May 4, 1873, Northampton, Old Age, 74, Abel & Susan Bunting, Accomac Co., Single, H. Sample, Neighbor source

READ, Smith CM Aug. 8, 1895, Northampton, Consumption, 49, Arthur & Maria, Acco., Co., Farmer, Married, Geo. Read, Brother source

REDDEN, Dolly M. WF June 27, 1893, Northampton, Inflammation of Bowels, 15 months, J. J. & Rosalie, Accomac, Single, J. J. Redden, Father source

REED, Ada BF Apr. 1880, Northampton, Consumption, 60, Parents Unkn., Va., Va., Va., Servant, John W. Husband, source unkn.

REID, ------- WM 1872, Northampton, Infantile, 1 month, Jno. W. & Jane, Birth Unkn., Single, source unkn.

REID, Anna WF Sept. 1871, Northampton, Diphtheria, 7, Jno. W. & Ada, Northampton, Single, Jno. W. Reid, Father source

REID, Edward WM Sept. 1871, Northampton, Diphtheria, 9, Jno. W. & Ada, Northampton, Single, Jno. W. Reid, Father source

REID, Jno. W. WM Oct. 1871, Northampton, Diphtheria, 15, Jno. W. & Ada Reid, Northampton, Single, Jno. W. Reid, Father source

REID, Tena WF Aug. 1871, Northampton, Congestion, 4, Jno. W. & Jane, Northampton, Single, Jno. W. Reid Father source

REVEL, Custis CM June 1875, Northampton, Cause Unkn., 1, Custis & Martha Revel, Birth Unkn., Single, Custis Revel Father source

RHEA, Rebecca WF Dec. 15, 1892, Northampton, Consumption, 22, Parents Unkn., Birth Unkn., Married, Columbus Rhea, Husband source

RHEA, Rebecca H. WF Dec. 14, 1891, Halifax Co., Pneumonia, 24, Parents Unkn., Halifax Co. Va., Married, Wm. H. Rhea, Father-in-Law source

RICHARDSON, ------- WF Dec. 14, 1878, Northampton, Cause Unkn., 3 days, Johnathan & Mary, Birth Unkn., Single, Johnathan Richardson, Father source

RICHARDSON, ------- WF Dec. 30, 1875, Northampton, Cause Unkn., 1 day, Nathan & Anna, Birth Unkn., Single, Nathan Richardson, Father source

RICHARDSON, ------- WF Feb. 10, 1891, Northampton, Cause Unkn., 2 days, Thos. & Mary, Northampton, Single, Thos. Richardson, Father source

RICHARDSON, ------- WM July 27, 1894, Northampton, Cause Unkn., 2 days, E. D. & Mary, Northampton, Single, E. D. Richardson, Father source

RICHARDSON, Emily S. WF Nov. 10, 1876, Northampton, Child Birth, 22, Thos. & Emily, Northampton, Thos. Richardson, Father source

RICHARDSON, Georgiana WF Mar. 11, 1873, Northampton, Congestion, 10, Thomas Richardson, Northampton, Single, J. R. Richardson, Cousin source

RICHARDSON, Infant WF July 1879, Northampton, Convulsions, 11 days, Nathan & Anna, Va., Va., Va., Single, source unkn.

RICHARDSON, James CM Jan. 21, 1882, Shot, 5 yrs. 6 mos., Eliza Richardson, Northampton, Single, Father source

RICHARDSON, James A. WM Jan. 1880, Northampton, Gun Shot wound, 20, Parents Unkn., Elijah Father, Va., Va., Va., Sailor, source unkn.

RICHARDSON, Major WM Mar. 15, 1873, Northampton, Measles, 25, Jno. & Sarah, Northampton, Sailor, Single, John Richardson, Father source

RICHARDSON, Major WM May 1873, Northampton, Old Age, 80, John & Hessy, Northampton, Farmer, Single, J. R. Richardson, Nephew source

RICHARDSON, Mary E. WF Feb. 22, 1892, Northampton, Pneumonia, 52, Wm. & Eliza Scott, Northampton, Married, J. Wash. Richardson, Husband source

RICHARDSON, R. B. WM July 17, 1894, Northampton, Typhoid Fever, 17, J. W. & Elizabeth, Northampton, Farmer, Single, J. W. Richardson, Father source

RICHARDSON, Richard CM May 1, 1882, Northampton, Consumption, 8 days, R. Richardson, Northampton, Single, Mother source

RICHARDSON, Sarah WF Feb. 18, 1891, Northampton, Old Age 65, Parents Unkn., Northampton, Laborer, Married, Thos. Richardson, Husband source

RICHARDSON, Tabitha S. WF Jan. 1880, Northampton, Dropsy, 46, Parents Unkn., Va., Va., Va., At Home, Thos. A. Husband, source unkn.

RICHARDSON, Thomas WM Dec. 31, 1873, Northampton, Consumption, 50, John & Hessy, Northampton, Farmer, Single, J. R. Richardson, Son source

RICHARDSON, Thomas WM Jan. 1, 1874, Eastville Township, Dropsy, 58, Jno. & Sally, Eastville Township, Farmer, Tabitha wife, Leon'd Richardson, source

RICHARDSON, Tobertha WF Jan. 25, 1882, Northampton, Heart Disease, 46, Abel & Susan Belote, Northampton, House Keeper, Married, Daughter source

RIDDICK, ------- CM Nov. 21, 1893, Northampton, Croup, 7 days, William & Nannie, Northampton, Single, Wm. Riddick, Father source

Northampton County, VA, Deaths from Death Register and Wills, 1871-1896

RILEY, ------- CF Oct. 14, 1878, Northampton, Infantile, 14 days, Unkn. & Fluvianna, Birth Unkn., Single, Fluvianna Riley, Mother source

RILEY, Dianna BF Oct. 1879, Northampton, Typhoid Fever, 55, Parents Unkn., Va., Va., Va., Keeping House, Aron Husband, Dr. S. P. Nottingham, Physician source

RILEY, Dinah CF Oct. 14, 1882, Northampton, Typhoid Fever, 55, Parents Unkn., Northampton, Married, Mrs. Carpenter, source

RILEY, Peter CM 1882, Northampton, Dropsy, 70, Parents Unkn., Northampton, Farmer, S. James, source

RILEY, Peter CM Dec. 5, 1892, Northampton, Consumption, 39, Parents Unkn., Northampton, Laborer, Single, Dr. G. P. Moore, Physician source

RIPPON, Peggie WF Feb. 12, 1891, Northampton, Croup, 3, Thos. & Sadie E., Northampton, Single, Thos. Rippon, Father source

ROBBINS, A. CM July 16, 1878, Northampton, Old Age, 89, Parents Unkn., Birth Unkn., Laborer, Single, Ephram Stephens, Friend source

ROBBINS, Geo. M. WM Feb. 4, 1895, Northampton, Gen. Dibility, 81, Isaac D. & Elizabeth, Northampton, Mechanic, Single, W. T. Robbins, Son source

ROBBINS, W. F., Rev. WM Mar. 6, 1895, Northampton, Heart Failure, 58, Parents Unkn., Birth Unkn., Clergyman, Married, G. P. Moore, Neighbor source

ROBERSON, Virginia WF Aug. 15, 1894, Northampton, Consumption, 25, Geo. & Hennie Eshom, Northampton, Married, W. T. Roberson, Husband source

ROBERTS, ------- CM Sept. 1, 1882, Northampton, Cause Unkn., 4 days, Jno. H. Roberts, Northampton, Single, source unkn.

ROBERTS, ------- WM Aug. 2, 1884, Northampton, 1 mo. 24 days, Geo. L. & Margt. E., Northampton, Geo. L. Roberts, Father source

ROBERTS, ------- WM July 4, 1891, Northampton, Cholera Infantum, 3 months, Geo. L. & M. E., Northampton, Single, Geo. L. Roberts, Father source

ROBERTS, ------- WM May 1873, Northampton, Infantile, 10 days, Geo. & Maggie, Northampton, Single, source unkn.

ROBERTS, Arthur M. WM July 14, 1894, Northampton, Typhoid Fever, 21, Geo. L. & Margaret E., Northampton, Farmer, Single, Geo. L. Roberts, Father source

ROBERTS, E. T. WM Apr. 12, 1893, Northampton, Pneumonia, 22, Geo. L. & Margaret E., Northampton, Farmer, Single, Geo. L. Roberts, Father source

ROBERTS, Edmd. T. WM July 1, 1872, Northampton, Typhoid, 3 mos. 28 days, Edmd. U. & Florence M., Northampton, Edmd. U. Roberts, Father source

ROBERTS, Edwd. P. WM May 16, 1872, Northampton, Consumption, 56, Edmd. & Sally, Farmer, Married, Eliz. Wife, Jno. H. Roberts, Son source

ROBERTS, Grace M. WF Apr. 17, 1893, Northampton, Spinal Meningitis, 3 months, H. W. & Mollie E., Northampton, Single, H. W. Roberts, Father source

ROBERTS, John L. WM Sept. 10, 1896, Northampton, Consumption, 41, Arthur & Mary, Northampton, Farmer, Married, Isaac Moore, farm hand source

ROBERTSON, William WM Apr. 1873, Northampton, Infantile, 3 days, Jno. R. & Rebecca, Northampton, Single, Jno. R. Robertson, Father source

ROBINS, ------- CM Jan. 11, 1876, Northampton, Cause Unkn., Age Unkn., John & Tiny, Northampton, Jno. Robins, Father source

ROBINS, ------- CM Sept. 1874, Eastville Township, Cause Unkn., Age Unkn., Jno. & Irving, Eastville Township, Jno. Robins, Father source

ROBINS, ------- WF June 5, 1892, Northampton, Cause Unkn., 1 day, Isaac D. & Mary N., Northampton, Single, Isaac D. Sr., Grandfather source

ROBINS, Abraham J. WM Mar. 21, 1894, Northampton, Consumption, 78, John & Jennie, Northampton, Sailor, Married, Isaac D. Robins, Cousin source

ROBINS, Charles WM Mar. 20, 1894, Northampton, Consumption, 78, Isaac & Betsy Robins, Northampton, Waterman, Single, Isaac D. Robins, Brother source

ROBINS, Essie WF Oct. 1, 1883, Northampton, Croup, 4 yrs. 4 days, O. K. & Emory, Birth Unkn., O. K. Robins, Father source

ROBINS, Lafe WM Mar. 5, 1894, Northampton, Cause Unkn., 66, Arthur & Julia, Acc. Co., Farmer, Married, A. M. Robins, son source

ROBINSON, Delia CF 1888, Northampton, Malarial, 1, Michael Robinson, [Farmer?], Northampton, Single, Michael Robinson, Parent source

ROBINSON, Estelle CF Sept. 16, 1894, Northampton, Crying Fits, 8 months, John & Maggie, Northampton, Single, Caroline Robinson, Grandmother source

ROBINSON, Mary E. WF Dec. 17, 1873, Northampton, Pneumonia, 42, Thomas & Betsy Eshom, Northampton, Single, Geo. S. Robinson, Friend source

ROBINSON, Wm. K. WM Feb. 16, 1895, Northampton, Absass of Liver, 42, Parents Unkn., Phil., Pa., Farmer, Married, Dr. Chas. Smith, Father-in-law source

RODGERS, Lucy WF Jan. 9, 1877, Northampton, Dropsy, 29 yrs. 8 mos., Samuel & Margt. Dunton, Northampton, John Husband, Wm. T. Dunton, Brother source

ROGERS, ------- CF Nov. 17, 1892, Northampton, Cause Unkn., 7 days, Lewis & Susie, Northampton, Single, Lewis Rogers, Father source

ROGERS, ------- CM May 14, 1892, Northampton, Cause Unkn., 1 month, John & Cora, Northampton, Single, John Rogers, Father source

ROGERS, John CM Dec. 15, 1893, Northampton, Pneumonia, 8, John & Cora, Northampton, Laborer, Single, Geo. Rogers, Grandfather source

ROLLEY, ------- WF May 15, 1876, Northampton, Cause Unkn., 1 day, Francis & Margt., Northampton, Single, Frank C. Rolley, Father source

ROLLEY, ------- WM Dec. 15, 1876, Northampton, Cause Unkn., 10 days, Raymond & Clara, Northampton, Single, Clara Rolley, Mother source

ROLLEY, C. P. WM Oct. 28, 1891, Northampton, Thrush, 4 days, F. J. & A. E., Northampton, Single, F. J. Rolley, Father source

ROLLEY, Wm. S. WM May 9, 1896, Northampton, Norfolk, Va., Cancer, 70, Wm. & Polly, Acco. Co., Farmer, Married, Mary A. Rolley, Wife source

ROLLY, ------- WF June 2, 1895, Northampton, Cholera E., 1 month, Luther & Estelle, Northampton, Single, J. E. Mister, Grandfather source

ROLLY, Nettie WF May 12, 1877, Northampton, Measles, 7, Francis & Margaret, Northampton, Single, Francis Rolly, Father source

ROOKS, ------- WF Apr. 22, 1894, Northampton, Cause Unkn., 2 days, O. L. & Fannie S., Northampton, Single, O. L. Rooks, Father source

ROOKS, James WM Aug. 1879, Northampton, Drowned, 27, Parents Unkn., Va., Va., Va., Sailor, Navilla Wife, source unkn.

ROOKS, James WM Aug. 19, 1878, Northampton, Drowned, 39, James & Susan, Northampton, Sailor, Sallie Wife, John T. Bell, Friend source

ROOKS, Oliver P. WM Aug. 12, 1894, Northampton, Kidney Disease, 70, Wm. & Harriet, Northampton, Sailor, Married, Henry Rooks, Son source

ROSE, ------- WF Oct. 6, 1884, Northampton, Cause Unkn., 5 days, Oscar & Ida, Northampton, Single, Oscar Rose, Father soure

RUFUS, Lucinda CF Oct. 1871, Northampton, Child Birth 20, Parents Unkn., Northampton, Single, Gennie Stephens, Friend source

RUSSEL, Emily CF Feb. 20, 1876, Northampton, Debility, 23, Parents Unkn., Accomack, Single, Jno. Williams, Supt. of Poor source

SADDLER, Nathan CM May 4, 1876, Northampton, Cause Unkn., 45, Parents Unkn., Northampton, Laborer, Single, W. West, Neighbor source

SAMPLE, ------- CF Oct. 8, 1891, Northampton, Cause Unkn., 1 day, Jacob & Sarah, Northampton, Single, Jacob Sample, Father source

SAMPLE, ------- CM May 4, 1887, Northampton, Crying Fits, 2 months, Mary Sample, Northampton, Single, J. J. Scott, Neighbor source

SAMPLE, ------- CM Nov. 1, 1894, Northampton, Cause Unkn., 1 day, Jacob & Sarah, Northampton, Single, Sarah Sample, Mother source

SAMPLE, David CM Oct. 4, 1896, Northampton, Whooping Cough, 3, Arthur & Dora, Northampton, Single, Manie Brickhouse, Neighbor source

SAMPLE, Eliza CF Feb. 14, 1895, Northampton, Old Age 82, Parents Unkn., Acco. Co., Single, Lucy Wise, Neighbor source

SAMPLE, Lloyd CM Mar. 4, 1892, Northampton, Pneumonia, 24, Wm. & Frances, Northampton, Laborer, Married, Sam'l Sample, Brother source

SAMPLE, Octava CF Feb. 25, 1885, Northampton, Pneumonia, 2 months, Sam & Bettie, Northampton, Single, Sam Sample, Father source

SATCHEL, ------- CF July 4, 1895, Northampton, Cause Unkn., 4 days, Thos. & Nannie, Northampton, Single, Thos. Satchell, Father source

SATCHEL, ------- CM Mar. 13, 1892, Northampton, Cause Unkn., 9 days, Adolphus & Effie, Northampton, Single, Adolphus Satchel, Father source

SATCHEL, Carrie CF June 1, 1895, Northampton, Typhoid Fever, 10, Rich'd & Rebecca J., Northampton, Single, Rich'd Satchel, Father source

SATCHEL, Julia CF May 16, 1892, Northampton, Pneumonia, 32, Geo. & Laura Jarvis, Northampton, Laborer, Married, Bennett Satchel, Husband source

SATCHEL, Leah CF Apr. 4, 1892, Northampton, Abscess on lungs, 25, Peter & Charlotte Smith, Northampton, Laborer, Married, Southey Satchel, Husband source

SATCHEL, Southey CM Dec. 22, 1895, Northampton, Knife wound, accident, 42, Isaac & Grace, Northampton, Laborer, Married, Lucy Wise, Neighbor source

SATCHELL, ------- CF Oct. 20, 1873, Northampton, Cause Unkn., Age Unkn., Henry Henderson & Sarah Satchell, Northampton, Single, Sarah Satchell, Mother source

SATCHELL, ------- CM Feb. 1872, Northampton, Infantile, 10 days, Levin & Anice?, Birth Unkn., Single, source unkn.

SATCHELL, ------- CM Jan. 15, 1885, Northampton, Cause Unkn., 0, Bob & Bettie, Northampton, Single, Robt. Satchell, Father source

SATCHELL, ------- CM June 23, 1896, Northampton, Cause Unkn., 21 days, Levin R. & Caroline, Northampton, Single, Levin R. Satchell, Father source

SATCHELL, Dasey CF 1888, Northampton, Disease of Bowels, 7 months, R. J. Satchell, [Farming?], Northampton, Single, R. J. Satchell, Parents source

SATCHELL, Emily S. WF Feb. 15, 1876, Northampton, Cause Unkn., Age Unkn., Thos. & Rosa, Northampton, Laborer, Th. Satchell, Father source

SATCHELL, Ester BF Mar. 1880, Northampton, Enteritis, 13, Parents Unkn., Va., House Servant, Single, Jas. M. McNutt, source (PR)

SATCHELL, Geo. Jr. CM Dec. 1891, Northampton, Hemorrhage, 14, Geo. & Ellen, Northampton, Single, Geo. Satchell, Father source

SATCHELL, George CM Mar. 15, 1873, Northampton, Drowned, 80, Southey Bell & Louisa Scisco, Northampton, Laborer, Single, Geo. Nottingham, Friend source

SATCHELL, Juliet CF Mar. 12, 1893, Northampton, Asthma, 76, Parents Unkn., Northampton, Married, Bennett Satchell, son source

SATCHELL, Leah CF Apr. 1874, Northampton, Consumption, 20, Levin Satchell, Northampton, Single, source unkn.

SATCHELL, Leonard CM Apr. 2, 1894, Northampton, Gen. Debility, 75, Amos & Susan, Northampton, Farmer, Married, Wm. Stratton, Friend source

SATCHELL, Nelson CM Mar. 1, 1873, Northampton, Old Age, 83, Southey Bell & Louisa Scisco, Northampton, Laborer, Single, Geo. Nottingham, Friend source

SATCHELL, Prissy CF Nov. 1875, Northampton, Consumption, 35, wife of Jno. Satchell, Birth Unkn., John Satchell. Husband source

SATCHELL, Schailothe BF May 1880, Northampton, Dropsy, 12, Ames & Laura, Va., Va., Va., Domestic Servt., Single, S. P. Nottingham, source

SATCHELL, Thos. J. WM Apr. 27, 1893, Northampton, Pneumonia, 67, Thos. & Sallie, Northampton, Mechanic, Married, Chas. Killmon, Son-in-Law source

SAUNDERS, ------- WF Oct. 29, 1876, Northampton, Cause Unkn., 1 day, Stewart J. & Laura, Northampton, Single, Stewart J. Saunders, Father source

SAUNDERS, Arthur WM Nov. 25, 1895, Northampton, Cholera E., 2 months, Arthur & Elizabeth, Acco. Co., Single, Arthur Saunders, Father source

SAUNDERS, Effie CF Nov. 15, 1893, Northampton, Dropsy, 63, Jas. Slack & Maria Smith, Northampton, Married, City Saunders, Husband source

SAUNDERS, Jas. T. WM Nov. 14, 1891, Northampton, Paralysis, 48, J. T. & Maria, Northampton, Drummer, Married, Arthur Saunders, Son source

SAVAGE, ------- (2) WM's Dec. 2, 1896, Northampton, Cause Unkn., 1 day, J. B. & Anne M., Northampton, Single, J. B. Savage, Father source

SAVAGE, ------- C Sex Unkn. Dec. 1873, Northampton, Infantile, 1 day, Jos. & Anna, Northampton, Single, source unkn.

SAVAGE, ------- CF Aug. 2, 1896, Northampton, Cause Unkn. , 5 days, Geo. L. & Betsy, Northampton, Single, George L. Savage, Father source

SAVAGE, ------- CF July 1872, Northampton, Infantile, 1 day, Henry & Adaline, Northampton, Single, Gennie Stephens, Friend source

SAVAGE, ------- CF June 2, 1895, Northampton, Cause Unkn., 2 days, Emanuel & Rachel, Northampton, Single, Emanuel Savage, Father source

SAVAGE, ------- CM Apr. 1874, Northampton, Infantile, 1 day, Henry & Adelin, Northampton, Single, A. Savage, Mother source

SAVAGE, ------- CM Mar. 1875, Northampton, Cause Unkn., 2 days, Geo. & ----- Savage, Birth Unkn., Single, Neighbor source

SAVAGE, ------- CM May 10, 1891, Northampton, Cause Unkn., 8 days, Walker & Laura, Northampton, Single, Walker Savage, Father source

SAVAGE, ------- WM May 3, 1887, Northampton, Cause Unkn., 1 day, Joseph & Jane, Northampton, Single, Joseph Savage, Father source

SAVAGE, ------- CM June 8, 1895, Northampton, Cause Unkn., 6 days, Emanuel & Rachel, Northampton, Single, Emanuel Savage, Father source

SAVAGE, Ann CF May 10, 1893, Northampton, Heart Disease, 60, Parents Unkn., Northampton, Married, Ed. Nichols, Son-in-Law source

SAVAGE, Anna CF Oct. 10, 1872, Northampton, Diphtheria, 3, Rose Savage, Northampton, Single, Leon'd. J. Nottingham, where died source

SAVAGE, Edward CM July 10, 1895, Northampton, Old Age, 70, Peggie Savage, Northampton, Farmer, Married, John Savage, Grandson source

SAVAGE, Edward WM Oct. 1874, Northampton, Cause Unkn., 8, Edwd & Katie, Northampton, Single, H. P. Wescoat, Uncle source

SAVAGE, Elizabeth WF July 1874, Northampton, Consumption, 60, Wm. & Ester, Northampton, James T. husband, Emory E. Thomas, Daughter source

SAVAGE, Ella CF Oct. 2, 1895, Northampton, Typhoid Fever, 26, Isaac & Pollie Fitchett, Northampton, Married, Bridget Scott, Friend source

SAVAGE, Fannie CF May 9, 1877, Northampton, Congestive, 4, George & Sallie, Northampton, Single, George Savage, Father source

SAVAGE, Geo. T. WM Nov. 1873, Northampton, Diphtheria, 7 mos. , Jas. K. & Emory, Northampton, Single, Jas. K. Savage, Father source

SAVAGE, Geo. W. CM July 10, 1893, Northampton, Dropsy, 35, Jos. & Rachel, Northampton, Laborer, Married, Lavenia Evans, Mother-in-Law source

SAVAGE, George WM Oct. 12, 1872, Northampton, Old Age, 74, Geo. Savage & --, Northampton, source unkn.

SAVAGE, Indiana CF Jan. 14, 1876, Northampton, Typhoid Fever, 13, Peter & Mary, Northampton, Laborer, Single, Mary Savage, Mother source

SAVAGE, Isaac CM Mar. 20, 1885, Northampton, Pleurisy, 57, Isaac & Nellie, Northampton, source unreadable

SAVAGE, James W. WM Oct. 1875, Northampton, Fever, 2, Jas. K. & Emory, Birth Unkn. Single, Jas. K. Savage, Father source

SAVAGE, Jas. H. WM Sept. 23, 1883, Northampton, Typhoid, 6 yrs. 7 mos., Jas. K. & Emory, Birth Unkn., Jas. K. Savage, Father source

SAVAGE, Julious CM Mar. 9, 1878, Northampton, Pneumonia, 9, Henry & Adaline, Northampton, Laborer, Single, Henry Savage, Father source

SAVAGE, Kate WF Sept. 24, 1893, Northampton, Consumption, 27, Wm. S. & Margaret Sarah Wilson, Northampton, Married, W. R. Savage, Husband source

SAVAGE, Lettie CF Sept. 1875, Northampton, Cause Unkn., 60, Parents Unkn., Birth Unkn., Neighbor source

SAVAGE, Liddie CF May 12, 1896, Northampton, Consumption, 72, George & Silvia Sample, Acco. Co., Married, Horace Garrison, Son source

SAVAGE, Lilia WF Nov. 1873, Northampton, Diphtheria, 4 mos., Jas. K. & Emory, Northampton, Single, Jas K. Savage, Father source

SAVAGE, Margaret S. WF Mar. 10, 1878, Northampton, Fall, 84, John & Ann Wilson, Northampton, Single, Edwd T. Nottingham, Friend source

SAVAGE, Mary CF June 18, 1893, Northampton, Asthma, 21, Geo. & Ellen, Northampton, Single, Geo. Savage, Father source

SAVAGE, Nelson BM May 1880, Northampton, Dysention, 85, Parents Unkn., Va., Va., Va., Laborer, Widower, source unkn.

SAVAGE, Peter CM Mar. 12, 1891, Northampton, Spine Disease, 18, Emanuel & Rachel, Northampton, Laborer, Single, E. Savage, Father source

SAVAGE, Robt. CM June 12, 1895, Northampton, Cholera E., 1, Bell S. Savage, Northampton, Single, Jas. Giddings, Father source

SAVAGE, Rufus K. CM 1888, Northampton, Consumption, 21, R. K. Savage, [Laborer?], Northampton, R. K. Savage, Parent source

SAVAGE, Sam CM Nov. 1873, Northampton, Heart Disease, 70, Parents Unkn., Northampton, Laborer, E. Savage, Friend source

SAVAGE, T. P. WM Feb. 2, 1895, Northampton, Brain Fever, 30, Preston & India, Northampton, Farmer, Married, E. B. Savage Brother source

SAVAGE, Thos. WM Sept. 3, 1893, Northampton, Consumption, 10 months, W. R. & Kate Savage, Northampton, W. R. Savage, Father source

SAVAGE, Walker CM July 11, 1893, Northampton, Pneumonia, 45, Parents Unkn., Northampton, Laborer, Married, Chas. Kellam Neighbor source

SAVAGE, William CM Jan. 1, 1887, Northampton, Dropsy, 38, Parents Unkn., Northampton, Laborer, Sarah Savage, Wife source

SAVAGE, William L. WM July 1, 1876, Northampton, Congestion Brain, 23, Thos. D. & Mary L., Northampton, Farmer, Single, Jno. T. Savage, Brother source

SCARBORO, Emeline CF May 25, 1896, Northampton, Consumption, 58, Louis & Maria Johnson, Northampton, Married, Henry Bayly, Son source

SCARBORO, William CM Nov. 15, 1896, Northampton, Consumption, 48, Shadrack & Laura, Northampton, Laborer, Single, Laura Scarboro, Mother source

SCARBOROUGH, ------- CM Aug. 14, 1887, Northampton, Crying Fits, 5 days, J. & Hariet, Northampton, Single, J. Scarborough, Father source

SCARBOROUGH, Hennie CF Aug. 1871, Northampton, Diphtheria, 5, Luke & Tamar, Northampton, Single, Luke Scarborough, Father source

SCARBOROUGH, Henny BF Mar. 1880, Northampton, Cause Unkn., 9 months, Unkn. & Dianna, Va., Va., Va., source unkn.

SCISCO, ------- CM Jan. 8, 1876, Northampton, Crying Fits, 1 day, Henry & Laura, Northampton, Single, Henry Scisco, Father source

SCISCO, Annie CF Mar. 2, 1887, Northampton, Child Birth, 24, Preston & Mary Scisco, Northampton, Servant, Hariet Scisco, Mother source

SCISCO, Etha L. CF Nov. 1885, Northampton, Cause Unkn., 3 months, Preston & Ellen, Northampton, Single, Preston Scisco, Father source

SCISCO, Henry CM May 12, 1878, Northampton, Diarrhea, 67, Parents Unkn., Northampton, Laborer, Single, Harriet Scisco, Friend source

SCISCO, Michael BM Dec. 1879, Northampton, Apoplexy, 60, Parents Unkn., Va., Va., Va., Laborer, Juliet Wife, Dr. Geo. W. Smith, Physician source

SCISCO, Russell CM Oct. 25, 1896, Northampton, Inf. Rheumatism, 10, G. C. & Virginia, Northampton, Single, George C. Sisco, Father source

SCOTT, ------- CF Aug. 5, 1887, Northampton, Crying Fits, 1 month, Jesse Scott, Northampton, Single, Jesse Scott, Father source

SCOTT, ------- CF May 14, 1877, Northampton, Infantile, 4 days, Unkn. & Lizzie, Northampton, Single, Lizzie Stott, Friend source

SCOTT, ------- CM June 17, 1884, Northampton, Cause Unkn., 7 days, Nim & Bridget, Northampton, Single, Nim Scott, Father source

SCOTT, ------- WF July 1874, Eastville Township, Cause Unkn., 1 day, E. O. & Eliza, Eastville Township, Single, E. O. Scott, Father source

SCOTT, ------- WF Oct. 1, 1893, Northampton, Cholera Infantum, 10 days, Thos. & Sarah, Northampton, Single, Thos. L. Scott, Father source

SCOTT, ------- WF Oct. 1874, Northampton, Infantile, 1 day, Dr. & Ella, Northampton, Single, Dr. Scott, Father source

SCOTT, ------- WM June 3, 1887, Northampton, Cause Unkn., 4 days, Edward & Sarah, Northampton, Single, Edward Scott, Father source

SCOTT, Annie CF Dec. 14, 1896, Northampton, Cause Unkn., 40, Parents Unkn., Northampton, Married, Jesse Scott, Husband source

SCOTT, Ella WF Dec. 27, 1882, Northampton, Cause Unkn., 35, Jno. W. Tankard, Northampton, Housekeeper, Mrs. Edmonds, source

SCOTT, Ella T. WF Dec. 1879, Northampton, L , 35, Parents Unkn., Va., Va., Va., Keeping House, Married, P. F. Scott, Stratton B. Downing, source

SCOTT, Ellen CF July 12, 1892, Northampton, Consumption, 56, Parents Unkn., North Carolina, Laborer, Married, Dolly Hebard, Friend source

SCOTT, Ellen G. WF July 10, 1876, Northampton, Cause Unkn., 7 days, Thos. M. & Hennie, Northampton, Single, Thos. M. Scott, Father source

SCOTT, Geo. W. CM Apr. 4, 1892, Northampton, Consumption, 28, Jas. & Annie, Northampton, Laborer, Married, Jas. H. Scott, Brother source

SCOTT, H. Hy "Henry " CM June 15, 1884, Northampton, Cause Unkn., 3, Edwd. & Tabitha, Northampton, Single, Edwd. Scott, Father source

SCOTT, Ibbie CF Jan. 20, 1893, Northampton, Cause Unkn., 2 months, Edward & Tabitha, Northampton, Single, Edward Scott, Father source

SCOTT, Infant BM Feb. 1880, Northampton, Debility, 6 days, Henry & Candis, Va., Va., Va., Single, source unkn.

SCOTT, James B. WM Mar. 17, 1891, Northampton, Dyspepsia, 63, Benj. & Ann, Northampton, Farmer, Single, Clinton Scott, Son source

SCOTT, Jno. E. WM Dec. 1873, Northampton, Cause Unkn., 38, Parents Unkn., Birth Unkn., Farmer, source unkn.

SCOTT, John T. P. WM July 1879, Northampton, Apoplexy, 55, John & Sally S., Va., Va., Va., Farmer, Virginia Wife, Dr. N. Henderson, Physician source

SCOTT, John T. P. WM June 10, 1878, Northampton, Insane, 54, John & Sallie, Northampton, Virginia Wife, John F. Bell, Stewart of Alms House source

SCOTT, Lucile WF Apr. 14, 1892, Northampton, Measles, 9 months, L. E. & Sarah, Northampton, Single, L. E. Scott, Father source

SCOTT, Maggie WF Aug. 10, 1871, Northampton, Dysentery, 1, James & Emily, Northampton, James Scott, Father source [Farmer?]

SCOTT, Nim I. WM Feb. 10, 1874, Northampton, Typhoid Fever, Thos. L. & Sarah A., Northampton, Farmer, Single, Thos. Scott, Brother source

SCOTT, S. H. WM Sept. 1, 1893, Northampton, Dysentery, 2, Geo. L. & Lillie, Northampton, Single, Geo. L. Scott, Father source

SCOTT, Seth. G. CM Dec. 16, 1896, Northampton, Cause Unkn., 5 days, S. R. & Rosa, Northampton, Single, S. R. Scott Father source

SCOTT, V. A., Mrs. WF Sept. 2, 1891, Northampton, Dropsy, 64, Jacob & Rosie Nottingham, Northampton, Married, B. T. Nottingham, Brother source

SCOTT, Victoria J. WF May 26, 1893, Northampton, Congestive Lungs, 49, John & Mary Moore, Isle of Wight Co., Va., Married, Dr. W. J. Scott, Husband source

SCOTT, Wesley U. WM Oct. 3, 1892, Northampton, Cause Unkn., 3 months, Geo. H. & Alice, Northampton, Single, Geo. H. Scott, Father source

SCOTT, Willie H. WM June 7, 1885, Cholera Infantum, 4 months, Peter & Peggie W., Northampton, Single, Peter F. Scott, source

SCOTT, Wm. H. WM 1872, Northampton, Diphtheria, 2, Peter & Ella, Northampton, Single, source unkn.

SEARS, Fairfield CM Mar. 4, 1894, Northampton, Cause Unkn., 10 months, Joseph & Ellen, Northampton, Single, Jos. Sears, Father source

SEATON, ------- CM Mar. 1875, Northampton, Cause Unkn., 7 days, Cornelius & Lettie, Birth Unkn., Single, Cornelius Seaton, Father source

SEATON, Tabitha CF Oct. 10, 1871, Northampton, Bilious Fever 1 yr. 8 mos., Corn's (Cornelius) & Alice Seaton, Northampton, Single, Corn's Seaton, Father source [Laborer?]

SEDGEWICK, Florence WF July 10, 1894, Sussex Co., Del., Consumption, 3 months, E. G. & Rebecca C., Sussex Co., Del., Single E. G. Sedgewick, Father source

SEEDS, Samuel WM Sept. 12, 1876, Northampton, Sore Throat, 5, Amanda Seeds, Birth Unkn., Single, Amanda Seeds, Mother source

SEYMOUR, Abe CM Apr. 6, 1896, Northampton, Pneumonia, 62, Abe & Mary, Northampton, Laborer, Married, Ned Seymour, Brother source

SHACKELFORD, -------, WF June 4, 1893, Northampton, Cholera Infantum, 30 days, Thos. H. & Elizabeth, Northampton, Single, T. H. Shackelford, Father source

SHACKLEFORD, LeCato WM July 12, 1895, Northampton, Cholera E., 10 months, T. H. & Elizabeth, Northampton, Single, T. H. Shackleford, Father source

SHACKLEFORD, Milley CF July 18, 1871, Northampton, Typhoid Fever, 39, Sallie Shackleford, Northampton, Single, Friend Physician source

SHARPLEY, Bettie WF Jan. 8, 1894, Northampton, Dyspepsia, 40, John & Mary Robins, Northampton, Married, John H. Robins, Brother source

SHARPLEY, James E. WM Oct. 9, 1893, Northampton, Drowned, 41, James & Nancy, Acco. Co., Waterman, Married, P. H. Bool, Friend source

SHEPPARD, ------- CM Aug. 2, 1894, Northampton, Cause Unkn., 1 day, Severn & Glace, Northampton, Single, Severn Sheppard, Father source

SHEPPARD, Agnes CF May 18, 1891, Northampton, Dropsy, 25, Parents Unkn., Northampton, Laborer, Married, Geo. Sheppard, Brother-in-Law source

SHEPPARD, James CM July 21, 1893, Northampton, Cause Unkn., 1 month, James & Maggie, Northampton, Single, James Sheppard, Father source

SHEPPARD, Lloyd CM Dec. 1, 1885, Northampton, Heart Disease, 21, Jas. & Esther, Northampton, Single, Jas. Sheppard, Father source

SHEPPARD, Mary E. CF Apr. 2, 1895, Northampton, Dropsy, 3, James & Maggie, Northampton, Single, James Sheppard, Father source

SHIELDS, Infant CM Mar. 3, 1873, Northampton, Cause Unkn., 6 days, ----- & Martha Shields, Northampton, Single, Martha Shields, Mother source

SHIVERS, John CM Aug. 2, 1895, Northampton, Typhoid Fever, 16, ----- & Gertrude Shivers, Northampton, Single, Jack Addison, Friend source

SIMKINS, ------- CM Nov. 28, 1877, Northampton, Measles, 4 yrs. 2 mos., John & Linda, Northampton, Single, John Simkins, Father source

SIMKINS, Margaret S. WF May 30, 1876, Northampton, Consumption, 48, Thos. & Hannah Fitchett, Northampton, Widow, Mary Simkins, Daughter source

SIMPKINS, ------- CM Jan. 3, 1887, Northampton, Crying Fits, 10 days, John & Annie, Northampton, Single, John Simpkins, Father source

SIMPKINS, Geo. CM Aug. 1875, Northampton, Dysentery, 2, Jno. & Litey, Birth Unkn., Birth Unkn., Single, Jno. Simpkins, Father source

SIMPKINS, Jno. A. WM Nov. 29, 1874, Northampton, Congestive Chill, 62 yrs. 4 mos., Arthur & Sallie, Northampton, Farmer, Margariet S. wife, Jno. R. Fitchett, Friend source

SIMPKINS, Laura WF May 10, 1872, Northampton, Consumption, 55, Betsy & William Jarvis, Northampton, Married, Physician source

SISCO, ------- CM May 1875, Northampton, Croup, 8 months, Preston & Alexine, Birth Unkn., Preston Sisco, Father source

SISCO, Henry CM Jan. 12, 1892, Northampton, Burned to death, 4, Geo. H. & Virginia, Northampton, Single, Geo. H. Sisco, Father source

SISCO, Leonard CM Oct. 12, 1893, Northampton, Cause Unkn., 9 months, Preston & Alexine, Northampton, Single, Preston Sisco, Father source

SISCO, Louisa CF Oct. 15, 1895, Northampton, Consumption, 45, Isaac & Mary Bayly, Northampton, Married, L. J. Willis, Neighbor source

SISCO, Margt. CF Aug. 1875, Northampton, Cause Unkn., 21 days, Henry & Louisa, Birth Unkn., Single, Louisa Sisco, Mother source

SIX, Sallie CF July 12, 1894, Northampton, Cholera Infantum, 18 months, John & Susan, Northampton, Single, Jas. Sheppard, Neighbor source

SKIDMORE, ------- WF Dec. 23, 1884, Northampton, 6 days, Isaac & Ann, Northampton, Isaac Skidmore, Father source

SKINNER, William CM Jan. 2, 1896, Northampton, Catarrh, 8 Months, Thomas & Maggie, Northampton, Single, Maggie Skinner, Mother source

SMAW, ------- CM July 4, 1894, Northampton, Cause Unkn., 1 day, J. H. & Jennie, Northampton, Single, J. H. Smaw, Father source

SMAW, Edward CM July 6, 1892, Northampton, Dropsy, 50, Bennett & Rosie, Northampton, Laborer, Married, Jennie Smaw, Wife source

SMAW, Emily CF Jan. 9, 1878, Northampton, Crying Fits, 4 days, Unkn. & Emily, Northampton, Single, Emily Smaw, Mother source

SMAW, Spencer CM Oct. 2, 1894, Northampton, Thrush, 11 months, Spencer & Rachel, Northampton, Single, Spencer Smaw, Father source

Northampton County, VA, Deaths from Death Register and Wills, 1871-1896

SMITH, ------- CF Apr. 7, 1895, Northampton, Cause Unkn., 3 days, W. A. & Annie, Northampton, Single, W. A. Smith, Father source

SMITH, ------- CF Dec. 29, 1874, Northampton, Cause Unkn., 23 days, Samuel & Lauretta, Northampton, Single, Nim H. Downs, Friend source

SMITH, ------- CF Mar. 1, 1876, Northampton, Cause Unkn., 2 days, Appy & Leah, Northampton, Single, Appy Smith, Father source

SMITH, ------- CF Oct. 1874, Northampton, Infantile, Age Unkn., Tob Smith, Northampton, A. Savage, Neighbor source

SMITH, ------- CF Oct. 21, 1896, Northampton, Cause Unkn., 4 days, Severn & Nellie, Northampton, Single, Severn Smith, Father source

SMITH, ------- CM Apr. 28, 1883, Northampton, Crying Fits, 7 days, Joshua & Alice, Birth Unkn., Joshua Smith, Father source

SMITH, ------- CM July 6, 1874, Northampton, Cause Unkn., 1 day, Nim & Tabby, Northampton, Single, Leo. T. Fitchett, Friend source

SMITH, ------- CM June 14, 1893, Northampton, Cause Unkn., 4 days, James & Margaret, Northampton, Single, James Smith, Father source

SMITH, ------- CM June 8, 1885, Northampton, Cause Unkn., 2 months, Peter B. & Charlotte, Northampton, Single, Peter B. Smith, Father source

SMITH, ------- CM Oct. 2, 1893, Northampton, Croup, 1, James & Jennie, Northampton, Single, Rachel Smaw, Neighbor source

SMITH, ------- WF Jan. 1876, Northampton, Cause Unkn., 15 days, John & Ginny, Northampton, Single, John Smith, Father source

SMITH, ------- WM Nov. 14, 1876, Northampton, Cause Unkn., 2 days, Jas. H. & Elizabeth, Northampton, Jas. H. Smith, Father source

SMITH, Abe CM Feb. 19, 1878, Northampton, Enlarged Head, 18 months, Abram & Margaret, Northampton, Single, Abram Smith, Father source

SMITH, Alfred CM Apr. 2, 1894, Northampton, Consumption, 57, Geo. & Maria, Northampton, Farmer, Married, Nat Smith, Friend source

SMITH, Alfred CM Nov. 21, 1894, Northampton, Consumption, 58, Geo. & Maria, Northampton, Laborer, Single, Mary Press, niece source

SMITH, Annie CF Apr. 9, 1877, Northampton, Burned, 4 yrs. 6 mos., William & Sallie, Northampton, Single, Sallie Smith, Mother source

SMITH, Appy CM May 2, 1878, Northampton, Cause Unkn., 58, Parents Unkn., Accomac Co., Laborer, Single, John T. Bell, Friend source

SMITH, Caty "Catherine" WF Mar. 1874, Northampton, Old Age, 64, Wm. & Sally Wecoat, Northampton, George, Husband Jas. Smith, Son source

SMITH, Diann CF 1888, Northampton, Paralysis, 45, Parents Unkn., Northampton, Laborer, Alfred Savage, Neighbor source

SMITH, Dinah CF 1882, Northampton, Heart Disease, 55, Parents Unkn., Northampton, Housekeeper, Mrs. Carpenter, source

SMITH, Ed. WM Oct. 9, 1896, Northampton, Drowned, 28, Isaac & Adah, Northampton, Farmer, Married, Geo. F. Smith, Brother source

Northampton County, VA, Deaths from Death Register and Wills, 1871-1896

SMITH, Edward CM Jan. 31, 1892, Northampton, Consumption, 54, Geo. & Leah, Northampton, Farmer, Married, William Smith, Son source

SMITH, Edward WM June 28, 1872, Northampton, Cholera Infantum, 7 months, Peter & Kate, Northampton, Single, Peter Smith, Father source

SMITH, Elton B. WM Apr. 6, 1894, Northampton, R. R. accident, 32, Peter B. & Kate, Northampton, R. R. Service, Married, Charlie Smith, Brother source

SMITH, Fanny WF Sept. 15, 1876, Northampton, Old Age, 70, Benj. & Peggy Haley, Northampton, Widow, Jas. H. Smith, Son source

SMITH, George CM May 5, 1896, Northampton, Cause Unkn., 25, John & Lizzie, Northampton, Laborer, Single, Lizzie Smith, Mother source

SMITH, Golden WM June 12, 1882, Northampton, Brain Fever, 4 months, Robert & Ellen, Northampton, Single, Robert Smith, Father source

SMITH, Goldust BM June 1879, Northampton, Brain Fever, 4 months, Robert & Ellen, Va., Va., Va., Single, Dr. Wm. A. Thom, Physician source

SMITH, Grace WF Nov. 1871, Northampton, Convulsions, 1, Jas. A. & Ella, Northampton, Single, Jas. A. Smith, Father source

SMITH, Hariet BF Aug. 1879, Northampton, Whooping Cough, 3, Parents Unkn., Va., Va., Va., Single, source unkn.

SMITH, Henry BM June 1879, Northampton, Cause Unkn., 1 month, Nathaniel & Adar, Va., Va., Va., source unkn.

SMITH, Infant BM Feb. 1880, Northampton, Cause Unkn., 5 days, William & Tobitha, Va., Va., Va., Single, source unkn.

SMITH, Infant June 20, 1871, Northampton, Crying Fits, 2 days, Severn & Nancie, Northampton, Single, Severn Smith, Father source [Laborer?]

SMITH, Isaac WM Mar. 9, 1876, Northampton, Pleurisy, 50, John Smith, New Jersey, Carpenter, Widower, John Nottingham, Friend source

SMITH, J. W. WM Feb. 24, 1892, Northampton, Rheumatism, 43, John & Susan, Northampton, Shoemaker, Single, Rich'd Smith, Brother source

SMITH, Jacob CM Mar. 2, 1878, Northampton, Drunkeness, 70, Parents Unkn., Birth Unkn., Laborer, Bridget Taylor, Robt. B. Taylor, Friend source

SMITH, Jno. CM 1888, Northampton, Malerial, 6 months, Jas. Smith, [Laborer?], Northampton, Single, Jno. Smith, Parent source

SMITH, Joseph CM Oct. 4, 1878, Northampton, Pneumonia, 24, Josiah & Susan, Northampton, Laborer, Single, Susan Smith, Mother source

SMITH, Julius A. WM June 1879, Northampton, Typhoid Fever Hemorrhage, 15, Parents Unkn., Va., Va., Va., at home, Single, William E. Brickhouse, source

SMITH, Leah CF Oct. 22, 1896, Northampton, Cause Unkn., 43, Abe & Mahaley Fitchett, Northampton, Married, Patience Kellam, Daughter source

SMITH, Major WM June 16, 1874, Northampton, Dysentery, 10 mos., Geo. A. & Virginia F., Northampton, Single, Geo. A. Smith, Father source

SMITH, Mary CF July 12, 1895, Northampton, Diarrhea, 6 months, Tobe & Maggie, Northampton, Single, Tobe Smith, Father source

SMITH, Moses CM Feb. 24, 1878, Northampton, Consumption, 33, Unkn. & Lizzie, Accomac Co., Laborer, Susan Wife, Wm. T. Nottingham, Friend source

SMITH, Patience BF Aug. 1879, Northampton, Heart Disease, 23, Parents Unkn., Va. Va., Va., Domestic Servt., Single, S. P. Nottingham, source

SMITH, Peter CM Sept. 1882, Northampton, Dropsy, 70, Parents Unkn., Northampton, Farmer, Single, Den James, source

SMITH, Sallie CF Nov. 18, 1871, Northampton, Diphtheria, 2 yrs. 4 mos., Severn & Margaret, Northampton, Single, Severn Smith, source [Laborer?]

SMITH, Severn CM Apr. 16, 1896, Northampton, Pneumonia, 40, Parents Unkn, Northampton, Laborer, Single, Ellen Smith, Sister source

SMITH, Toby CM July 16, 1894, Northampton, Drowned, 20, Toby & Patience, Northampton, Laborer, Single, Jas. Smith, Undertaker source

SMITH, Virginia CF Mar. 15, 1891, Northampton, Dropsy, 50, Custis & Margaret, Northampton, Severn J. Smith, Son source

SMITH, William. G. WM Feb. 29, 1876, Northampton, Softening Brain, 77 yrs. 5 mos. 16 days, Isaac & Maria, Northampton, Physician, Elizabeth W. Smith, widow source

SOLOMON, Adah CF Dec. 13, 1877, Northampton, Typhoid Fever, 34 yrs. 9 days, Unkn., & Lucy, Northampton, Laborer, Single, Nath'l Sample, Friend source

SOMERS, ------- WF Sept. 1876, Northampton, Choleramorbus, 9 months, Wm. T. & Mary, Single, Birth Unkn., Wm. T. Somers, Father source

SPADY, ------- CF Apr. 6, 1893, Northampton, Cause Unkn., 2 days, ----- & Mollie, Northampton, Single, Washington Smith, Uncle source

SPADY, ------- CF Dec. 22, 1877, Northampton, Infantile, 19 days, Unkn. & Jane, Northampton, Single, Jane Spady, Mother source

SPADY, ------- CF Jan. 30, 1896, Northampton, Cause Unkn., 10 days, Josiah & Lola, Northampton, Single, Josiah Spady, Father source

SPADY, ------- CF July 16, 1896, Northampton, Cause Unkn., 4 days, Sol & Gussie, Northampton, Single, Sol. Spady, Father source

SPADY, ------- CF May 1875, Northampton, Cause Unkn., 3 months, Alfred & Mary, Birth Unkn., Single, Alfred Spady, Father source

SPADY, ------- CF Oct. 9, 1878, Northampton, Infantile, 7 days, Unkn. & Fannie, Northampton, Single, Fannie Spady, Mother source

SPADY, ------- CM 1888, Northampton, Premature Birth, 0, Robt. Spady, [Laborer?], Northampton, Single, Robt. Spady, Parent source

SPADY, ------- CM Aug. 19, 1891, Northampton, Cause Unkn., 3 days, Jno. & Patience, Northampton, Single, Jno. Spady, Father source

SPADY, ------- CM Aug. 6, 1896, Northampton, Cause Unkn., 8 days, Sol & Gertie, Northampton, Single, Sol. Spady, Father source

SPADY, ------- CM June 29, 1887, Northampton, Ague, 1 month, James & Elizabeth, Northampton, Single, James Spady, Father source

SPADY, ------- CM Mar. 1875, Northampton, Cause Unkn., 2 months, Chas. & Mary, Birth Unkn., Single, Neighbor source

SPADY, ------- CM Oct. 8, 1887, Northampton, Cause Unkn., 7 days, Arthur & Sylvia, Northampton, Single, Arthur Spady, Father source

SPADY, Betsy CF May 10, 1893, Northampton, Paralysis, 70, Parents Unkn., Northampton, Married, Wm. White, Son-in-Law source

SPADY, Edgar J. WM Nov. 23, 1878, Northampton, Cause Unkn., 2 months, Edgar J. & Annie, Northampton, Single, E. J. Spady, Father source

SPADY, Edy BF July 1879, Northampton, Cause Unkn., 70, Parents Unkn., Va., Widow, Wm. J. Scott, source (PR)

SPADY, Ella CF Oct. 2, 1893, Northampton, Croup, 3 months, Lottie, Northampton, Single, Eugene Spady, Grandfather source

SPADY, Ella CF Sept. 2, 1894, Northampton, Malaria, 15, Horace & Rachel, Northampton, Single, Horace Spady, Father source

SPADY, George CM June 30, 1887, Northampton, Typhoid Fever, 56, Parents Unkn., Northampton, Laborer, Married, Eliz. Widgen, Friend source

SPADY, Grace CF Feb. 19, 1893, Northampton, Burned, 70, Parents Unkn., Northampton, Married, Rachel Smaw, Daughter source

SPADY, Infant CF Jan. 8, 1873, Northampton, Cause Unkn., 5 days, Jim & Maria, Northampton, Single, Jim Spady, Father source

SPADY, Infant CM Sept. 11, 1873, Northampton, Cause Unkn., 7 days, George & Fanny, Northampton, Single, Abe Spady, Friend source

SPADY, Infant WF Aug. 10, 1872, Northampton, Crying Fits, 6 days, Susan & John, Northampton, John Spady, Father source [Farmer?]

SPADY, John CM May 10, 1877, Northampton, Crying Fits, 4 days, Unkn., & Nancy, Northampton, Single, Nancy Spady, Mother source

SPADY, Joseph CM Oct.22, 1877, Northampton, Measles, 1 yr. 6 mos., Joseph & Lucy, Northampton, Single, Joseph Spady, Father source

SPADY, Joseph D. CM Apr. 13, 1893, C. Lunatic Ayslum, Fits, 38, Levin & Ibbie Jackson, Northampton, Laborer, Single, Mary A. Fitchett, Sister source

SPADY, Leolin CF Mar. 21, 1895, Northampton, Thrush, 2, Smith & Bell, Northampton, Single, Smith Spady, Father source

SPADY, Louisa BF Aug. 1879, Northampton, Colic, 2, Parents Unkn., Va., Va., Va., Single, source unkn.

SPADY, Major BM Aug. 1879, Northampton, Drowned, 21, Parents Unkn., Va., Va., Va., Sailor, Single, source unkn.

SPADY, Patience CF Feb. 6, 1892, Northampton, Dropsy, 27, Jas. & Patience, Northampton, Laborer, Single, John Spady, Brother source

SPADY, Robert C. WM June 8, 1876, Northampton, Bilious Fever, 5 months, Edgar J. & Annie, Northampton, Single, Edgar J. Spady, Father source

SPADY, Sallie CF Oct. 14, 1877, Northampton, Measles, 5, George & Sallie, Northampton, Single, George Spady, Father source

SPADY, Sallie WF Aug. 15, 1878, Northampton, Diarrhea, 3, John T. & Sallie, Birth Unkn., Single, John T. Spady, Father source

SPADY, Sam'l CM Mar. 27, 1893, Northampton, Fits, 9 days, Sam'l & Sarah, Northampton, Single, Sarah Spady, Mother source

Northampton County, VA, Deaths from Death Register and Wills, 1871-1896

SPADY, Susan CF Sept. 30, 1887, Northampton, Cause Unkn., 54, Parents Unkn., Northampton, Daniel Spady, Husband source

SPADY, Thos. CM Apr. 1885, Northampton, Cholera Infantum, 11 months, Alfred & Mary A., Northampton, Single, Alfred Spady, Father source

SPADY, Thos. N. WM Nov. 1875, Northampton, Heart Disease, 57, Parents Unkn., Birth Unkn., Physician, Son source

SPRATLEY, Marion CF Dec. 27, 1883, Northampton, Cause Unkn., 1 mo. 5 days, Jno. & Julia, Birth Unkn., Jno. Spratley, Father source

STAFFORD, Melvina CF June 10, 1871, Northampton, Dysentery, 2, Daniel & Melvina, Northampton, Daniel Stafford, Father source [Laborer?]

STAKES, ------- WM June 12, 1878, Northampton, Crying Fits, 11 days, John W. & Mollie, Northampton, Single, John W. Stakes, Father source

STARCHEY, ------- CM Ap. 7, 1891, Northampton, Croup, 7 months, Jacob & Maggie, Northampton, Single, Jacob Starchey, Father source

STEPHEN, Robert CM Oct. 11, 1871, Northampton, Diphtheria, 3, Robt. & Adah, Northampton, Single, Robt. Stephens, Father source

STEPHENS, ------- CF Dec. 5, 1877, Northampton, Diarrhea, 6 months, Unkn. & Puss, Northampton, Single, George Upshur, Step Father source

STEPHENS, ------- CF Nov. 1874, Northampton, Infantile, 1 day, Margt. Stephens, Northampton, Single, D. Harman, Neighbor source

STEPHENS, ------- CF Sept. 1875, Northampton, Cause Unkn., 2 months, Unkn. & Bailey Stephens, Birth Unkn., Single, Neighbor source

STEPHENS, ------- CM Oct. 30, 1871, Northampton, Infantile, 5 days, Robt. & Ada, Northampton, Single, Robt. Stephens, Father source

STEPHENS, Adah CF Mar. 9, 1876, Northampton, Cause Unkn., 60, Adah Stephens, Northampton, Laborer, Widow, Dennis James Friend source

STEPHENS, Jno. CM Oct. 1875, Northampton, Cause Unkn., 1 month, Unkn. & Ann Stephens, Birth Unkn., Single, Neighbor source

STEPHENS, Sallie WF Nov. 28, 1877, Northampton, Dropsy, 10 yrs. 3 mos. 8 days, Unkn. & Mary, Northampton, Single, Mary Stephens, Mother source

STEPHENS, Susan CF Oct. 10, 1878, Northampton, Cause Unkn., 6 months, Wesley & Mary, Birth Unkn., Single, Wesley Stephens, Father source

STERLING, ------- WM Sept. 12, 1893, Northampton, Cause Unkn. 2 days, Thos. & Sallie, Northampton, Single, Thos. Sterling, Father source

STERLING, L. R. WM May 15, 1892, Northampton, Cholera Infantum, 3, William & Susan, Northampton, Single, William Sterling, Father source

STEVENS, ------- CF Feb. 25, 1896, Northampton, Cause Unkn., 3 days, Jno. T. & Josephine, Northampton, Single, Jno. T. Stevens Father source

STEVENS, ------- CF Mar. 4, 1895, Northampton, Dysentery, 3 months, John & Josephine, Northampton, Single, John Stevens, Father source

STEVENS, ------- CF Sept. 1891, Northampton, Cause Unkn., 9 days, Phoebe Stevens, Northampton, Single, Jacob Ephraim, Grandfather source

STEVENS, ------- CM Dec. 1891, Northampton, Cholera Infantum, 2 months, Annie Stevens, Northampton, Single, Littleton Stevens, Uncle source

STEVENS, ------- CM Feb. 22, 1892, Northampton, Cause Unkn., 1 month, Walter & Rosa, Northampton, Single, Rosa Stevens, Mother source

STEVENS, ------- CM Jan. 26, 1893, Northampton, Cause Unkn., 4 days, Isaac & Arintha, Northampton, Singles, Arintha Stevens, Mother source

STEVENS, ------- CM Mar. 25, 1892, Northampton, Cause Unkn., 2 days, J. A. & Mary, Northampton, Single, J. A. Stevens, Father source

STEVENS, -------CM Jan. 30, 1896, Northampton, Dropsy., 3, Walter & Rosa, Northampton, Single, Jno. T. Stevens, Father source

STEVENS, Alice CF May 12, 1883, Northampton, Consumption, 19, Lit & Sarah, Northampton, Servant, Geo. Simkins, Friend source

STEVENS, Dara WF Nov. 1879, Northampton, Delirium Fever, 4, Georgianna Stevens & Henry Thomas, Va., Va., Va., Single, Wm. A. Thom, source

STEVENS, Geo. CM Aug. 13, 1892, Northampton, Old Age, 79, Parents Unkn., Northampton, Laborer, Married, Ed Stevens, Nephew source

STEVENS, Infant BF May 1880, Northampton, Cause Unkn., 6 months, Unkn. & Susan Stevens, Va., Va., Va., Single, source unkn.

STEVENS, John CM Aug. 12, 1896, Northampton, Typhoid, 12 days, Len & Mary, Northampton, Single, Len Stevens, Father source

STEVENS, Josephine CF Dec. 13, 1896, Northampton, Dropsy, 31, Horace & Lavenia Sample, Northampton, Married, Jno. T. Stevens, Husband source

STEVENS, Lavenia CF Feb. 2, 1896, Northampton, Burn, 6, Jno. T & Josephine, Northampton, Single, Jno. T. Stevens, Father source

STEVENS, Lillian WF Nov. 1879, Northampton, Delirium Fever, 1, Georgianna Stevens & Henry Thomas, Va., Va., Va., Single, Wm. A. Thom, source

STEVENS, Nancy CF 1888, Northampton, Premature Birth, 10 days, Parents Unkn., Northampton, Single, Custis Stevens, Neighbor source

STEVENS, Raymond CM July 4, 1893, Northampton, Run over by cart, 2, ----- & Annie Stevens, Northampton, Single, Annie Stevens, Mother source

STEVENS, Robert CM Jan. 25, 1887, Northampton, Burned, 5, Walter & Rose, Northampton, Single, Walter Stevens, Father source

STEVENSON, Blanche WF July 13, 1896, Northampton, Cause Unkn., 5 months, J. R. & Roberta, Northampton, Single, J. R. Stevenson, Father source

STEVENSON, Ella CF Sept. 2, 1894, Northampton, Child Birth, 24, Southey & Jane Goffigon, Northampton, Married, Geo. E. Wilson, Brother source

STEVENSON, Susan WF Nov. 1879, Northampton, Malarial Fever, 2, Parents Unkn., Va., Single, W. W. Wilkins, source (PR)

STEWART, ------- CF June 16, 1892, Northampton, Cause Unkn., 1 day, Ben & Maggie, Northampton, Single, Ben Stewart, Father source

STEWART, ------- CM Feb. 10, 1895, Northampton, Cause Unkn., 8 days, Chas. & Tabitha, Northampton, Single, Chas. Stewart, Father source

STEWART, ------- (2) WM Oct. 1874, Northampton, Infantile, Age Unkn., Virgil & Mary, Northampton, Single, Virgil Stewart, Father source

STEWART, Herbert WM Apr. 2, 1893, Northampton, Burned, 15 months, J. M. & Georgianna, Northampton, Single, John M. Stewart, Father source

STEWART, James H. WM Jan. 19, 1876, Northampton, Cause Unkn., Age Unkn., James Stewart, Birth Unkn., Single, A. Ashby, Neighbor source

STEWART, Joseph CM July 28, 1876, Northampton, Yellow Jaundice, 70, Parents Unkn., Accomack, Laborer, Widower, Dennis James, Son source

STEWART, Mary CF Apr. 23, 1892, Northampton, Measles, 11, Charles & Tabitha, Northampton, Single, Charles Stewart, Father source

STEWART, Mary WF July 2, 1883, Northampton, Dysentery, 8 months, Virgil & Mary, Birth Unkn., Single, Virgil Stewart,Father source

STEWART, Thos. CM Aug. 12, 1891, Northampton, Drowned, 7, Chas. & Tabitha, Northampton, Single, Chas. Stuart, Father source

STILES, Nellie WF 1888, Northampton, Heart Disease, 2 yrs. 5 mos., J. W. Stiles, New Jersey, Single, J. W. Stiles, Parent source

STOAKLEY, Alfred CM Mar. 14, 1893, Northampton, Consumption, 51, Joshua & Milly, Northampton, Laborer, Married, John Stoakley, Brother source

STOAKLEY, Alfred CM Mar. 9, 1893, Northampton, Kidney Trouble, 60, Parents Unkn., Northampton, Laborer, Single, Handy Drummond, Neighbor source

STOAKLEY, Henry CM Jan. 12, 1892, Northampton, Grippee, 76, Parents Unkn., Northampton, Laborer, Married, E. Savage, Friend source

STOAKLEY, Milley CF Jan. 10, 1892, Northampton, Grippee, 82, Hugh & Comfort Savage, Northampton, Laborer, Married, E. Savage, Nephew source

STOAKLEY, Sarah CF Aug. 11, 1873, Northampton, Cause Unkn., 40, Parents Unkn., Northampton, Housekeeping, Michael Stoakley, Husband source

STOAKLEY, Thos. A. WM Feb. 24, 1884, Northampton, Cause Unkn., 5 days, Thos. J. & Sally S., Northampton, Thos. J. Stoakley, Father source

STOAKLEY, Thos. S. WM Mar. 1, 1876, Northampton, Cancer, 75, Parents Unkn., Northampton, Wm. S. Stoakley, Son source

STOCKLEY, Henry CM Dec. 16, 1893, Northampton, Consumption, 67, Jos., & Priscilla, Northampton, Farmer, Married, Ed Stockley, Son source

STOKELY, Thomas S. WM Mar. 21, 1887, Northampton, Cholera Infantum, 2, Thos. & Mary, Northampton, Single, Thomas Stokely, Father source

STOTT, Lizzie CF May 10, 1878, Northampton, Cramp Colic, 40, Parents Unkn., Birth Unkn., Laborer, Single, Fred Waddy, Friend source

STOTT, Maritta WF Dec. 1879, Northampton, Croup, 1, Unkn. & Mary, Va., Va., Va., Single, Dr. G. W. Smith, Physician source

STRATTON, ------- CF July 20, 1896, Northampton, Cause Unkn., 10 days, Chas. & Adah, Northampton, Single, Chas. Stratton, Father source

STRATTON, ------- WF Jan. 25, 1896, Northampton, Yellow Jaundice, 9 days, Ed & Emma, Northampton, Single, Ed Stratton, Father source

STRATTON, Chas. CM July 4, 1883, Northampton, Cholera Infantum, 2, Jacob & Sabra, Birth Unkn., Jacob Stratton, Father source

STRATTON, David CM Sept. 14, 1878, Northampton, Cause Unkn., 50, Parents Unkn., Northampton, Laborer, Bridget Stratton, Sister source

STRATTON, Infant Sept. 24, 1871, Northampton, Crying Fits, 2 days, Daniel & Bridget, Northampton, Single, Daniel Stratton, Father source [Laborer?]

STRATTON, Jennie CF June 6, 1891, Northampton, Croup, 2, Daniel & Carrie, Northampton, Single, Daniel Stratton, Father source

STRATTON, Peter BM Feb. 1880, Northampton, Dropsy, 70, Parents Unkn., Va., Va., Va., Farm Laborer, Tweezer Wife, Dr. S. P. Nottingham, Physician source

STRATTON, Peter CM Jan. 1, 1882, Northampton, Dropsy, 70, Parents Unkn., Northampton, Farmer, Miss Sadie Ames, source

STRAUSBURY, C. H. WM Sept. 12, 1894, Northampton, Dropsy, 32, Parents Unkn., North Carolina, Laborer, Single, E. S. Herald County paper source

STRINGER, Sallie WF June 1879, Northampton, Paralysis, 60, Hilary B. & Sally B., Va., Va., Va., Keeping House, Geo. W. Husband, Dr. P. A. Fitzhugh, Physician source

STURGIS, ------- WF Feb. 2, 1887, Northampton, Congestive Chill, 3, Henry & Ida, Northampton, Single, Henry Sturgis, Father source

STURGIS, ------- WM July 15, 1896, Northampton, Cause Unkn., 1 month, C. F. & Minnie, Northampton, Single, C. F. Sturgis, Father source

STURGIS, Alma WM Aug. 14, 1877, Northampton, Typhoid Fever, 8 yrs. 6 days, William & Lizzie, Northampton, Single, William Sturgis, Father source

STURGIS, Effie Lee WF Sept. 10, 1872, Northampton, Brain Fever, 3 yrs. 9 mos., Jas. K. & Missouri, Northampton, Single, Jas. K. Sturgis, Father source

STURGIS, Leonard WM Sept. 16, 1892, Northampton, Bronchitis, 10 months, C. F. & M. C., Northampton, Single, C. F. Sturgis, Father source

STURGIS, Lillian L. WF Aug. 23, 1885, Northampton, Congestive Chill, 12, Jas. & Indie, Northampton, Single, Jas. M. Sturgis, Father source

STURGIS, Mary WF Mar. 14, 1877, Northampton, Typhoid Fever, 29, Jacob & Molly Spady, Northampton, Wm. H. Husband, Richard O. Nottingham, Friend source

STURGIS, Samuel Jr. WM 1876, Month/Day of Death Unkn., Northampton, Cause Unkn., Age Unkn., Wm. T. H. & Katy, Northampton, Wm. T. H. Sturgis, Father source

STURGIS, Vianna WF Sept. 20, 1885, Northampton, Old Age, 72, Jno. & Vianna, Northampton, Married, Oswald Sturgis, source

STURGIS, William WM Oct. 4, 1887, Northampton, Congestive Chill, 2, Henry & Ida, Northampton, Single, Henry Sturgis, Father source

STURGIS, Wm. H. WM Mar. 9, 1877, Northampton, Typhoid Fever, 39, William & Mary, Northampton, Farmer, Mary Wife, Richard O. Nottingham, Friend source

SUNKET, ------- CM June 1885, Northampton, CM June 1885, Cause Unkn., 0, Jno. & Ledy, Northampton, Single, Jno. H. Sunket, Father source

SUNKETS, ------- CM Oct. 14, 1878, Northampton, Crying Fits, 6 days, John & Litia, Northampton, Single, John Sunkets, Father source

SUNKETT, Mack CM Mar. 22, 1894, Northampton, Malaria, 5 months, John & Lelia, Northampton, Single, Lelia Sunkett, Mother source

SUTTON, ------- CM 1888, Northampton, Cause Unkn., 6 months, Nat Sutton, [Laborer?], Northampton, Single, Nat Sutton, Parent source

SUTTON, Hennie CF Dec. 12, 1892, Northampton, Consumption, 50, Parents Unkn., Northampton, Laborer, Married, Chas. Smith, Neighbor source

SUTTON, Peter CM 1888, Northampton, Croup, 6 months, Nat Sutton, [Laborer?], Northampton, Single, Nat Sutton, Parent source

TANKARD, ------- CM July 16, 1875, Northampton, Cause Unkn., 2 days, Calino & Mary, Birth Unkn., Single, Mary Tankard, Mother source

TANKARD, ------- CM July 4, 1894, Northampton, Cause Unkn., 10 days, Sam & Esther, Northampton, Sam Tankard, Father source

TANKARD, Adah CF Feb. 10, 1876, Northampton, Inflammation Bowels, 31, Sarah Tankard, Northampton, Laborer, Sarah Tankard, Mother source

TANKARD, Alfred CM Mar. 28, 1883, Northampton, Typhoid, 1, Calno & Mary, Birth Unkn., Calno Tankard, Father source

TANKARD, Calno CM July 4, 1893, Northampton, Consumption, 68, John & Mary, Northampton, Laborer, Geo. Hutchenson, Neighbor source

TANKARD, Ezekiel CM May 6, 1892, Northampton, Consumption, 60, Parents Unkn., Northampton, Laborer, Married, Newspaper report source

TANKARD, Maria CF Apr. 1, 1887, Northampton, Old Age, 84, Parents Unkn., Northampton, Laborer, Married, Peter Doughty, Friend source

TANKARD, Mary G. WF Aug. 14, 1894, Northampton, Malaria Fever, 54, Luther & Mary Nottingham, Northampton, Married, P. B. Tankard, Husband source

TANKARD, Roland WM Apr. 20, 1894, Northampton, Blood Poison, 38, P. B. & Elizabeth, Northampton, Farmer, Married, P. B. Tankard, Father source

TANKARD, Sophie E. WF Aug. 29, 1895, Northampton, Billious Dystenery, 6, E. G. & Annie D., Northampton, Single, E. G. Tankard, Father source

TAYLOR, ------- CF Dec. 18, 1887, Northampton, Cause Unkn., 3 days, Thomas & Ida, Northampton, Single, Thomas Taylor, Father source

TAYLOR, ------- CM Dec. 14, 1876, Northampton, Whooping Cough, 4 months, Arthur & Ann, Northampton, Single, Arthur Taylor, Father source

TAYLOR, ------- WM Dec. 18, 1877, Northampton, Infantile, 13 days, Samuel & Isabella, Northampton, Single, Samuel Taylor, Father source

TAYLOR, Adelaide CF Aug. 16, 1892, Northampton, Dropsy, 40, Parents Unkn., Northampton, Laborer, Married, Laura Morris, Friend source

TAYLOR, Elizabeth B. WF Feb. 15, 1894, Northampton, Pneumonia, 63, M. J. & Eliza Dunton, Northampton, Married, Geo. B. Taylor, Son source

TAYLOR, Harry WM Oct. 16, 1894, Northampton, Typhoid Fever, 18, Chas. L. & Jennie, Penn., Hotel Clerk, Single, C. L. Taylor, Father source

TAYLOR, Henry CM Sept. 1871, Northampton, Bilious, 80, Sam & Violet, Northampton, Laborer, Single, Jas. Taylor, when died source

TAYLOR, Jas. W. WM Nov. 10, 1892, Northampton, Typhoid, 31, Wm. M & Catherine, Northampton, Waterman, Married, Frank Colona, Father-in-Law source

TAYLOR, Levin CM Apr. 10, 1893, Northampton, Cause Unkn., 40, Annie, Northampton, Dina Williams, Aunt source

TAYLOR, Mary CF Aug. 1891, Northampton, Consumption, 60, Parents Unkn., Northampton, Laborer, Married, Harry Taylor, Husband source

TAYLOR, Mary WF Aug. 4, 1892, Northampton, Consumption, 31, Parents Unkn., Northampton, Married, G. A Taylor, Husband source

TAYLOR, Peter CM June 8, 1892, Northampton, Cause Unkn., 2 months, Smith & Nellie, Northampton, Single, Smith Taylor, Father source

TAYLOR, Wesley WM Jan. 20, 1896, Northampton, Old Age, 84, Died at Alms House, Northampton, Laborer, Single, Wm. G. Bell, Overseer of Poor source

TAYLOR, William WM Sept. 1879, Northampton, Atrophy of Liver, 68, Parents Unkn., Va. Farmer, Married, Jas. M. McNutt, source (PR)

TAYLOR, Wm. E. WM Sept. 1871, Northampton, Brain Fever, 6 mos., Robt. B. & Lelia A., Northampton, Single, Robt. B. Taylor, Father source

TAZEWELL, Infant BF Mar. 1880, Northampton, Debility, 2 days, Harry & Mary, Va., Va., Va., Single, source unkn.

TAZWELL, Emma BF Aug. 1879, Northampton, Whooping Cough, 7 months, Parents Unkn., Va., Va., Va., Single, source unkn.

TAZWELL, John CM Mar. 6, 1894, Northampton, Consumption, 2, Henry & Kerin, Northampton, Single, Henry Tazwell, Father source

THOM, Annie P. WF Jan.9, 1894, Northampton, Pneumonia, 63, Alfred & Annie Parker, Northampton, Married, W. A. Thom, Husband source

THOMAS, ------- CF Dec. 1871, Northampton, Infantile, 15 days, Adaline Thomas, Northampton, Single, Geo. H. Thomas, Neighbor source

THOMAS, ------- CM Aug. 1, 1887, Northampton, Cause Unkn., 6 days, Arthur & Maria, Northampton, Single, Arthur Thomas, Father source

THOMAS, ------- CM June 1873, Northampton, Infantile, 10 days, Henry & Ad., Northampton, Single, Ellen Savage, Neighbor source

Northampton County, VA, Deaths from Death Register and Wills, 1871-1896

THOMAS, ------- CM Mar. 29, 1894, Northampton, Cause Unkn., 14 days, Alice, Northampton, Single, H. Buchanan, Neighbor source

THOMAS, ------- CM May 1875, Northampton, Cause Unkn., 3 days, Geo. Savage & Areline Thomas, Birth Unkn., Single, Areline Thomas, Mother source

THOMAS, ------- CM Sept. 1873, Northampton, Infantile, 5 days, Bell Thomas, Northampton, Single, source unkn.

THOMAS, ------- WM Mar. 29, 1873, Northampton, Infantile, 12 days, Joseph W. & Emma, Northampton, Single, Jos. W. Thomas, Father source

THOMAS, Caleb Jr. BM May, 1880, Northampton, Trismus Narcentium, 9 days, Caleb & Nannie, Va., Va., Va., Single, Dr. W. W. Wilkins, Physician source

THOMAS, Dennis CM Nov. 1871, Northampton, Congestive Fever, 6, Peggie Thomas, Northampton, Single, Peter Thomas, Grandfather source

THOMAS, Geo. CM Mar. 1891, Northampton, Pneumonia, 35, Ada Jarvis, Northampton, Laborer, Married, Geo. Willis, Neighbor source

THOMAS, George CM Jan. 19, 1877, Northampton, Bilious Fever, 2 yrs. 6 mos., Peter & Sarah, Northampton, Single, Peter Thomas, Father source

THOMAS, John C. WM Mar. 27, 1873, Northampton, Dropsy of the Chest, 23 yrs. 8 mos. 19 days, John W. & Sophia E., Northampton, Farmer, Single, Jos. W. Thomas, Brother source

THOMAS, Levin WM July 1873, Northampton, Shot, 21, Geo. L. J. & Mary, Northampton, Single, Geo. H. Thomas, Friend source

THOMAS, Luke CM Apr. 1891, Northampton, Consumption, 55, Parents Unkn., Northampton, Laborer, Married, O. R. Tankard, Neighbor source

THOMAS, Solomon CM Sept. 2, 1893, Northampton, Typhoid Fever, 43, Sol. & Sarah, Northampton, Laborer, Single, John R. Read, Neighbor source

THOMAS, Sophia CF 1891, Northampton, Cause Unkn., 46, Robt. & Amy Rogers, Northampton, Laborer, Single, Robt. Rogers, Brother source

THOMAS, Virginia E. CF Dec. 20, 1872, Northampton, Dropsy, 9 mos. 1 day, Mary Thomas, Northampton, Single, Mary Thomas, Mother source

THOMAS, Wm. H. WM April. 17, 1872, Northampton, Typhoid, 30, Parents Unkn., Bedford Co., Minister, Anna Wife, Rich'd T. Dunton, where died source

THOMPSON, ------- WF June 29, 1885, Northampton, Crying Fits, 6 days, O. A. & S. E., Northampton, Single, O. A. Thompson, Father source

THOMPSON, ------- WM Aug. 16, 1891, Northampton, Cause Unkn., 6 days, Obed & Sarah, Northampton, Single, Obed Thompson, Father source

THOMPSON, Ella WF Sept. 15, 1892, Northampton, Typhoid, 11, Willis & Annie P., Northampton, Single, Willis Thompson, Father source

THOMPSON, Geo. CM Sept. 11, 1893, Northampton, Cause Unkn., 51, Parents Unkn., Northampton, Laborer, Single, John R. Read, Neighbor source

Northampton County, VA, Deaths from Death Register and Wills, 1871-1896

THOMPSON, Peter C. CM 1888, Northampton, Consumption, 28, Wm. Thompson, Northampton, Laborer, Single, Wm. Thompson, Father source

TOLIVER, John H. CM June 9, 1896, Northampton, Meningitis, 5 months, Henry & Mary A., Northampton, Single, Mary A. Toliver, Mother source

TOMAS, Bettie WF Mar. 6, 1893, Northampton, Cause Unkn., 28, Henry & Lettie Robinson, King Wm. Co., Married, Henry Robinson, Father source

TOY, George WM Nov. 10, 1893, Northampton, Paralysis, 62, Parents Unkn., Near Balto. Md., Farmer, Single, James Toy, Brother source

TRAVIS, ------- Dec. 1891, Northampton, Cause Unkn., 3 months, Wm. & Sarah E., Northampton, Single, Wm. Travis, Father source

TRAVIS, ------- WM Mar. 5, 1874, Northampton, Cause Unkn., 4 days, Nim S. & Fanny, Northampton, Single, Nim S. Travis, Father source

TRAVIS, Charlotte WF June 18, 1893, Northampton, Old Age, 90 yrs. 6 mos. 18 days, Polly Costin, Northampton, Married, John T. Whitehead, Son source

TRAVIS, George WM Oct. 14, 1876, Northampton, Cause Unkn., 8, Severn B. & Missouri, Northampton, Single, Severn B. Travis, Father source

TRAVIS, Madaline WF Oct 4, 1891, Northampton, Croup, 3, Wm. & Sarah E., Northampton, Single, Wm. Travis, Father source

TREHERN, ------- CF June 30, 1887, Northampton, Crying Fits, 7 days, Len & Mary, Northampton, Single, Lenard Trehern, Father source

TREHERN, ------- CM 1888, Northampton, Cause Unkn., 1 mo. 13 days, Leonard Trehern, [Laborer?], Northampton, Single, Robin Trehern, Neighbor source

TREHURNE, ------- CM Dec. 28, 1891, Northampton, Pneumonia, 3 months, Alfred T. & Norow (Nora), Northampton, Single, Alfred T. Trehurne, Father source

TROWER, ------- CF Aug. 10, 1893, Northampton, Cause Unkn., 1 month, Alfred & Priscilla, Northampton, Single, Geo. Satchell, Neighbor source

TROWER, ------- CM April 1875, Northampton, Cause Unkn., 1 month, Harrison & Sarah, Birth Unkn., Single, Harrison Trower, Father source

TROWER, ------- CM June 2, 1896, Northampton, Cause Unkn., 43, James & Fannie, Northampton, Laborer, Single, James Trower, Father source

TROWER, ------- CM Mar. 13, 1895, Northampton, Cause Unkn., 8 days, Ben & Eliza, Northampton, Single, Ben Trower, Father source

TROWER, ------- CM May 12, 1893, Northampton, Cause Unkn., 1 month, James & Lottie, Northampton, Single, Geo. Satchell, Neighbor source

TROWER, Alfred CM June 4, 1891, Northampton, Dysentery, 4 months, Alfred & Priscilla, Northampton, Single, Alfred Trower, Father source

TROWER, Alfred CM Oct. 2, 1896, Northampton, Pneumonia, 35, John & Ann, Northampton, Laborer, Married, George Kellam, Friend source

TROWER, Annie L. WF Aug. 12, 1896, Northampton, Cause Unkn., 7 months, R. S. & Henrietta, Northampton, Single, R. S. Trower, Father source

TROWER, Clement CM Dec. 20, 1884, Northampton, Cholera Infantum, 1, Jim & Lottie, Northampton, Single, Jim Trower, Father source

TROWER, Daisy WF Dec. 1, 1884, Northampton, Cause Unkn., 4, Geo. W. & A. J. Trower, Northampton, Geo. W. Trower, Father source

TROWER, Fannie CF Oct. 14, 1877, Northampton, Measles, 3, Isaac & Sallie, Northampton, Single, Isaac Taylor, Friend source

TROWER, Infant Apr. 10, 1872, Northampton, Northampton, Crying Fits, 8 days, Mary Nelson Trower, Northampton, Father source [Laborer?]

TROWER, Infant BM Jan. 1880, Northampton, Debility Teething, 20 days, Henrietta Trower, Va., Va., Va., Single, L. A. Bissouly?, Physician source

TROWER, Infant CF Feb. 16, 1871, Northampton, Crying Fits, 1 day, Nelson & Mary, Northampton, Single, Nelson Trower, Father source [Laborer?]

TROWER, Jesse CM Sept. 1, 1884, Northampton, Drowned, 27, Nelson Trower & Mary Nottingham, Northampton, Nelson Trower, Father source

TROWER, Joseph CM June 1891, Northampton, Dropsy, 66, Parents Unkn., Northampton, Laborer, Married, Nat Churn, Neighbor source

TROWER, Luke CM Nov. 10, 1871, Northampton, Consumption, 70, Parents Unkn., Northampton, Friend Physician source

TROWER, Rachel CF Apr. 1875, Northampton, Cause Unkn., 50, Parents Unkn., Birth Unkn., wife of Keley Trower, Husband source

TURNER, ------- CF Mar. 14, 1874, Alms' House, Cause Unkn., 7 days, Kitty Turner, Eastville Township, Single, N. W. Wyatt source

TURNER, ------- CM June 5, 1872, Northampton, Infantile, 3 days, Ellen Turner, Northampton, Single, Geo. T. Turner, where died source

TURNER, ------- WF July 25, 1895, Northampton, Cholera E., 6 months, G. W. & Arintha, Northampton, Single, James Turner, Brother source

TURNER, ------- WM Apr. 20, 1883, Northampton, Cause Unkn., 5 days, Jno. T. & Mary E., Birth Unkn., Jno. T. Turner, Father source

TURNER, ------- WM Mar. 1891, Northampton, Cause Unkn., 3 days, Major & Malinda, Northampton, Single, Wm. T. Killmon, Neighbor source

TURNER, Henie WF Mar. 12, 1878, Northampton, Cancer, 45, Rob & Mary Nottingham, Northampton, Geo. T. Turner, Husband source

TURNER, Isaac CM Feb. 13, 1894, Northampton, Pneumonia, 61, Parents Unkn., Northampton, Farmer, Married, Fred Wright, Son-in-Law source

TURNER, Julia CF Apr. 17, 1896, Northampton, Pneumonia, 19, John & Jennie Scott, Northampton, Married, Israel Turner, Husband source

TURNER, Julia CF July 7, 1891, Northampton, Dropsy, 60, Parents Unkn., Alabama, Laborer, Married, Frank Hoskins, Son source

TURNER, Major WM Sept. 18, 1885, Northampton, Fits, 6, Major & Malinda, Northampton, Single, Major Turner, Father source

TURNER, Mary WF Feb. 1880, Northampton, Difficult Labor, 35, Parents Unkn., Va., Housekeeper, Married, G. W. Smith source (PR)

TURNER, Nancy CF 1888, Northampton, Old Age, 68, Cata Upshur, Northampton, Laborer, Single, Cata Upshur, Neighbor source

TURNER, Sarah CF Sept. 14, 1894, Northampton, Cholera Infantum, 2, Horace & Minnie, Acco. Co., Married, Arthur Read, Grandfather source

TYLER, ------- WF Dec. 2, 1894, Northampton, Cause Unkn., 2 months, Ben & Addie, Northampton, Single, Sam'l Townsend, Friend source

TYLER, John A. WM Dec. 20, 1893, Northampton, Cause Unkn., 1 mo. 15 days, Benj. & Addie, Northampton, Single, J. E. Tyler, Grandfather source

TYLER, Lillie WF May 17, 1872, Northampton, Typhoid, 80, Saml. Marshall, Birth Unkn., Single, Wm. J. Marshall, Nephew source

TYLER, Robt. E. WM May 10, 1874, Northampton, Worms, 2 yrs. 3 mos., Jno. E. & Sallie, Northampton, Single, Jno. E. Tyler, Father source

UNDERHILL, ------- WM 1888, Northampton, Cause Unkn., 1 day, M. E. Underhill, [Farmer?], Northampton, Single, M. E. Underhill, Father source

UNDERHILL, Richie P. WF Sept. 1874, Eastville Township, Confection Chill, 7, M. E. & Maggie, Eastville Township, Single, Michael E. Underhill, Father source

UNKNOWN, ------- WM Apr. 1882, Northampton, Dropsy, 60, Parents Unkn., Northampton, unkn. source

UPSHUR, ------- CF Aug. 10, 1896, Northampton, Cause Unkn., 9 Days, Henry & Liddie, Northampton, Henry Upshur, Father source

UPSHUR, ------- CF Oct. 2, 1891, Northampton, Bled to Death, 8 days, Geo. & Ella, Northampton, Single, Geo. Upshur, Father source

UPSHUR, Abraham CM Nov. 13, 1895, Northampton, Dysentery, 7 months, Jacob & Leah, Northampton, Single, Jacob Upshur, Father source

UPSHUR, Addie CF Feb. 29, 1894, Northampton, Burned, 7 months, Sarah Upshur, Northampton, Single, Ellen Upshur, Grandmother source

UPSHUR, Annie G. WF May 1880, Northampton, Cholera Infantum, 6 months, Henry & Alice S., Va., Va., Va., George Ker source

UPSHUR, Arthur CM June 12, 1892, Northampton, Dysentery, 63, Isaac & Adah, Northampton, Laborer, Married, Henry Upshur, Son source

UPSHUR, Bennett CM Apr. 20, 1873, Cobb Is., Va.,, Cause Unkn., 60, Frank & Nelly, Northampton, Laborer, Single, A. F. Cobb, Neighbor source

UPSHUR, Bill CM Oct. 1875, Northampton, Fits, 18, Parents Unkn., Birth Unkn. Neighbor source

UPSHUR, Caleb CM Jan. 23, 1893, Northampton, Consumption, 48, Parents Unkn., Northampton, Laborer, Single, John Stoakley, Friend source

UPSHUR, Caroline CF Aug. 2, 1887, Northampton, Consumption, 1, Henry & Alice, Northampton, Single, Henry Upshur, Father source

UPSHUR, Demory CF 1888, Northampton, Congestive Chill, 10, Alfred Upshur, [Farmer?], Northampton, Single, Alfred Upshur, Father source

UPSHUR, Elizabeth WF Aug. 25, 1887, Northampton, Congestion, 14, Thomas & Cary, Northampton, Single, Thomas Upshur, Father source

UPSHUR, Gaddy CF Dec. 14, 1876, Northampton, Old Age, 81, Parents Unkn., Maryland, Laborer, Widow, Harry Taylor, Son source

UPSHUR, Geo. CM Jan. 4, 1893, Northampton, Dysentery, 12, Parents Unkn., Northampton, Laborer, Single, Upshur Potter, Friend source

UPSHUR, Geo. CM Sept. 17, 1875, Northampton, Cause Unkn., 3 months, Geo. & Matilda, Northampton, Single, Neighbor source

UPSHUR, John M. WM Aug. 16, 1893, Northampton, Dysentery, 9 months, Henry L. & Alice, Northampton, Single, Henry L. Upshur, Father source

UPSHUR, Julia A. CF Feb. 15, 1893, Northampton, Cause Unkn., 5 months, Henry & Liddie, Northampton, Single, Henry Upshur, Father source

UPSHUR, Leah CF Oct. 8, 1876, Northampton, Old Age, 80 yrs. 5 mos. 10 days, Parents Unkn., Northampton, Laborer, Widow, Cato Upshur, Son source

UPSHUR, Leah CF Sept. 14, 1894, Northampton, Old Age, 78, Parents Unkn., Northampton, Single, Frank Upshur, Nephew source

UPSHUR, Levin CM Jan. 16, 1895, Northampton, Pneumonia, 62, Parents Unkn., Northampton, Laborer, Single, Geo. Read, Friend source

UPSHUR, Liddie CF Aug. 2, 1896, Northampton, Child Birth, 25, George & Jennie Jarvis, Northampton, Married, Henry Upshur, Husband source

UPSHUR, Mary E. CF Dec. 20, 1896, Northampton, Cause Unkn., 45, Parents Unkn., North Carolina, Married, Emily Poulson, Cousin source

UPSHUR, Mary E. WF Jan. 20, 1892, Northampton, Typhoid, 58, Geo. W. & Arintha Dunton, Married, T. W. Upshur, Husband source

UPSHUR, Nellie CF Sept. 6, 1894, Northampton, Dropsy, 80, Parents Unkn., Northampton, John Badger, source

UPSHUR, Patience CF June 21, 1891, Northampton, Consumption, 40, Geo. & Leah Satchell, Northampton, Laborer, Married, Alfred Upshur, Husband source

UPSHUR, Paul CM July 8, 1891, Northampton, Croup, 3 months, Alfred & Patience, Northampton, Single, Alfred Upshur, Father source

UPSHUR, Rachel CF Oct. 10, 1873, Northampton, Dropsy, 28 yrs., 4 mos., 11 days, George & Leah, Northampton, Housekeeping, Henry Sisco, Husband source

UPSHUR, Sallie CF July 14, 1895, Northampton, Cause Unkn., 1 month, Thos. C. & Clara, Northampton, Single, Thos. C. Upshur, Father source

UPSHUR, Sally WF July 1874, Northampton, Typhoid, 10, Arthur & Lucretia, Northampton, Single, E. Dunton, Neighbor source

UPSHUR, Sam'l CM Sept. 2, 1895, Northampton, Consumption, 72, Susan Upshur, Northampton, Farmer, Married, Lucy Wise, Neighbor source

Northampton County, VA, Deaths from Death Register and Wills, 1871-1896

UPSHUR, Sarah CF Feb. 29, 1894, Northampton, Burned, 17, Chas. & Ellen, Northampton, Cook, Single, Ellen Upshur, Mother source

UPSHUR, Sarah CF June 5, 1883, Northampton, Dropsy, 80, Parents Unkn., Birth Unkn., Chas. Upshur, Head of Family source

UPSHUR, Sarah P. WF Oct. 26, 1884, Northampton, Consumption, 2 mos. 23 days, Hy "Henry" L. & Ann, Northampton, Single, Hy L. Upshur, Father source

UPSHUR, William CM Nov. 14, 1892, Northampton, Typhoid, 24, Jacob & Sophia, Northampton, Single, Edward Upshur, Brother source

UPSHUR, William J. CM June 4, 1894, Northampton, Croup, 3 months, Wm. & Lizzie, Northampton, Single, Wm. Upshur, Father source

UPSHUR, Willie CM Mar. 13, 1877, Northampton, Measles, 5, Alfred & Nellie, Northampton, Single, Alfred Upshur, Father source

UPSHUR, Willie CM Mar. 19, 1878, Northampton, Large Head, 18 months, Abe & Sallie, Birth Unkn., Single, Abe Upshur, Father source

UPSHUR, Wm. B. CM Jan. 14, 1893, Northampton, Cause Unkn., 15 months, Henry & Liddie, Northampton, Single, Henry Upshur, Father source

VAN NESS, William WM Aug. 10, 1873, York Co., Va., Epileptic fits, 39 yrs. 5 mos., William J. Van Ness, Maryland, Laborer, Single, Wm. J. Van Ness, Father source

VANNESS, Jerusha WF Feb. 1875, Northampton, Consumption, 60, Parents Unkn., Birth Unkn., Married, Wm. Husband source

VAUGHN, Mary C. CF Nov. 1873, Norfolk, Va., Bilious Fever, 2 yrs. 5 mos., Jett & Mary L., Southampton, Va., Single, Jett Vaughn, Father source

VINCENT, Laura WF Jan. 11, 1894, Northampton, Pneumonia, 38, Parents Unkn., Birth Unkn., Married, E. S. Herald County paper source

WADDY, Mary E. WF May 21, 1896, Northampton, Paralysis, 66, John & Ann Griffith, Northampton, Married, Wm. E. Waddy, Husband source

WADDY, Priscilla CF June 16, 1894, Northampton, Diarrhea, 1, Maggie Waddy, Northampton, Single, Maggie Waddy, Mother source

WALKER, Annie WF Feb. 20, 1894, Northampton, Cause Unkn., 49, Parents Unkn., Birthplace Unkn., Married, C. H. Savage, Neighbor source

WALKER, Jno. CM Sept. 1875, Northampton, Dissipation, 50, Parents Unkn., Birth Unkn., Neighbor source

WALLACE, ------- CF Aug. 12, 1894, Northampton, Cause Unkn., 9 Days, Alfred & Margaret L., Northampton, Single, Alfred Wallace, Father source

WALLACE, Andrew CM Sept. 1871, Northampton, Diphtheria, 2, Wm. & Rose, Northampton, Single, Wm. Wallace, Father source

WALLACE, Rose CF Sept. 1871, Northampton, Diphtheria, 4, Wm. & Rose, Northampton, Single, Wm. Wallace, Father source

WALSTON, Maggie CF Nov. 1891, Acco. Co., Consumption, 35, Wm. Bayly & Susan Parker, Accomac, Laborer, Married, J. L. Brickhouse, Neighbor source

WALSTON, Sam'l J. WM Apr. 1880, Northampton, Apoplexy, 36, Parents Unkn., Va., Druggist, Married, Jas. M. McNutt source (PR)

WALSTON, Thos. C. WM Dec. 6, 1887, Richmond, Va., Blood Poisoning, 41, Parents Unkn., Accomac Co., Va., Lawyer, Married, Alfred Parker, Friend source

WARD, ------- WF Jan. 13, 1877, Northampton, Infantile, 4 days, Southey & Mary, Northampton, Single, Mary Ward, Mother source

WARD, Edgar WM Sept. 28, 1894, Northampton, Typhoid Fever, 21, S. W. & Tabitha, Northampton, Farmer, Single, S. W. Ward, Father source

WARD, Eliza WF June 1879, Northampton, Gastritis, 38, Parents Unkn., Va., Va., Va., Keeping House, Married, source unkn.

WARD, J. D. WM Sept. 20, 1878, Northampton, Inflammation, 44, Parents Unkn., Birth Unkn., Single, John W. Pearson, Friend source

WARD, John WM May 1880, Northampton, Typhoid Fever, 45, Parents Unkn., Va., Va., Va., Sailor, Married, source unkn.

WARD, Kate WF Jan. 1875, Northampton, Pneumonia, 6, Wm. Ward & Melinda, Birth Unkn., Single, Wm. Ward, Father source

WARD, Michael WM Nov. 1873, Northampton, Pneumonia, 55, Parents Unkn., Northampton, Merchant, source unkn.

WARD, Minny WM June 5, 1876, Northampton, Cause Unkn., 3 months, George G. & Ann, Northampton, Single, George Ward, Father source

WARD, Missouri WF Feb. 1872, Northampton, Child Birth, 28, Jno. L. & Eliz. Wescoat, Northampton, Wm. G. Ward, Husband source

WARD, Nettie WF Aug. 8, 1895, Northampton, Thrush, 3, Ben & Sadie, Northampton, Single, Sadie Ward, Mother source

WARD, Ruth S. WF June 15, 1895, Northampton, Croup, 3 months, W. B. & Nervilla, Northampton, Single, W. B. Ward, Father source

WARD, Sam'l D. WM Dec. 28, 1894, Northampton, Pneumonia, 39, Sam'l & Margaret, Northampton, Laborer, Married, C. J. Ward, Brother source

WARD, Sam'l N. WM Apr. 12, 1893, Northampton, Old Age, 91, Thos. & Henry "etta", Acco. Co., Farmer, Single, Berry Ward, Son source

WARD, Thomas WM Aug. 1872, Northampton, Infantile, 4 months, Wm. G. & Missouri, Northampton, Single, source unkn.

WARREN, Lukie CF Sept. 14, 1883, Northampton, Consumption, 70, Parents Unkn., Birth Unkn., Parker Morris, source

WARREN, Lukie CF Dec. 1884, Northampton, Cause Unkn., 50, Parents Unkn., Northampton, Parker Morris, source

WARREN, M. Sarah WF Oct. 20, 1896, Northampton, Cause Unkn., 2, T. E. & Mary E., Northampton, Single, T. E. Warren, Father source

WARREN, Mary WF June 15, 1887, Northampton, Consumption, 31, James & Frances Nottingham, Northampton, Richard Warren, Husband source

WARREN, Rebecca CF June 1885, Northampton, Dropsy, 1 yr. 1 mo., Ed & Martha, Northampton, Single, Ed Warren, Father source

WARRINGTON, Wissie May WF Nov. 29, 1887, Northampton, Cause Unkn., 13 days, John & Georgia, Northampton, Single, John Warrington, Father source

WASHINGTON, Geo. CM Apr. 1891, Northampton, Old Age, 75, --- & Fannie, Northampton, Laborer, Married, Fannie Washington, Wife source

WATSON, ------- CF Aug. 16, 1894, Northampton, Cause Unkn., 3 days, Joshua & Maria, Northampton, Single, Joshua Watson, Father source

WATSON, Ben CM Feb. 8, 1896, Northampton, Poison, 45, J. L. & Mary J., Northampton, Laborer, Single, J. L. Watson, Father source

WATSON, Daniel CM June 4, 1895, Northampton, Heart Dis., 26, Luke & Kate, Northampton, Farmer, Married, Luke Watson, Father source

WATSON, John B. WM Dec. 14, 1878, Northampton, Falling of a tree, 20, John C. & Mary, Nacy mon Co. Va., Farmer, Single, John C. Watson, Father source

WATSON, John B. WM Jan. 19, 1877, Northampton, Kill by the fall of a Tree, 24, John C. & Tabbith, Northampton, Farmer, Single, John C. Watson, Father source

WATSON, John C. WM Dec. 21, 1896, Northampton, Old Age, 84, Ben & Betsy, Acco. Co., Married, F. T. Matthews, Son-in-Law source

WATSON, Joseph WM July 7, 1885, Northampton, Typhoid, 19, Jno. & Polly, Northampton, Farmer, Jno. Watson, Father source

WATSON, Sally CF Feb. 1, 1873, Northampton, Crying Fits, 9 days, George & Sally, Northampton, Single, George Watson, Father source

WATSON, Thornton BM Jan. 1880, Northampton, Cause Unkn., 1 month, Parents Unkn., Va., Va., Va., Single, source unkn.

WATSON, Walter BM Jan. 1880, Northampton, Pleurisy, 4, George & Sarah, Va., Va., Va., Single, Dr. Geo. W. Smith, Physician source

WEBB, D. R. WM Apr. 17, 1892, Northampton, Consumption, 38, James & Louisa, Northampton, Surfman, Married, Mrs. Webb, Wife source

WEBB, Harriet CF Jan. 12, 1877, Northampton, Consumption, 42, Parents Unkn., Accomack, Laborer, Single, Sallie Webb, Friend source

WEBB, Jno. J. WM July, 1891, Northampton, Consumption, 45, Jas. & Sarah, Northampton, Laborer, Married, S. S. Wilkins, Friend source

WEBB, Rosa WF May 6, 1887, Northampton, Consumption, 36, John & Peggy Satchel, Northampton, John Webb, Husband source

WEEKS, ------- CM Oct. 10, 1871, Northampton, Bilious, 15 days, Francis Weeks, Northampton, Jno U. Gunter, when died source

WEEKS, ------- WM 1882, Northampton, Dropsy, 7 days, J. & T. Weeks, Northampton, Single, J. Weeks, Father source

WEEKS, Edmond BM Apr. 1880, Northampton, Dysentery, 80, Parents Unkn., Va., Va., Va., Laborer, Widower, Lucy W. Wife, source unkn.

WEEKS, Ellen CF Feb. 4, 1878, Northampton, Bilious Diarrhea, 2, Edmund & Mary, Northampton, Single, Mary Weeks, Mother source

WEEKS, Major CM Sept. 9, 1878, Northampton, Crying Fits, 7 days, Unkn. & Nellie Weeks, Birth Unkn., Single, Nellie Weeks, Mother source

WEEKS, Nelly BF Jan. 1880, Northampton, Child Birth, 30, Parents Unkn., Va., Va., Va., Major Husband, Drs. Smith & Scott, Physicians source

WEEKS, Solomon CM Dec. 9, 1877, Northampton, Cause Unkn., 2, Alfred & Susan, Northampton, Single, Alfred Weeks, Father source

WEEKS, Wm. CM Aug. 7, 1872, Northampton, Congestive Fever, 25, Edwd. Weeks, Northampton, Laborer, Single, Ezekiel Mason, where died source

WESCOAT, ------- CM June 1871, Northampton, Cause Unkn., 1, Rose Wescoat, Northampton, Single, H. P. Wescoat, Neighbor source

WESCOAT, ------- CM June 1871, Northampton, Cause Unkn., 1, Gennie Wescoat, Northampton, Single, H. P. Wescoat, Neighbor source

WESCOAT, Dennis CM July 1875, Northampton, Cause Unkn., 65, Parents Unkn., Birth Unkn., Neighbor source

WESCOAT, Easter CF Jan. 3, 1882, Northampton, Burnt, 5 yr. 5 mos., Rose Wescoat, Northampton, Single, Dr. Scott, Physician source

WESCOAT, Jno. B. WM Aug. 1873, Northampton, Cause Unkn., 60, Parents Unkn., Northampton, Farmer, Single, source unkn.

WESCOAT, Lizzie CF Mar. 1872, Northampton, Exposure, 18, Parents Unkn., Northampton, source unkn.

WESCOAT, Rich'd WM Jan 1875, Northampton, Whooping Cough, 3 months, Wm. R. & Mary, Birth Unkn., Single, Wm Wescoat, Father source

WESCOAT, Rose WF Sept. 13, 1887, Northampton, Consumption, 58, Parents Unkn., Northampton, Hez. Wescoat, Husband source

WESCOAT, Rose WF Sept. 17, 1875, Northampton, Consumption, 54, Parents Unkn., G. M. Wescoat, Husband source

WESCOAT, Sally T. WF Nov. 1873, Northampton, Cause Unkn., 3, E. D. & Gennie, Northampton, Single, Emory Thomas, Friend source

WESCOAT, Sarah CF June 23, 1884, Northampton, Heart Disease, 50, Parents Unkn., Northampton, Geo. Adair, source

WESCOTT, Comfort CF Aug. 15, 1885, Northampton, Sum Stroke, 41, Nim & Alice Wescott, Northampton, Severn Mapp Husband, Severn Mapp Senr., Source

WESCOTT, Jno. WM June 1883, Northampton, Old Age, 76, Parents Unkn., Birth Unkn., Farmer, W. W. Joynes, source

WESCOTT, Margaret CF Apr. 18, 1896, Northampton, Old Age, 82, Parents Unkn., Died at Alms House, Northampton, Widow, Wm. G. Bell, Overseer of Poor source

WESCOTT, Wm. B. WM Dec. 24, 1895, Northampton, Shot accident, 18, W. R. & Mary S., Northampton, Farmer, Single, W. R. Wescott, Father source

WESLEY, Estelle CF Aug. 28, 1895, Northampton, Brain Fever, 18, Geo. & Violet, Northampton, Single, Violet Wesley, Mother source

WESLEY, William CM 1873, Northampton, Cause Unkn., 37, Parents Unkn., Accomack, Va., Laborer, Single, Isaac Brown, Friend source

WEST, Caroline CF Jan 1875, Northampton, Cause Unkn., 30, Parents Unkn., Birth Unkn., Neighbor source

WEST, Comfort CF June 6, 1896, Northampton, Old Age, 105, Parents Unkn., Northampton, Widow, C. C. Read, Neighbor source

WEST, Daniel CM Nov. 15, 1894, Northampton, Consumption, 30, Ap. & Mary, Acco., Co., Laborer, Married, J. I. Mapp, Neighbor source

Northampton County, VA, Deaths from Death Register and Wills, 1871-1896

WEST, Mary A. WF June 29, 1885, Northampton, Inflammation of the Bowels, 65, John & Susan Scott, Jno. Edwd. Nottingham, source

WHITE, Annie CF Mar. 4, 1885, Northampton, Cause Unkn., 25, Jas. & Margt. Stevens, Northampton, Married, Jas. Stevens, Father source

WHITE, Annie E. WF May 8, 1891, Northampton, Grief, 76, J. W. & Mary Wilkins, Northampton, Married, S. S. White, Son source

WHITE, Edward T. WM July 1873, Northampton, Congestion, 21, E. T. & Margt., Northampton, Single, Boating, source unkn.

WHITE, Jas. H. WM Aug. 9, 1883, Northampton, Brain Fever, 65, Oh & Nancy, Birth Unkn., Farmer, Sidney S. White, Head of Family source

WHITE, John WM Feb. 2, 1895, Northampton, Thrush, 20 days, John W. & Mary J., Northampton, Single, John W. White, Father source

WHITE, John M. WM May 1896, Northampton, Brain Fever, 46, James H. & Anne E., Northampton, Journalists, Married, S. S. White, Brother source

WHITE, John W. WM July 31, 1893, Northampton, Thrush, 5 months, John W. & Emma J., Northampton, Single, John W. White, Father source

WHITE, L. S. WM 1888, Northampton, Congestive Chill, 54, Jas. C. White, Northampton, Farmer, Jas. C. White, Head of Family source

WHITEHEAD, ------- WM Apr. 5, 1874, Northampton, Thrush, 1 mo. 1 day, Sev. & Rose, Northampton, Single, Severn Whitehead, Father source

WHITEHEAD, Edgar WM Feb. 6, 1892, Northampton, Pneumonia, 22, John & Sarah, Northampton, Farmer, Single, John Whitehead, Father source

WHITEHEAD, Fannie WF Oct. 20, 1895, Northampton, Pneumonia, 48, R. F. & Veanna Dunton, Northampton, Married, J. R. Read, Neighbor source

WHITEHEAD, Talmadge WM Sept. 15, 1876, Northampton, Diphtheria, 9 mos. 5 days, Wm. M. & Fanny, Northampton, Single, Wm. M. Whitehead, Father source

WHITEHEAD, Wm. WM Aug. 3, 1892, Northampton, Cholera Infantum, 1 day, Wm. E. & Mary E., Northampton, Single, Wm. E. Whitehead, Father source

WHITMAN, Mary E. WF June 12, 1895, Northampton, Dysentery, 2, John & Georgiana, Northampton, Single, John Parkerson, Uncle source

WICKS, ------- CM Jan. 16, 1893, Northampton, Cause Unkn., 6 days, James & Elenora, Northampton, Single, Elenora Wicks, Mother source

WICKS, Carrie CF Feb. 2, 1893, Northampton, Measles, 13, Wm. & Emily, Northampton, Single, Emily Wicks, Mother source

WICKS, James Sr. CM Feb 17, 1893, Northampton, Paralysis, 64, Joseph & Harriet, Northampton, Farmer, Married, Robt. Wicks, Nephew source

WICKS, Mattie CF May 3, 1892, Northampton, Whooping Cough, 1, Wm. & Emily, Northampton, Single, William Wicks, Father source

WIDGEN, ------- CM Jan. 7, 1893, Northampton, Cholera Infantum, 10 days, John & Rinthia, Northampton, Single, John Widgen, Father source

WIDGEN, Alfred CM Dec. 2, 1887, Northampton, Congestive Chill, 70, Parents Unkn., Northampton, Laborer, Eliz. Widgen, Wife source

WIDGEN, Ernest WM Aug. 12, 1883, Northampton, Bilious Fever, 7, Thos. & Lucy, Birth Unkn., Thos. Widgen, Father source

WIDGEN, Fannie WF Dec. 28, 1893, Northampton, Consumption, 28, Frank & Emma Frost, Northampton, Married, Jeff Widgen, Husband source

WIDGEN, Gabe CM Sept. 1, 1873, Northampton, Lock Jaw, 33 yrs. 3 mos., Harry Taylor & Ibby Widgen, Northampton, Laborer, Single, Harry Taylor, Father source

WIDGEN, John WM Aug. 14, 1877, Northampton, Typhoid Fever, 27, Joseph & Sallie, Northampton, Blacksmith, Single, Joseph Widgen, Father source

WIDGEN, Kate CF Sept. 10, 1873, Northampton, Cause Unkn., 35, Harry Taylor & Ibby Widgen, Northampton, Laborer, Single, Harry Taylor, Father source

WIDGEN, Mary CF Apr. 3, 1895, Northampton, Consumption, 8, John & Arintha, Northampton, Single, John Widgen, Father source

WIDGEN, Sauky WM June 1, 1876, Northampton, Cause Unkn., 4 days, Southey & Mary E., Northampton, Single, Southey Widgen, Father source

WIDGEN, William CM Oct. 1, 1873, Northampton, Cause Unkn., 70, Ibby Widgen, Northampton, Laborer, Single. A. F. Cobb, Neighbor source

WIDGEON, Elizabeth WF Apr. 1880, Northampton, Irritative Fever, 78, Parents Unkn., Va., Va., Va., Widower, Thomas Widgeon, son, Dr. George W. Smith, Physician source

WIDGEON, Patsey E. WF May 9, 1874, Northampton, Meningitis, 31 yrs. 4 mos. 4 days, Walter & Susan, Northampton, Single, Geo. W. Widgeon, Brother

WILKINS, ------- CM May 10, 1896, Northampton, Cause Unkn., 6 months, Ed & Louisa, Northampton, Single, Ed. Wilkins, Father source

WILKINS, ------- WM Aug. 30, 1872, Northampton, Infantile, 4 days, Wm. E. & Kate, Northampton, Single, Wm. E. Wilkins, Father source

WILKINS, ------- WM Aug. 7, 1884, Northampton, Cause Unkn., 7 days, Wm. E. & Kate, Northampton, Single, Wm. E. Wilkins, Father source

WILKINS, ------- WM Dec. 12, 1871, Northampton, Infantile, 1 day, Geo. F. & Lottie, Northampton, Single, Geo. F. Wilkins, Father source

WILKINS, Anna B. WF Jan. 22, 1892, Northampton, Pneumonia, 13 months, W. J. & Essie L., Northampton, Single, W. J. Wilkins, Father source

WILKINS, Emily WF Nov. 10, 1893, Northampton, Cause Unkn., 66, Southey & Mary Spady, Northampton, Single, C. F. Wilkins, Nephew source

WILKINS, Fred CM Feb. 2, 1893, Northampton, Pneumonia, 61, Parents Unkn., Northampton, Farmer, Married, John R. Read, Neighbor source

WILKINS, Geo. W. WM Feb. 1894, Northampton, Pneumonia, 57, Parents Unkn., Northampton, Farmer, Married, Sam'l A. Jarvis, Neighbor

WILKINS, Jafus CM May 4, 1887, Northampton, Dysentery, 6 months, Peter & Sarah, Northampton, Single, Peter Wilkins, Father source

Northampton County, VA, Deaths from Death Register and Wills, 1871-1896

WILKINS, James E. WM Sept. 1874, Eastville Township, Cholera Infantum, 2, William E. & Kath., Eastville Township, Single, Wm. E. Wilkins, Father source

WILKINS, Laura WF Mar. 1880, Northampton, Erysipelas of Brain, 52, Parents Unkn., Va., Va., Va., Seamstress, Single, source unkn.

WILKINS, Lottie WF Mar. 5, 1876, Northampton, Paralysis, 30 yrs. 6 mos., Th. J. L. & Tabitha Nottingham, Northampton, Married, George F. Wilkins, source

WILKINS, M. S. WF Oct. 10, 1872, Northampton, Cancer, 55, Sallie & Thomas, Northampton, Physician source Thomas [Farmer?]

WILKINS, Maria CF Aug. 10, 1876, Northampton, Diphtheria, 3, Ann Wilkins, Northampton, Single, Ann Wilkins, Mother source

WILKINS, Mary A. WF Feb. 1875, Northampton, Consumption, 50, Parents Unkn., Birth Unkn., Robt. E. Wilkins, Husband source

WILKINS, Nancey WF Sept. 18, 1871, Northampton, Typhoid, 76 yrs. 6 mos., Jno. & Sally Trower, Northampton, Married, Wm. E. Wilkins, Husband source

WILKINS, Origen J. WM Oct. 1879, Northampton, Croup, 3, Parents Unkn., Va., Va., Va., Single, source unkn.

WILKINS, Sallie WF Nov. 20, 1872, Northampton, Inflammation of Brain, 35, Marg't & John Spady, Northampton, Joakim Wilkins Husband source

WILKINS, Sarah CF July 5, 1878, Northampton, Whooping Cough, 14 months, Unkn. & Sallie, Northampton, Single, Sallie Wilkins, Mother source

WILKINS, Thos. WM Oct. 5, 1893, Northampton, Cause Unkn., 16 months, W. T. & Missouri, Northampton, Single, W. T. Wilkins, Father source

WILLETT, ------- WM June 15, 1884, Northampton, Cause Unkn., 2 days, Jas. H. & Nannie, Northampton, Single, Jas. H. Willett, Father source

WILLIAMS, ------- CF Oct. 9, 1876, Northampton, Crying Fits, 2 days, Henry & Sarah, Northampton, John B. Williams, Neighbor source

WILLIAMS, E. J. WM Apr. 4, 1896, Northampton, Dropsy, 35, E. J. & Susan, Northampton, Farmer, Single, Mary Williams, Sister source

WILLIAMS, Edward CM Aug. 25, 1874, Northampton, Drowning, 50, James & Eady, Northampton, Laborer, Lucy wife, Alfred Wilkins, Friend source

WILLIAMS, Edward CM Oct. 14, 1877, Northampton, Bilious Fever, 5 yrs. 3 mos., Cutter & Sarah, Northampton, Single, Cutter Williams, Father source

WILLIAMS, George CM Aug. 4, 1887, Northampton, Dysentery, 2, Parents Unkn., Northampton, Single, Peter Savage, Friend source

WILLIAMS, Jesse WM Mar. 1, 1893, Northampton, Cause Unkn., 8 days, J. S. & Mary, Northampton, Single, Jesse S. Williams, Father source

WILLIAMS, Jno. H. CM Mar. 22, 1885, Northampton, Pneumonia, 2 yrs. 2 mos., Jno. H. & Lucy, Northampton, Single, Jno. H. Williams, Father source

WILLIAMS, Levin CM Apr. 15, 1893, Northampton, Dropsy, 40, Parents Unkn., Northampton, Married, Annie Wife, Mack Robinson, Friend source

WILLIAMS, Lloyd W. WM Mar. 10, 1893, Northampton, Old Age & Heart Failure, 78, Wm. & Mary, Northampton, Lawyer, Married, Dr. A. Brockenbrough, Son-in-Law source

WILLIAMS, Mrs. Maria P. H., WF Mar. 24, 1893, Northampton, Old Age Heart Failure, 68, Parents Unkn., Baltimore, Md., Married, Dr. A. Brockenbrough, Son-in-Law source

WILLIAMS, Nannie B. WF May 23, 1892, Northampton, Child Birth, 28, John A. & Virginia, Northampton, Married, W. A. Wise, Friend source

WILLIAMS, Puss CF Dec. 26, 1876, Northampton, Crying Fits, 7 days, George & Mary, Northampton, Single, George Williams, Father source

WILLIAMS, Sarah CF Mar. 4, 1894, Northampton, Congestive Chill, 42, Jas. H. & Eliza Williams, Northampton, Married, Margaret Only, Sister source

WILLIAMS, Wm. J. WM Oct. 13, 1894, Northampton, Typhoid Fever, 49, John & Mary, Northampton, Farmer, Married, Wm. I. Melson, Neighbor source

WILLIS, ------- WF Dec. 1875, Northampton, Cause Unkn., 2 months, Wm. & Julia, Birth Unkn., Single, Wm. Willis, Father source

WILLIS, ------- WF Jan. 1875, Northampton, Cause Unkn., 7 days, Custis & Emily, Birth Unkn., Single, Custis Willis, Father source

WILLIS, ------- WM Jan. 1875, Northampton, Cause Unkn., 7 days, Jno. & Arinthia, Birth Unkn., Jno. Willis, Father source

WILLIS, ------- WM Jan. 9, 1876, Northampton, Crying Fits, 8 days, John & Arinthia, Northampton, Single, John Willis, Father source

WILLIS, ------- (2) WM June 11, 1873, Northampton, Dysentery, 1 mo., 0 days, Jno. & Arinthia, Northampton, Single, John Willis, Father source

WILLIS, Ella M. WF July 11, 1893, Northampton, Measles, 1 yr. 2 mos., Luther & Anna, Northampton, Single, Anna Willis, Mother Mother source

WILLIS, Emily CF Jan. 10, 1876, Northampton, Typhoid Fever, 34, Sarah Willis, Northampton, Laborer, Single, Sarah Willis, Mother source

WILLIS, Emily Susan WF Jan. 1875, Northampton, Child Birth, 40, Parents Unkn., Birth Unkn., Custis Willis, Husband source

WILLIS, Harriet CF Nov. 10, 1891, Northampton, Accident, 13, Luke & Mary, Northampton, Single, Luke Willis, Father source

WILLIS, Harriett CF Jan. 8, 1876, Northampton, Cause Unkn., 1 month, John & Sarah, Northampton, Single, Sarah Willis, Mother source

WILLIS, Leonard WM Dec. 25, 1871, Northampton, Crying Fits, 5 days, Leon'd J. & Marg't. S., Northampton, Single, Leon'd J. Willis, Father source

WILLIS, Lola CF July 4, 1892, Northampton, Cause Unkn., 7, Lewis & Mary, Northampton, Single, Lewis Willis, Father source

WILLIS, Susan WF Feb. 1875, Northampton, Consumption, 66, Parents Unkn., Birth Unkn., Son source

WILSON, ------- CF Dec. 17, 1874, Eastville Township, Crying Fits, 8 days, Joe & Ellen, Eastville Township, Single, Jos. Wilson, Father source

WILSON, ------- CM Feb. 8, 1894, Northampton, Cause Unkn., 6 days, John & Patience, Northampton, Single, John Wilson, Father source

WILSON, Annie WF Nov. 21, 1887, Northampton, General Debility, 81, Parents Unkn., Northampton, Widow, William Wilson, Son source

WILSON, Ellen CF May 25, 1894, Northampton, Bronchitis, 3, Geo. A. & Tabitha, Northampton, Single, Geo. A. Wilson, Father source

WILSON, Ellen CF Nov. 11, 1891, Northampton, Consumption, 20, Joe & Ellen, Northampton, Laborer, Single, Joe Wilson, Father source

WILSON, Emily BF Nov. 1879, Northampton, Cobillsy Bronchitis, 61, Parents Unkn., Va., Va., Va., Keeping House, James Husband, Dr. Thomas Mapp, Physician source

WILSON, Emily CF Oct. 9, 1882, Northampton, Dropsy, 60, Parents Unkn., Northampton, Housekeeper, Husband source

WILSON, Fannie CF Apr. 12, 1895, Northampton, Dropsy, 62, Geo. & Agnes Thomas, Northampton, Married, Silva Costin, Neighbor source

WILSON, Fannie CF Sept. 14, 1891, Northampton, Consumption, 14, Leonard & Lelia, Northampton, Single, Leonard Wilson, Father source

WILSON, Geo. WM Jan. 4, 1892, Northampton, Cholera Infantum, 6 months, Jas. & Florence E., Northampton, Single, James Wilson, Father source

WILSON, Hennie WF Mar. 30, 1885, Northampton, Cause Unkn., 3 yrs. 8 mos., Wm. J. & Florence, Northampton, Single, Wm. J. Wilson, Father source

WILSON, James B. WM June 1875, Northampton, Old Age, 76, Parents Unkn., Birth Unkn., Son source

WILSON, John CM Feb. 22, 1878, Northampton, Measles, 4, Geo. & Martha, Northampton, Single, Geo. Wilson, Father source

WILSON, John W. CM July 3, 1893, Phil., Pa., Consumption, 21, Matilda Wilson, Northampton, Druggist, Single, Matilda Wilson, Mother source

WILSON, Margaret WF May 10, 1877, Northampton, Consumption, 41, Obed & Lizzie Kelly, Northampton, William Wilson, Husband source

WILSON, Martha CF Sept. 4, 1892, Northampton, Typhoid, 45, Parents Unkn., Surry Co. Va., Married, Henry Wilson, Husband source

WILSON, Mary CF June 23, 1894, Northampton, Old Age, 75, Grace Ferby, Northampton, Married, Geo. Wilson, Son source

WILSON, Mary E. WF Jan. 2, 1891, Northampton, Croup, 16, E. H. & Mary E., Northampton, Single, E. H. Wilson, Father source

WILSON, Michael CM May 10, 1885, Northampton, Asthma, 76, Parents Unkn., Northampton, Farmer, Robt. Wilson, source

WILSON, Nancey WF Jan. 24, 1874, Northampton, Cause Unkn., 63 yrs. 10 days, Charles & Nancey Dilard, Northampton, Single, Moses Wilson, son source

WILSON, Ricca "Fredrica" WF June 5, 1885, Northampton, Cause Unkn., 8 days, Wm. J. & Florence, Northampton, Single, Wm. J. Wilson, source

WILSON, Ricca "Fredrica" WF Apr. 23, 1885, Northampton, Congestion of Brain, 19, Frederick F. & Charlotte Fauth, Portsmouth, Va., House Keeper, Jesse W. Husband, F. U. Wilson, source

WILSON, Sam'l CM Mar. 2, 1895, Northampton, Cause Unkn., 68, Parents Unkn., Northampton, Laborer, Married, Geo. Wilson, Friend source

WILSON, Samuel CM May 22, 1877, Northampton, Consumption, 33, Samuel & Margaret, Northampton, Laborer, Emily Wife, Isaac Upshur, Friend source

WILSON, Severn BM Aug. 1879, Northampton, Dropsy, 25, Parents Unkn., Va., Va., Va., Laborer, Single, P. F. Scott, source

WINDER, ------- CF 1888, Northampton, Born Dead, 0, Ed Winder, [Farming?], Northampton, Single, Ed. Winder, Father source

WINDER, ------- CM Apr. 1872, Northampton, Infantile, 3 months, Wesley & Maria, Northampton, Single, source unkn.

WINDER, ------- CM Feb.24, 1893, Northampton, Cause Unkn., 4 days, Lewis & Leah, Northampton, Single, Mary Brown, Neighbor source

WINDER, Alice CF Mar. 4, 1892, Northampton, Measles, 12, Edward & Susan, Northampton, Single, Edward Winder, Father source

WINDER, E. L. WM Sept. 3, 1892, Northampton, Consumption, 31, William & Mary, Northampton, Black Smith, Married, J. Lee Winder, Uncle source

WINDER, Edith CF July 8, 1896, Northampton, Old Age, 89, Nat & Edith Smith, Northampton, Married, Jay Nottingham, Son-in-Law source

WINDER, Georgianna CF May 12, 1893, Northampton, Consumption, 43, Parents Unkn., Northampton, Married, Geo. White, Son-in-Law source

WINDER, Jno. CM Dec. 27, 1895, Northampton, Malaria, 18, Ed & Georgie, Northampton, Laborer, Single, Thos. Scott, Neighbor source

WINDER, John B. WM Nov. 3, 1891, Northampton, Congestive Chill, 17 months, J. L. & S. J. Northampton, Single, J. L. Winder, Father source

WINDER, Joseph WM Oct. 10, 1895, Northampton, Dropsy, 57, Parents Unkn., Hungary Europe, Laborer, Single, L. F. Godwin, Friend source

WINDER, Lizzie BF Apr. 1880, Northampton, Whooping Cough, 2, Edward & Georgeanna, Va., Va., Va., Single, source unkn.

WINDER, Maggie G. WF Mar. 10, 1893, Northampton, Bronchitis, 8 months, J. L. & Sarah, Northampton, Single, J. Lee Winder, Father source

WINDER, Maria CF Sept. 16, 1893, Northampton, Consumption, 51, Parents Unkn., Northampton, Single, Geo. E. Finney, Neighbor source

WINDER, Wesley CM Aug. 14, 1887, Northampton, Dysentery, 50, Parents Unkn., Northampton, Farmer, Emily Winder, Wife source

WINDER, William CM Aug. 6, 1887, Northampton, Dropsy, 50, Parents Unkn., Northampton, Farmer, Alice Winder, Wife source

WINDER, William WM Aug. 2, 1896, Northampton, Malaria, 8, Ed & Mollie, Northampton, Single, J. C. Mapp, Father-in-law source

Northampton County, VA, Deaths from Death Register and Wills, 1871-1896

WINDOW, Alonzo WM Mar. 12, 1876, Northampton, Pneumonia, 14, Levin & Sally, Northampton, Single, Sally Window, Mother source

WISE, ------- CF Apr. 28, 1896, Northampton, Cause Unkn., 10 days, Jesse & Grace, Northampton, Single, Jesse Wise, Father source

WISE, ------- CF Jan. 16, 1893, Northampton, Cause Unkn., 10 days, Henry A. & Maria, Northampton, Single, Henry A. Wise, Father source

WISE, ------- CF Mar. 15, 1891, Northampton, Cause Unkn., 3 months, Luther & Lena, Northampton, Single, Luther Wise, Father source

WISE, ------- CM Aug. 15, 1884, Northampton, Cause Unkn., 11 days, Hy "Henry" & Maria, Northampton, Single, Hy Wise, Father source

WISE, ------- CM Aug. 27, 1896, Northampton, Cause Unkn., 8 days, Henry & Maria, Northampton, Single, Henry Wise, Father source

WISE, ------- CM Jan. 15, 1894, Northampton, Cause Unkn., 10 days, Henry & Maria, Northampton, Single, Henry Wise, Father source

WISE, ------- CM July 11, 1894, Northampton, Cause Unkn., 11 days, John & Lucy, Northampton, Single, Lucy Wise, Mother source

WISE, ------- CM July 2, 1891, Northampton, Croup, 6 days, Kate Wise, Northampton, Single, J. Andrews, Neighbor source

WISE, Arintha S. WF June 8, 1896, Northampton, Dysentery, 7 months, J. B. & Adalade B., Northampton, Single, J. B. Wise, Father source

WISE, Charles CM Aug. 31, 1876, Northampton, Inflammation Bowels, 7, Peter & Charlotte, Northampton, Single, Charlotte Wise, Mother source

WISE, Charlotte S. CF June 30, 1876, Northampton, Bilious Fever, 2 months, Henry & Rhinie, Northampton, Single, Henry A. Wise, Father source

WISE, Eleanor CF Oct. 11, 1876, Northampton, Cause Unkn., 2 yrs. 3 mos., Peter & Charlotte, Northampton, Single, Charlotte Wise, Mother source

WISE, Horace WM Apr. 11, 1887, Northampton, Abcess, 3 months, Bowden & Addie, Northampton, Single, Bowden Wise, Father source

WISE, James CM July 4, 1894, Northampton, Pneumonia, 18 months, John & Lucy, Northampton, Single, Lucy Wise, Mother source

WISE, Seymour CM Mar. 1874, Northampton, Typhoid, 3, Sam & Susan, Northampton, Single, Sam Wise, Father source

WISE, W. H. WM Oct. 8, 1894, Northampton, Diabetes, 71, Solomon & Nancy, Acc. Co., Farmer, Married, J. B. Wise, Son source

WISE, William CM Apr. 2, 1895, Northampton, Burned to death, 6, Luther & Lena, Northampton, Single, Lena Wise, Mother source

WISE, William CM Feb. 10, 1894, Northampton, Burned, 5, Luther & Lena, Northampton, Single Lucy Wise, Aunt source

WRIGHT, Fred CM July 14, 1895, Northampton, Diarrhea, 40, Tenny Wright, Acco. Co., Farmer, Married, Custis Wright, Brother source

WRIGHT, Isaac CM July 4, 1892, Northampton, Asthma, 65, John & Leah, Northampton, Laborer, Married, Mary Wright, Wife source

WRIGHT, J. C. CM June 30, 1893, Northampton, Dysentery, 1 mo. 20 days, Levi & Sarah, Northampton, Single, Levi Wright, Father source

WRIGHT, James CM Apr. 16, 1892, Northampton, Drowned, 40, Levi & Grace, Northampton, Laborer, Married, Henry Bailey, Friend source

WRIGHT, Mary E. WF Aug. 15, 1873, Northampton, Bilious Fever, 2 yrs. 6 mos., James B. & Emma, Single, James R. Wright, Father source

WRIGHT, William CM Mar. 14, 1893, Northampton, Pneumonia, 35, Parents Unkn., Northampton, Farmer, Married, John R. Read, Neighbor source

WYATT, ------- CM Sept. 9, 1878, Northampton, Infantile, 12 days, Smith & Sarah, Northampton, Single, Smith Wyatt, Father source

WYATT, ------- WF Nov. 1873, Northampton, Diphtheria, 3, Wm. J. & Amelia, Northampton, Single, Wm. T. Ashby, Friend source

WYATT, ------- WF Nov. 1873, Northampton, Diphtheria, 6, Wm. J. & Amelia, Northampton, Single, Wm. T. Ashby, Friend source

WYATT, ------- WF Sept. 10, 1872, Northampton, Infantile, 1 day, Nath'l U. & Esther A., Northampton, Single, Nath'l U. Wyatt, Father source

WYATT, Amelia WF Nov. 1873, Northampton, Diphtheria, 24, Jos. B. & Laura Brittingham, Northampton, Wm. J. Husband, Wm. T. Ashby, Friend source

WYATT, Betsy WF Aug. 10, 1871, Northampton, Typhoid, 12, Thos. & Susan, Northampton, Single, Thos. Wyatt, Father source

WYATT, Estelle P. CF Dec. 16, 1891, Northampton, Cause Unkn., 3 months, Geo. & Mary, Northampton, Single, Geo. Wyatt, Father source

WYATT, Isma G. WM July 19, 1878, Northampton, Consumption, 55, Parents Unkn., Accomack, Farmer, Bell Wyatt Wife, C. L. Wyatt, Friend source

WYATT, Isma G. WM July, 1879, Northampton, Pneumonia & Consumption, 52, Parents Unkn., Va., Va., Va., Farmer, Married, source unkn.

WYATT, Jas. T. WM 1888, Northampton, Crying Fits, 11 days, Jas. H. Willett, [Waterman?], Northampton, Jas. H. Wyatt, Father source

WYATT, Robert CM Apr. 23, 1896, Northampton, Dropsy, 25, Died at Alms House, Northampton, Laborer, Single, Wm. G. Bell, Overseer of Poor source

WYATT, Thos. H. WM Oct. 2, 1893, Northampton, Cause Unkn., 63, Parents Unkn., Northampton, Waterman, Married, Polly Wyatt, Daughter-in-Law source

WYATT, Virginia E. WF Nov. 1885, Northampton, Pneumonia, 62, Wm. & Betsy, Northampton, Wm. Wyatt, Son source

WYATT, Wilmer WM Sept. 15, 1883, Northampton, Croup, 8, Pem & Mary, Birth Unkn. Pem Wyatt, Head of Family source

WYATT, Wm. E. WM July 7, 1896, Northampton, Consumption, 47, Parents Unkn., Northampton, Farmer, Married, Effie White, Wife source

YERBY, Tabby CF Aug. 30, 1872, Northampton, Eusipilus, 65, Parents Unkn., Northampton, House Servant, Single, Jas. U. Thomas, where died source

YOUNG, Mary E. WF May 7, 1878,
Northampton, Dropsy, 48 yrs. 1 mo. 8 days,
Severn & Sallie, Northampton, Single, Phillip B.
Tankard, Friend source

YOUNG, Peggy CF Mar. 26, 1874,
Northampton, Cause Unkn., 70, Jno. & Sallie,
Northampton, Single, Michel Stoakley,
Grandson source

YOUNG, Peggy WF Dec. 2, 1871,
Northampton, Pneumonia, 50, Parents Unkn.,
Northampton, Single, Thos. B. Fisher, Friend
source

Note: Initially the 1871-96 Death Registry contained 25 married females with no surname listed for their parents. After research this has been reduced to 15 and noted in the list and in the index. Here are the Deceased and their parents with reference page where they can be found.

Page	Name	Death	Parents
5	Barrott, Tabitha	'85	Thos. & Unknown ???
8	Bell, Lottie E.	'85	James S. & Lottie ???
12	Brickhouse, Mary	'91	Robt. & Eveline ???
14	Burton, Annie	'91	Garrison & Mary ???
53	Killmon, Polly	'91	Isoriah & Juliet ???
54	Lewis, Margaret	'76	William & Mary ???
55	Major, Clara	'92	Robt. W. & Mary ???
57	Matthews, Adah	'96	Robt. & Peggie ???
59	Miles, Eliza	'87	Richard & Mary ???
68	Pead, Georgeanna	'91	Mitchel & Mary ???
78	Savage, Elizabeth	'74	Wm. & Ester ???
86	Smith, Virginia	'91	Custis & Margaret ???
91	Stringer, Sallie	'79	Hilary B. & Sally B. ???
91	Sturgis, Vianna	'85	Jno. & Vianna ???
105	Williams, Nannie B.	'92	John A. & Virginia ???

111

I N D E X

BAILEY "cont'd"

Phillip 5

BAILY

Edith 5

Emily 5

Seth 5

BAKER

Edith 5

Edy 5

George 5

Nancy 5

Peter 5

Sarah 5

Shadrack 5

Thos. S. 5

BALDWIN

Shadrack 62

BALL

Lettie 5

BANISTER

Annie 5

Nannie 5

Wm. 5

BANKS

Shelly 5

BAPTIST

Caddy 5

Jacob 5

Jim 5

BARCRAFT

Jno. 5

BARROTT

Thos. 5

BAXTER

Bettie 6

Isaac W. 6

BAYLY

Arthur 7

Arthur R. 7

Bethanie 14

Betsy 6

Edward 6

Edy 6

Elizabeth 6

Emily 6

Esther 6

Fannie/Fanny 6

Georgie 6

Harry 6

Henry 6, 49, 80

BAYLY "cont'd"

Ida 7

Isaac 83

J. B. 6

Jackson 6

James 6, 7

Jane 6

John A. 6

L. A. 6

Louisa 7

M. J. 7

Mary 6, 7, 51, 83

Pamelia 6

Sally 6

Sam 14

Sarah 7

Seth M. 6

Thomas 6, 7

Wm. 99

Zed 6

BEACH

Geo. 54

BECKET

Abram 7

Alice 7

Charity 9

Emily 7

Geo. 36, 64

Jacob 7

James 7

Jno. 10, 33

Kessiah 7

Susan 7

William 7

BECKETT

Arthur 7

Geo. 7, 36, 67

James 7

Maggie 7

Maria 7

S. B. 7

Virginia 7

BELL

A. T. 8

Alfred 31

Alice 8

Edwd. 8

Elizabeth/Eliza 8

Ellen 8

Geo. 8, 30

BELL "cont'd"

H. A. 8

H. N. 8

Harriet 8

Haven 37

Hettie 8

J. L. 21

James 8

Jane 8

Jas. B. 8

Jno. F. 8, 81

John 8, 38

John H. 8

John T. 57, 76, 84

Lottie 8

M. M. 8

Margt. 51

Margaret A. 8

Maria 8

Nelson 8

Olivia 8

Peggie 8

Peter 7, 8

R. W. 9

Robert W. 8

Smith 51

Southey 77

Susan 8, 21

T. P. 26

Tabbie 7

W. G. 15

Wm. G. Alm's House

"Overseer of Poor"

30, 50, 93, 102, 110

BELOAT

Amanda 8

Fannie 9

Hezakiah 4

Laban J. 8, 9

Maggie 9

Margt. 4

Tom 9

BELOTE

Abel 73

Fannie 9

G. T. 9

L. J. 9

Laban 9

Lizzie 9

P. S. 9

BELOTE "cont'd"

Susan 73

Victoria 9

BENSON

Edward 9

Sally 9

BERRY

Geo. H. 9

Margaret 9

R. H. 9, 10, 56

BEVANS

Edith 9

Sam'l 9

BINGHAM

Louisa 9

Maria 9

Mary 9

S. 7

Southey 9

BIRD

Jas. L. 9

Mary 9

BISSOULY

L. A., Dr. 96

BIVANS

Emma 9

Lit. 9

Lizzie 17

BIVVINS

Matilda 9

BLEW

Spencer 27

Va. 27

BLOXOM

E. 9

BOGGS

J. E. 9

N. G. 9

BONWELL

Chas. 10

Jane 10

BOOKER

Arthur 7

Fontaine 10

Harriet 10

Sophia 10

BOOL

David 10

J. D. 10

Janie 10

BOOL "cont'd"
P. H. 10, 82
Rosa A. 10
Sarah 10
Wm. F. 10
BOTT
Georgie 10
Jas. 10
BOWDOIN
Easter 10
Ed 10
Edie 10
BOWEN
Benj. 30
BOYTT
Annie 10
J. T. 10
BRADFORD
Abel 11
Amanda 10
Angeline 11
Geo. 10
Geo. W. 10, 11
Joana 10
Julia 5
Mary 11
Nancy 11
William 11
Wm. W. 11
BRADY
Emma 11
Frank 11
BRAGG
Charles 11
Susan 11
BRAXTON
Jas. P
P. "Pricilla" 11
Thomas 11
BRICKHOUSE
Ann 12
Ben 11
Catherine C. 53
Comfort 11
Emily 12
Eveline 12
Geo. 12
Georgeanna 11, 12
Hugh 11

BRICKHOUSE "cont'd"
J. L. 99
J. N. 53
Jack 12
Jacob 12
James M. 11
Jane 12
Janie 11
Jennie 11
John 11
John E. 11
John L. 11, 12
Johnson 12
Juliet 10, 12
Leah 11, 12
Manie 76
Mary 11, 12
Mary E. 12
Polly 11, 12
Robt. 12
Sallie 11
Severn 12
Susan 11, 12
Thomas E. 12
Virginia 11, 12
W. H. 12
Wm./William 11, 12
William E. 36, 85
BRITTINGHAM
Elijah 13
Jos. B. 110
Laura 110
Peggy 13
Susan 13
BROCKENBROUGH
A., Dr. 106
BROOKS
Annie 13
Augustus 13
Lucy 13
Pat 13
BROWN
Alex 13
Annie 13
Horace 13
Isaac 102
J. E. 13
Leah 13
Lewis 13

BROWN "cont'd"
Mary 13, 108
Mary W. 13
P. H. 13
Priscilla 13
Runie 13
Sophia 13
Thos. 13, 39
W. A. 13
Wm. A. 13
BUCHANAN
H. 94
BULL
Bagwell 39
Roland 14
BULLMAN
R. C. 14
Virginia 14
BUNTING
Abe 72
Mary 14
Susan 72
BURBRIDGE
Elizabeth 14
Henry 14
BURR
Ella 14
Warren 14
BURRIS
Eugenie 14
BURROWN
Caleb 14
Geo. P. 14
Mary E. 14
BURROWS
Geo. P. 14
Mary E. 14
BURRUSS
Geo. 14
Hary 33
Mary 14, 33
BURTIN
James 14
Mariah 14
Mary 14
Sarah 14
BURTON
Adah 15
C. A. 10

BURTON "cont'd"
Ed 61
Garrison 14
Geo. 44
Hennie 14
Lit 14
Robin 15
Sophia 44
BYRD
Betsy 15
Jennie 41
Lloyd 15

CARPENTER
A.C. 15
Alexine 15
Arlene 15
Caroline 15
Dinah 15
G. V. 15
G. W. 25
Henrietta 15
Jacob 15
Jas. 4, 15
Jas. R. 15
Jas. S. 15, 34, 46
Jno. P. 15
Kate 15
L. T. 23, 24
Leah 15
Mary 4, 15
Morris 13
Mrs. 74, 84
Nellie 15
Richard 15
Stephen 15
T. F. 15
CARTER
Abel 16
Alfred 16
Eliza 16
Geo. 16
Jane 16
Lizzy 16
Peter 16
Peter J. 16
Silla 16
Tamer 16
Victor 16

CHAMBERS
David 16
Georgia 16
CHANDLER
Bowdoin 6
J. W. 2
John 16
John J. 16
Jos. W. 16
Joseph 16
Joseph C. 16
Louis 16
Lucy 6
Maggie 16
Margaret 16
Missouri 16
CHARNICK
Jno. T. 17
CHARNOCK
Ann 17
Charlotte 17
Jas. 17
Lafayette 17
Mary V. 17
W. J. 17
W. T. 17
Wm. 17
CHEA
Geo. W., Mrs. 55
CHRISTIAN
Arthur 17
Mary Susan 17
CHURCH
Abe 17, 18
Ada 17
Alexine 18
Ann 17
Anthony 18
Bethany 17
Bettie 18
C. N. 17
Eliza 17
George 13, 17, 18
James 17, 44
John 17
Lizzie 4
Margt. 17, 18
Mary 17
Sol. 46

CHURCH "cont'd"
Susan 17, 44
Tony 4
CHURN
Essie 18
Jno./John 18
Nat 69, 96
Peggie/Peggy 18
Sev. B. 18
Tama 52
Walter 18
Wm. 52
CISCO
Bettie 18
George 18
Mary 18
CLEGG
Ann 57
Major 57
COBB
A. F. 97, 104
Emily 18
Warren 18
COFFER
Fanny 18
Patrick 18
COLAWAY
A. B. 18
Susan 18
COLBOURN
Jno. 39
Mary 39
COLEMAN
Jane 18
COLES
Colbert 19
Jno. 18
Mary 19
Mary A. 19
COLEY
Samuel 19
COLLINS
Adah 19, 20
Amy 19, 20
Betsy 20
Bettie 19
Caleb 20
Elizabeth 19
Ellison 19

COLLINS "cont'd"
Garnett 19
Geo/George 19, 20
Griffin 20
Griffith 19
Henry 19, 71
Horace 19
Ibby 69
John 19, 20
Jas/James 19, 20, 57
Laura 1
Lauretta 20
Lizzie 19
Maggie 19
Major 69
Margaret 20, 57
Mary 19, 20
Melvina 19
Noah 20
Peter 20
Rachel 19
Ralph 19
Rose 20
Sarah 20
Severn 57
Smith 19, 20
Stephen 20
Susan 19, 20
Tobitha 19
Victor 19
Welcher 20
Wilsher 20
Wm/William 19, 20
COLONA
Alice 21
Arthur 52
Frank 93
Geo. H. 21
Major 17
Sallie 17
Virginia 20
W. T. 20
COLONNA
Wm. E. 21
COLONY
Marg't A. 21
Wm. F. 21
CONNER
C. H. 21

CONNER "cont'd"
Tabitha 21
CONWAY
Eli 21
COOK
Martha 21
COPES
Elizabeth 15
L. D. 15
Margaret 21
CORNELL
Ben 21
Sally 21
COSTIN
Caleb 22
Cove 22
Eldred 22
Ella 22
Ellison L. 21
Emma 21
George 21
Ibby 49
James 22
John 21
Juliet 22
Lucretia 21
Lucy 22
Madora 21
Margt. 21
Maria 21
Mary 22
Mary E. 21
Polly 95
Rich. 23, 69
Samuel 21, 22
Samuel J. 21
Sarah 21, 22
Seth 21
Severn 21
Silvia 107
Thos. H. 22
Thos. W. 38
Wesley 21
Wm. 21
Wm. F. 22
COSTON
Wm. 22
COTTINGHAM
Betsy 21

COTTINGHAM "cont'd"
- Henry 21, 22
- Mollie 22

COTTRELL
- Eliz. 26
- Jno. 26

CROSBY
- Ella 22
- Thomas 22

CROW
- James 22
- Mariah 22

CUSTIS
- Andrew 22
- Ben 23
- C. S. 23
- Elizabeth 19, 22, 23
- Emily 22
- Georgianna 22
- Henry 22
- Patience 23
- Peter 12, 22
- Philip 22
- Sallie 23

CUTLER
- Ada 23
- Ann 66
- Ed 23
- Luke 23
- Sue 23
- Wm. 66

CYPRESS
- Henry 23

DALBY
- Benj. 48
- Eliza/Elizabeth 9, 23
- Ellen 23
- Emeline 23
- Emma D. 23
- Geo. R. 23
- H. 23
- Hezzie 23
- Isaac 23
- J. B. 9
- Jacob 23
- Jno. L. 23
- Luther 23
- Margaret 23

DALBY "cont'd"
- Maria 23
- Mary 48
- Mary A. 23
- Nathaniel 23
- Nelly 23
- Peter 23
- Susan 23
- Thos. 23

DARBY
- Nelly 69
- Peter 69

DAVIS
- Jno. 23
- Mary 23, 24
- Robert 24

DENNIS
- Adah 24
- Archie 24
- Frank 24
- Mary 24
- R. G. 24

DEXTER
- Emily 24

DILARD
- Charles 107
- Nancey 107

DILLIARD
- Susan 24

DILLION
- Betsy 11
- Chas. 11

DIX
- Arthur 24
- Asa 24
- Asa Jr. 24, 47
- Emily 24
- John 24
- John H. 24
- Martha 24
- Martha S. 24
- Mary 24
- Wm. 24, 65
- Wm. T. Jr. 24

DIXON
- Bell(e) 24, 25
- Ginny 25
- Henry 25
- Jacob 25

DIXON "cont'd"
- James 25
- Lavenia 25
- Lucy 25
- Madora 25
- Mary 24, 25
- Mary P. 41
- Samuel 25
- Thomas 24
- Wm. 24, 25
- Wm. W. 41

DORSEY
- Margt. 46
- R. W. 46

DOUGHTY
- A. B. 59
- Amanda 25
- Annie 25
- Archie 26
- B. U. 25
- Ben 25
- Ben U. 25
- E. J. 25
- Eli 25, 26, 52
- Geo. L. 25, 26
- Geo. T. 26
- Geo. W. 25
- J. C. 26
- J. H. 26
- James 26
- Jane 25, 26
- Jno. W. 26
- John 3, 26
- John H. 11, 12, 26
- Lizzie 26
- Mary 25, 26
- Mollie 26
- Nancy D. 26
- Peggie 25
- Peter 25, 26, 92
- S. A. 25
- Sallie 26
- Sorin 26
- Susan 52
- W. 25
- Wm. 25
- Wm. J. 26

DOUGLASS
- James 26, 27

DOUGLASS "cont'd"
- Kate 26
- Madora 27
- Sallie 26
- Sarah 27

DOUTY
- Ann 49
- Mich'l 49

DOWNES
- Diana 27
- Guy 27
- Jane 27
- Mary 27
- Nathaniel 27
- Thos. 27

DOWNING
- A. W., Dr. 27 phy.
- Clara 55
- E. W. 27
- Edmond 27
- Henry 27
- John 27
- John C. 27
- Jos. 27
- Lizzie 27
- Lucy 27
- Margt. 27
- Maria 27
- Martha 27
- Mary 27
- Milla 27
- S. 55
- S. B. 27
- Stratton B. 28, 81
- Susan 27
- W. A. 28 phy.
- Wm. 27

DOWNS
- Albert 27
- Anna 27
- Nath. G. 27
- Nim. H. 84

DRENNAN
- Sarah 28
- Wm. 28

DRUMMOND
- G. W. 28
- Handy 90
- Mary 28

DUNNE	EAST "cont'd"	FATHERLY	FISHER "cont'd"
H. W. 28	Maggie 29	Geo. J. 30	Thos. B. 111
Sarah 28	Mary 29	Patsy 30	U. N. 31
DUNTON	**EASTON**	Patsy F. 30	Walker 31
Annie 28	Lorana 29	Wm. J. 30	Wallace 30, 31
Arinthia 28, 98	Pat 29	**FAUTH**	**FITCHETT**
Caroline 40	**EATES**	Charlotte 108	Abe 23, 85
Custis 28	Catherine 29	Frederick F. 108	Abram 33
E. 98	Fritz 29	**FENDERSON**	Alfred 33
Eliza 93	**EDMONDS**	Adelaide 30	B. T. 32, 33
Ellen 28	Mrs. 8, 14, 81	James 30	Betsey 32
Em 28	**EICHELBERGER**	Jas. F. 30	Caroline 32
Emeline 29	J. A. 26	M. F. 30	Chas. 56
Geo. W. 98	Jno. A. 29	**FERBY**	Cordelia 32
Hanna 28	**ELLIOTT**	Ed 30	Dan'l 32
Isaac 28	Ellen 29	Grace 107	Dennard 33
Jacob B. Senr. 28	H. W. 29	Mary 30	Dora 31
James M. 43	Jerry 29	**FEREBY**	Elizabeth 29, 32, 33
Jas. 28	Rachel 29	Americas 30	Fannie 23
John 28	Sallie 29	Maria 30	Frank 33
John R. 28, 29	Thos. 29	**FINNEY**	Geo. 32, 33
Jos. B. 28	W. D. 29	Ann 39	Georgie 32
Jos. B. F. 28	**ELSNER**	Chas. 39	Hannah 33, 83
K. 28	Lizzie 29	Geo. 30	Isaac 32, 33, 78
Lucy 28	Martin 29	Geo. E. 30, 62, 108	Jacob 32
Luke 20	**ENNIS**	Henry 30	Jno. R. 83
M. E. 24	E. E. 29	Isaac 30	John 33, 63
M. J. 93	I. S. 71	Nora 30	Julia 33
Major 40	Joseph 29	**FISHER**	Laura 32
Margt. 75	Mary 29	Abe 31	Leah 56, 63
Mary 28, 29	**EPHRAIM**	Amy 30	Lelia 32
Mike 29	Emily 30	Eliza 31	Leo. T. 84
Patsy 28	Jacob 29, 30, 88	Esther 31	Leon 32
Peter 28	James 30	Geo. 31	Leon'd T. 32
R. F. 103	Sarah 29	James 31	Lew 32
Rich'd T. 94	Susan 30	Jas. U. 1	Lewis 32
S. F. 29	**ESHOM**	John 31	Lucinda 33
Samuel 75	Betsy 75	Joseph 31	Maggie 32, 33
Sarah 28, 29	Geo. 74	Leah 31	Mahaley 85
Veanna 103	Hennie 74	Maria 31	Mammie 33
Wm. T. 28, 75	Thomas 75	Mary 31	Margaret 32
	EVANS	N. H. 8	Maria 32
E. S. HERALD	LaVenia 79	Nena 30	Mariah 32
13, 44, 45, 62, 91, 99	**EXALL**	Sallie 31	Mary 32, 33
EAST	Geo. 30	Sam 31	Mary A. 46, 87
Ed 29		Sam'l. P. 31	Melvina 32
Edward R. 29	**FACE**	Selma 31	Minnie 33
Edward T. 29	Eliz. 66	Susan 31	N. P. 33
Kitty 29	Sam'l 66	Thomas 31	Nathaniel 30, 33, 46

FITCHETT "cont'd"

Nelson 33
Parker 32
Patrick 14, 31, 33
Pollie 78
Prisey 31
Rachel 32
Sallie 33, 46
Sam'l 33
Spencer 31
Susan 33
Sydney 13
Thos. 83
Thos. J. 55
W. J. 29
W. P. 33
W. P. J. 33
W. T. 33
Wm. 13
Wm. J. 32
Wm. P. 33

FITZHUGH

P. A., Dr. 30, 91

FLETCHER

Sally 34
Thos. 34

FLOYD

Comfort 30
Emily 34
F. P. 34
Fluvanna 34
G. Fred, Phy. 10, 34
Geo. 34
Jas. B., Dr. 50, 51, 72
Jim 34
Jno. F. 38
Jno. H. 37
John 34
John E. 34
Levin 30, 34
Lucille 34
Lydia 34
Martha 34
Mary 34
Nancy 34
Philus 34
R. E. 34, 57
Susan 34
Thomas 34

FLOYD "cont'd"

Wm. E. 34

FOREMAN

Laura 34
Lemuel 34

FORTUNE

Lewis 34
Peggie 34

FOSQUE

John 42
Mary 42

FOWLER

John E. 34

FOX

Betsy 34
J. W. 3
Levin 33
Sallie 33
William 34

FRANCES

Abel 35
Bridget 35

FRANCIS

Belford 49
Emily 35
George L. 35
Georgianna 35
Hennie 35
Horace T. 35
Maggie S. 35
Mary 35
Thos. 35

FROST

Emma 104
Frank 104
John 35

FRY

James H. 35
Winney K. 35

GARRETT

J. F. 35
Mary A. 35
Wm. T. 35

GARRISON

Geo. 59
Horace 79

GASKINS

G. S. 35

GASKINS "cont'd"

Lettitia 35

GAYLE

C. C. 35
Christopher 35
Lucy 35

GIBB

Emma 16
Frank 35
Joseph 16
Julia 35

GIBBINS

Eliza 35

GIDDINGS

Aaron 36
Alfred 36
Ellison 36
George 35, 36
Hester 35
James 36, 79
Maggie 36
Maria 36
Mary 36
Rena 36
Rose 7
Sam'l 36
Sarah 36

GIDDINS

Jim 36
Mahala 36

GLADDEN

Edwd. 36
Eliz. 36
Jas. T. 36
Susan 36

GLADSON

Edward 36
Edward E. 36
Edwd. O. 40
Emily 36
Henrietta 36
J. E. 36
Jno. J. 36
Margaret E. 36
Wm. 36

GLADSTONE

Bettie 37
John 37
William 37

GODWIN

A. G. 58
Alex G. 37
Edmd. 37
Edwin 37
Elton B. 37
J. M. 24
Julia 37
L. F. 108
Mariah 21
Robert 37
Robin 37
Rosa 37

GOFFIGON

Arinthia 37, 38
Arthur 37, 38
Fred G. 38
H. S. 22
Ibby 37, 38
Jane 89
John 37
John H. 22, 37
L. H. 37
L. J. 58, 68
Laura 37
Lucy 38
Luther 37
Mary 38
Mary B. 37
Obed 37
Polly 38
Sallie 37
Severn 38
Southey 89
Spencer 37
W. J. 22
William 38

GOOCH

Archie 53
Mary 53

GOODY

Louisa 38
Wm. 38
Wm. T. 38

GORDON

Jno. 29
Mary 29

GORDY

L. C. 38

GORDY "cont'd"

M. E. 38

GREEN

James 38

Margaret 38

GRIFFIN

Adah 41

Annie 38

Bennett 41

Bettie 38

Edward 38

Jacob 38

Lucy 38

Solomon 38

GRIFFITH

Ann 99

Anna 39

Benj. 38, 39

Emily 39

Henrietta 38

James 38

Jacob 39

John 38, 39, 41, 99

Lelia A. 39

Levin 38, 39

Luke 39

Lucy 38, 39

Mary 39

Missouri 38, 39

Nancy 41

Nathan 39

Sallie 38, 39

Sarah 27

Severn 39

Walter 39

William M. 39

Wm. 38

GRIMMER

Conrad 39

Fannie 39

GUNTER

Charlotte 31

E. V. 40

Edwd. L. 40

Edwd. V. 11

Geo. 39

Jas. L. 40

Jno. U. 48, 101

John 39, 40

GUNTER "cont'd"

Laban I. 39

Peggie 40

Sally 40

Sukey 39

Virginia 40

Wesley 40

Wm. R. 40

GUY

Alice 40

Bettie 40

Edward 40

Edward J. 40

John W. 40

Mary 40

Peter 40

HACK

Jacob 40

Jno. 40

John H. 40

Thos. 40

Willanna 40

HALEY

Benj. 85

Mary A. 40

Peggy 85

HALLETT

Abe 41

Abel 41

Caleb 40

Easter 40

Ed. M. 41

Elias 41

Elizabeth 41

Ella 41

Ellen 41

Emily 40

Emma 41

Esther 40

Len 41

Leonard 41

Maria 41

Robt. 41, 42

Robt. I. 41

Sabra 41

Spencer 40

Tamar 41

HAMBLETON

Andrew 5

Sallie 5

HAMILTON

John S. 41

L. J. 41

Mary 41

Patsie 41

Virginia 41

W. J. 41

HANBY

Nancy 41

Nannie T, 41

Wm. L. 32, 41

HANDY

R. B. 47

HARCUS (HARGIS?)

Ella 41

Thos. J. 41

HARGIS

C. H. 42

J. W. 42

Jno. W. 42

John 68

L. S. 42

L. T. 42

Maggie 42

Margt. 42

Mary A. 42

Nancy 42

HARMAN

Annie 42

Amey 42

Charlotte 42

Custis 42

D. 88

Dublin 42

Geo. 42

Harriet 42

Isaac 42

Jas. 42

John 42

Laura 42

Leon 42

Lucy 42

Martin 42

Mary 42

Nervilla 42

Nim 42

HARMAN "cont'd"

Susan 42

HARMON

Arthur 19, 43

Ben 43

Edward 43

Jane 43

John 43

Lizzie 19

Lloyd 43

Lucinda 31

Phillis 43

Tobitha 43

HARMANSON

Eliz. 43

Ellison 10

Henry 43

HARRISON

Fanny 43

Jno. T. 43

Wm. 43

HASTINGS

Ano. 43

E. M. 43

Liddie 43

Martha 43

HATANY

Ann 43

James 43

HAYES

Chas. 43

Mary 43

Susan 43

HEATH

Augustus 43

Esther 43

Hannah 7

Horace 32

J. S. 44

Jas. 44

Jasper 43

John 7, 43, 44

Julius C. 43

Kitty 44

Louisa 44

Lucinda 43

Mary 44

Mary W. 32

Ruth 44

HEATH "cont'd"	HORSEY "cont'd"	JACKSON "cont'd"	JAMES "cont'd"
Sarah 43	T. G. 45	Henry 10	Hez. P. Jr. 47
Virginia 43	**HOSIER**	**JACOB**	Jacob 19
W. H. 40, 43	Comfort 35	Ann 46	Jno. 47
HEBARD	John 35	Betsy 46	Lewis 14
Dolly 81	**HOSKINS**	E. S. 37	Louis 47
HEMINGS	Frank 96	Edwin S. 46	Lydia 47
J. W. 44	**HOUSE**	Eliza 46	Margaret 56
Matilda 44	George 45, 72	Geo. 46, 68	Murray 47
HENDERSON	Mary 45	Geo. R. 46	Patience 48
A. D. 44	**HUMPHREYS**	Hancock 46	Rachael 47
Arelius 5, 56	Meta 45	Jas/James 27, 46	S. 74
Henry 77	Thomas 45	Job 16	S. M. 47
J. M. 44	**HUNT**	Lloyd 46	Sallie 47
Jack 44	Henry 45	Louis 46	Sarah C. 47
Jno. 44	Ida 45	Maggie 46	Susan 47
Louisa 44	Jane 45	Malinda 16	William 31, 47
Margaret 44	Jesse 45	Mary 46, 47, 68	**JARVIS**
Mary 44	John 45	Polly 36	Ada 94
N. P., Dr. 36, 48, 81	Mary 45	Rachiel 46	Betsy 48, 83
Susan 5, 56	Nannie 45	Robt. C. 46	Bettie 48
HENRY	Peggie 45	Sallie A. 47	Caroline 48
Annie 44	Washington 45, 58	Solomon 46	Elizabeth 48
James 44	Wm. M. 45	Susan 46	Emily 48
HICKMAN	**HURTT**	T. A. 46	G. N. 40
Geo. 44	C. H. 45	Wm. T. 47	Geo. 8, 48, 76, 98
Jno. 44	W. G. 45	Zor. 27	Geo. T. 48
Lila 44	**HUTCHENSON**	**JACOBS**	Harriet 48
Mary 44	Geo. 92	Adah 47	J. Ambler 53
Severn 44	**HYSLOP**	Caroline 47	J. N. 48
HODGES	J. T. B. 72	Emeline 47	Jane 48
Edith 44	James 45	Henry 47	Jas. A. 48
Joseph 44	Lottie 45	Jas. 47	Jennie 98
HOLLAND		Lloyd 47	Jessie N. 48
Juliet 44	**IIIFF**	**JAMES**	Laura 76
N. L. 44	John W. 46	Caroline 46	Mary 48
HOLT	**IRELAND**	Charles 47	Peggie 48
George 44, 45	E. B. 46	Cordie 47	S. A.- Sheriff 28, 104
Susan 44, 45	**ISDELL**	Den 86	Sam'l A. 48
HOPKINS	Fannie 46	Dennis 88, 90	Sarah 48
Harriet 45	Geo. 46	Dianna 47	Severn 48
Henry 45	Jas. 46	Edmond 17	Virginia 48
Jennie 45	Lovey 46	Eliza 47	Virginia A. 48
Mary 45	Mary 46	Ellis 48	Wm. 48, 83
Peter 45	S. P. 46	Emily 47	**JEFFERSON**
Sarah 45	Sally 46	George 8, 47	J. D. 48
Wright 45		H. P. 47, 56	Martha 48
HORSEY	**JACKSON**	Henry 47	Mary 49
L. J. 45	Ann 36	Hez. 5	Mary S. 48

JEFFERSON "cont'd"	JONES "cont'd"	KELLAM "cont'd"	KISHPAUGH
T. D. 48	George 50	Sallie 51	Anthony 53
JOHNSON	Gorton 50	Sam'l 52	Martha 53
Alfred 49	H. E. 50	Sarah 51	W. D., Mrs. 53
Clorissa 50	Horace C. 50	Thomas 52	**KNIGHT**
Dallas 50	Sarah 50	**KELLEY**	Mary E. 53
Delitha 49, 50	**JOYNES**	Annie 52	Wm. 53
Edwd. B. 57	B. L. 51	Edward 52	
Eliza 49	Cath. 51	James 52	**LaFORGE**
Ellen 49, 50	Edwd. 51	Obed 52	Ellen 53
Fannie 49, 68	Eleanora 51	Virginia U. 52	**LAMBERTSON**
Henry 50	Emily 51	**KELLY**	Essie 53
J. C. Sr. 49	Hez. 51	Alice 52	Wm. H. 53
J. H. 49	Jesse 51	Geo. 52, 68	**LANE**
Jas. F. 49, 50	Jno. H. 51	Geo. E. 52	John 53
Jas. R. 49	Julia 51	Lizzie 107	Kittie 53
Jeff 49	Louisa 51	Mary 53, 68	**LaPETERS**
Jno. C. 49	R. C. 51	Mary E. 52	Ella 53
Jno. E. M. 49	W. W. 51, 102	O. 52	Jacob
John H. 49, 50	Wm. 51	Obed 53, 107	**LAWSON**
John T. 49	Wm. P. 51	Timothy 52, 53	A. D. 54
L. H. 16	**JUBILEE**	**KENDALL**	Edwin 54
L. T. 5, 49, 56	Harriet 51	G. S. 53	Martha 54
L. W. 50	Wm. H. 51	Hannah 53	Mary 54
Laban 49	**JUSTICE**	John 53	Sarah 54
Littleton 49	Thomas 51	Lucius 53	**LEATHERBURY**
Lizzie 49		Lucretia 53	A. T. 43
Louis 80	**KELLAM**	Mary 53	Lit. 54
Louisa 49	A. W. 51	William 53	Matthew 54
M. E. 49	Abel 51	**KER**	Nancy 54
Maggie 49	Chas. 42, 80	Ames 1	Perry 33
Maggie V. 50	E. D. 52	Esther 1	Sally 33
Maria 80	Emely 52	George 97	T. E. 54
Martha 50	Esther 51, 52	**KERR**	Vianes 54
Mary 49	Frank 52	Geo., Dr. 19	**LeCATO**
Rosa 49	George 95	George 49	Cordelia 54
S. T. 49	Harry 51, 52	Hugh 53	Jennie 54
Sally 50	Henry 38	Margaret 53	L. T. 54
Sudie M. 50	J. E. 51	**KETCHAM**	Susan 54 (2)
Susan A. 49	Jno. C. P. 60	John W. 53	Wm. 54
Sydney 50	John 51	Mary 53	**LEE**
W. T. 50	John H. 7, 12, 17, 51	Nathan 53	Isaac 54, 56, 57
Wm. F. 50	Levi 52	**KILLMON**	Josephine 54, 57
Wm. T. 50, 56	Mary 52	Chas. 77	**LEWIS**
JONES	Nim T. 52	Isoriah 53	Chas. 54
Elizabeth 50	Patience 85	Juliet 53	John R. 54
Emily 50, 51	Peggy 52	S. V. 53	Laban T. 54
G. B. 50	Raechel 52	Wm. T. 96	Louisa 54
Geo. T. 50, 51	Sadie 51		Mary 54

LEWIS "cont'd"
Mattie 54, 69
Rachel 54
William 54
LILISTON
E. C. 54
E. C., Mrs. 54
Mahala 54
LINDSAY
Frank 54
Mattie B. 54
Seymour 54
Susan 54
W. C., Rev. 54
LINGO
Ben. F. 55
Ed. 55
Eliza 55
J. E. 55
James 54
Maria 55
Mary 55
Robt. 55
Susan 54, 55
LIPSCOME
Chas. 55
Lucey 55
LITTLE
David L. 55
Mary S. 55
LITTLETON
Betsy 14
Wm. 14
LOTHAND
Mary 55
Wm. T. 55
LUKER
Cordie 55
Geo. 55

MAJOR
James C. 55
Mary 55
Olevia 55
Robt. W. 55
MALLETT
J. T. 55
Mamie 55
Nannie 55

MANNING
Fannie 55
Wm. 55
MAPP
A. N. H. 56, 57
Adah 56
Alfred 47, 56
An. H. 40
Betsy 56
E. W. 56
Edwd. 56
Ellen 57
Emily 56
Esther 56
F. A. 56
F. B. 56
F. G. 56
Fred 56
Geo. R. 57
George 55
Hellen 55
J. C. 56, 108
J. I. 102
James 57
Jas. H. 56
Jno. A. 56
Jno. R. 46, 56
John H. 56
Laura 47, 56
Lloyd A. 28
M. Sue 56
Margt. T. 57
Mary 55, 56
Natilia 57
Peggy 33, 56
R. W. 56
Robins 33, 56
S. M. 56
Sallie 20
Sally 56
Sam 56
Sarah 56, 57
Sarah J. 56
Severn 56, 102
Severn Sr. 102
Thomas, Dr. 45, 57,
67, 107
Thos. 55
V. A. 56, 70

MAPP "cont'd"
Victor A. 56
W. J. Jr. 56
William 56
Wm. W. 57
MARINER
Jno. T. 57
M. L. 57
MARRINER
Maria L. 57
Sallie 57
MARSH
Fred 57
Maggie 57
MARSHALL
Sam'l 97
Wm. J. 97
MASON
Emma 57
Ezekiel 102
Jas. 57
Jas. T. 57
John E. 57
Maggie 57
W. H. 57
Wm. T. 57
MASSEY
Jas. W. 57
MATTHEWS
Delia 58
F. T. 101
Geo. J. 58
Maria 58
Peggie 58
Robt. 58
Thos. 58
William 58
McGUIRE
Anderson 58
Martha 58
McKANDESS
Martha 8
Wm. 58
McKOWN
Annie 58
Betsey 58
Herbert 58
Sallie 58
Sev. 58

McMATH
John 58
Samuel 58
Susan 58
Virginia 58
McNUTT
Jas. M., Dr. 27, 55,
77, 93, 100
MEARS
Emily 58
Geo. 58
Jas. T. 58
Jemima 58
Lizzie 58
Margie 58
Mary 58
Shadrick 58
W. T. 58
MELSON
Annie 59
J. T. 59
Maggie 59
W. I. 59
Wm. I. 106
MESSICK
J. T. 59
METCALF
Lucy 59
Thos. 59
MILBY
R. 59
Rebecca 59
Rich'd 48
MILES
Esther 59
Esther D. 6
H. C. 28
John W. Sr. 59
Mary 59
R. E. 6, 7, 59
Richard 59
MILLIGAN
Ida 59
J. H. 59
MILLS
Emory 59
England 59
MINGO
Amy 59

MINGO "cont'd"
Emeline 59
Jas. 59
MISTER
J. E. 76
MOODY
Florence 59
Henry 59
MOORE
Abraham 59
Abram 60
Adain 60
Betsy 60
Bettie 60
Drucilla 61
Emily 60
G. P., Phy. 24, 53, 56, 58, 74
Geo. U. 60
Harriet 60
Hennie 59, 60, 61
Isaac 74
Isaac T. 60
J. E. 60
James 60
Jane 59
Jesse 60
John 59, 81, 85
John N. 60
L. W. 61
Lottie 60
Mack 60
Major 60
Margaret 60
Mary 59, 60, 81
Mathew 60
Matilda 60
Peggy 60
Robert B. 60
Sarah 60
Severn 60
Susan 60
Thos. 61
Wash. 60
Willamina 71
William 60
William P. 60
Wm. H. 60

MORRIS
Caleb 61
Cornelius 61
Ellen 61
Geo. 61
Henrietta 61
Henry 61
Jacob 61
James 61, 62
Jane 61
Laura 93
Lucy 61
Luke 61
Martha 61
Mollie 61
Nat 61
Parker 100
Rosa 61
Sallie 61
Sam'l 62, 72
Sarah 61
Sillie 61
Susan 61
Virgie 61
W. H. 61
MOSES
Adah 47
Catharine 62
Cyrus 62
Fannie 62
Francis 62
Jas. 8
Levin 62
Nat 62

NEAL
Elizabeth B. 62
H. S. 62
Hamilton S. 62
NEILASS
John 62
Mary 62
NELSON
David 62
James 62
Jim 62
Mary (2)
Ruth 62
Sallie J. 37

NELSON "cont'd"
Southey 37
Susan 62
Wesley 62
NEWSPAPER REPORT
6, 15, 47, 52, 92
NICHOLS
Ed 78
NICKERSON
Dora 62
Handy 62
NOCK
Mary 62
William 62
NOTTINGHAM
Abram 64
Adam 64
Agnes 62, 63
Ann 65, 68
Annie 64, 65
B. F. 66
B. T. 32, 81
B. V. 63
Bennett 64, 65
Betsey 65
Bettie 63, 64
Bridget 55
Candis 62
Cary 65
Cary F. 63
Clay 63
Comfort 67
Ed. W. 62
Edwd. T. 79
Eliza 6, 64, 66
Ellen 65
Ellena 63
Emily 63, 65, 66
Emmy 64
Emory 66
Esther A. 110
Fannie 64
Frances 100
Francis 65
Fred E. 32, 65
Gennie 65
Geo. 66, 67, 77
Geo. U. 63
Geo. W. 2

NOTTINGHAM "cont'd"
Henry 63, 64, 67
Herbert 16
Isaac 3
Isadora 63, 65
Isadora A. J. 64
Jacob 9, 64, 65, 81
James 100
Jane 63
Jay 108
Jno. 63, 64, 65, 66
Jno. Edwd. 63, 103
John A. 65, 66
John E. 66, 67
John R. 14, 63, 64, 65, 66
Joseph 65
Joshua 17, 65
Julia 63
Juliet 63
L. J. 65
L. W. 53, 66
Leah 66
Leon'd J. 78
Lev. T. 66
Lizzie 64, 65, 66
Lloyd 63
Lucius S. 65
Lucretia 63, 64
Lucy 65
Luther 92
Luther L. 65
Margaret 17, 67
Maria 66
Mary 3, 4, 32, 63, 65, 66, 67, 92, 96
Mary A. 66
Nath'l U. 110
Nelson 62
Peggy 66
R. 65
R. V. 63
Richard O. 91, 92
Richard V. 63
Rinie 64
Robt. 62, 65, 96
Rosa 64
Rosie 81

NOTTINGHAM "cont'd"
S. P., Dr. 27, 58, 59
60, 62, 74, 77, 86, 91
S. W. 33, 62
Sallie 63, 65, 66, 67
Sam 66
Samuel 62, 63
Sarah 62, 64
Sev. F., Dr. 15
Sev. T. 64, 66
Severn 64, 65
Severn E. 55, 63
Silla 64
Sol. 20, 64
Sue 64
Susan 9, 62
Susie 67
T. E. 64
Tabitha 105
Thomas 4, 66
Thos. H. 62
Thos. J. L. 105
Vandalia 65
W. C. 66
W. R. 66
W. T. 66
William Thos. 63, 65
Wm. 63, 64, 67, 68
Wm. P. 66
Wm. T. 64, 66, 86
Zeb. 66

ONLY
Esther 67
Frank 67
Jno. 67
Jno. H. 67
Lovey 67
Margaret 67, 106
Mary 67
OUTEN
Annie 67
Isaac 67
OUTTEN
Mary 67
W. D. 67

PALMER
Bethane 67

PALMER "cont'd"
Henry 67
Joseph 67
Mary 67
Peter 67
PARKER
Alfred 68, 93, 100
Annie 93
Henry G. 68
Jno. J. 68
R. H., Dr. 5, 21
Sarah 66
Sev. 68
Susan 99
Susan R. 68
Wm. 66
PARKERSON
John 103
PARKS
Chas. 8
Eliza 8
J. P. 68
Marietta 68
PARRAMORE
James 68
Rosa 68
PARSONS
Frank 68
John 68
Julious 22
Mary 68
Rosey 68
S. H. 3
S. S. 29
Sallie 3
Wm. 3
PEAD
Mary 68
Mitchel 68
PEARSON
John W. 100
Zac. 68
PEED
Cordelia 68
Elisha 68
Isaac 68, 69
Mary 69
Severn 68

PERKINS
Clara 69
Emily 69
Henry 69
Jas. 19
Mary 69
PHILIPS
Abel R. 69
Margt. 69
Patsy 69
PHILLIPS
Catharine 69
Celia 69
Custis 69
Geo. R. 69
George C. 69
Mrs. 69
Sadie A. 69
PITTS
Annie 69
Edward 70
Geo. 69
Jno. 69, 70
Leah 70
Margaret 70
Nellie 69
Parker 70
Peggie 69, 70
Rebecca 69
Sallie 69
Sarah 69
Susan 70
Wm. 69
POOL
Margaret 70
Sally 70
Wm. 70
POTTER
Upshur 98
POULSON
Emily 98
POWELL
Adah 71
Arintha 70
Ben 70
Bennett 70
C. D. 70
Claudie 70
Eady 70

POWELL "cont'd"
Frank 70
G. H. 70
Geo. H. 70
Hannah 70
Isaac 70
John 70
Lynnie 70
Nervella 70
Richard 70
Sallie 70
Susan 70
PRESS
Edmund 71
Mary 84
Sarah 71
PRINCE
Albert 71
Juliet 71
PYLE
Isaac 71
Julia 71

RANDALL
Fanny 71
George 71
RANDOLPH
Elizabeth 71
James 71
RAYFIELD
Cath. 71
Henry S. 71
Leon'd 71
Lettie 71
Wesley 71
Wm. A. 71
READ
Agnes 37
Anna T. 71
Arthur 72, 97
C. C. 23, 102
Enoch 71
Esther 71
Geo. 71, 72, 98
J. R. 9, 103
Jane 71
Jno. R. 10, 22, 27, 41,
50, 51, 53, 68, 70,
94, 104, 110

READ "cont'd"
- Jno. T. 72
- Jno. W. 10
- Jno. W., Mrs. 72
- John 6, 25, 71, 72
- L. S. 72
- Louis 37
- Lucy 72
- Luther 72
- Maria 72
- Mary 71, 72
- Severn 72
- Smith 71
- Wm. 71

REDDEN
- J. J. 72
- Rosalie 72

REED
- George 18
- John W. 72

REID
- Ada 72
- Jane 72
- Jno. W. 72
- William 14

REVEL
- Custis 72
- Martha 72

RHEA
- Columbus 72
- Wm. H. 72

RICHARDSON
- Anna 73
- E. D. 73
- Elijah 73
- Eliza 73
- Elizabeth 73
- Emily 73
- Hessy 73
- J. 22
- J. R. 73
- J. W. 73
- J. Wash. 73
- Jno. 73
- Johnathan 73
- Leon'd 73
- Mary
- Nathan 73
- Patsy 53

RICHARDSON "cont'd"
- R. 73
- Robert 35
- Sally 73
- Sarah 73
- Tabitha 73
- Thos. 73
- Thos. A. 73
- Wm. 73

RIDDICK
- Nannie 73
- Wm. 73

RILEY
- Alfred 33
- Aron 74
- Eliza 71
- Fluvianna 74
- Isaac 71

RIPPON
- Sadie E. 74
- Thos. 74

ROBBINS
- Arthur 7
- Elizabeth 74
- Geo. M. "Undertaker" 70
- Isaac D. 74
- Julia 7
- W. T. 74

ROBERSON
- W. T. 74

ROBERTS
- Ann 32
- Arthur 74
- Arthur E. 4
- Edmd. U. 74
- Eliz. 74
- Florence M. 74
- Geo. 74
- Geo. L. 4, 74
- H. W. 74
- Henry 68
- J. H. 32
- Jake 20
- Jno. H. 74
- Louis 56
- M. E. 74
- Maggie 74
- Margt. 4

ROBERTS "cont'd"
- Margt. E. 74
- Mary 74
- Mollie E. 74
- Sally 74
- Sarah 56

ROBERTSON
- Geo. 23
- Jno. R. 75
- Rebecca 75

ROBINS
- A. M. 75
- Arthur 75
- Betsy 75
- Emory 75
- Irving 75
- Isaac 75
- Isaac D. 75
- Isaac D. Sr. 75
- Jennie 75
- John 16, 75, 82
- John H. 26, 82
- Julia 75
- Mary 82
- Mary N. 75
- O. K. 75
- Tiny 75

ROBINSON
- Caroline 75
- Geo. S. 75
- Henry 95
- John 75
- Lettie 95
- Mack 60, 106
- Maggie 75
- Michael 75

RODGERS
- John 75

ROGERS
- Amy 94
- Cora 75
- Geo. 75
- Jno. T. 28
- John 75
- Lewis 75
- Robt. 94
- Susie 75

ROLLEY
- A. E. 75

ROLLEY "cont'd"
- Clara 75
- F. J. 75
- Francis 75
- Frank C. 75
- Margt. 75
- Mary A. 75
- Polly 75
- Raymond 75
- Wm. 75

ROLLY
- Estelle 76
- Francis 76
- Luther 76
- Margaret 76

ROOKS
- Fannie S. 76
- Harriet 76
- Henry 76
- James 76
- Navilla 76
- O. L. 76
- Sallie 76
- Susan 76
- Wm. 76

ROSE
- Ida 76
- Oscar 76

SAMPLE
- Arthur 76
- Bettie 76
- Dora 76
- Frances 76
- George 79
- H. 72
- Jacob 76
- Major 17
- Mary 76
- Nath'l 86
- Sam'l 76
- Sarah 76
- Silvia 79
- Wm. 76

SATCHEL
- Adolphus 76
- Bennett 76
- Effie 76
- Grace 77

SATCHEL "cont'd"	SAVAGE "cont'd"	SAVAGE "cont'd"	SCOTT "cont'd"
Isaac 77	Anna 78	Sarah 3, 80	J. J. 76
John 101	Anne M. 78	Thos. D. 80	Jas. 81
Nannie 76	Asa 69	W. R. 79	Jas. H. 81
Peggy 101	Bell S. 79	Walker 78	Jennie 96
Rebecca J. 76	Betsy 78	Wm. 78	Jesse 80, 81
Rich'd 76	C. H. 39, 99	**SCARBORO**	John 81, 96, 103
Southey 77	Chas. 7	Laura 80	L. E. 81
Thos. 76	Comfort 90	Shadrack 80	Lillie 81
SATCHELL	E. 79, 90	**SCARBOROUGH**	Lizzie 80
Ames 77	E. B. 79	Dianna 80	Mary 29, 52
Amos 77	Edwd. 78	Hariet 80	Nim 80
Anice? 77	Eliz. 72	J. 80	P. F. 31, 81, 108
Bennett 77	Ellen 17, 58, 79, 93	Luke 80	Peggie W. 82
Bettie 77	Emanuel 78, 79	Tamar 80	Peter 82
Bob 77	Emory 78, 79	**SCHROEDER**	Peter F. 52, 82
Caroline 77	Ester 78	Nat 71	Rosa 81
Ellen 77	George 3, 78, 79, 94	**SCISCO**	S. R. 81
Geo. 77, 95, 98	Geo. G. 53	Ellen 80	Sally/Sallie 12, 81
Isaac 47	Geo. L. 78	G. C. 80	Sally S. 81
John 77	Henry 78, 79	George C. 80	Sarah 80, 81
Julia 47	Hugh 90	Harriet 80	Susan 103
Laura 77	India 79	Henry 80	Tabitha 81
Leah 98	Isaac 79	Juliet 80	Thomas 52, 80, 108
Levin 77	J. B. 78	Laura 80	Thos. L. 80, 81
Levin R. 77	James T. 78	Louisa 77	Thos. M. 81
R. J. 77	Jane 78	Mary 80	Virginia 81
Richard 67	Jas. K. 18, 78, 79	Preston 80	Wm. J., Dr. 5, 13, 22
Robt. 77	Jno. T. 80	Virginia 80	34, 52, 60, 61,
Rosa 77	John 78	**SCOTT**	70, 80, 81, 87,
Sallie 77	Jos. 78, 79	& Wilkins 64	101, 102.
Sarah 77	Kate 79	Alice 82	**SEARS**
Susan 77	Katie 78	Ann 81	Ellen 82
Thos. 77	Laura 78	Annie 81	Joseph 82
Wm. 7	Litt. 72	Benjamin 12, 81	**SEATON**
SAUNDERS	M. A. 17	Bridget 78, 80	Alice 82
A. 13	Martha 7	Candis 81	Cornelius 82
Arthur 77, 78	Mary 79	Clinton 81	Corn's 82
City 78	Mary L. 80	E. O. 80	Lettie 82
Elizabeth 77	Nellie 79	Edward 80, 81	**SEDGEWICK**
J. T. 78	P. W. 28	Eliza 80	E. G. 82
Laura 77	Patrick 70	Elizabeth 56	Rebecca C. 82
Maria 78	Peggie 78	Ella 80, 82	**SEEDS**
Stewart J. 77	Peter 79, 105	Emily 81	Amanda 82
SAVAGE	Preston 79	Geo. H. 82	**SELBY**
A. 78, 84	R. K. 79	Geo. L. 81	Sallie 24
Adaline 78, 79	Rachel 78, 79	George 56	Tr. 24
Adelin 78	Rose 78	Hennie 81	**SEYMOUR**
Alfred 84	Sallie 78	Henry 81	Abe 82

SEYMOUR "cont'd"	SIX "cont'd"	SMITH "cont'd"	SOLOMON
Mary 82	Susan 83	Ginny 84	Lucy 86
Ned 82	**SKIDMORE**	Isaac 84, 86	**SOMERS**
SHACKLEFORD	Ann 83	James 84	Mary 86
Elizabeth 82	Isaac 83	Jas. "Undertaker"	Wm. T. 86
Sallie 82	**SKINNER**	4, 37, 42, 86	**SPADY**
T. H. 82	Maggie 83	Jas. A. 10, 28, 64, 85	Abe 87
Thos. H. 82	Thomas 83	Jas. H. 84, 85	Abel 2
SHARPLEY	**SLACK**	Jennie 84	Alfred 86, 88
James 82	James 78	Jno. C. 4	Annie 87
Nancy 82	**SMALL**	John 84, 85	Arthur 87
SHEPPARD	V. 13	Joshua 84	Bell 87
Esther 82	**SMALLWOOD**	Josiah 85	Chas. 86
G. 82	Susan 46	Kate 85	Daniel 37, 49, 88
Geo. 82	Wilson 46	Lauretta 84	Edgar J. 87
Jas. 2, 82, 83	**SMAW**	Leah 84, 85	Elizabeth 86
Maggie 82	Bennett 83	Levin 13	Eugene 87
Mary 2	Emily 83	Lizzie 85, 86	Fannie 86, 87
Severn 82	J. H. 83	Maggie 85	George 87
SHIELD	Jennie 83	Margaret 84, 86	Gertie 86
Frank 2	Rachel 83, 84, 87	Maria 78, 84, 86	Gussie 86
SHIELDS	Rosie 83	Nancie 85	Horace 87
Martha 83	Spencer 83	Nat 84, 85, 108	Ibbie 87
SHIVERS	**SMITH**	Nellie 84	James 86, 87
Gertrude 83	Abram 84	Nim 84	Jane 86
SIMKINS	Adah 84	Patience 86	Jim 67, 87
Geo. 89	Adar 85	Peter 77, 85	John 86, 87, 105
John 83	Alice 84	Peter B. 84, 85	John T. 87
Linda 83	Annie 84	Rich'd 85	Joseph 87
Mary 83	Appy 84	Robert 85	Josiah 86
SIMPKINS	Charles 49, 92	Sallie/Sally 84	Levin 87
Annie 83	Charles, Dr. 75	Samuel 84	Lola 86
Arthur 83	Charlie 85	Severn 84, 85, 86	Lottie 87
George 16	Charlotte 77, 84	Severn J. 86	Lucy 87
John 83	Custis 86	Spencer 38	Marg't. 105
Litey 83	Dr. 101	Susan 85, 86	Maria 67, 87
Margaret S. 83	Druetta 4	Tabby 84	Mary 86, 104
Sallie 83	E. U., Mrs. 10	Tob 84	Mary A. 88
Sarah 67	Edith 108	Tobe 85, 86	Mollie 86
SISCO	Elizabeth 84	Tobitha 85	Nancy 87
Alexine 83	Elizabeth W. 86	Virginia F. 85	Patience 86, 87
Geo. H. 83	Ella 85	W. A. 84	Rachel 87
Henry 83, 98	Ellen 85, 86	Washington 86	Robt. 86
Louisa 83	Geo. 84, 85	Wm. 66, 84, 85	Sally/Sallie 65, 87
Preston 83	Geo. A. 85	Wm. G., Phy. 1	Sam'l 87
Rhodie 67	Geo. F. 84	**SNEAD**	Sarah 2, 87
Virginia 83	Geo. W., Dr. 3, 16,	Mary 26	Smith 25, 87
SIX	69, 80, 90,	Tully 26	Sol. 86
John 83	97, 101.		Southey 104

SPADY "cont'd"
Susan 87
Sylvia 87
Thomas W. 45
Thos. 65
W. H. 38
Wm. H. 38

SPARROW
Dillia 21
Jacob 21

SPRATLEY
Jno. 88
Julia 88

STAFFORD
Daniel 88
Melvina 88

STAKES
John W. 88
Mollie 88

STARCHEY
Jacob 88
Maggie 88

STEPHEN
Adah 88
Robt. 88

STEPHENS
Ada 88
Ann 88
Bailey 88
Ephram 74
Gennie 6, 15, 31, 35,
 76, 78.
Geo. 65
Margt. 88
Mary 88
Peggie 71
Puss 88
Robt. 88
Virginia 56
Wesley 88

STERLING
Margt. 43
Sallie 88
Susan 88
Thos. 88
Wm. 43, 88

STEVENS
Annie 89
Arintha 89

STEVENS "cont'd"
Custis 89
Ed 89
Eliza 13
Georgianna 89
Horace 89
Isaac 89
J. A. 89
Jas. 103
Jno. T. 88, 89
John 13
Josephine 88, 89
LaVenia 89
Len 89
Lit. 89
Littleton 89
Margt. 103
Mary 22, 89
Phoebe 88
Rose 89
Sarah 89
Susan 89
Walter 89

STEVENSON
J. R. 89
Roberta 89

STEWART
Ben 89
Chas. 90
Georgianna 90
Henry B. 4
J. M. 90
James 90
John M., Capt. 30, 90
Maggie 89
Mary 90
Tabitha 90
Virgil 90
W. B. 18

STILES
J. W. 90

STOAKLEY
Geo. A. 3
John 90, 97
Joshua 90
Michael 90, 111
Mitty 90
Sally S. 90
Thos. J. 90

STOAKLEY "cont'd"
Wm., Dr. 4 Phy.
Wm. S. 90

STOCKLEY
Jos. 90
Priscilla 90

STOKELY
Mary 90
Thos. 90

STOTT
Abel 11
Lizzie 80
Margaret 11
Mary 90

STRATTON
Adah 91
Bridget 91
Carrie 91
Chas. 91
Daniel 91
Ed 91
Emma 91
Jacob 91
Jno. 68
Lucy 68
Sabra 91
Tweezer 91
Wm. 12, 77

STRINGER
Geo. W. 91
Hilary B. 91
Sally B. 91

STUART
Chas. 90

STUARTT
Fanny 12
J. M. 12

STURGIS
C. F. 91
Henry 91, 92
Ida 91, 92
Indie 91
Jacob 91
James 28
Jas. 91
Jas. K. 91
Jas. M. 91
Jno. 91
Katy 91

STURGIS "cont'd"
L. N. 54
Lizzie 91
M. C. 91
Mary 92
Minnie 91
Missouri 91
Molly 91
Oswald 91
Vianna 28, 91
William 91, 92
Wm. H. 91
Wm. T. H. 91

SUNKETS
Jno. H. 92
John 92
Ledy 92
Litia 92

SUNKETT
John 92
Lelia 92

SUTTON
Nat. 92

SWANGER
A. E. 34
E. B. 34

TANKARD
Annie D. 92
Calino 92
E. G. 92
Elizabeth 92
Esther 92
Ha 70
J. R. 5
Jno. W. 4, 81
John 92
Major 5
Mary 92
O. R. 94
P. B. 92
Phillip B. 111
Sam 92
Sarah 92
Susan 4
Tinny 5

TAYLOR
Ann 92
Annie 93

TAYLOR "cont'd"
Arthur 92
Bridget 85
C. L. 93
Catherine 93
Chas. L. 93
G. A. 93
Geo. B. 93
Harry 93, 98, 104
Ida 92
Isaac 96
Isabella 93
Jas. 93
Jennie 93
John 59
Laura 64
Lelia A. 93
Louis B. 53
Mary 59
Nellie 93
Richard 12
Robt. B. 46, 85, 93
Samuel 93
Smith 93
Thomas 92
Violet 93
Wm. 45
Wm. M. 93
TAZEWELL
Harry 93
Henry 93
Kevin 93
Mary 93
THOM
A. P. 70
Wm. A., Phy. 9, 18,
 22, 35, 67,
 85, 89, 93.
THOMAS
A. 67, 70
Ad. 93
Adaline 93
Agnes 31
Alice 94
Anna 94
Arthur 93
Aveline 94
Bell 94
Caleb 94

THOMAS "cont'd"
Emma 94
Emory 102
Emory E. 78
G. H. 52
Geo. H. 26, 93, 94
George L. J. 94
Henry 89, 93
J. W. 66
Jas. U. 110
John W. 94
Jos. W. 94
Joseph W. 94
L. J. 94
Maria 93
Mary 94
Mary A. 15
Nannie 94
Peggie 94
Peter 94
Sarah 94
Sol. 94
Sophia E. 66, 94
THOMPSON
Annie P. 94
O. A. 94
Obed 94
S. E. 94
Sarah 94
Willis 94
Wm. 95
TOLIVER
Henry 95
Mary A. 95
TOWNSEND
Sam'l 97
TOY
James 95
TRADER
Eliza 46
L. T. 46
TRAVIS
Fanny 95
Missouri 95
Nim S. 95
Sarah E. 95
Severn B. 95
Wm. 95

TREHERN
Alfred T. 95
Len 95
Lenard/Leonard 95
Mary 95
Nora 95
Robin 95
TREHURNE
Lloyd 32, 33
TROWER
A. J. 96
Alfred 95
Ann 95
Ben 95
Benjamin 27
Eliza 95
Fannie 95
Geo. W. 96
Harrison 95
Henrietta 95, 96
Henry 23
Isaac 96
James 95
Jim 96
John 95, 105
Keley 96
Lavenia 24, 25
Lottie 95, 96
Mary Nelson 96
Nelson 96
Priscilla 95
R. S. 95
Sallie/Sally 96, 105
Sarah 95
TURLINGTON
Levi 58
Rachel 58
TURNER
A. T. 50
Arintha 96
E. T., Mrs. 55
Edward 34
Ellen 96
G. W. 96
Geo. T. 96
Horace 97
Israel 96
Jno. T. 96
Joshua B. 59

TURNER "cont'd"
Kitty 96
Major 96
Malinda 96
Margaret 34
Mary E. 96
Minnie 97
Sallie 59
T. W. 38
TYLER
Addie 97
Ben 97
Benj. 97
J. E. 97
Jno. E. 97
Sallie 97

UNDERHILL
M. E. 97
Maggie 97
Michael E. 97
Polly 13, 72
UPSHUR
Abe 99
Adah 97
Alice 97, 98
Alice S. 97
Alfred 98, 99
Ann 99
Arthur 98
Cary 98
Cata 97
Cato 98
Chas. 99
Clara 98
Edith 45
Edward 99
Ella 97
Ellen 97, 99
Frank 97, 98
George 88, 97, 98
Henry 97, 98, 99
Henry L. 98, 99
Isaac 97, 108
Jacob 97, 99
Joseph 45
Leah 97, 98
Liddie 97, 98, 99
Lizzie 99

UPSHUR "cont'd"	WARD "cont'd"	WEEKS	WHITE "cont'd"
Lucretia 98	S. W. 100	Alfred 102	Geo. 28, 108
Matilda 98	Sadie 100	Edmund 101	Jas. C. 103
Nelly 97, 99	Sam'l 100	Edwd. 102	James H. 103
Patience 98	Southey 100	Francis 101	John W. 103
Sallie 99	Tabitha 59, 100	J. 101	Margt. 103
Sarah 97	Thos. 100	Lucy W. 101	Mary J. 103
Sophia 99	W. B. 100	Major 101	Nancy 103
Susan 98	Wm. 100	Mary 101	Oh 103
T. W. 98	Wm. G. 100	Nellie 101	S. S. 103
Thomas 98	**WARREN**	Spencer 16	Sidney S. 103
Thos. C. 98	Ed 100	Susan 102	Wm. 87
Wm. 99	Martha 100	T. 101	**WHITEHEAD**
	Mary E. 100	**WESCOAT**	Fanny 103
VAN NESS	Richard 100	E. D. 102	John 103
William J. 99	T. E. 100	Edmd. 41	John T. 95
Wm. 99	**WARRINGTON**	Elizabeth 41, 100	Mary E. 103
VAUGHN	Georgia 100	G. M. 102	Rose 103
Jett 99	John 100	Gennie 102	Sarah 103
Mary L. 99	Rich'd 4	Geo. M. 70	Severn 103
	WASHINGTON	H. P. 78, 102	Wm. E. 103
WADDY	Fannie 101	Hez. 102	Wm. M. 103
Fred 24, 90	**WATSON**	Hezh. P. 10, 17	**WHITMAN**
Hamilton 7	Ben 101	Jno. L. 100	Georgiana 103
Maggie 99	Betsy 101	Mary 102	John 103
Wm. E. 99	Dan'l 5	Rose 102	**WICKS**
WALLACE	George 101	Wm. R. 102	Elenora 103
Alfred 99	J. L. 9, 101	**WESCOTT**	Emily 103
Margaret L. 99	Jno. 101	Alice 102	Harriet 103
Rosa 99	John C. 101	Geo. M. 50	James 103
Wm. 99	Joshua 101	Mary S. 102	Joseph 103
WARD	Kate 101	Nim 102	Major 37
Albert 26	Luke 101	Rosa 50	Mary 37
Ann 100	Maria 101	W. R. 102	Robt. 103
Ben 100	Mary 101	**WESLEY**	Violette 34
Berry 100	Mary J. 101	Geo. 102	Wm. 34, 103
C. J. 100	Polly 101	Violet 102	**WIDGEN**
George G. 100	Sally 101	**WEST**	Arintha 104
Henry 100	Sarah 5, 101	Ap. 102	Eliz. 87, 104
Jas. 59	Tabbith 101	Mary 102	Fannie 65, 66
John 68	**WEBB**	W. 76	Ibby 104
Lellia 26	D. R., Mrs. 101	**WESTON**	J. T. 66
Margaret 100	James 101	Jos. 45	Jeff 104
Mary 100	John 13, 101	**WHITE**	John 103, 104
Melinda 100	Louisa 101	Anne E. 103	Joseph 54, 66, 104
Millie 68	Sallie 101	E. T. 40, 103	Lucy 104
Missouri 100	Sarah 101	Effie 110	Mary E. 104
Nervilla 100		Emma J. 103	Mrs. 66
		Esther 33	Nora 66

WIDGEN "cont'd"	WILLIAMS "cont'd"	WILSON "cont'd"	WISE
Rinthia 103	Cutter 105	Florence 107	A. W. 27
Sallie 104	Dina 93	Florence E. 107	Adalade B. 109
Southey 66, 104	E. J. 105	Geo. 39, 107, 108	Addie 109
Thos. 104	Eady 105	Geo. A. 107	Bowden 109
WIDGEON	Elizabeth 71, 106	Geo. E. 89	Charlotte 109
Geo. W. 104	George 106	Henry 107	Grace 109
Susan 104	Henry 105	James 107	Henry 109
Thomas 104	J. S. 105	Jesse W. 108	Henry A. 109
Walter 104	James 105	Joe 106, 107	J. B. 27, 109
WILKINS	Jas. H. 106	John 32, 79, 107	Jesse 109
Alfred 105	Jesse S. 105	Jos. 106	John 109
Ann 105	Jno. "Supt. Of Poor"	Lelia 107	Kate 109
C. F. 104	17, 21, 34, 76,	Leonard 107	Lena 109
Ed 104	106.	Margaret 108	Lucy 27, 76, 77, 98,
Elen 18	Jno. H. 105	Margaret Sarah 79	109.
Eliz 46	John A. 106	Martha 107	Luther 109
Essie L. 104	John B. 105	Mary E. 107	Maria 109
Geo. F. 104, 105	Lucy 105	Matilda 107	Nancy 109
J. W. 103	Mary 105, 106	Moses 107	Peter 109
Joakim 105	Sarah 105	Patience 107	Rhinie 109
Jno. B. 38	Severn 17	Robt. 107	Sam 109
Kate 104	Susan 105	Samuel 108	Solomon 109
Kath. 105	Virginia 106	Tabitha 107	Susan 109
Lelia 23	Wm. 106	Wm. 107	W. A. 106
Lottie 104	**WILLIS**	Wm. J. 107	W. D. 45
Louisa 104	Anna 106	Wm. S. 79	**WRIGHT**
Mary 49, 103	Arintha 106	**WINDER**	Custis 20, 22, 109
Missouri 105	Custis 106	Alice 108	Emma 110
Peter 104	Emily 106	Ed 108	Fred 96
Robt. 46	Geo. 94	Edward 108	Grace 110
Robt. E. 105	Jno. 106	Emily 108	James B. 110
S. S. 20, 53, 101	Julia 106	Georgeanna 108	James R. 110
Sallie 105	L. J. 83	Georgie 108	John 109
Sarah 65, 104	Leon'd J. 106	J. L. 108	Leah 109
Thos. 105	Lewis 106	J. Lee 108	Levi 110
Thos. W. 65	Luke 106	Leah 108	Mary 109
W. J. 104	Luther 106	Lewis 57, 108	Sarah 110
W. T. 105	Marg't. S. 106	Maria 108	Tenny 43, 109
W. W. 24, 65	Mary 106	Mary 108	Wm. 37
William W. "Phy."	Sarah 106	Mollie 108	**WYATT**
8, 14, 31, 35,	Wm. 106	S. J. 108	Amelia 110
41, 89, 94.	**WILSON**	Sarah 108	Bell 110
Wm. E. 104, 105	Agnes 107	Susan 108	Betsy 110
WILLETT	Ann 79	Wesley 108	C. L. 68, 110
Jas. H. 105, 110	E. H. 107	William 108	Geo. 110
Nannie 105	Ellen 106, 107	**WINDOW**	Isma 5, 15
WILLIAMS	Emily 108	Levin 109	Mary 110
Annie 106	F. U. 108	Sally 109	N. W. 8, 96

WYATT "cont'd"
   Pem 110
   Polly 110
   Sarah 110
   Smith 15, 110
   Susan 110
   Thos. 110
   Wm. 110
   Wm. J. 110

YOUNG
   Ezekiel 40
   George 3
   Jno. 111
   Matilda 37
   Rachel 40
   Sallie 111
   Severn 111

447 Surnames

Last Will & Testament

Deaths 1871 - 1901

from Will Book #39 (1854 – 97) & Will Book #40 (1897 – 1901)

ADAIR, G. H. Wit: Aug. 6, 1898 db June 12, 1899, Harriet Susan Adair, wife; Gordon H., son; Edgar P. Adair's 3 daughters Mary A., Rozena & Baine L. Adair; WB40 p. 23.

ASHBY, Benjamin Wit: Oct. 22, 1880 db Mar. 8, 1886, William T., Asa S., George W., John H. & James F. Ashby, sons; Mary A. & Peggy S. James, Elizabeth S. Fisher, daughters; Judson M. Ashby, grandson; WB39 p. 298.

BAGWELL, Heley D. Wit: Dec. 12, 1873, db Apr. 11, 1881, Heley P. Bagwell, son; Thos. H., son; Imogen (Thos. Wife), WB39 p. 219.

BAILY, Henry Wit: Dec. 16, 1896 db Oct. 18, 1899, Nancy Baily, wife; George, youngest son, Nancy his stepmother; Henry & Albert illegitimate children; WB40 p. 28.

BECKET, Edmund Wit: May 1899 db Aug. 14, 1899, Georgianna Johnson & son Sargent WB40 p. 24.

BELL, Elizabeth P. Wit: Jan. 26, 1898 db May 18, 1901, of Marionville, Margaret Elizabeth w/of Benjamin Thomas & Martha E. Bell, daughters; George S., William P. & Henry P. Bell sons; WB40 p. 54.

BELOTE, John C. Wit: Dec. 28, 1898 db Sept. 10, 1900, Frank, brother; Melissa Belote, sister; WB40 p. 46.

BIBBINS, Sam'l Sr. Wit: June 5, 1879 db Oct. 13, 1879, "DUPLICATE" Family: Lyttleton, Jno., Sam, Joseph, William & James, sons; Susan Wormly, Mary Ann Stephens, Margaret, Edith Bibbins, daughters; WB39 p. 212.

BLANKS, Estell M. Wit: Aug. 18, 1891 db Jan. 10, 1900, Edward M. Blanks, husband; WB40 p. 31.

BLUE, Tamer Wit: July 16, 1898 db Dec. 14, 1899, Arinthia Blue Fitchett & her children; Georgeanna Jarvis of Baltimore, Md., Lucile Blue, William Edward Blue, Georgeanna Simkins; WB40 p. 29.

BOWDOIN, Susan M. "Linden", Wit: Oct. 15, 1878 db July 13, 1885, John R. Bowdoin, son; John A. Bowdoin, grandson; WB39 p. 244.

BRADFORD, Harriet Wit: Aug. 15, 1889 db Sept. 12, 1892, Nellie M. Smith, friend; Almer Willis Smith, little friend; Ella Smith; WB39 p. 332.

BROWNE, ORRIS A. Wit: May 6, 1898 db Oct. 10, 1898, Nannie Howard Browne, wife; Elisabeth Josephine Browne, daughter; WB40 p. 13.

BURRIS, Caleb Wit: Apr. 3, 1873 db ?, Eugenia Burris, wife; children; WB39 p. 197.

CAMPBELL. Elizabeth W. Wit: Apr. 26, 1894 db July 9, 1894, Tabitha R. Jacob, Tabitha O. Bayley, Mrs. Susan J. Bell, Mrs. Amanda M. Bull, Miss. Mary B. Bell; WB39 p.348.

CARPENTER, Elizabeth Wit: June 27, 1894 db Mar. 16, 1899, Laurn Bayly & Susan Holt, daughters; WB40 p. 16.

CARPENTER, Elizabeth W. Wit: Jan. 20, 1873 db Apr. 14, 1873, John A. Carpenter, son; Alonzo G. Nottingham, grandson; Lauretta V. Nottingham, daughter; WB39 p. 176.

CARTER, Peter J. Wit: July 19, 1886 db Nov. 9, 1886, Maggie F. Carter, wife; Jessie S., Stanly L., Mallie C., William M. sons, WB39 p. 257.

COBB, Albert F. "Cobb Island", Wit: July 28, 1890 db Nov. 10, 1890, Ellen A. Cobb, wife; Sarah Travis, daughter & wife of William T.; Thomas S., son; WB39 p. 300.

COBB, Nathan F. Sr. Wit: July 10, 1870 db June 13, 1881, Nancy, wife, WB39 p. 221.

COLLINS, Elizabeth S. Wit: Feb. 10, 1900 db Oct. 14, 1901, James Collins, nephew; Florence Joynes, dear friend she raised; WB40 p. 57.

COLLINS, Esther, free woman of color Wit: Nov. 10, 1865 db March 8, 1886, John Collins, friend, relative & trustee for Roxaline, daughter; WB39 p. 246.

COLLINS, Philip in Capeville Township, Wit: July 2, 1888 db Sept. 10, 1888, Mary Hillyer; Betsy, wife; Ann T. Bentley, step-daughter of Ward, N.Y., John J. Gregory step-son; WB39 p. 270.

COPES, Thomas Wit: Apr. 10, 1879 db Jan. 13, 1891, Elizabeth S., wife; Mary S. Warren, Peggie J. & Annie T. Copes, daughters; WB39 p. 302.

COTTINGHAM, William H. Wit: Mar. 30, 1894 db Oct. 16, 1895, Mary A. Cottingham, wife; WB39 p. 362.

DALBY, Maggie J. Wit: Aug. 6, 1895 db ?, 1898, John L. Dalby, brother and John's children Mattie E. & Luther G. Dalby; WB40 p. 7.

DISHAROON, Mary H. Wit: Apr. 15, 1891 db Mar. 22, 1899, Sallie E. Disharoon, mother; WB40 p. 18.

DIXON, Thomas H. Wit: Mar. 27, 1899 db Aug. 12, 1901, Margaret Sarah Dixon, wife; William W. & Thomas J., sons; WB40 p. 55.

DOUGHTY, William J. of Hog Island, Wit: Jan. 3, 1888 db Sept. 14, 1888, Matilda Ann Doughty, Sarah wife of John, daughters; George, son; WB39 p. 275.

DOWNING, A. W. Wit: Mar. 10, 1896 db Dec. 9, 1901, Mary G. Downing, wife; Harriet B. Buss & Mary E. Fisher, daughters; WB40 p. 60.

DUNTON, Caroline B. Wit: Nov. 9, 1896 db May 12, 1902; John R. & Albert W. Dunton, sons; WB40 p. 64

DUNTON, Rosie Wit: July 22, 1896 db Sept. 14, 1896, Edward, George Ellis, Alfred, Severn, Joseph & Edmond Bowdoin, John Baker, sons; Sarah Skinner, Keran Tazwell, Mary Bayly & Harriet Scisco, daughters; WB39 p. 369.

ENNIS, Susan A. Wit: Jan. 1900 db Feb. 10, 1902, Elizabeth H. Reed, daughter; Irving S., Joseph, Elmer, Ara & Charlie Ennis, 5 sons; Hattie W. Reed, Nannie R. Ennis & Elizabeth S. Ennis, granddaughters; WB40 p. 62

FISHER, Miers W. Wit: Aug. 22, 1871 db July 14, 1873, "Woodburn", "DUPLICATE" Family: Nathaniel H. Fisher, son; Lafayette Harmanson, stepson; Juliet A. Parramore & Mary L. McNutt, daughters; George Fisher Parramore & William Winder Parramore, grandsons; Sally S., Juliet & Susan Cary, granddaughters; children of deceased daughter Susan; WB39 p. 158.

FISHER, Sally A. of Franktown, Wit: Apr. 10, 1885 db June 8, 1885, widow of Thomas B.; John Edward Nottingham Jr. son of J. E. & Malinda Catharine & Benjamin T. Gunter friends; Susan E. & James A Fisher; George H. & Bettie E. Read; Margaret Susan Harris, Warrenton, Va.; Marion B. Henderson & Susan E. Fisher, nieces; Arthur, Thomas & John Addison & Nathaniel P. Henderson, nephews; Louisa, N. P. Henderson's daughter, Codicil May 16, 1885, WB39 p. 239.

FISHER, Samuel P. Wit: Dec. 7, 1882 db Jan. 8, 1883, Rosa Fisher, wife; Samuel P., son, Fanny Fisher, daughter; Wilmer W., oldest son, WB39 p. 226.

FITCHETT, Jacob J. Wit: May 2, 1892 db July 12, 1892, Tabitha, wife; Lauretta Collins, daughter & wife of William H.; WB39 p. 330.

FITCHETT, James Wit: June 7, 1880 db Nov. 14, 1881, Cordelia J. Fitchett, daughter, WB39 p. 222.

FLOYD, Charlotte B. Wit: Dec. 27, 1893 db Aug. 8, 1898, Dr. James B., husband; Edward Bayly Floyd, son; WB40 p. 10.

FOX, William Wit: Feb. 2, 1901 db Feb. 10, 1902, Mary Fox, wife; Mary S. Turner, William T. Fox, Soule B. Fox & Ivan C. Fox, grandchildren; WB40 p. 63

HALLETT, James D. Wit: Apr. 18, 1884 db July 14, 1884, Maggie, Thomas, Curtis & Virginia Hallett, brother's children; Sarah Hallett, sister; Nellie Latimer, James Latimer; WB39 p.232.

HARMANSON, Wm. Wit: Oct. 4, 1876 db Nov. 13, 1876, "DUPLICATE" Family: Margaret, wife; Virginia S. Leatherbury, Elizabeth Dunton, David A. wife, daughters; James R. Harmanson dec. son's children Margaret & James Lewes Harmanson; Alonzo T. Leatherbury grandson; WB39 p. 194.

HOLLAND, Clara J. Wit: June 30, 1886 db Oct. 11, 1886, E. Holland, husband deceased; Nath'l L., son; Hattie J. Trower, daughter; Flossie R., granddaughter, WB39 p. 254.

JACKSON, Ibby Wit: June 6, 1893 db Aug. 14, 1893, Mary Fitchett, daughter; James Bell & Isaac James, grandsons; Ginnie& Fannie James, granddaughters; WB39 p. 344.

JAMES, Hez. P. Wit: Jan. 11, 1882 db Aug. 10, 1885,"DUPLICATE" Family: William I., John Robt., Samuel M.,Hezekiah P. James, sons; Levenia C., wife; Delitha T. Johnson, Susan A. Ashby, Virginia S. Heath, Margaret S, Mapp, daughters; WB39 p. 247.

JAMES, Lavania Wit: May 30, 1890 db June 11, 1890, J. Llewellyn Mapp &Kezekia P. James, friends; Alfred M. James, minor friend; WB39 p. 288.

JARVIS, George, man of color, Mar. 3, 1885 db Feb. 14, 1888, Virginia, present wife; Arthur, Liddie, Bettie, George, Mary, Severn, Sarah, Roberta & Isidora Jarvis, children; Sally Jarvis & Juliet Satchell, children of 1st wife; p. WB39 264 & 279.

JOHNSON, Arthur M. Wit: June 1900 db Apr. 14, 1902; Harriet Amanda Johnson, wife; WB40 p. 64

KELLAM, Margaret Wit: Aug. 25, 1886 db Dec. 12, 1887, Thomas Warren, nephew & son of Hezekiah; WB39 p. 261.

MAPP, Alfred N. H. "Darby's Wharf", Wit: June 1, 1875 db Dec. 15, 1876, Laura, wife; children; WB39 p. 199.

MASON, Ezekiel Wit: Dec. 22, 1891 db Mar. 9, 1897, Charles E. Godwin sell Birds Nest Station store house; Sallie Satchell & daughter Sadie, Tabbie Collins wife of Horace and son Albert; WB39 p. 379.

MASON, Thomas J. Wit: Feb. 1880 db Nov. 21, 1881, Anna Mason, wife; Susan Wescoat, sister, WB39 p. 224.

MEARES, James Wit: Dec. 29, 1882 db Dec. 13, 1886, William & George, sons; Lizzie Smith, Rosie Whitehead, Lovey Whitehead & Caroline Mears, daughters; Mary, wife of son James, WB39 p. 255.

MOORE, Severn of Bayview, Wit: June 9, 1878 db Nov. 10, 1879, Rachel, wife; Margaret S. & Catherine, daughters; WB39 p. 218.

MOORE, William P. Wit: Nov. 1, 1872 db Nov. 11, 1872, Anne H. Smith, daughter; Susan Rogers, Granddaughter; Edmund Potter "Stringer Land", William P. Moore 3rd "Red Bank" farm, "Fisher Land, Hills Land", William P. M. Kellam& Stewart Kellam, Grandsons; WB39 p. 148.

MORRIS, Thomas Wit: Nov. 3, 1892 db May 13, 1901, Susan Morris, wife; Wm., son; WB40 p. 53.

NOCK, Harriett Wit: Nov. 11, 1898 db Jan. 9, 1899, Isaac Nock, husband; WB40 p. 14.

NOCK, Isaac Wit: Mar. 4, 189 db Mar. 16, 1899, Lucy Nock, wife; WB40 p. 17

NOTTINGHAM, Comfort Q. G. Wit: Feb. 10, 1897 db Sept. 13, 1897, Robinson, husband; John E. Winder, maternal uncle; WB40 p. 1

NOTTINGHAM, Esther S. B. Wit: Apr. 15, 1885 db June 11, 1888, Juliet A. Bell, daughter & wife of George W., Peggy Mapp Jacob, daughter & wife of Thomas H.; grandchildren; WB39 p. 267.

NOTTINGHAM, J. L. L. Wit: May 1873 db Sept. 17, 1877 Tabitha, Wife (dec.); Elizabeth S. B. Nottingham, Daughter "Lebanon"; Peggy J., daughter w/o Thomas Henry Nottingham "Lebanon"; Codicil: Wit: Sept. 3, 1873 Clara J. Nottingham, daughter; WB39 p. 208.

NOTTINGHAM, Missouri S. Wit: Sept. 25, 1888 db Apr. 17, 1890, Howard, husband; WB39 p. 286.

NOTTINGHAM, Robert B. Wit: Feb. 12, 1872 db May 13, 1872,Hennietta P. Turner, daughter; William Nottingham, little boy; E. W. Nottingham, brother; WB39 p. 145.

PARKER, Alfred Wit: Dec. 9, 1896 db Sept. 17, 1897, Sarah P. Upshur, sister "Elkington"; Henry L. Upshur, Alfred P, Thom, nephews; Sydney Nottingham, A. T. Leatherbury, friends; WB40 p. 1.

PARKER, Anne E. Wit: Mar. 3, 1896 db Nov. 14, 1896, Jacob G. Parker, son; Margaret Eyre, Lucy Willard, Nannie Parker, sisters; WB39 p. 374.

PARKER, John J. Wit: Nov. 13, 1891 db June 12, 1899, William & Emily Parker, grandchildren, children of Henry by 1st wife; WB40 p. 24.

PARKER, John. S. Wit: Nov. 5, 1888 db Sept. 9, 1889, Jacob G. Parker, son: Annie "Nannie" Floyd Parker, daughter; Caleb C. Willard, son-in-law; Willie, Grace & Mary Eyre, grandchildren, WB39 p. 280.

PARSONS, Saml. H. Wit: May 26, 1888 db Nov. 14, 1898, Lucie A, wife; Sally E Parsons, niece; John R. Parsons, son of Julius F. Parsons, nephew; WB40 p. 12.

PITTS, Parker H. Wit: 1878 db Apr. 14, 1881, Leah Pitts, wife; Nat Pitts, brother; William Pitts, grandson; WB39 p. 220.

READ, Margaret L. Wit: Aug. 1, 1848 db Oct. 14,1872,Pamala J. Bayly, Elizabeth Jane Savage & Margaret S. Read, daughters;Daniel, Slave, my man; Littleton S. Read & John Calvin, sons; WB39 p. 151.

RICHARDSON, Thos. J. age 44 Wit: Apr. 17, 1899 db Feb. 12, 1900, Mary E. Richardson, wife; children not named; WB40 p. 31.

RIPPON, Thos. Wit: Nov. 21, 1876 db Aug. 14, 1893, Elizabeth, wife; children; WB39 p. 345.

ROBERTS, Eliza Wit: Jan. 25, 1879 db Sept. 18, 1879, William E., Walter & Edward, sons; Cordelia Roberts, Augusta Pannel, Mary E. Wescoat, Emily Scott, daughters; WB39 p. 211.

ROBERTS, Shepard Wit: Sept. 2, 1884 db Oct. 15, 1889, Arthur B. Roberts, brother; Margaret Roberts, sister; James E. Bull, nephew; Margaret Elizabeth Roberts, niece; WB39 p. 284.

ROBINS, John Wit: Nov. 20, 1897 db July 11, 1898, Tinie, wife; John H. Robins, son & John H. children Vasser Talmage Robins, Estell Robins & John Gaines Robins; Mattie Nottingham, daughter and her children Christine Jenn Nottingham & Fannie Langston Nottingham; WB 40 p. 7.

ROBINS, Margaret T. Wit: Mar. 5, 1874 db June 16, 1879, Emily & Susan T. Robins, niece; Maria Anne Spady w/Dr. Thos. F. Spady: Bettie Jarvis d/o Wm. S. Jarvis; Maggie Jarvis d/o Jesse N. Jarvis; Gilmor S. Kendall s/o Thos. L.; WB39 p. 210.

ROLLEY, Mary Wit: Dec. 22, 1869 db June 9, 1890, Raymond M., Francis C., William S. & Charles, sons; Harriet Elliot, Emeline Erwin, Mary W. Bloxam, daughters; Mary E. Bloxam, granddaughter; WB39 p.287.

SATCHELL, Nelson Wit: July 1870 db Feb. 1871, Fanny, Comfort, Peggy, Elizabeth & Sarah Satchell, daughters; Jim Satchell, son; WB39 p. 137

SAVAGE, Rachel Wit: Jan. 7, 1886 db Feb. 14, 1887, Walker Savage, son, Abel Costin, brother, WB39 p. 259.

SAVAGE, Sallie S. Wit: Apr. 25, 1900 db June 12, 1900, P. W. Savage, husband; WB40 p. 33.

SCHROEDER, Henry B. Wit: Apr. 5, 1894 db Apr. 9, 1901, Kate Schroeder, wife; WB40 p. 46

SCOTT, John T. Wit: July 23, 1885 db June 14, 1886, Eliza O. Scott, wife; John W. & Thomas M., sons, WB39 p. 249.

SCOTT, Sallie Wit: Jan. 6, 1896 db Apr. 10, 1899, Hennie Reid, daughter; WB40 p. 19.

SHAW, Julius E. Wit: Mar. 6, 1883 db June 9, 1884, Harriet Ann, wife; Henry O. Shaw, Sarah Jane Nichols, children; WB39 p. 231.

SMITH, Severn Wit: Dec. 28, 1895 db Jan. 8, 1900, Susan Smith, wife; children not named; WB40 p.30.

SPADY, Harry Wit: Apr. 13, 1888 db June 11, 1888, Anis Beckett, Elen Morris & Sally West, daughters; Suzen Widgens heirs; WB39 p. 266.

STEVENS, Sarah Wit: Apr. 21,1885db May 9, 1887, Walter & Thomas, sons, WB39 p. 259.

STEWART, Henry B. Wit: Apr. 9, 1880 db Aug. 16, 1901, Ann H. Stewart, wife; WB40 p. 56.

TANKARD, J. W. Wit: June 6, 1901 db Dec. 9, 1901, Susan Tankard, wife; Effie, daughter; Mary Frances, dec. daughter; Mary Frances' children Thomas N. & John T. Badger; Richard "Dickey" E. Floyd, grandson; John H. Roberts; WB40 p. 59.

TANKARD, Philip B. Wit: Apr. 17, 1897 db Feb. 14, 1898, Eming, wife; children not named; WB40 p. 6.

TEAKLE, Margaret S. Wit:Oct. 18, 1865 db Mar. 9, 1874, Harriet S. Teakle, sister; Kate Bell, grandniece; Thomas T. & Elizabeth Upshur, Ann S. & Sally B. Upshur daughters; John & Thomas T. Upshur sons; WB39 p. 183.

THOM, Wm. Alexander Wit: Nov. 12, 1894 db June 12, 1899, Alfred P. Thom, son; Alfred's children Anne Parker, Lucy Latane & William Thom; Marion E. Thom, daughter; F. Maria Thom, Alexander's daughter-in-law, wife of deceased son William A. Thom; William's son Alexander; WB40 p. 20.

TURNER, Elizabeth Wit: Dec. 1, 1897 db Mar. 13, 1899, William T. Jacob, son; Mary E. Wilkins, daughter; WB40 p. 15.

UPSHUR, Elizabeth Wit: July 22, 1898 db Nov. 14, 1898, Arthur B., Thomas C. & Henry T., sons, Henry T's wife Caroline; Berlie Elizabeth Chisom, daughter; WB40 p. 14.

UPSHUR, William Brown of Brownsville,Wit: Oct. 28, 1878 db Sept. 9, 1884, Catharine "Kate", wife "Mockon" farm near Eastville; Ann E. Upshur, Sally B. Handy, sisters; Thomas T. Upshur, brother, Thomas T. Jr. & John Upshur, nephews; Codicil-1 Aug. 11, 1882 Hamilton S. Neale, brother-in-law; Florence Irving, Ann E. & Sally B. Upshur, nieces; Codicil-2 Sept. 28, 1882 Wm. C. Handy, nephew; Judge Levin T. H. Irving, nephew-in-law; WB39 p. 234.

WARD, Eliza Wit: July 26, 1885 db Sept. 14, 1885, Nannie R. &Ludie M. Wescoat, friends; Rebecca Ward, sister; George G. Ward, brother; WB39 p. 245.

WARD, John C. Wit: Apr. 16, 1897 db July 12, 1897, Virginia, wife; Wm. Carpenter, nephew; Carie Philips, widow sister; Patsie Haley & parents Widgen& Mary Haley; WB39 p. 380.

WARREN, Leonard Wit: May 4, 1891 db Jan. 10, 1898, Joshua Warren, brother; Richard Warren ½ brother; John G. Warren, Sarah Armenia White & Pansey White, daughters of George E. & Lucy; Emma D. Whitehead, daughter of Ella Whitehead; WB40 p. 5.

WATSON, Sallie Wit: Nov. 20, 1891 db Jan. 13, 1892, Mary Susan Carpenter, daughter; Steven Carpenter son-in-law; WB39 p. 307.

WESCOAT, Edward P. Wit: Sept. 30, 1871 db Oct. 9, 1871, Elizabeth Hamby, sister w/o William Hamby Sr.; 5 children of sister Margaret Bell, dec. w/o Smith Bell; Vianna Dunton, half sister; William Hamby Jr., nephew; WB39 p. 137.

WHITEHEAD, Edward D. Wit: Jan. 23, 885 db May 14, 1888, Sally E. White, wife; Emma D. Whitehead, daughter; WB39 p. 265.

WHITEHEAD, William S. Wit: Nov. 17, 1885 db June 9, 1890, Sally P., wife, WB39 p. 289.

WIDGEN, Thomas E. Wit:Jan. 30, 1886 db Oct. 11, 1886, Solomon Widgen, Littleton Leatherbury, Ann E. Collins d/o Luky Collins; Maggie L. Widgen d/o Diana Scarburg; John E. Nottingham s/o Leonard; Dr. Robert B. Taylor to sell farm Orphan Retreat, WB39 p. 252.

WILKINS, Geo. F. "Lealand" 500 ac., Wit: July 24, 1894 db Apr. 12, 1897, Dr. William W. Wilkins, George F. Wilkins Jr.Dr's. son, Hettie Wilkins, Dr's. daughter; George R. & Thomas H. Jacob, Mary Sue Mapp "Aspin Grove"; Mary Ellen Russell & Annie Edwards, daughters of James Poulson; Vienna Wescoat, servant; Peggie J. & Severn O. Nottingham; WB39 p. 376.

WILKINS, Robert Wit: Feb. 11, 1885 db May 10, 1886, Margaret Wilkins, wife; Sarah Morris, Ellen Burtin & Georgianna Wilkins, daughters, WB39 p. 251.

WILLIAMS, John Walter Wit: Feb. 8, 1876 db July 17, 1890, John L. Wilkins &Benj. T. Scott, nephews; Sally, wife of John T. Nottingham, Emily, wife of James B. Scott nieces; Codicil 3 Sept. 1889, Walter, William, George, John & Clinton Scott, Chas. D. Nottingham, nephews; WB39 p. 290.

WINDER, John E. Wit: Sept. 23, 1897 db: Nov. 8, 1897, John Winder Garrett, nephew; Susan Garrett deceased sister's 5 children Mary Winder Garrett, Charlotte Garrett, Susan Garrett, Van Winder Garrett & Robinson Garrett; WB40 p. 3.

WISE, William A. Wit: Nov. 14, 1895 db Oct. 9, 1899, Emma Sheppard Wise, wife; WB40 p. 25.

WISE, William H. Wit: Oct. 14, 1893 db Nov. 12, 1894, Adelaide B., wife; J. B. & William A., sons; Emma S. Portlock, daughter; WB39 p. 360.

William W. Andrews p. 177	Bettie E. Moore p. 347
Edward P. Bayly p. 156	Levin Moses p. 364
John C. Coleburn p. 269	John E. Nottingham Sr. p. 242
William H. Cottingham p. 362	Leonard B. Nottingham p. 203
James B. Dalby p. 375	Samuel Y. Nottingham p. 170
Edward Preston Downes p. 196	Thomas H. Nottingham p. 345
George W. Dunton p. 139	Thomas J. L. L. Nottingham p. 208
Mary S. Dunton p. 232	Virginia F. Nottingham p. 339
William J. Fatherly p. 227	Anne Gertrude Parker p. 228
Mary A. Fitchett p. 278	John W. Reid p. 304
Arthur Goffigon p. 262	Edward P. Roberts p. 155
Elizabeth S. Griffith p. 198	William S. Rolley p. 365
Nathan Griffith p. 207	Abel Seymour p. 368
Bell Gunter p. 201	Laura M. Simkins p. 147
Tamar Hallett p. 192	Alfred Stoakley p. 341
William E. Isdell p. 144	Thomas S. Stoakley p. 186
Hezekiah James p. 308	Thomas C. Walston p. 260
George T. Jarvis p. 179	John B. Wescoat p. 178
Obed C. Kelly p. 303	George F. Wilkins p. 376
George Kerr p. 331	William E. Wilkins p. 184
Robin Mapp p. 168	

Will Book

INDEX

COPES
  Annie T. 134
  Elizabeth S. 134
  Peggie J. 134
COSTIN
  Abel 137
COTTINGHAM
  Mary A. 134

DALBY
  John L. 134
  Luther G. 134
  Mattie E. 134
"DANIEL" (Slave) 136
"DARBY'S WHARF" 135
DISHAROON
  Sallie E. 134
DIXON
  Margaret Sarah 134
  Thomas J. 134
  William W. 134
DOUGHTY
  George 134
  John 134
  Matilda Ann 134
  Sarah 134
DOWNING
  Mary G. 134
DUNTON
  Albert W. 134
  Alfred 134
  David A. 135
  Edmd. Bowdoin 134
  Edward 134
  Elizabeth 135
  George Ellis 134
  John Baker 134
  John R. 134
  Joseph 134
  Severn 134
  Vianna 138

EDWARDS
  Annie 138
"ELKINGTON" 136
ELLIOT
  Harriet 137

ENNIS
  Ara 134
  Charlie 134
  Elizabeth S. 134
  Elmer 134
ENNIS "cont'd"
  Irving S. 134
  Joseph 134
  Nannie R. 134
ERWIN
  Emeline 137
EYRE
  Grace 136
  Margaret 136
  Mary 136
  Willie 136

FISHER
  Elizabeth S. 133
  Fanny 134
  James A. 134
  Mary E. 134
  Nathaniel H. 134
  Rosa 134
  Samuel P. 134
  Susan E. 134
  Thomas B. 134
  Wilmer W. 134
"FISHER LAND" 135
FITCHETT
  Arinthia Blue 133
  Cordelia J. 135
  Mary 135
  Tabitha 135
FLOYD
  Edward Bayly 135
  James B., Dr. 135
  Richard E. 137
FOX
  Ivan C. 135
  Mary 135
  Soule B. 135
  William T. 135
"FRANKTOWN" 134

GARRETT
  Charlotte 138
  John Winder 138
  Mary Winder 138
  Robinson 138
  Susan 138
  Van Winder 138
GODWIN
  Charles E. 135
GREGORY
  John J. 134
GUNTER
  Benjamin T. 134

HALEY
  Mary 138
  Patsie 138
  Widgen 138
HALLETT
  Curtis 135
  Maggie 135
  Sarah 135
  Thomas 135
  Virginia 135
HAMBY
  Elizabeth 138
  William Jr. 138
  Wm. Sr. 138
HANDY
  Sally B. 137
  Wm. C. 137
HARMANSON
  James Lewes 135
  James R. 135
  Lafayette 134
  Margaret 135
HARRIS
  Margaret Susan 134
HEATH
  Virginia S. 135
HENDERSON
  Louisa 134
  Marion B. 134
  Nathaniel P. 134
"HILLS LAND" 135

HILLYER
  Mary 134
"HOG ISLAND" 134
HOLLAND
  E. 135
  Nath'l L. 135
HOLT
  Susan 133

IRVING
  Florence 137
  Levin T. H., Judge 137

JACOB
  George R. 138
  Peggy Mapp 136
  Tabitha R. 133
  Thomas H. 136, 138
  William T. 137
JAMES
  Alfred M. 135
  Fannie 135
  Ginnie 135
  Hezekiah P. 135
  Isaac 135
  John Robt. 135
  Levenia C. 135
  Mary A. 133
  Peggy S. 133
  Samuel M. 135
  William I. 135
JARVIS
  Arthur 135
  Bettie 135, 136
  George 135
  Georgeanna 133
  Isidora 135
  Jesse N. 136
  Liddie 135
  Maggie 136
  Mary 135
  Roberta 135
  Sally 135
  Sarah 135
  Severn 135
  Virginia 135

JARVIS "cont'd"
Wm. S. 136
JOHNSON
Delitha T. 135
Georgianna 133
Harriet Amanda 135
JOYNES
Florence 134

KELLAM
Stewart 135
William P. M. 135
KENDALL
Gilmor S. 136
Thos. L. 136

LATANE
Lucy 137
LATIMER
James 135
Nellie 135
"LEALAND" 138
LEATHERBURY
A. T. 136
Alonzo T. 135
Littleton 138
Virginia S. 135
"LEBANON" 136
"LINDEN" 133

MAPP
Laura 135
Llewellyn Mapp 135
Margaret S. 135
Mary Sue 138
MASON
Anna 135
McNUTT
Mary L. 134
MEARES
Caroline 135
George 135
James 135
Mary 135
William 135

"MOCKON" 137
MOORE
Catherine 135
Margaret S. 135
Rachel 135
William P. 135
MORRIS
Elen 137
Sarah 138
Susan 136
Wm. 136

NEALE
Hamilton S. 137
NICHOLS
Sarah Jane 137
NOCK
Isaac 136
Lucy 136
NOTTINGHAM
Alonzo G. 133
Chas. D. 138
Christine Jenn 136
Clara J. 136
E. W. 136
Eliz. S. B. 136
Fannie Langston 136
Howard 136
J. E. 134
John E. 138
John Edward Jr. 134
John T. 138
Lauretta V. 133
Leonard 138
Malinda Cath. 134
Mattie 136
Peggy 136
Peggy J. 138
Robinson 136
Sally 138
Severn O. 138
Sydney 136
Tabitha 136
Thomas Henry 136
William 136

"ORPHANS RETREAT" 138

PANNEL
Augusta 136
PARKER
Anne 137
Annie Floyd 136
Emily 136
Jacob G. 136
Nannie 136
William 136
PARRAMORE
Geo. Fisher 134
Juliet A. 134
Wm. Winder 134
PARSONS
John R. 136
Julius F. 136
Lucie A. 136
Sally E. 136
PHILIPS
Carie 138
PITTS
Leah 136
Nat 136
William 136
PORTLOCK
Emma S. 138
POTTER
Edmund 135
POULSON
James 138

READ
Bettie E. 134
George H. 134
Littleton S. 136
Margaret S. 136
"RED BANK" farm 135
REED
Elizabeth H. 134
Hattie W. 134
REID
Hennie 137

RICHARDSON
Mary E. 136
RIPPON
Elizabeth 136
ROBERTS
Arthur B. 136
Cordelia 136
Edward 136
John H. 137
Margaret 136
Margaret Eliz. 136
Walter 136
William E. 136
ROBINS
Emily 136
Estell 136
John Gaines 136
John H. 136
Susan T. 136
Tinie 136
Vasser Talmage 136
ROGERS
Susan 135
ROLLEY
Charles 137
Francis C. 137
Raymond M. 137
William S. 137
RUSSELL
Mary Ellen 138

SATCHELL
Comfort 137
Elizabeth 137
Fanny 137
Jim 137
Juliet 135
Peggy 137
Sadie 135
Sallie 135
Sarah 137
SAVAGE
Elizabeth Jane 136
P. W. 137
Walker 137

Deaths 1902 – 1906
in Will Book #40

Kendall F. Addison Wit: Apr. 12, 1898 db: May 10, 1905 p. 88

Henry Baily Wit: May 15, 1906 db: Aug. 10, 1906 p. 102

Thos. H. Braxton Wit: Sept. 15, 1904 db: Oct. 31, 1904 p. 82

Bagwell Bull Wit: Aug. 18, 1904 db: July 10, 1905 p. 93

George Burton Wit: Apr. 20, 1902 db: May 16, 1902 p. 65

Wm. S. Christian Wit: Nov. 20, 1906 db Feb. 27, 1907 p. 107

Severn Costin Wit: Feb. 14, 1903 db: Jan. 3, 1905 p. 85

Isaac Custis Wit: Nov. 1, 1900 db: Sept. 15, 1905 p. 95

Alexine N. Dennis Wit: July 21, 1898 db: Nov. 28, 1906 p. 106

Esther Drighouse Wit: no date given db: Apr. 20, 1906 p. 101

R. T. Dunton Wit: Feb. 7, 1902 db: Nov. 13, 1905 p. 96

George W. Garrett Wit: Sept. 15, 1905 db: Dec. 4, 1905 p.97

Alexander Gray Godwin Wit: Oct. 27, 1902 db: Feb. 9, 1903 p. 72

Isaac Gunter Wit: Dec. 14, 1900 db: Jan. 24, 1905 p. 86

James E. Heath Wit: May 22, 1901 db: Aug. 23, 1906 p. 103

Anna Henderson Wit: Jan. 20, 1906 db: Dec. 11, 1906 p. 107

Tabitha R. Jacob Wit: Dec. 7, 1896 db: Sept. 8, 1902 p. 68

Mary E. Johnson Wit: Nov. 17, 1899 db: Nov. 10, 1903 p. 74

Delaware Kellam Wit: Sept. 23, 1903 db: Dec. 14, 1903 p. 79

Henry Kellam Wit: May 19, 1899 db: Aug. 23, 1906 p. 103

Floyd A. Mapp Wit: Apr. 15, 1901 db: July 22, 1904 p. 105

George Harris Mapp Wit: Nov. 17, 1905 db: Dec. 27, 1905 p. 98

Sallie T. Mapp Wit: June 23, 1885 db: Apr. 28, 1904 p. 81

Carleton R. Moore Wit: Oct. 31, 1901 db: Sept. 25, 1905 p. 94

Elizabeth S. B. Nottingham Wit: Christmas 1897 db: Jan. 23, 1903 p. 71

John H. Offer Wit: Feb. 20, 1896 db: June 13, 1902 p. 67

Ann Walter Reid Wit: Aug. 2, 1893 db: June 16, 1904 p. 82

John C. Roberts W: Feb. 28, 1905 db: Oct.25, 1905 p. 96

Susan Sample Wit: Aug. 22, 1901 db: Jan. 12, 1903 p. 71

Virginia A. Scisco Wit: Aug. 21, 1905 db: Dec. 29, 1905 p.99

William N. Thomas Wit: Oct. 30, 1900 db: Apr. 13, 1903 p. 73

Thomas Widgeon Wit: Oct. 13, 1902 db: Nov. 13, 1902 p. 69

Emily P. T. Willis Wit: Sept. 8, 1902 db Dec. 14, 1903 p. 76

John Willis Sr. Wit: Nov. 4, 1901 db: Dec. 14, 1903 p. 77

Leonard J. Willis Wit: Aug. 17, 1901 db: Dec. 28, 1904 p. 84

Rose A. Winder Wit: May 15, 1902 db: June 9, 1902 p. 66

"1882" Death Discrepancies
(race/ sex, cause of death, age)

	Chart A	Chart B	Chart C
Ashby, Charles	CM Unkn. 3	CM Unkn. 30	CM Unkn. 3
Becket, Mary	CF Pneumonia 30	CF Unkn. 6 mos.	CF Unkn. 30
Bell, Maggie			--Cons. 61
Bell, Major	CM Congestive Chill 65	CM Congestive Chill 65	
Braxton, Richard	CM Sunstroke 1 yr. 6 mos.	CM Cons. 1 yr. 6 mos.	CM Brain Fever 1yr. 6mos.
Brickhouse, Carrie	CF Fever 8 mos.	CF Fever 61	CF Congestive Chill 8 mos.
Brooks, Adline	CF Pneu. 39	CF Pneu. 39	CF Pneu. 39
Bull, Leah	WF Cons. 61	WF Cons. 65	WF Typhoid Fev Pneu. 65
Cisco, Henry	CM Cons.. 65	CM Cons. 65	CM Cons. 65
Collins, Ann	CF Typh. Pneu. 65	CF Typh. Pneu. 3 yr. 5 mos.	CF Burnt 65
Collins, Henry	CM Unkn. 1 yr. 4mos.	CM Unkn 2 yr. 6 mos.	CM Unkn. 4 mos.
Collins, Jacob Henry	CM Pneu. 22 yr. 6 mos.	CM Unkn. 1 yr. 4 mos.	CM Unkn. 22 yr. 6 mos.
Collins, James	CM Unkn. 21 yr. 6 mos.	CM Unkn. 20 yr.	CM Unkn. 21 yr. 6 mos.
Collins, Sallie	CF Unkn. 2 yr. 6mos.	CF Unkn. 4	CF Unkn. 2 yr. 6 mo.
Costin, Nat.	WM Pneu. 28	WM Pneu. 28	WM Pneu. 28
Custis, James	CM Cons. 9 yr. 8 mos.	CM Cons. 9 yr. 8 mos.	CM Cons. 9 yr. 8 mos.
Downs, Nellie	CF Child Birth 30	CF Child Birth 30	CF Child Birth 30
Easter, Mary	CF Unkn. 1 yr. 2 mos.	CF Unkn 1 yr. 2 mos.	CF Unkn 1 yr. 1 mo.
Floyd, Jno. M.	WM Cons. Age unkn.	CM Cons. Age unkn.	WM Cons Age unkn.
Gladson, Annie F.	WF Child Birth 34	WF Cons. 21 yr. 6 mos.	WF Brain Fever 5 yr. 6 mo.
Gunter, Charles	CM Unkn. 20	CM Unkn. 3	CM Unkn. 20
Jarvis, Sam'l	CM Unkn. 4	CM Scar. Fever 5 yr. 6 mo.	CM Unkn. 4
Kellam, Sam'l E. D.	WM Dysentery 52	WM Disen. 35	WM Unkn. 50
Morris, Nat	CM F. F. W. 70	CM Typhoid Pneu. 70	CM F F Pneu. 70
Nottingham, Unkn.		CM Unkn. 4 days	CM Unkn. 4 days
Nottingham, Unnam	WF Pneu. 6 days		
Richardson, James	CM Shot 5 yr. 6 mos.		CM Brain Fever 21
Richardson, Richard		CM Cons. 8 days	
Richardson, Tobertha	WF Heart Disease 46	CF Heart Disease 46	WF Heart Disease 46
Riley, Dinah	CF T F Fever 55	CF Typh. Fever 55	
Riley, Peter			CM Dropsy 70
Roberts, Unname	CM Unkn. 4 days		
Scott, Ella	WF Unkn. 35	WF Unkn. 21 yr. 6 mos.	WF Unkn. 35
Smith, Golden	CM Brain Fever 4 mos.	WM Brain Fever 4 mos.	CM Brain Fever 4 mos.
Smith, Dinah			CF Heart Disease 55
Smith, Peter		CM Dropsy 70	
Stratton, Peter	CM Dropsy 70		
Unkn./Unkn.		WM Dropsy 60	
Weeks, Unnamed			WM Dropsy 7 days
Wescoat, Easter	CF Burnt 5 yr. 5 mos.	CF Burnt 52	CF Heart Dis. 5 yr. 5 mos.
Wilson, Emily	CF Dropsy 60	CF Pneu. 22 yr. 6 mos.	CF Pneu. 60 yr. 6 days

There are 33 listed on each chart for a total of 41 in 1882

"1882"

	Chart A	Chart B
Ashby, Charles	Feb. 10, 1882	Aug. 1882
Becket, Mary	Apr. 18, 1882	Feb. 1882
Bell, Major	Jan. 25, 1882	Jan. 1, 1882
Braxton, Richard	Sept. 1, 1882	Nov. 1882
Brickhouse, Carrie	June 18, 1882	June ? 1882
Brooks, Adline	Feb. 1, 1882	Feb. 1, 1882
Bull, Leah	July 24, 1882	Jan. 25, 1882
Cisco, Henry	Apr. 4, 1882	Sept. 1882
Collins, Ann	May 1, 1882	July 24, 1882
Collins, Henry	May 3, 1882	Jan. 16, 1882
Collins, Jacob Henry	Jan. 16, 1882	Oct. 20, 1882
Collins, James	Sept. 11, 1882	Dec. 27, 1882
Collins, Sallie	May 9, 1882	May 1882
Costin, Nat.	Jan. 22, 1882	Jan. 22, 1882
Custis, James	Sept. 1, 1882	Apr. 21, 1882
Downs, Nellie	Jan. 8, 1882	Jan. 8, 1882
Easter, Mary	Dec. 9, 1882	Apr. 1882
Floyd, Jno. M.	Apr. 3, 1882	Apr. 1882
Gladson, Annie F.	Nov. 5, 1882	Oct. 1882
Gunter, Charles	Aug. 9, 1882	Sept. 1882
Jarvis, Sam'l	Oct. 18, 1882	May 1882
Kellam, Sam'l E. D.	Oct. 12, 1882	Jan. 1882
Morris, Nat	Apr. 28, 1882	Jan. 21, 1882
Nottingham, Unkn.	Jan. 6, 1882	
Nottingham, Unnamed		Sept. 1882
Richardson, James	Jan. 21, 1882	
Richardson, Richard		May 1, 1882
Richardson, Tobertha	Jan. 25, 1882	Jan. 25, 1882
Riley, Dinah	Oct. 14, 1882	Dec. 17, 1882
Roberts, Unnamed	Sept. 1, 1882	
Scott, Ella	Dec. 27, 1882	Oct. 1882
Smith, Golden	June 12, 1882	June 1882
Smith, Peter		Sept. 1882
Stratton, Peter	Jan. 1, 1882	
Unkn./Unkn.		Apr. 1882
Wescoat, Easter	Jan. 3, 1882	May 1882
Wilson, Emily	Oct. 9, 1882	June 6, 1882

Above are discrepancies in the dates of death listed on Chart A & B.
Chart C is same as A or B.